Edmonton Transit LRT 1012 is northbound at 91 Street. This cold New Year's Day 1979 is quickly giving way to evening, and Edmonton's "blue cold" is caught in this dramatic photograph. *(Colin K. Hatcher)*

Photo below:
Edmonton Transit System car 64 is shown travelling eastbound on 118 Avenue near 66 Street, North Edmonton, January 18th 1951. *(A. Clegg)*

Edmonton's Electric Transit

The Story of Edmonton's Streetcars and Trolley Buses

**by Colin K. Hatcher
and Tom Schwarzkopf**

Copyright 1983 by
Railfare Enterprises Limited,
Toronto, Canada. Mailing address:
Box 33, West Hill, Ontario, Canada. M1E 4R4
All rights reserved. Printed and manufactured in Canada.

Book design by Cathy Wilson and David R. Henderson.

ISBN 919130-33-X

A Railfare ❋ Book

Copyright 1983 by
Railfare Enterprises Limited,
Toronto, Canada. Mailing address:
Box 33, West Hill, Ontario, Canada. M1E 4R4

All rights reserved. Printed and manufactured in Canada.

Canadian Cataloguing in Publication Data

Hatcher, Colin K., 1939-
  Edmonton's electric transit
Bibliography: p.
ISBN 0-919130-33-X

1. Street-railroads — Alberta — Edmonton — History — 20th century.
2. Edmonton (Alta.) — Transit systems — History — 20th century.
I. Schwarzkopf, Tom, 1943- II. Title.

HE4509.E35H37   388.4'6'0971233   C83-098232-9

Photo left:

Jasper Avenue, at First (101) Street in the heart of Edmonton's business and shopping district, during the early years of the Twentieth Century (circa 1912). (Canadian Pacific)

Right:

Looking down 100 Street towards the CN Tower, located on 104 Avenue. The Tower was one of the first of Edmonton's new modern skyscrapers built in the 1960s. It houses the CN station in the ground floor of the building. (A. Clegg)

Contents

Chapter		**Page**
	Introduction	4
1	From Ordinance to Construction	7
	Street Names in Edmonton	12
2	The First Car Operates	13
3	Streetcar Service Begins	17
4	Preston Cars Introduce PAYE Fare Collection	21
5	The Railway and the Cities Grow	31
6	Plans Become Reality	41
7	The High Level Bridge Opens	53
8	Edmonton Interurban Railway	69
9	Economic Instability	75
10	Stability Returns	87
11	The Twenties and Thirties	94
12	Streetcar Service Declines	109
	Mileage and Passenger Statistics	124
	How to Rebuild a Streetcar	126
13	Streetcar Epilogue	128
14	Return to the Rails	135
15	The Trolley Bus	147
16	The War Years and Beyond	155
17	The Not-So-Final Years	165

Appendix		**Page**
I	Equipment Roster — Rail	180
II	LRT Extensions	193
III	Trolley Coach Roster	195
IV	Trolley Coach Extensions	196
V	Footnotes	198
VI	Acknowledgements	205
VII	Bibliography	207

Maps

1908	Track Diagram	20
1912	Track Diagram	57
1913	Edmonton Interurban Railway	71
1924	Track Diagram	86
1938	Track Diagram	106
1950	Track Diagram	117
1978	LRT Line	144
1945	Trolley Coach Wire Diagram	163
1970	Trolley Coach Wire Diagram	171
1981	Clareview LRT Extension	193
1943	Route Map — Rail	208
1982	Trolley Coach Network	209

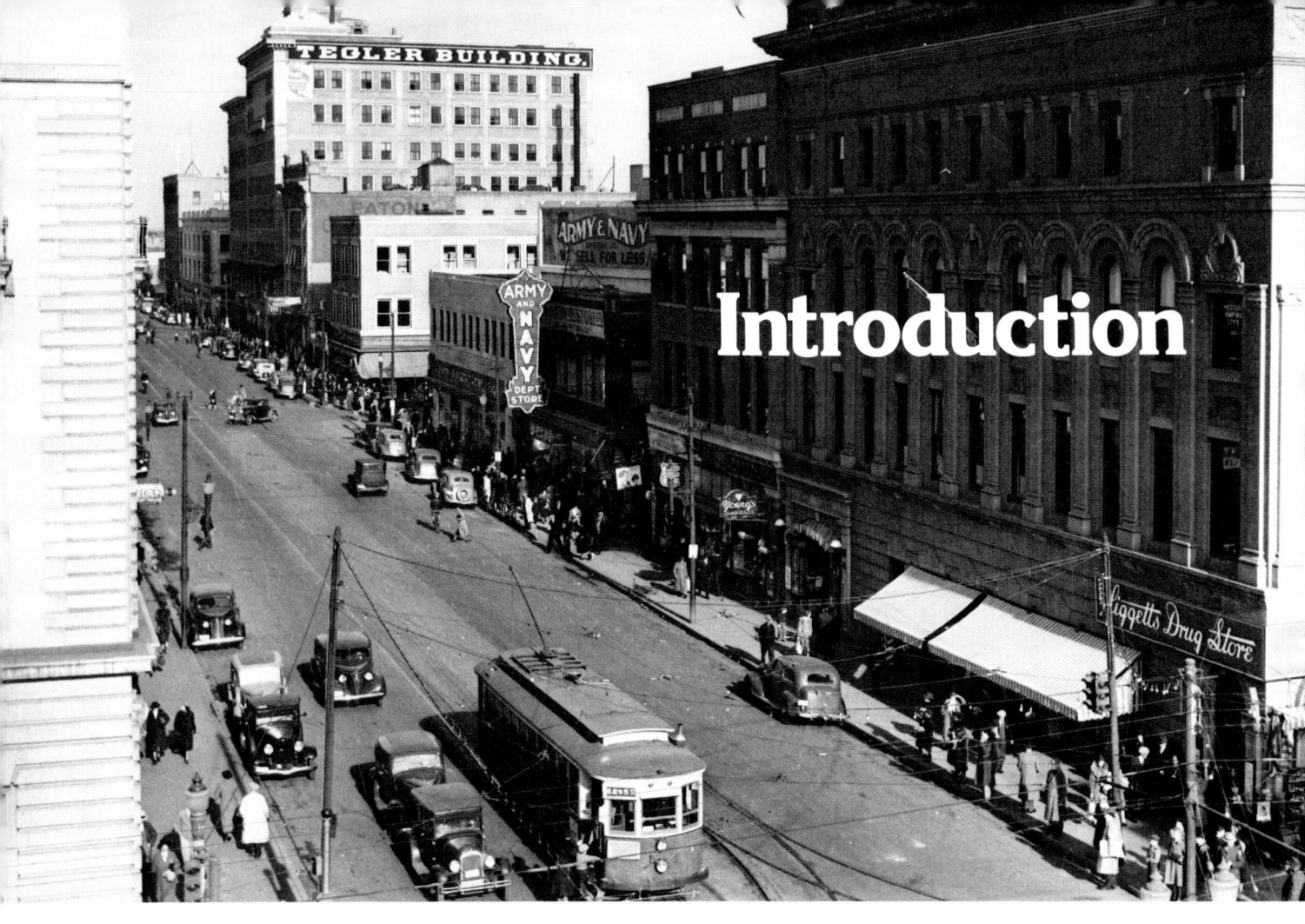

Introduction

WHEN the Edmonton Radial Railway was conceived, it was to serve an Edmonton comprising 18,500 inhabitants, and Strathcona numbering 4,500. When operations began in 1908, the streetcars served and connected four population clusters. The largest cluster was in the area east of 101 Street and north from Jasper Avenue, to about 118 Avenue. This included the major business district of Edmonton, then centred around 97 Avenue and Jasper Avenue. The second group tended to be a thinner one, spread out along Jasper Avenue to 116 Street.

The line to Strathcona served another group of residents in the river valley flats. However, the new transportation system did not speed their downtown journey very much. People in that area could reach the downtown area just as quickly by walking, as by taking the circuitous car ride west to 109 Street, then doubling back along Jasper Avenue. The lengthy routing was necessary to take the car line from the valley floor, after crossing the Low Level bridge, to higher ground on Jasper Avenue.

This routing took the car line past the Fort Edmonton area, south of present-day 97 Avenue, between 108 and 109 Streets. The Strathcona line — in addition to serving the 4,500 people living in that town — also provided residents with transportation to and from the Calgary and Edmonton Railway (Canadian Pacific Railway) terminal in Strathcona.

The story of the development of Edmonton from a fort to a city is well detailed in J.G. MacGregor's *Edmonton, A History,* published by Hurtig of Edmonton in 1967 and 1975. The events leading up to Edmonton's need for a public transportation system are briefly sketched in this introduction.

In the late 1700s and early 1800s, any British, French or European settlement in the area west of the Great Lakes was initiated almost exclusively to support the fur trade. Such settlement usually took place along the waterways, since the rivers and lakes provided the most expedient means of moving supplies west and furs east.

The two major fur trade companies, the Northwest Company and the Hudsons's Bay Company, first established trading posts for the purpose of obtaining furs from the Indian fur traders in the present-day Edmonton area in 1795. The Hudson's Bay Company established Edmonton House in October of that year, at the confluence of the Sturgeon River and the North Saskatchewan River. Edmonton House rivalled the adjacent Fort Augustus built a few months earlier

Car No. 1, operating on the red-sign route, takes on passengers at 101 Street. It will then turn eastbound onto Jasper Avenue to continue its belt line run via Jasper Avenue, 95 Street, 111 Avenue and 101 Street. The noon sun casts long shadows as it hangs low in the southern sky. This, and the absence of snow, suggests a late fall day in 1937 or 1938. Red-sign car service was terminated in the summer of 1939, as work began to prepare 95 Street for the trolley coaches.
(Provincial Archives of Alberta)

by the Northwest Company. These two forts were located near the present-day Fort Saskatchewan, on the North Saskatchewan River some twenty miles downstream from present-day Edmonton.

In 1802, both companies moved their respective installations to the low river flats immediately downstream from today's Walterdale bridge in Edmonton. Eight years later, in 1810, this site was also abandoned in favour of one further downstream. In 1832, after the amalgamation of both the Northwest Company and the Hudson's Bay Company under the latter's name, the expanded company established a new fort high above the river bank, just below the site of the present-day Legislature Buildings. A portion of this fort is illustrated on page eight.

River traffic changed in 1875, when the steamer *Northcote* began to churn its way along the North Saskatchewan. It linked Edmonton with Grand Rapids, at the mouth of the Saskatchewan River on Lake Winnipeg. Here, goods were transshipped to and from Lake Winnipeg steamers for the trip to Winnipeg. This increased river trade attracted independent traders and entrepreneurs to the Fort Edmonton area. Edmonton's first hotel was built in 1876 to accommodate this traffic.

Fort Edmonton also became the south end of a ninety-mile land bridge between the North Saskatchewan and Athabasca River systems. From the Athabasca River, traders and settlers could also gain access to the Peace River country, through the Lesser Slave River.

The Hudson's Bay Company influenced the settlement pattern of Edmonton, as the Company held a large 3,000 acre reserve extending north from the river bank to about present-day 125 Avenue. It was bounded on the west by present-day 124 Street, and on the east by today's 101 Street. Most early settlers tended to take land to the east of this reserve, while a few settled west of it. These two settlements — plus the surveying of the 100-foot-wide Jasper Avenue as the main thoroughfare across the southern portion of this reserve — influenced the routing and operation of the Edmonton Radial Railway for many years.

In February 1892, the hamlet became incorporated as the Town of Edmonton. A decade earlier, Edmontonians had anticipated (incorrectly) that the Canadian Pacific Railway transcontinental line, as surveyed by Sanford Fleming, would pass through Edmonton. With that disappointment behind them, they later looked forward to the arrival of the Calgary and Edmonton Railway from Calgary in 1891. It soon became evident that the C&ER would not cross the river for some time. A new community called Strathcona grew up around the rail head on the south bank of the river.

Strathcona grew very rapidly, and became incorporated as a town on April 29th 1899. That population cluster, too, would influence the future of the Edmonton Radial Railway. Both communities flourished briefly in 1897, as the Klondike gold rush attracted prospectors through the area via the C&ER, on their way north.

Many prospectors outfitted themselves from suppliers on both sides of the river, before setting out on the long trail north to the Klondike. Cross-river transportation was, for many years, provided solely by a ferry located near the Walterdale bridge. In 1900, the Low Level bridge was built. In 1902, the tracks of the Edmonton, Yukon and Pacific Railway — a MacKenzie and Mann property — were laid across the bridge, providing the first rail line into Edmonton.

Edmonton continued to grow. The year 1905, however, was a very significant one. On September 1st of that year, part of the large prairie area west of Ontario, known as the Northwest Territories, was divided to form the provinces of Alberta and Saskatchewan. Edmonton became the capital of the new Province of Alberta. On November 7th 1905, Edmonton became incorporated as a City.

The Fort Edmonton buildings located below the Legislature Buildings, and illustrated on pages 8 and 62, were completely dismantled about 1915. However, Edmontonians have recognized the importance of their city's early history by recreating the fort and other early buildings, to represent various eras of Edmonton's development, in the well-planned Fort Edmonton Park.

Following the restoration of streetcar number 1 in 1979, the Edmonton Radial Railway Society was formed. The Society was interested in maintaining Car 1 in operating condition. It also set out to restore other streetcar bodies which, since their retirement from active streetcar service, were found in varying stages of disrepair on a number of farm properties in the Edmonton area. The Society contracted with Fort Edmonton Park to supply transit services in the park area, using these restored vehicles.

A streetcar barn, based on the design of the early four-track ERR south side barn illustrated on page 19, has been completed. It provides shop and storage space for the streetcar restoration program. This structure is furnished with tools which were found stored in the former ERR Cromdale car barn.

Streetcar number 1 was operated at Fort Edmonton during the 1980 season. The Society expects to have two cars operating on electrified street track in the near future. Edmontonians and visitors will have an opportunity to experience a ride on an Edmonton streetcar in a recreated, historically-accurate, Edmonton city setting. At the same time, two modern, efficient modes of electric transportation — trolley coach and light rail transit — continue to provide service on the main routes of today's Edmonton Transit.

Photo above:
Downtown Edmonton about 1896, looking east from the roof of Laurie & Pichar's store. Quite a contrast to the same scene today! (Canadian Pacific)

Photo below:
Another view of the growing community before the need for urban transit became of pressing concern. This view was taken from the tower of the Fire Hall. (CN photo)

From Ordinance to Construction

*E*DMONTON'S DESIRE to have a tramway system goes back as far as 1893. On September 16th of that year, the government of the Northwest Territories passed "An Ordinance to Empower the Municipality of the Town of Edmonton to Construct and Operate a Tramway." With the passage of this legislation, the Town of Edmonton was "authorized and empowered to construct, maintain, equip and operate and from time to time to remove, change and renew, as may be found necessary or expedient, a single or double track tramway . . ."[1] The tramway could operate anywhere within the town and upon lands acquired outside the town but not beyond a distance of five miles from the town limits based upon the limits existing at the time the ordinance was passed. It appears that a desire to transfer freight and passengers to and from the Calgary and Edmonton Railway at its northern terminus in Strathcona was the reason for providing for the extension beyond the town boundaries, as servicing the Calgary and Edmonton Railway is specifically mentioned in the ordinance. The tramway was empowered to construct and operate ferries across the North Saskatchewan River during summer and to lay tracks upon the ice during winter in order to reach the Calgary and Edmonton Railway line which was operated by the Canadian Pacific Railway. The ordinance also provided for the town Council through a bylaw to enter into a franchise agreement with a private company empowered by the Parliament of Canada to construct and operate the railway.[2]

While a tramway under authority of this ordinance was never completed, the intent of the document was clear and it provided a basis for subsequent more venturesome radial tramway proposals. The transport of passengers and goods between Edmonton and Strathcona was left entirely to the operators of horse drawn drays and buses from 1891 until 1908.

The question of a tramway showed up again on the Edmonton Council's agenda in 1902, but was dropped apparently because of a concern that a tramway would not pay its way.[3] Late in 1903, William G. Tretheway, a Montreal real estate agent, presented a proposal to secure a franchise for the construction and operation of a street railway service in Edmonton. Tretheway paid out $10,000 to the City to secure that right and agreed to have a line in operation by the close of 1905. Edmonton Town Council passed a bylaw approving the franchise agreement giving Tretheway the authority to proceed with construction and operation of the line. Nothing came of this proposal; the Town was left with Tretheway's $10,000 but no tramway system.[4] Immediately following the failure of this proposal, City Council considered a municipally-operated system, but that too failed.[5]

Finally, in 1907 Council again decided to move ahead with a municipally-owned and operated street railway system, and the Commissioners were asked on February 26th, 1907 to recommend the most suitable route for the line.[6] A proposed route for the street railway was approved at a special session of City Council on March 7th, 1907.

On Jasper Avenue from St. Catharine's east to Government Avenue (92 St.)

On First Street (101 St.) from Jasper Avenue to Isabella Street (104 Avenue)

On Namayo Avenue (97 St.) from Jasper Avenue to Norwood Boulevard

On Isabella Street (104 Ave.) from First Street (101 St.) to Namayo Avenue (97 St.)

A belt line be made by a line on Syndicate Avenue (95 St.) from Jasper Avenue to Norwood Boulevard, thence westerly to Namayo Avenue (97 St.)

Clauses were included, requiring that the curves be ordered for Syndicate Avenue (95 St.) and be installed at the same time as the others.

It was also specified that the next extension of the Street Railway be on Jasper Avenue from Government Avenue to View Point and on Namayo Avenue from Norwood Boulevard to Alberta Avenue.[7]

Some impetus was given to the street railway issue as Edmonton was embarking upon its first street paving program that summer. It was necessary to establish the route of the car lines so that the rails could be appropriately laid as the paving program progressed. Following the approval of a route, City Council on March 12th, 1907 approved a motion that a bylaw be submitted to raise $224,000 to complete the street railway.[8]

Grading for a double track line on Jasper Avenue between First Street and Ninth Street actually began in May 1907 as the paving program was getting underway. A total of .58 miles of track was laid that year, all of it in pavement. The Bitulithic Paving Company laid the pavement and paved the track allowance with wood blocks. Two city blocks in the city centre were finished with stone blocks as a test.[9]

Until construction of trackage was actually underway, City Council was still open to consider the disposal of the street railway franchise to a private operator.

P. Cronin, a Toronto financial agent, approached Council on behalf of George Balfour, a civil engineer of London, England, who apparently held franchises for the operation of several street railway systems in Great Britain. Dundee, Scotland, was cited as one of his major franchise holdings.[10] The offer triggered a very spirited debate for a few days in Edmonton. Council discussed the issue while sitting as a "Committee of the Whole" and based its position largely on the expired agreement between the Town of Edmonton and Mr. W.G. Tretheway.[11] The talk of the town was over municipal vs. private ownership and operation of the street railway system. Municipal ownership would require the raising of considerable sums of money to invest in the system, and while the city's credit rating was good, money was not easily available at the time. On the other hand, if the street railway franchise was sold, the city could take the revenue from the franchise to reduce interest on indebtedness or to finance other municipal projects. Many citizens, however, felt that the Edmonton franchise was too valuable to be sold.[12] It would appear that the British interest in the Edmonton Street Railway franchise eventually faded, as there was no further reference to this proposal.

Meanwhile, in 1904 a group of Edmonton, Fort Saskatchewan and Strathcona businessmen had formed a corporate body called the Strathcona Radial Tramway Company Limited. This Company had authority to lay out, construct and operate a single or double track tramway from a point at or near the town of Strathcona to five specified points, among them the town of Fort Saskatchewan and the Village of Morinville. In addition the Strathcona Radial Tramway could lay out, construct and operate the railway to any point in the district of Alberta not more than eighty miles distant from the boundaries of the town of Strathcona as the boundaries existed at the time of the passing of the ordinance. The Strathcona Radial Tramway was obligated by the terms of the ordinance to receive authority from the municipal council of any municipality before constructing or operating within that municipality, and likewise from the Commissioner of Public Works before constructing or operating lines outside the boundaries of a municipality. A municipal council was empowered to enter into an agreement with the Tramway respecting all aspects of the construction and operation of the Tramway within the municipality. The municipal council could also pass by-laws to carry into effect any agreements with the Tramway Company. The 1904 ordinance would cease unless at least fifteen miles of line were actually constructed within three years. After a lapse of seven years the powers granted by the ordinance with respect to all lines excluding turnouts, switches and side tracks not then constructed would also cease.[13]

The Strathcona Radial Tramway Company remained inactive for some period of time following the passing of the ordinance, as it was obvious that the radial lines to the places named could not

Photo left:

Fort Edmonton and stage-coach transit during the early years of the century. The newly-constructed Provincial Legislature Building in the background dates the photo circa 1914.
(Canadian Pacific)

Photo above:

Looking westward along Whyte Avenue in Strathcona from CP crossing near Main Street (later 104 Street), South Edmonton. Note the suspended arc lamps, the old Canadian Pacific boxcar, and the unattended horse in front of Strathcona House. No doubt his rider was refreshing himself at the adjacent Strathcona saloon. *(Canadian Pacific)*

in fact generate enough traffic to sustain operations on their own merits. The directors of the Radial Company, however, were very interested in obtaining the rights to operate a street railway system within the City of Strathcona itself, and made continuing efforts throughout 1907 to obtain the franchise rights from the City of Strathcona to do so. Finally in September 1907 the Strathcona Radial Tramway Company made a specific offer to Strathcona Council. This offer was precipitated by the fact that Edmonton was giving serious thought to the question of retaining the franchise to its already partly-built system versus disposing of it to British interests.[14] The offer was difficult to refuse but Strathcona Council decided to take the matter to the ratepayers for final approval.

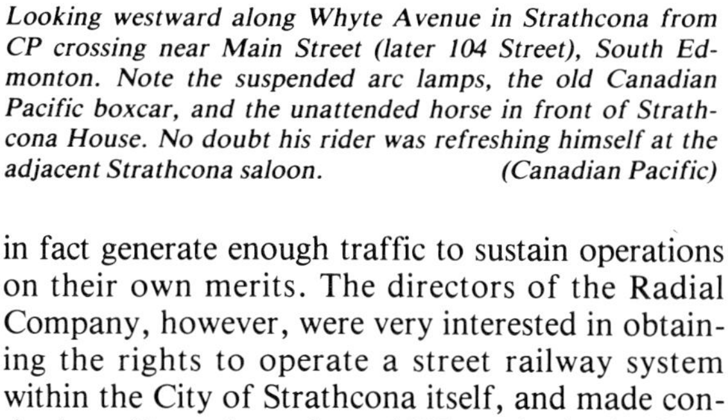

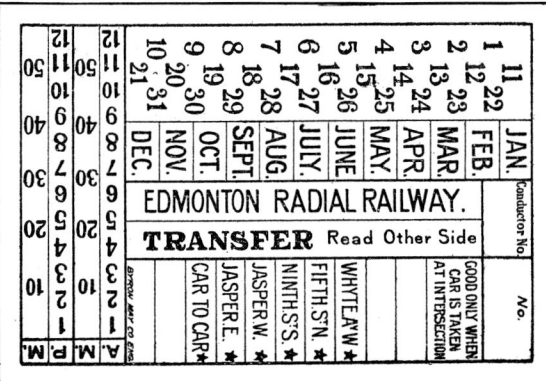

The terms of the resulting bylaw provided that the Company must commence work not later than August 1st, 1908 and that by November 1909, track must be laid down and in operation. The first part of the line constructed would be from a point at or near the south terminus of the Saskatchewan bridge at the corner of Cameron Street and Short Avenue and on Whyte Avenue from Cameron Street west. After 1924 the Company would be required to pay to the City an annual fee of 4% on gross earnings up to $500,000; 5% on gross earnings over $500,000 up to $800,000 and 7% on gross earnings over $800,000. The franchise was exclusive and would last for a period of thirty years, with the City of Strathcona receiving the right to acquire the system at any time upon giving two years' notice in writing.[15] While not part of the terms of the bylaw, the Strathcona Radial Tramway Company did indicate an intention to build a line to Cooking Lake, a popular cottage and resort area east of Strathcona. This was one of the destinations noted in the 1904 SRT Ordinance.[16]

The City of Edmonton showed an active interest in the outcome of the Strathcona decision. Edmonton's City Council dispatched a Committee consisting of Mayor Griesbach and Aldermen Manson and Gariepy to meet with Strathcona Council to discuss the franchise.[19] According to the Edmonton Journal, Mayor Griesbach was anxious to see Edmonton and Strathcona work together on the building and operation of a street railway system in and between the two cities. He was therefore anxious that Edmonton and Strathcona deal with the same company if they agreed to sell their respective franchises. Mayor Greisbach also advocated the possibility of the City of Edmonton purchasing the Strathcona franchise. Thus, if the franchise was later sold, one company would look after street railway services in and between both cities, while if the system remained in municipal hands, the resources of both cities would be available to go into one system.[18]

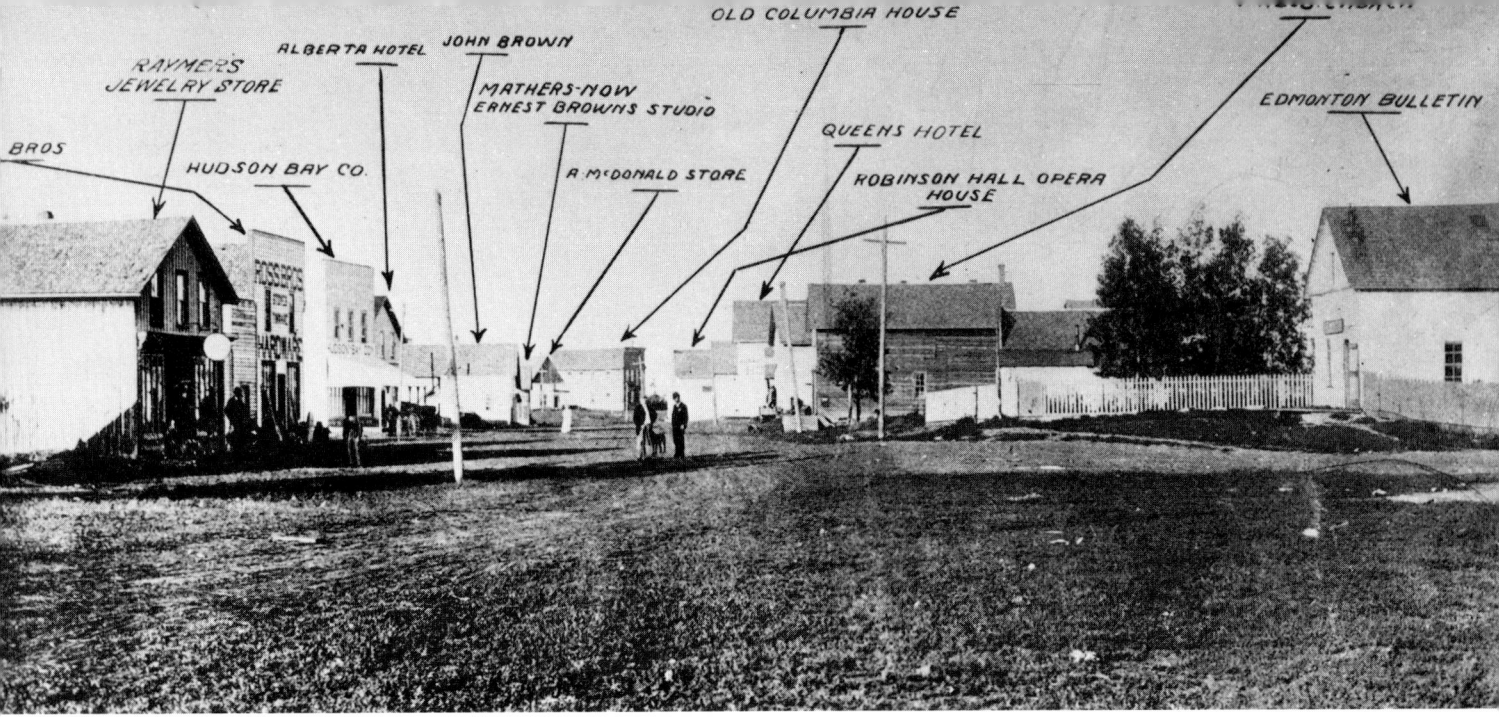

Edmonton, in one final attempt to influence the Strathcona ratepayers, presented an alternate specific franchise proposal to them just a few days before they voted on the Strathcona Radial Tramway Company bylaw. The Edmonton proposal provided for one mile of line in Strathcona built before the end of 1908 to the same standards as the Edmonton lines for every 2,000 people in the south bank municipality. Car service would be provided every fifteen minutes on the connecting line between the two cities; the basis for determining car service frequency within Strathcona would be the same as that for Edmonton. The eventuality of Edmonton wishing to dispose of the franchise was covered by suggesting that no agreement for sale of the franchise would be approved unless it was signed by both cities.

The Edmonton proposal was presented to encourage the ratepayers to reject the private Strathcona Radial Tramway Company proposal. The ratepayers went to the polls on Wednesday, September 30th, 1907 with the clear choice of accepting or rejecting the Strathcona Radial Tramway Company proposal. The official count indicated that 781 had cast their vote in favour of the proposal while 186 voted against it.[20] In Strathcona, the street railway issue had been settled. The following Monday it was announced that the Strathcona Radial Tramway Company had purchased land in Edmonton immediately adjacent to the Low Level Bridge, thus eventually giving their cars direct access to Edmonton.[21] Strathcona Council's street railway concerns were now limited to ensuring that the Strathcona Radial Tramway Company met the terms of its franchise.

Edmonton City Council had yet to make a firm decision about the franchise issue. Possibly in an effort to make the eventual sale of an Edmonton tramway franchise more attractive to prospective buyers, Edmonton City Council applied to the Government of Alberta to pass the Edmonton Radial Tramway Act. This act was assented to on March 5th, 1908. It gave the City authority to extend tramway lines much further beyond its boundaries than did the original 1893 Ordinance.

Above:

Jasper Avenue looking east about 1890.   *(Canadian Pacific)*

Opposite:

The same area of the City in 1914.   *(Canadian Pacific)*

The Edmonton Radial Tramway Act gave the City of Edmonton powers to build its tramway lines to any points in Alberta not more than eighty miles away from the existing (1908) city boundaries. Specific points noted in the Act were Stony Plain, White Whale (Wabamun) Lake, Lac St. Anne, St. Albert and Morinville, Namayo, Athabasca Landing, Fort Saskatchewan, Saddle Lake, Lacombe and Gull Lake and finally Daysland.[22]

Throughout the last quarter of 1907 and into 1908, street railway planning and the ordering of supplies for the system drew heavily upon Council's time. Rail and fittings were ordered, including the special work for intersections on Jasper Avenue at First Street (101 Street) and at Namayo Avenue (97 Street).[23]

Delegations were heard from time to time suggesting changes in the routing of the car lines or expanding existing plans from single track lines to double track lines.[24] Council was anxious to complete paving on First (101) Street between Jasper Avenue and Isabella Street (104 Ave.) and on Namayo Avenue (97 St.) between Jasper Avenue and Clark Street (105 Avenue). Therefore track laying requirements had to be conducted and necessary money bylaws passed to cover the additional cost of track laying in pavement.[25]

Paving contracts for First Street (101 Street) and Namayo Avenue (97 Street) were finally let out to the Bitulithic and Contracting Ltd. while the laying of the street railway trackage for these projects was contracted out to W.J. Carter.[26] The method adopted for laying trackage in the pavement deviated considerably from standard railway track laying. Once the grading had been completed, concrete was poured into trench-like runners about 9'' deep and 13'' across the bottom located so that they would be directly under each rail.

Then every fifteen feet, a 6-foot-long steel tie was placed across the road bed. Half way between each steel tie, a 10 x 10" wooden block was placed on each concrete runner. The rails were then bolted to the steel ties and spiked to the wooden blocks. Once the rail had all been laid, securely bolted and properly gauged, the whole area including the devilstrip and the area between the rails was filled with concrete to a point about half-way up each rail. The final topping between the rails, on the devilstrip, and for about eighteen inches away from each outer rail consisted of wooden blocks. This brought the pavement level with the top of the rail.[27]

An event of significance occurred on July 29th 1908, when arrangements were completed enabling the City of Edmonton to purchase the rights, privileges and property of the Strathcona Radial Tramway Company Ltd.[28] Charles E. Taylor was taken on as the Superintendent of Construction and, with the Commissioners, had full authority to engage the necessary clerical and engineering assistance required. In addition, the Superintendent and Commissioners were empowered to let all contracts for construction and to purchase materials for the building and equipping of the street railway system in Edmonton and Strathcona.[29] The amalgamated operation was to be known as the Edmonton Radial Railway.

City Council at its August 4, 1908 meeting gave first, second and third reading to Bylaw 184 which authorized the execution of an agreement between the Strathcona Radial Tramway Company Ltd., the City of Edmonton, John Walter and other directors of the Company. Council then promptly gave first, second and third reading to Bylaw 185 authorizing $135,000 for the purchase of the Strathcona Radial Tramway Company Ltd., for the construction of that line, for the extension of the Edmonton lines and to provide equipment for the system.[30] The Edmonton Bulletin reported that two to three miles of railway were expected to be operating by the end of 1908. The plan was to operate one car in Strathcona along Whyte Avenue to the top of the grade on Cameron Street (99 St.). Two cars were to operate from this point across to Edmonton and three or four additional cars would serve Edmonton. Mayor McDougall of Edmonton stated publicly that the interurban line between Edmonton and Strathcona would be in operation by November 1908. The interurban line was to be built south on 9th Street (109 Street) to Saskatchewan Avenue (97 Avenue) then east to the Low Level Bridge. In Strathcona, the line would run from the Bridge south on Cameron Street (99 Street) to Whyte Avenue and then west to the University grounds. It was further noted that construction of the line in Strathcona had already begun and would continue in anticipation of receiving approval from the ratepayers on August 26th 1908.[31]

The Edmonton ratepayers overwhelmingly approved Bylaw 185, with 710 favouring the bylaw and 7 voting against it. From the $135,000 bylaw, $10,000 was earmarked for the purchase of the Strathcona Radial Tramway Company while $125,000 went toward the purchase of cars and the extension of the Edmonton system on Namayo Avenue (97 Street) to Alberta (118) Avenue; on Jasper Ave. from 9th (109) Street to Twenty-First (121) Street; the connecting line at the Low Level Bridge over the North Saskatchewan River with the Strathcona system.[32]

With a specific mandate in the form of money bylaws, target dates and a superintendent, the Edmonton Radial Railway finally came into being as the City of Edmonton's municipal street railway system servicing both Edmonton and Strathcona.

Street Names in Edmonton

During the early years of its history, some Edmonton streets were designated by name and some by number. Jasper Avenue, Namayo Avenue, Syndicate Avenue, Spruce Avenue and Alberta Avenue are examples of some of the named thoroughfares. Westward from present-day 101 Street, Edmonton's streets (north - south thoroughfares) were numbered progressively from First Street at least as far as Forty-second Street although Twenty-fourth Street was also referred to as Edward Street.

The south side community of Strathcona employed a somewhat different system. The main east-west thoroughfare was called Whyte Avenue while the principal north-south route was called Main Street. Generally speaking, all of Strathcona's north-south streets took progressive numbers eastward and westward from Main Street; e.g., First Street West, Second Street West and First Street East, Second Street East. The same pattern was followed for the east-west avenues using Whyte Avenue as the centre; e.g., First Avenue North, Second Avenue North and First Avenue South, Second Avenue South.

Following amalgamation of the two communities to form the expanded City of Edmonton in 1912 a plan was introduced to integrate street and avenue designations on both sides of the river. During 1914 the current designation of numbered avenues (east-west) and streets (north-south) went into general use. Jasper (101) Avenue retained its name and 101 Street became the centre of the new city. Street numbers ascend west, and descend east, from 101 Street. Similarly numbered avenues ascend northward and descend southward from Jasper Avenue. Jasper Avenue is rarely referred to as 101 Avenue, but Whyte Avenue is often referred to as 82 Avenue.

Throughout the first eight chapters of this publication, the street and avenue names describing Edmonton Radial Railway routes and turning points have been shown in the pre-1914 terms, supplemented, in some cases, by the current designations. The following listing relates old and new names of streets, avenues and roads in the text. After the 1914 change, only the present nomenclature has been shown.

Named Thoroughfares

Formerly	*Present Day Numbers*
Agnes St.	79 St.
Albany Ave.	110 Ave.
Alberta Ave.	118 Ave.
Athabasca Ave.	102 Ave.
Algonquin Ave.	137 Ave.
Brandon Ave.	127 Ave.
Clarke St.	105 Ave.
Curry St. (also Currie)	100 St. south of 100 Ave.
Douglas St.	78 St.
Duparau St.	68 St.
Edmiston St.	110A Ave.
Edward St. (also 24 St.)	124 St.
Elm Ave.	113 Ave.
Fox St.	89 St.
Gallagher St.	109A Ave.
Government Ave.	92 St. (south of Norwood Blvd.)
Irwin St.	63 St.
Isabella St.	104 Ave. (east of 101 St.)
James St.	81 St.
John St.	80 St.
Kelly Ave.	124 Ave.
Kennedy St.	93 St.
Kinnaird St.	82 St.
Kirkness St.	95 St. (north of Norwood Blvd.)
Knox	112 Ave.
Leggett St.	87 St.
Lorne St.	92 St. (north of Norwood Blvd.)
Main St. (Strathcona)	104 St.
McDougall Ave.	100 St. (north of 100 Ave.)
McKay Ave.	99 Ave.
McKenzie Ave.	104 Ave. (west of 101 St.)
Morgan Ave.	123 Ave.
Namayo Ave.	97 St.
Nelson Ave.	107 Ave.
Nipigon Ave.	112 Ave.

Named Thoroughfares

Formerly	*Present Day Numbers*
Norton St.	66 St.
Norwood Blvd.	111 Ave.
Oak Ave.	116 Ave.
Pine Ave.	112 Ave.
Portage Ave.	Kingsway Ave. (changed 1939)
St. Catherine's St.	92 Ave.
Saskatchewan Ave.	97 Ave.
Short Ave.	107 Ave. (west of 124 St.)
Spruce Ave.	114 Ave.
Sutherland St.	106 Ave. (east of 97 St.)
Syndicate Ave.	95 St. (south of Norwood Blvd.)
Vermillion Ave.	106 Ave. (west of 101 St.)
Whyte Ave. (Strathcona)	82 Ave.
Willow Ave.	115 Ave.

Edmonton: *Formerly* — *Present Day Numbers*

First Street through Forty-second Street	101 Street through 142 Street

Strathcona: *Formerly* — *Present Day Numbers*

Fifth Street East	99 St.
Eleventh Street East	91 St.
Fifth Street West	109 St.
Sixth Street West	110 St.
Seventh Street West	111 St.
Eighth Street West	112 St.
Twelfth Street West	116 St.
First Avenue North	83 Ave.
Sixth Avenue North	88 Ave.
Sixth Avenue South	76 Ave.

Photo above:
A panorama of the growing metropolis, with the skyline dominated by the Alberta Legislature Building and the Grand Trunk Pacific Railway's MacDonald Hotel. (CN Photo)

2

The First Car Operates

THE EDMONTON RADIAL RAILWAY was scheduled to begin operating on November 1st 1908. By mid-August tenders had been called to obtain the rail and electrical overhead supplies required to complete the new Edmonton-Strathcona interurban line. Contracts had been awarded for the provision of power-generating equipment, while grading contractors were well into their respective tasks on both the Edmonton and Strathcona portions of the interurban connection.[1] Fifty-two iron support poles for the overhead trolley wires were being erected along the centre of Jasper Avenue between Namayo Avenue (97 Street) and 9th (109) Street, while the section west of the latter street was being lined with fifty-three wooden poles.[2]

The fare structure called for riders to pay a 5¢ fare within each city during the day. Whenever a rider crossed from Edmonton to Strathcona or vice-versa, he would be required to pay an additional 5¢ fare. After 11 p.m. these fares were increased to 10 cents.[3]

The official track layout plans established by Edmonton City Council in March 1907 were superseded by an amended layout approved by Council on August 18, 1909:

On Jasper Avenue from Namayo Avenue (97 Street) to 21 (121) Street.

On Namayo Avenue (97 Street) from Jasper Avenue to Sutherland Street (106 Avenue).

On Sutherland Street (106 Avenue) from Namayo (97 Street) to Syndicate Avenue (95 Street).

On Syndicate Avenue (95 Street) from Sutherland Street (106 Avenue) to Norwood Boulevard.

On Kirkness (95) Street from Norwood Boulevard to Alberta (118) Avenue.

On 9th (109) Street southerly from Jasper Avenue to Saskatchewan (97) Avenue.

On Saskatchewan (97) Avenue to Curry (100) Street.

On McDougall Avenue (100 Street) to the bridge (Low Level Bridge) and across to Stratchona.[4]

At the same meeting notice was given by one of the aldermen that he would move to rescind all previous motions regarding the street railway route. These two motions were carried at the September 1st 1908 meeting and all further construction proceeded under authority of that motion. The Strathcona trackage was built as agreed upon in the Strathcona Radial Tramway Company purchase, but the new track plan had immediate implications on the development of the Edmonton Radial Railway. The trackage in pavement along First (101) Street from Jasper Avenue now dead-ended at Isabella Street (104 Avenue) near the Canadian Northern Railway station with no immediate prospects for further extension. Secondly, and perhaps of most significance, the Edmonton City Council had adopted a radial or "out-and-back" system of operation for its street railway system in place of the belt system the original plan had, in part, suggested. The influence of the radial system was reflected in the design of the first rolling stock ordered for the railway.

The first street cars, numbered 1 through 7, were built by the Ottawa Car Company Limited of Ottawa, Ontario. The order was contracted by the City of Edmonton through Gorman, Clancey and Grindley, well-known street railway and construction equipment suppliers of the day. All cars were semi-convertible, that is, the side windows could be dropped into wall pockets, allowing plenty of air to circulate during hot weather. Under inclement weather conditions the cars could be completely enclosed by lifting all the window sash up into place. These street cars were built with two trolley poles for double-end operation, so that they did not have to be turned at the end of the line. When the car was operating the trolley pole at the rear was on the overhead line while the pole at the front was hooked down clear of the overhead wire. At the end of the line, the motorman simply reversed the position of the trolley poles, raising the pole on the former front end to the overhead wire and lowering the pole at the former trailing end of the car. A complete set of equipment for operating the car was installed inside at both ends, and the motorman simply moved the controller handle and reverse key from the end he was formerly operating to the opposite end. The car was now ready to operate in the opposite direction, without having to be physically turned. This system eliminated the need for building and maintaining loop or wye trackage and overhead wire at the end of the line. The double-ended car was a very flexible vehicle, as it could operate just as

Photo above:

The Edmonton Radial Railway's original car barns on Syndicate Avenue (95 Street) at 109A Avenue. This facility was closed in 1913 when Cromdale shop opened as the new headquarters for the ERR. (Glenbow Alberta Institute)

readily on a "belt line" system where its double-ended features were not actually required, as the car simply operated in the same direction around a large circuit. It was a necessity on "radial" systems for "out-and-back" routes where facilities to turn the car physically did not exist. Since the order for the Edmonton street cars was not signed until August 20th 1908, the flexibility provided by the double-end feature was important, as Edmonton City Council vacillated between the belt and radial styles of track layout, up to the last moment. When Council finally decided upon the radial style layout, the double-ended car was justified; consequently, turning loops and wyes were not built at the extremities of the system for some years to come.

Cars numbered 1 through 6 were large double truck trams, 38' 6 1/2" long, capable of seating forty passengers each. Number 7 was a single truck car, 31' 10" long, with a seating capacity of thirty-two. Car 7 had only one trolley pole fixed to the centre of its roof. In order to change the operating direction of this car, the motorman untied the trolley rope, pulled the trolley off the wire, then walked around to the other end with trolley rope in hand to set the pole back to the wire and secure the trolley rope at the other end. Car 7 had been ordered to provide the service in Strathcona from Sixth Street West (110 Street) along Whyte Avenue to Cameron (99) Street and then south to the top of the hill on Cameron Street where it was to connect with the interurban car to and from Edmonton. All of the cars were equipped with hand brakes only. The colour scheme on these original cars when they were delivered is uncertain, but it is thought to have been two tones of brown. The words EDMONTON RADIAL RAILWAY appeared in gold lettering centred on each side of the body below the window sill. The road numbers were prominently displayed on both sides of both platform dashes. They also appeared on each side beneath the first and last body window posts in line with and at each end of the railway name. Initially, the cars relied entirely on electric heaters for warmth during the winter months. The underframing consisted of georgia pine side and intermediate sills while end sills and cross joints were of white oak. The side sills were reinforced the full length of the car body with 7" x 5/8" steel plate. The platform framing was all of white oak with centre and side knees reinforced with steel angle. The interior of the car, including all sash, was finished in natural cherry. Vestibules were finished in birch, stained to match the interior of the car body. Ceilings were finished in three-ply bird's-eye maple veneer.[5]

Each double truck car was powered by four 40 h.p. electric motors, while the smaller single-truck car had two motors — one for each axle. All electrical equipment including the motors was supplied by Canadian General Electric Company of Peterborough, Ontario.[6] The platforms were of equal length, with a single folding door on each side. Passengers boarded the car and paid their fares to the conductor as he passed through the car to collect them.

Final assembly of the cars such as setting the car bodies on their trucks and connecting up the electrical equipment actually took place in Edmonton. It was thus necessary to establish a storage and maintenance shop before the car bodies began to arrive. A site was chosen on the east side of Syndicate Avenue (95 Street) at Gallagher Street (109 Avenue). The barn was a four-track white frame structure with blue trim, 60' x 90', set on a brick foundation and capable of accommodating eight cars. The office wing was 20' x 64'. The whole structure provided facilities for two repair pits, a general repair shop, a car storage area, a drafting room, a waiting room for car crews, a general office and a private office.[7] A second two-track storage barn was to be built in Strathcona so that cars serving that city could be stored there. It was located at 6th (110) Street West and First (83) Avenue North[8] but was not actually completed and ready for service until early in 1909.

Work progressed very rapidly throughout August, September and October. Electrical equipment was installed for the overhead line, final track laying completed and the first pair of street cars was shipped from the Ottawa Car Company on October 14th 1908.[9]

Final adjustments are made to Edmonton's first streetcar before it sets out on one of its trial trips. The early snowfall has encouraged the installation of the storm windows on the car body, but trolley catchers and even trolley rope cleats are in the future, as the worker in the foreground secures the trolley rope to the hanger for the Providence fender. Since the first two trial runs on October 29th and 30th took place at night, it is probable that this scene depicts the preparations somewhere near the Syndicate Avenue (95 Street) car barns for the first trip to Strathcona on October 31st 1908.

The shipment of these first two cars was divided between the two transcontinental railways. At that time, Canadian Northern had extensive trackage in Western Canada and some trackage in central and eastern Canada, but the two segments had not yet been connected across Northern Ontario. Nevertheless Canadian Northern desired to convince its customers that it had a transportation system which could deliver goods from central Canada to western Canada as quickly as the Canadian Pacific Railway with its all-rail link. In order to prove the point, Edmonton Radial Railway car number 1 was loaded aboard a Canadian Northern train at Ottawa, while car number 2 went via Canadian Pacific. Car 1 had to be transferred from rail to ship, possibly at Key Harbour on Georgian Bay, Ontario, to travel over Lakes Huron and Superior picking up the Canadian Northern Railway again at Port Arthur.

The first car, number 2, arrived in Strathcona via CPR on Saturday, October 24th. It was immediately transferred by the Canadian Northern, across the Low Level Bridge to the CN's downtown Edmonton yards and then to the city warehouse on Kinistino (96 Street).[10] Here the street car was unloaded from the flat car and assembled.

Car number 1 arrived in Edmonton on the afternoon of Halloween (October 31st) exactly a week after car 2's arrival.[11] The Canadian Northern route from Ottawa to Edmonton could thus not yet be considered competitive. Hence the balance of the cars in the original order of seven for the ERR was shipped by the CPR to Strathcona.

The final work of installing the motors in car 2 was completed during the evening of Thursday, October 29th 1908. This work had fallen behind the anticipated time frame for completion, as some oversized parts which had been shipped with the car had to be cut down before final assembly could be completed.[12] Later that same evening car 2 made its way haltingly out of the city warehouse yards and proceeded a short distance up Syndicate Avenue. Some finer adjustments had yet to be made, so the car was left out all night on Syndicate Avenue.[13] In this inauspicious way, Edmonton's first street car, number 2, made its first run.

Superintendent Charles Taylor and a crew of eight men had been working long days, particularly since the arrival of car 2. It was not unusual for work to go on until midnight in the excitement to see the car operating as soon as possible. The long work hours were probably not entirely self-motivation on the part of Superintendent Taylor. Edmonton City Council had a strong mandate from the citizens of Edmonton and Strathcona to complete the line for operation by November 1st 1908, and time was running out on that promise. Superintendent Taylor and his crew were no doubt being encouraged by Mayor John A. McDougall to have the car ready to operate by November 1. The newspapers of the day gave due credit to Superintendent Taylor and his foreman, Oscar Barrstend. The men on the crew were N. Hougan, C. Jones, H. Kjo, A. Bogart, C. Hildebrand, M. Curfman, E.R. Johnson, C. Erickson, B. Brunless, A. Johnson and J. Wetteberg.[14]

(Provincial Archives of Alberta)

The first halting operations of the Edmonton Radial Railway on October 29th prepared the way for a smooth debut on Jasper Avenue at 10:00 p.m. on Friday, October 30th 1908. Motorman, W.J. Fountain, with six years' operating experience in Toronto, was the senior motorman in Edmonton. He guided the car from the car barns along Syndicate Avenue (95 Street), Sutherland (106 Avenue), Namayo (97 Street) and finally into Jasper Avenue. One reporter noted that car number 2 ". . . swept down Jasper Avenue to the Opera House running with a grace and ease which can only be compared with the most modern systems in Eastern Canada and the United States."[15] At 3rd (103) Street a fuse blew and the car stopped. The crowd of excited citizens who had been following the car's progress literally mobbed the car. When someone yelled "Fares please", the first one challenged presented a quarter saying "Never mind the change, it's worth a quarter to ride on the first car." Superintendent Taylor then ordered everyone off the car, the poles were changed, the fuse was repaired, and the car headed back to Sutherland Street (106 Avenue). Here the car was reversed again. Another trip was made toward Jasper Avenue with a large group of young ladies who had hailed it on Sutherland Street. Children on bicycles rode along beside and ahead of the car. People paced the car, clambering aboard whenever they could as it coasted along Jasper Avenue again. The female passengers were somewhat fearful when the trolley pole slipped off the wire throwing the vehicle into darkness and bringing it to a silent halt. The only fear they openly expressed is that they might have to walk back. All apprehension was dissipated when the pole was placed back on the wire and the car continued on its journey. The theatre crowds added their cheers to the excitement as they made their way home. At the Opera House the car was reversed again for its return to the barns. It could go no further west as the tracks beyond the Opera House had not been cleared of snow and sand.[16] Edmonton was finally about to enjoy an amenity common to only those urban centres which had achieved a measure of maturity. It was the first city between Winnipeg and the west coast to have a street railway system. Citizens were justifiably excited.

A "triumphal entry" into Strathcona carried the excitement over to Saturday, October 31st, 1908. Motorman Fountain set out from the car barns for Strathcona with Mayor McDougall, Civic Commissioners, members of the press, Superintendent Taylor and other street railway officials aboard.

It was indeed a "triumphal entry" as the trip went very smoothly and fulfilled McDougall's promised November 1st deadline. From Jasper Avenue the car turned into 9th (109) Street, over the hill to Saskatchewan (97) Avenue, and along Curry (100) Street to the Low Level Bridge where it shared a gauntlet track with the Canadian Northern Railway.

Once off the bridge, the car line followed the steep roadway up Strathcona hill to Fifth (99) Street East and then to Whyte Avenue. When car 2 turned into Whyte Avenue many people from Strathcona turned out to welcome its arrival. The car stopped just short of the CPR crossing where Mayor Duggan and members of the Strathcona Council boarded to congratulate Mayor McDougall. On the return trip the car was crowded with passengers, many of them Edmonton children who had run behind the car all the way from Edmonton. Superintendent Taylor had let it be known that Edmonton children would be given a ride back. He suddenly found the car jammed with children. He began to challenge his riders. One little girl told him she lived in Strathcona but was going to Edmonton to visit her aunt. She produced the money to pay her fare, so the Superintendent couldn't refuse her a ride.

Without incident, the crowded car returned to Edmonton and the Syndicate Avenue car barns. It finished its duty for the day by hauling car number 1 from the city yards to the car barn where the task of placing the second car in working order immediately got under way.[17]

3 Streetcar Service Begins

SEVERAL OUTSTANDING DETAILS required attention before regular operation of ERR trams could begin. Permission to cross the Low Level Bridge and the CPR on Whyte Avenue had yet to be officially granted by the Railway Commission. Installation of the overhead on First (101) Street between Jasper Avenue and Isabella (104) Avenue was incomplete, while operation of the second car, number 1, was not anticipated before Wednesday, November 4th.[1]

Superintendent Taylor announced a formal route structure and time table. Two routes were outlined. One began at Alberta (118) Avenue, south on Kirkness and Syndicate (95 Street) to Sutherland (106 Avenue); west to Namayo (97 Street); south to Jasper Avenue; and west to Twenty-First (121) Street. A round trip was expected to take one hour; four cars would provide a fifteen-minute service on the route. The other route provided for a half-hourly interurban service between Ninth (109) Street and Jasper Avenue and the Strathcona CPR station. Service was to be provided between 6 a.m. and midnight. This schedule was slated for implementation on Monday, November 9th 1908 but did not materialize because of a severe power shortage, lack of cars and no confirmation on the crossing of the Low Level Bridge.[2] The official opening of the system was postponed again and again and never really took place in a ceremonial way. Service began as it became expedient to provide it. Regular service did begin at 7 a.m. on November 9th with two trams (cars 1 and 2) operating between the car barns on Syndicate Avenue (95 Street) and 21st (121) Street until midnight. Receipts amounted to four dollars per car per hour. Motormen on the first day of regular service were Fountain, Miller, Moyer and Robinson while the conductors were Andrew, York, Horne and Bromley.[3] The two cars were providing a half-hourly service, and took in a total of $150 during the first day of revenue operation.[4]

The first few days of operation were not without the odd minor passenger mishap. For safety's sake, passengers were encouraged to board only from the outside instead of attempting to embark from between the double tracks,[5] and for safe and efficient operations, patrons were urged to board

Photo above:
In wet weather, unpaved streets became sticky, slippery pathways of mud. The streetcars brought reliable transportation to the many areas of Edmonton where such streets existed.

trams only at car stops. Car stops were located so that street cars always passed over the cross street intersections before halting on the far side.

Car number 3, the fourth delivered, arrived on Tuesday evening November 10th.[6] By Saturday, November 21st all four cars were operating providing fifteen-minute service.[7] Edmontonians made good use of the service that Saturday, as some 4,177 passengers were carried bringing in $178.[8]

But there were problems. Lack of power troubled the new service often during the latter part of November. An explosion occured at the gas producer plant (one of the important generators of electricity) which curtailed car service for a time when the demand for power from all other utilities was high. The steam generator plant could not meet the City's total power demand. This delayed the opening of service to Strathcona, which was to have begun on November 30th. Edmonton service was cancelled, too, when rain and snow formed ice on the rails and had to be removed with picks.[9] In addition to power and ice problems, the wood pavement blocks between the rails and for about eighteen inches on either side of the outermost rails along Jasper Avenue and Namayo Avenue (97 Street) were beginning to heave. The contractor blamed dirty streets for the problem, which became a serious concern to motormen. The blocks sometimes heaved as a street car passed, threatening to cause a derailment.[10]

Strathcona service began on Friday, December 4th 1908.[11] One car operated from the east side of the Whyte Avenue crossing near the CPR depot in Strathcona, via Whyte Avenue, Cameron (99) Street, the Low Level Bridge, Curry (100) Street, Saskatchewan (97) Avenue, 9th (109) Street, Jasper Avenue, Namayo Avenue (97 Street), to the corner of Sutherland (106 Avenue) and return, providing service every 1 1/2 hours. It was necessary to make the long trip through Edmonton because switches had not been installed at Jasper Avenue and First (101) Street nor at Jasper and Namayo (97 Street). The interurban car was labelled "Edmonton" at one end and "Strathcona" at the other. These white signs with dark contrasting lettering were fixed to the letterboard above the centre windows at each respective end. About three weeks later, interurban cars were further identified by a route colour system, a red glass installed in the centre panel of the transom of the deck roof at each end of the car. Smaller pieces of white glass flanked the larger red glass panel.[12]

The day that Strathcona street car service began, word came from the CPR granting permission for the ERR to cross its tracks at Strathcona.[13] William Whyte, Vice President of the CPR (and for whom Whyte Avenue was named) expressed concern about adequate protection at the crossing, and it was this issue which had prevented the ERR from crossing the CPR and continuing west along Whyte Avenue. Mr. Whyte continued to recommend that the ERR install a derail on the street car tracks approaching the crossing, as well as semaphore signals on the railway line, interlocked with the derail. The ERR had permission, however, to cross the railway on Whyte Avenue without the interlocking devices.

By early December, the producer gas plant had returned to normal, again supplying sufficient power to the street railway to commence the service to Strathcona and to restore full service (four cars operating on a fifteen-minute headway) in Edmonton.[14]

The Strathcona service as it was inaugurated reflected a change in the original plans for car service in and to that community. The through service was received well by its residents as it eliminated two transfers; one planned for the top of Scona Hill on Cameron (99) Street and one at 9th (109) Street and Jasper Avenue.[15] The run-through service offered more convenient service to passengers travelling between the CPR station at Strathcona and downtown Edmonton or the Canadian Northern station in Edmonton. Daily reports indicated that 973 passengers travelled on the interurban car on Monday, December 7th 1908 and 925 travelled the following day. The cars handled these loads without making any schedule revisions to handle traffic from the trains. Based on a schedule published on Thursday, December 10th 1908, the car left Strathcona 7:30 a.m., 9:00 a.m., 10:30 a.m., 12 noon, 1:30 p.m., 4:30 p.m., 6:00 p.m., 7:30 p.m., 9:00 p.m., and 10:30 p.m.[16] The above figures indicate that the car averaged some 44 passengers on each trip to and from Edmonton. Superintendent Taylor announced that in order to provide more reliable service, the interurban car would not stop on its northbound trip for local passengers in Edmonton. By December 10th, the cars were operating across the CPR tracks in Strathcona and west as far as Main (104) Street.[17]

The last car of the original order arrived in Strathcona on December 13th, 1908. Car 7 was immediately sent across to Edmonton to be fitted up for service.[18] On Wednesday evening, December 16th, two cars operated on the interurban line for the first time, offering a 45-minute service.[19] This service turned out to be a temporary measure, being subsequently withdrawn due to the power shortage.

The street cars were very popular and a bit of a novelty for residents of Strathcona and Edmonton. The young people of Queens Avenue Presbyterian Church sponsored a car ride party on December 28th 1908 to bind the ties between the two cities, now joined together by the new interurban car line. Plans were announced that the young people would meet at the Edmonton church at 7:45 p.m. to catch the car leaving Namayo Avenue at 8:00 p.m.[20] The "mystery tour" for a 25¢ return fare, actually terminated at Whyte Avenue and Main (104) Street where the group walked the two blocks north to Strathcona's Knox Church. Two full car loads of young people made the trip without mishap, but on the return trip the cars stalled due to a powerhouse failure. The group was forced to resort to the old horse-drawn bus to carry them back to Edmonton.[21]

"Gremlins" continued to plague the system. Car 5 ran right off the end of the track at Alberta (118) Avenue in Edmonton late Saturday, December 26th. The motorman reported that he was watching for a landmark light in a shack. The light was not there and when the motorman discovered he had reached the shack, it was too late. The car skidded on the frosty rails, running off the end of

EDMONTON RADIAL RAILWAY

Return Trip Transfer for Purchasers
FROM
THE CITY MARKET
This date, good only on Saturdays from 7 a.m. to 6 p.m.
Positively not good for Market Employees, Dealers or Retailers of any kind.
CITY COMMISSIONERS

JAN.	1	13	25
FEB.	2	14	26
MAR.	3	15	27
APR.	4	16	28
MAY	5	17	29
JUNE	6	18	30
JULY	7	19	31
AUG.	8	20	
SEPT.	9	21	
OCT.	10	22	
NOV.	11	23	
DEC.	12	24	

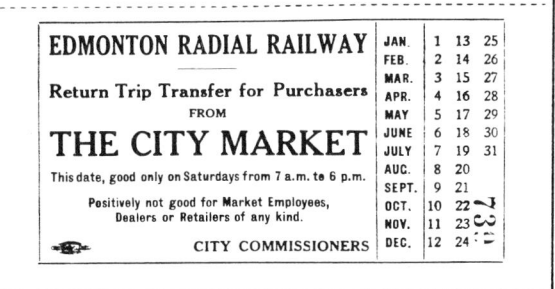

Photo left:

Car 14, a product of the Preston Car and Coach Company, travels eastbound along Jasper Avenue east of Namayo Avenue (97 Street). The Syndicate Avenue (95 Street) route began service on September 15th 1909. The then-fashionable Alberta Hotel appears immediately behind the streetcar.
(Provincial Archives of Alberta)

Photo below:

The south side car barn, located on 6th (110) Street West and 1st (83) Avenue North, was built in 1908 and went into service early in 1909 to house cars assigned to south side runs. Inspection and light repairs could be carried out in this facility, but its main function was for car storage. The two-track addition to the right was constructed in 1912. The tracks lead out into 6th (110) Street West. The ERR declared the barn surplus in 1921, centralizing all storage, dispatching and maintenance at Cromdale. *(Glenbow Alberta Institute)*

the line. It took an hour for a spare car to pull the derailed tram back onto the tracks again,[22] but the story carried in the Edmonton Journal, reported that it took a full 24 hours to get car 5 back on the rails.[23] This erroneous report justifiably annoyed Superintendent Taylor.

The intermittent service, however, did not discourage people from riding the cars. Whenever the cars were operating, people were there to ride them. In fact, on the Saturday before Christmas, the crowded cars left many hopefuls standing at the car stops, forcing them to walk to their destinations.[24]

During the week of December 14th-19th, 1908, the cars carried an average of 4,151 passengers per day. Receipts for that same week totalled $1,100.[25] In the following week, daily ridership averaged 4,784 bringing some $1,270 into the fare boxes.[26] Interurban cars picking up passengers from the trains in Strathcona became so crowded that conductors could not collect fares from all their passengers before the car reached the bridge.[27]

This popularity moved Mayor McDougall to predict that the Edmonton Radial Railway would be one of the best-paying utilities of the City of Edmonton. Some Strathcona financiers and some members of the Strathcona Council even expressed an open interest in buying back the charter of the Strathcona Radial Railway from the City of Edmonton. No formal proposal was ever presented; but since the City of Edmonton clearly favoured a single system in and between the two cities, acceptance of such a proposal seemed somewhat remote.[28]

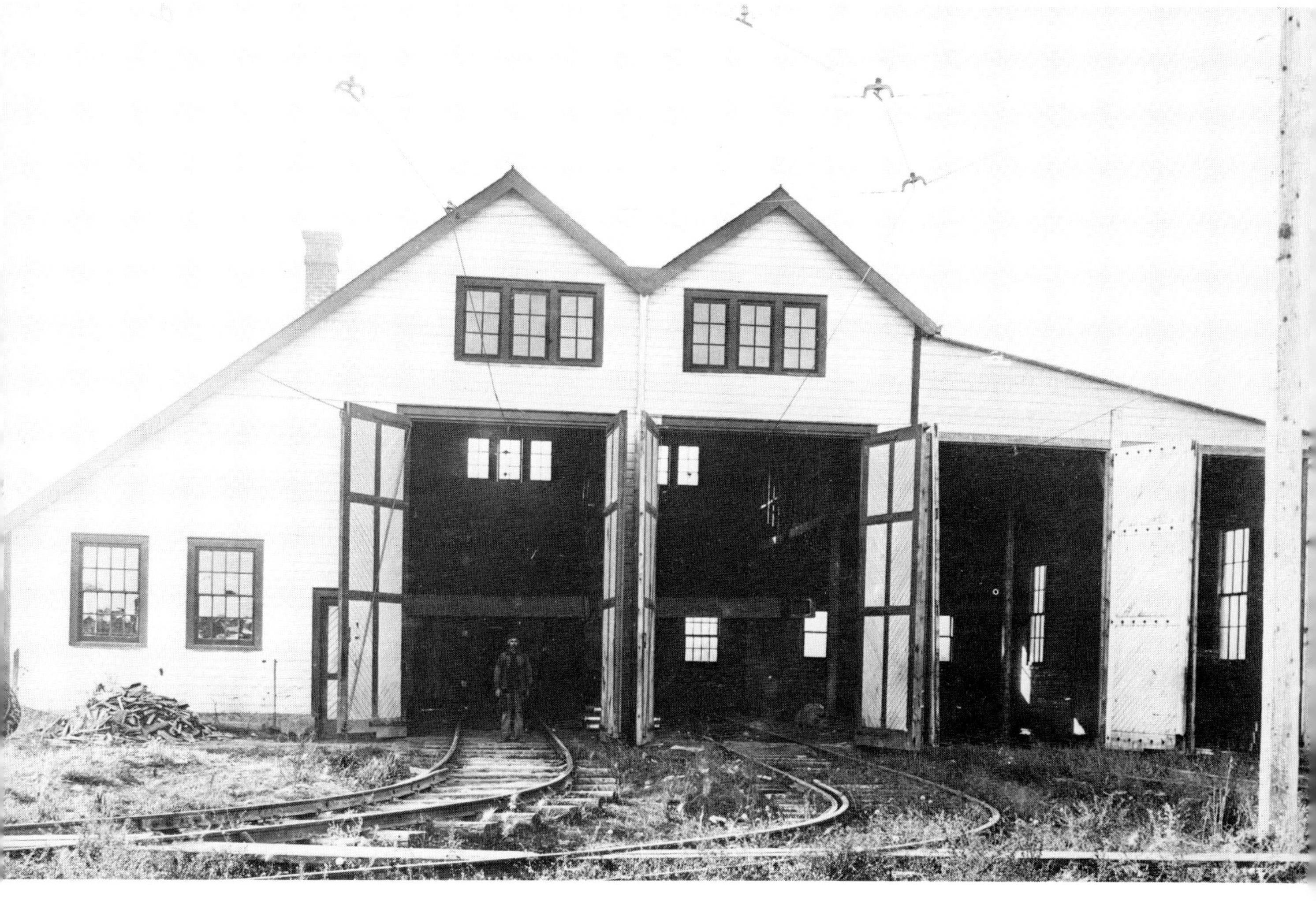

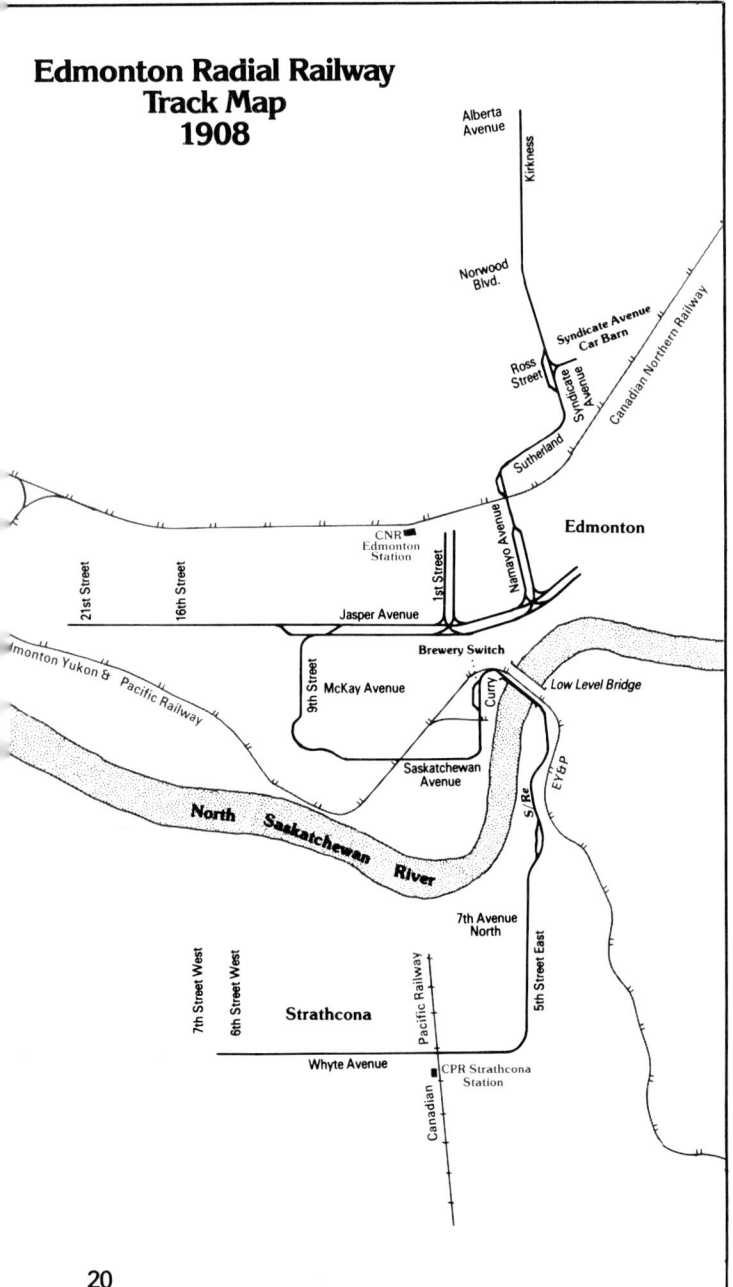

Photo above:

Single track has been laid in this scene looking north on Ninth (109) Street from Saskatchewan (97) Avenue in 1913. Preparations are being made for the laying of a second track as grading has been completed to accommodate the concrete base. Ties from the original alignment are stacked at the side of the right-of-way. The alignment of the original Ninth (109) Street trackage can be traced from the overhead line still in place in the top left corner. The white building at centre left is the original, temporary CPR north side station used from July until September 1913 before completion of the new station at Ninth (109) Street and Jasper Avenue.

(Glenbow Alberta Institute)

By the close of 1908, all eleven miles of Edmonton Radial Railway trackage was in service except for the six-block section on Whyte Avenue from Main (104) Street to 6th (110) Street west and 1st (101) Street from Jasper Avenue to Isabella (104) Avenue. Early January 1909 marked the completion of the Strathcona car barns at the corner of 6th Street west and First (83) Avenue north. Installation of some 200 yards of overhead wire and trackage from Whyte Avenue remained incomplete pending moderation of the cold weather,[29] and service to 6th (110) Street west in Strathcona began during January or February 1909. During the spring, the cars terminated at 4th (108) Street west due to poor track conditions beyond, but by mid-April they had resumed service to the end of the line again.[30] The south side barn expedited late evening and early morning service in Strathcona by obviating the need to dispatch the car providing such service from the distant Syndicate Avenue (95 Street) barn in Edmonton.[31]

The future of the Edmonton Radial Railway looked very bright indeed as citizens of Strathcona and Edmonton took to the new service enthusiastically. Before the close of 1908, four new cars had been ordered to keep up with passenger demand and a new motor-generator was being installed to supply a more dependable source of electric power for the street cars.

Preston Cars Introduce P-A-Y-E Fare Collection

THE NEED FOR more rolling stock became very evident soon after the first street car made its inaugural run. Superintendent Taylor expressed the need for four additional cars with air brake equipment, plus air brake equipment for the two cars from the original group normally assigned to the Strathcona run. The hills leading to the Low Level Bridge over the North Saskatchewan River from both Edmonton and Strathcona made air brakes almost a necessity for the cars assigned to this route. In December 1908 a contract for four new cars was awarded to the Preston Car and Coach Company of Preston, Ontario, a relative newcomer to the car building industry. Preston's low bid, coupled with its promise to improve on the quality of workmanship compared to those cars already operating on the system, convinced the Edmonton Radial Railway and City Council to purchase from it. Preston bid $3,225 per car, the Ottawa Car Company $3,528, the Brill Car Company of Philadelphia $4,060 and the St. Louis Car Company of St. Louis, Missouri $4,985. The bids were for car bodies only and did not include trucks, electrical or air brake equipment.[1] The final price of each Preston car in this order delivered to Edmonton and ready for service was estimated at $6,500.[2]

The Preston cars introduced the pay-as-you-enter fare concept to the Edmonton Radial Railway, which in turn resulted in some very apparent changes in car design. Inside the car body, longitudinal seating at each end with transverse seating in the centre, allowed greater freedom of movement for passengers.[3] The cars in service up to that time had transverse seating only. The longer vestibules, six feet in length compared to 4'8" on the original cars, provided the necessary space for two doorways, to allow passengers to embark and disembark simultaneously. The longer vestibules also permitted the conductor to collect fares as passengers boarded the car.[4] The Montreal Street Railway had experimented with and actually introduced this system of fare collection to public transportation in 1905.[5] Foreseeing its potential success, Messrs. Ross and McDonald of the MSR patented this method of fare collection, with the result that other electric railway systems adopting the use of this system had to pay a royalty on each car utilizing this method of fare collection. In Edmonton, concern was initially expressed about the pay-as-you-enter system because of fear that passengers would have to stand lined up in the cold for longer periods of time waiting to board the car, while those ahead stopped to pay their fares, but this concern proved to be unfounded.

Power shortages had been plaguing the Edmonton system from the start. Extension of trackage and introduction of new services in 1909, the use of new equipment and Sunday operations were all destined to be affected by the availability of power. The City's new producer gas plant apparently could generate sufficient power to serve all of Edmonton's electrical needs including those of the street railway, but it was not until late December 1908 that the 300-kilowatt Westinghouse motor generator arrived. This unit was designed to take the alternating current from the producer gas plant and convert it to direct current for the street railway.[7] Until the installation of this motor generator, the street cars had to rely upon limited power produced from the steam generators, but when these had to supply power to service all of the City's needs because of breakdowns at the producer gas plant, there simply was not enough power to go around. During one frosty January day for example, citizens let their water run continuously to prevent plumbing from freezing. This created a tremendous on-going demand for power to operate the electric pumps, and the ensuing shortage of power once again forced street car service to be halted for the day at 4:00 p.m.[8] Eventually, even the gas producer plant could not supply the necessary power for these peak demand situations, so it was announced that the new motor generator would be removed to Walter's Mill where idle steam boilers could operate it and supply all the current for the street railway system.[9] Anticipating a constantly growing demand for power, City Council accepted a tender for two 400 kilowatt generator units from Crocker-Wheeler Company for $7,100 for the street railway power plant.[10]

One street railway generator had indeed been installed at Walter's Mill and went into operation on January 30th 1909, enabling two-car service to Strathcona. Frozen pipes, however, shut the generator down the following day and the increased service had to be curtailed after 11:00 p.m. This turn of events brought strong criticism of the power department. Superintendent Taylor, supported by street car patrons, urged that control of street railway power be once again put into the hands of the street railway department. The aldermen of Strathcona recorded their displeasure

Photo above:

ERR sprinkler S-1 gives a fine display of its sprinkling prowess on Jasper Avenue at 21 (121) Street in 1909. Note the distinctive passenger shelter to the left of the sprinkler.
(Glenbow Alberta Institute)

Opposite page, right:

Sweeper 1, clearing a path through the snow on 124 Street south of 118 Avenue. This view was taken in later years, during the severe winter conditions of 1942. (Les Corness)

Photo below:

Edmonton Sweeper 3 stands with brooms poised, ready to do battle with the season's first fall of snow. (Bob Walker)

at the deteriorating and intermittent car service. On February 2nd 1909 the power was again ordered off by the power department at 11:00 p.m. In order to get to the barns before the deadline, the last car to Strathcona terminated its trip at the Whyte Avenue railway crossing instead of proceeding the seven blocks further west to its usual terminus. Passengers waiting for the car at stops further west expressed extreme consternation when they saw the car start back toward Edmonton before completing its trip.[11] This was not the last unannouced power failure to affect the street cars, but by the end of March 1909, power availability and reliability had improved enough to allow the operation of three cars on the interurban line, offering service every twenty minutes on Saturday afternoons.[12]

While power shortages caused most of the service problems during the first winter that the Edmonton Radial Railway operated, snow also played its part in tieing up services from time to time. Each of the cars carried flanger devices fixed to the leading truck frame just ahead of the wheels. Small amounts of snow posed no problem for these scrapers, but severe drifting and heavy snowfalls called for a more substantial means of snow removal. The city ordered a large double-truck sweeper from McGuire-Cummings, a Chicago car builder. Large, stiff, rattan brooms, driven by a powerful electric motor, cleared the snow off the tracks very effectively. The new sweeper was subjected to a "dry" test run on March 24th 1909,[13] while a mid-April snowfall put the sweeper to its first operating test. The whole system was cleared quite readily in one trip[14] as the machine shrouded itself in a huge cloud of white snow. Another piece of work-equipment ordered early in 1909 was a street sprinkler. This unit, powered and operated in the same manner as the street cars, consisted of a 5,000-gallon water tank which sprayed water under pressure over the streets ahead of it. Purchased primarily to flush the paved sections of the street railway system, it occasionally sprinkled some of the unpaved streets in order to keep down the dust during the hot dry summer season. This unit came from the Preston Car and Coach Company toward the end of September 1909,[15] and created enough interest in the early years of its operation to be the subject of a postcard illustrating its spraying prowess at the west end of the Jasper Avenue line.

Proposals for extensions to the Edmonton Radial Railway created considerable controversy. The J.Y. Griffith Packing Plant had an extensive operation in North Edmonton, and the need for a car line to the plant was pressing. Coal mining interests, notably Rosedale Coal Company and the Edmonton Standard Coal Company, favoured an extension of the car line east on Jasper Avenue then north to the packing plant, with rail connections to their mines.[16] Superintendent Taylor, however, was most adamant about having the line extended east on Alberta (118) Avenue from the end of the line at Kirkness (95) Street to Norton (66) Street and then north to the packing plant at 124 Avenue. In addition to the heavy rush hour traffic, the Alberta Avenue route offered more potential passenger revenue that the East Jasper Avenue route, as the Dominion Government held a large unsettled reserve of land along the proposed Jasper Avenue east extention. Taylor pointed out that the river also restricted any population growth along this stretch. The Alberta Avenue route traversed an area with high potential for an intensive residential population. In opposition, citizens of the Jasper Avenue east area pointed out

Photo above:

Excavation for double-tracking the streetcar line on Saskatchewan (97) Avenue is carried out by hand with the aid of horse-drawn vehicles in this 1913 scene.
Glenbow Alberta Institute

that a line through their areas would serve City Park (Borden Park). They singled out Guelph, Ontario as a case in point, where a street railway system became a paying proposition because it carried large summer crowds to a park on its street car line. Taylor countered that argument by suggesting that Edmonton summer evenings were not hot enough to draw large numbers of people to the parks. He noted, too, that the Alberta Avenue route would actually serve City Park as it touched the park's northern boundary.[17] The Alberta Avenue route was finally adopted.

Additional extensions approved for construction in 1909 included: Syndicate Avenue (95 Street) between Sutherland (106) Avenue and Jasper Avenue; First (101) Street north to Vermillion (106) Avenue and then west to Eighth (108) Street.[18] A west end resident convinced City Council to approve the construction of a line from either Jasper and Twenty-first (121) Street or Vermillion (106) Avenue and Eighth (108) Street to a point on Albany (110) Avenue and West end City Park. Council authorized Superintendent Taylor to determine the most appropriate route to be followed,[19] but construction on this proposed extension was not undertaken in 1909.

Transfers made their debut to the Edmonton Radial Railway on Monday, April 1st 1909. Up to that time, passengers, transferring from one car to another to continue their journey to or from the interurban line, paid a second fare or — in the case of riders going to or coming from Strathcona — a third fare. A Strathcona passenger paid a five-cent fare in Strathcona before the car crossed the Low Level Bridge. Then another five-cent fare after the car crossed the bridge into Edmonton which would take him or her to the interurban car terminus at Namayo Avenue (97 Street) and the CNR crossing. If one wanted to continue to the end of the street car line at Alberta (118) Avenue or go west on Jasper Avenue from Ninth (109) Street, one simply paid another five-cent fare upon boarding the car going to that point. A Strathcona passenger paid fifteen cents to get from Strathcona to the northern or western extremity of the street car line. Likewise a passenger going to or coming from a point on the Edmonton side of the bridge on the interurban line paid ten cents to get to the north or west end of the line. The introduction of transfers enabled passengers to transfer to or from the interurban car without paying an extra fare.[20] Transfer or not, passengers were still required to put an extra nickel in the fare box when the car crossed the Low Level Bridge. In April, only two transfer points existed; Jasper Avenue and Ninth (109) Street and the Namayo Avenue (97 Street) CNR crossing. As the system expanded the number of transfer points increased.

April 1st 1909 also marked the introduction of extended hours of operation. Service began an hour earlier at 6:00 a.m. from the Alberta (118) Avenue terminus, while the last car left the western terminus at 12 midnight instead of 11:45 p.m.[21]

Track maintenance and extension work began early in 1909. Much of the wooden block paving along Jasper Avenue and Namayo Avenue (97 Street) was taken up. The heaving which had occurred in November 1908 became worse as the frost left the ground in the spring of 1909. The heaving and swelling of the wooden blocks reportedly forced rail alignment out from 3/4" to 1" in some places. Gravel and ashes temporarily replaced the removed blocks.[22] By mid-May contractors with teams of horses and equipment began to build up the existing line along Fifth (99) Street east in Strathcona to Whyte Avenue.[23] Plans were finalized for the placement of the line east on Alberta (118) Avenue and north on Norton (66) Street to the packing plant in North Edmonton. The centre of the car tracks was to be eleven feet from the south boundary of Alberta Avenue and the same distance from the east boundary of Norton Street.[24] This packing plant line was completed, except for ballasting, by July 20th 1909, and officials expected the line to be open for service during the last week of that month.[25]

While track work proceeded, the arrival of the new street cars attracted much favourable comment for the Edmonton Radial Railway. Two of the the new cars arrived in Edmonton on May 31st via Canadian Northern from Preston, Ontario.[26] The pay-as-you-enter feature attracted considerable interest.

These cars also introduced a new colour scheme to Edmonton, green below the window sill and red above. On Tuesday, June 29th 1909, the opening day of the Edmonton Fair, the first Preston-built car in western Canada made its inaugural run on the ERR as a Strathcona special.[27] Like the first Preston cars delivered to Calgary that same year, the Edmonton trams came equipped with Bemis trucks. The coat of arms of the City, with the words "Industry, Energy, Enterprise" was displayed on the centre of each side in gold lettering. The words "Edmonton Radial Ry" flanked the crest. Road numbers 10, 12, 14 and 16 appeared on the left and right dash at each end of each respective car. No apparent reason has been found for assigning these particular numbers to the new trams.

"In the interior of the cars . . . Aside from having the pay-as-you-enter feature the cars are fitted up in a style which would be a credit to a C.P.R. parlour car."[27] The Edmonton Journal of the day appeared to regard parlour cars as the pinnacle of the railway car builders' art in Canada. The reporter went on to describe the new street cars in glowing terms. The interior lights on these cars were located on either side of the car interior, as opposed to clusters in the centre of the ceilings in the original cars. Push buttons at each window seat enabled passengers to signal their wish to disembark at the next stop.[28] Rosewood and mahogany finished interiors lent that parlour car "class" to these new trams.[29]

The new fare collection system and the new paint scheme were not the only innovations, as two new safety features were introduced as well. The steps on the left or blind side of the car as it travelled forward could be drawn in under the platform, preventing passengers from attempting to board the car from the wrong side.[30] At least one injury had already been reported involving a passenger being thrown against the overhead wire support poles in the centre of the road while attempting to board a moving car from the wrong side. The windows were all protected by gilded iron bars to prevent passengers from poking their heads out the side windows. When there were no bars, passengers had a propensity to do just that, exposing themselves to serious injury as the car passed a centre-of-the-road pole or an oncoming vehicle. Last, but certainly not least, these cars introduced the use of air brakes to the ERR. The air brakes were not immediately serviceable however, possibly because of the lack of power to operate the compressors.[31]

Photo below:

Interior of ERR No. 48, one of Edmonton's large Preston-built trams.
(Les Corness)

The additional services made feasible by the arrival of the new cars created a need for double tracking the car line on Jasper Avenue West between Ninth (109) Street and Sixteenth (116) Street. The intention to double-track this section appeared in the press on June 17th 1909[32] and on June 25th street cars began to use the new trackage.[33] At the same time a new route began operating between Sixteenth (116) Street and Jasper to the Namayo Avenue (97 Street) crossing giving eight-minute service over this portion of the system.[34] A new Preston car went into regular service on this new route on June 29th releasing an older car to the interurban line. The Edmonton Fair Grounds at that time were located on the flats between the river and Saskatchewan (97) Avenue, and were served by the interurban car line. During the four days of the fair, June 29th through July 2nd 1909, the eight cars operating carried some 45,000 passengers. Had sufficient power been available, all nine cars on the roster at the time could have been in service. As it was, the power system was being strained to its utmost, particularly because of the heavy loads of passengers on the hills of the interurban line.[35]

The second pair of pay-as-you-enter trams arrived from Preston via the CPR on July 4th completing the delivery of the four cars.[36] Air brakes were installed on the new cars under the supervision of a Westinghouse representative at the end of July 1909.[37] With the new units on the roster, more car barn space was required, so the third switch to the barns was installed in mid-June 1909.[38] By the end of the year, all four tracks into the barns were serviceable.

Motormen and conductors carried through with the parlour-car class tradition established by the new Preston cars, when the ERR issued them with dark blue uniforms trimmed with gold braid. At the time of issue on July 19th, cap emblems and buttons had not yet arrived but were to display the city coat of arms.[39] Rigid dress regulations demanded that full uniform be worn when on duty, winter or summer.

Photo below:

Controls of a typical Edmonton car: power and reverse handles on the G.E. controller to the left, with air brake valve and manual door control to the right. (A. Clegg)

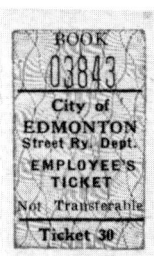

First (101) Street trackage, after laying idle since the opening of the system, finally went into service on Monday, July 12th 1909,[40] after businessmen along First Street had exerted pressure on City Council to place the expensive, paved, double track line into service. A special machine cut down the edges of the wooden paving blocks to make room for the flanges of the street car wheels. Then workers swept out the tracks.[41] The car assigned to this service began its trip at 6:30 a.m. from the Syndicate Avenue (95 Street) car barns and ran past First Street to the switch in front of the brewery on Curry (100) Street on the interurban line to accommodate men working at the brewery. From here the car turned back to the Canadian Northern Railway depot on First (101) Street. After the arrival of the CNR express at 7:40 a.m. the car left for the CPR Strathcona depot to connect with the train for Calgary. Another trip was made from the CNR depot at 2 p.m. arriving at the CPR station for 3 p.m.[42] It left Strathcona again at 4:10 p.m. and returned to the CNR depot. The car then finished its day by making a run to the brewery switch to pick up workers at 6:00 p.m.[43] This intermittent service would hardly have brought much business to the doors of the First (101) Street businessmen, but the line was in service and provided a direct connection between the Edmonton and Strathcona railway depots.

The second extension to be opened for service was the Jasper Avenue East-Syndicate Avenue (95 Street) line. Two cars went into regular service between the Syndicate Avenue (95 Street) railway crossing via Syndicate and Jasper Avenues to Sixteenth (116) Street on Wednesday, September 15th 1909.[44] The Vermillion (106) Avenue line from Eighth (108) Street via Vermillion Avenue and First (101) Street to Jasper Avenue opened on September 23rd. This was the third and last of the new extensions to go into service in 1909. Completion of this extension and construction of the Namayo Avenue (97 Street) extension north from Sutherland (106) Avenue to Norwood Boulevard was delayed pending the outcome of the September 20th 1909 money bylaws authorizing expenditures to pave a short one block section of First (101) Street north of the CNR tracks and the five-block section on Namayo Avenue (97 Street).[45] The public voted against authorizing the funds for the paving projects,[46] although the short gap in the tracks on First (101) Street was quickly completed and the line went into service immediately. Construction of the Namayo Avenue (97 Street)-Norwood Boulevard line, however, was cancelled for 1909 as the expense of laying the tracks with the distinct possibility of taking them up within a year to permit paving was considered an unnecessary expense.

Some assurance of a steady and plentiful source of power came early in September 1909 when Commissioner McNaughton announced that two new street railway power generators were about to go into service.[47] A 450-kilowatt engine from the Robb Engine Company of Amherst, Nova Scotia had arrived in Edmonton in June 1909,[48] but the powerhouse staff discovered that the boilers themselves which were to power the generators needed to be replaced. This boiler problem postponed delivery of full power to the Edmonton Radial Railway until September.[49] Up to this time Superintendent Taylor was limited to the operation of eight cars at any given time.

Since the delivery of the four new cars from Preston brought the number of cars on the roster up to eleven, three cars were always standing idle at the barns. During this energy crisis Taylor experimented with different schedules, particularly on the interurban line. Street car schedules were changed to coincide with CPR schedule changes so that street cars were on hand for train arrivals and departures. When two cars were running on a 45-minute schedule, they ususally passed each other at the siding on Curry (100) Street in front of the brewery just off the Edmonton side of the Low Level Bridge. A second siding located at the top of Scona hill on Fifth (99) Street east in Strathcona offered a passing point to delayed cars and for situations when three cars provided twenty-minute service on the interurban line.[50] Twenty-minute service was usually restricted to Saturday afternoons and special events such as the Edmonton Fair. In July 1909, a third interurban line passing siding went into use on Saskatchewan (97) Avenue between Seventh (107) and Eighth (108) Streets, directly in front of the Legislative Building, then under construction but nearing completion. This siding would allow the operation of four cars on the interurban line.[51] The increased amount of power after September 12th also resulted in more rapid service. Previously cars were permitted to operate on series circuit only (up to half speed) but the improved power situation made it possible for the motormen to advance their controllers to use the parallel circuit, enabling them to attain twice the speed both on level streets and on the hills.[52] Faster service made it possible for the interurban cars to make a one way trip in thirty minutes instead of taking forty-five minutes.[53] Further power difficulties during October 1909 made the speeded-up service impossible to maintain, but by mid-November restoration of full power assured passengers of continued better service.

This new power supply eventually enabled the street railway management to offer a more reliable service to the riding public and efforts were made to keep each car on a more punctual schedule. It had been common for Strathcona cars to operate as much as fifteen or twenty minutes late.[54] The Edmonton Bulletin, in an editorial calling for better car service, specifically criticized late running cars, crowded cars and bunching of cars.[55]

On Wednesday, November 17th 1909, fifteen-minute service began between First (101) Street and Jasper Avenue and Vermillion (106) Avenue and Eighth (108) Street, utilizing one of the large pay-as-you-enter cars. Although not a new route,

Above:

Andrew Robertson joined the Edmonton Radial Railway in 1909. Here he illustrates the style of uniform typical of the early years of the ERR. Wearing badge number 5, Mr. Robertson stands in a proud pose, the watch chain being the mark of a time-conscious railwayman and the gloves-in-hand typical of an electric railway motorman or conductor. Gloves were almost a necessity to prevent blistered hands while operating hand-brake equipped cars. Manually operated door controls could also call for a gloved hand. The conductor often wore gloves when he guided the trolley rope while the car passed through intersections or tight curves to ensure that the trolley-wheel remained on the wire.   (W. Robertson)

Photo above:

Ottawa-built car 20 travels south on First (101) Street toward its south side destination marked "WHYTE AVE. VIA HIGH LEVEL BRIDGE". The streetcar is in front of the Tegler Building south of the Athabasca Avenue and Elizabeth Street (102 Avenue) crossing. Note the bicycle with the side car in front of The Journal office. The scene dates back to about 1913.   (Provincial Archives of Alberta)

this change did represent a significant increase in service, since the increased power allowed faster running and therefore more trips per hour.[56]

It now appeared that for the first time in the Edmonton Radial Railway's one year history the entire system could be operated at its full potential. There were eleven cars on hand. Three were assigned each afternoon to the interurban line. Four cars provided service between Jasper Avenue and Twenty-first (121) Street to Kirkness (95 Street) and Alberta (118) Avenue. One car shuttled between Alberta Avenue and Kirkness Street and the packing plant in North Edmonton. One car was assigned to the Vermillion (106) Avenue service and one to the Syndicate Avenue (95 Street) line. This left only one car as a spare for emergency service or breakdowns.[57]

A spur line on First (103) Street East in Strathcona, south from Whyte Avenue, was proposed by Superintendent Taylor, in order that the ERR might pick up freight and express from the CPR freight sheds and deliver it to points in downtown Edmonton. The proposal, first presented in March 1909, initially found favour with the Strathcona aldermen on condition that it was to be used for freight only.[58] About the same time, a spur was actually constructed in Edmonton from the ERR line on Jasper Avenue at Ninth (109) Street to the Hardisty Brothers Warehouse, so that freight could be delivered or picked up by the street railway. The transferring of freight from the Strathcona freight shed to the warehouse raised the possibility of a lucrative income for the ERR.[59] Strathcona Council however, did not come to a hasty conclusion on the freight spur line request. They expressed concern that people might rush off the train onto a street car parked on the spur without getting a glimpse of the City of Strathcona. Council therefore reiterated the fact that the spur be used for freight purposes only.[60] Then Strathcona transfer men complained to Council that the street railway spur would put them out of business.[61] Finally, Strathcona Council refused the spur line application, in spite of Mayor Duggan's reasoning that the hauling of heavy loads by the transfer wagons contributed significantly to the poor shape of the road to Edmonton.[62] The spur line request did not disappear easily. While Superintendent Taylor was dealing with Strathcona Council about the spur line, Strathcona had been pressing the Edmonton Radial Railway about its obligation to replace the wooden poles with iron ones down the centre of Whyte Avenue as the paving program progressed.

These overhead wire support poles were to be the same as those on Jasper through downtown Edmonton. In retaliation for refusal to allow the spur line to the freight sheds, Superintendent Taylor refused to place iron poles along the paved portion of Whyte Avenue.[63] As it turned out, the spur line never materialized, but iron poles were eventually installed down the centre of Whyte Avenue. Even urgings from the Dominion Express Company of Montreal to the Strathcona Council to have the street railway handle its shipments from Strathcona depot via the disputed spur failed to evoke a change in Council's stance.[64] Taylor tried to force Strathcona Council's hand by applying to the letter the street railway agreement, and by instituting double fares to Strathcona after 11:00 p.m., a practice which had previously been waived. He was foiled by power shortages which forced curtailment of all services by 11:00 p.m., and the provision for double fare after that hour was revoked two weeks after he had announced that it would be applied.[65]

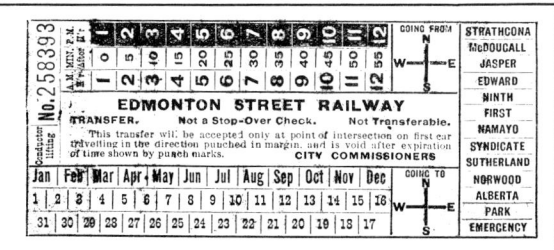

Freight service on the Edmonton Radial Railway began slowly. As early as April 1909, well before the packing plant line opened, the large snow-sweeper was used for freight carriage. It picked up meat shipped from the J.Y. Griffith packing plant in North Edmonton at the corner of Alberta (118) Avenue and Kirkness (95) Street and delivered it to Strathcona.[66] The Hardisty Brothers Warehouse spur gave an increased boost to the freight business as well. The handling of freight by the street railway became popular with shippers because wagon hauling over unpaved roads was at best slow and onerous. Wagon shipments did have the advantage of being more flexible and able to serve areas other than those along the car line, but many businesses adjacent to the car line had the advantage of receiving or sending goods with less probability of damage and certainly greater speed. The street railway could also handle heavier shipments than competing horse-and-wagon facilities.

Paving projects on street railway lines were minimal in 1909. Jasper Avenue east of Namayo Avenue (97 Street) to Syndicate (95 Street) and Syndicate (95 Street) northwards to the CNR/GTP crossing was all that was completed in Edmonton that year. On August 14th 1909 paving work on Whyte Avenue in Strathcona between First (105) Street West and Third (101) Street east got underway. A special car left Alberta (118) Avenue at 6:00 each morning to accommodate paving workers going to the work site on Whyte Avenue.[67] During the time this work was underway street car service on Whyte Avenue west of Second (102) Street east was curtailed much of the time.[68] On October 2nd street cars resumed service west of the CPR crossing.[69] Four days later the installation of the second diamond to accommodate double track operation of the ERR at the CPR crossing took place.[70] About mid-October the paved section on Whyte Avenue was opened to regular service but the double trackage did not actually go into service until Monday, March 21st 1910. At that time the flexibility of service on the interurban run increased quite considerably.

The cost of paving those streets where the car lines operated was borne in part by the Edmonton Radial Railway. Within the City of Edmonton, the ERR covered the cost of paving that part of the street upon which the tracks were laid plus a distance of eighteen inches on either side of the rails and the devil strip, (that portion of the roadway between the two sets of tracks). In Strathcona, a similar agreement applied except that the devil strip paving was covered by the City of Strathcona.

Provincial law in general prohibited operation of street cars in Alberta on Sundays, although a municipality could have Sunday street car service through specific approval by the voters. Edmonton held such a plebiscite in June 1909. The proposal received wide acceptance with 1510 favouring Sunday cars and 382 opposing.[71] The power shortage, however, prevented the inauguration of this service until Sunday, September 5th 1909. Cars were to operate between 8:00 a.m. and 11:00 p.m. over routes within Edmonton only, as plebiscites for service outside the city limits, to the packing plant in North Edmonton and to Strathcona, had not been taken. Five cars offered a fifteen-minute service between Twenty-first (121) Street and City Park on the packing plant line. A twenty-minute service operated between the Low Level Bridge and the CNR station on First (101) Street.[72] Three weeks later Sunday service was extended from the east end City Park terminal to the packing plant[73] offering half hourly service.[74]

Strathcona citizens turned down the Sunday street car proposal by a very narrow margin in December 1909. A total of 398 voters opposed the bylaw while only 355 indicated they favoured it. The clergy in Strathcona took up a very vocal stance against the bylaw, influencing their parishoners to register their opposition.[75] Ironically the City of Edmonton paid the expenses involved in presenting this bylaw to the Strathcona electorate. Superintendent Taylor and the CPR both loudly opposed the position of the Strathcona electorate. The CPR claimed that the Edmonton Radial Railway was diverting all rail passengers to the Canadian Northern Railway station in Edmonton on Sundays which, in fact, was true. Nothing, however, could be done to alter the situation, and Strathcona remained without car service on Sundays for a full year before the issue could be raised again. The first car in revenue service on a Sunday in Strathcona finally operated on December 20th 1910[76] after Strathcona voters finally gave their approval.

Edmonton Radial Railway tower wagon drawn by two horses carries the line crew as they make adjustments to the overhead line on Curry (100) Street in the valley near Low Level Bridge in 1912. H. Gilbert Sorenson, line foreman, stands on the tower, while Bill Brunlees, track foreman, is on the road beside the wagon's rear wheels. (H. Gilbert Sorenson)

5 | The Railway and the Cities Grow

In 1909, the Edmonton Radial Railway was in need of still more rolling stock and tenders were called for six additional passenger cars for use on the system. Three Canadian car builders bid as follows:

Ottawa Car Company, Ottawa, Ontario — $2,727 f.o.b. Ottawa.
Preston Car and Coach Company, Preston Ontario — $3,252 f.o.b. Preston.
Silliker Car Company, Halifax, Nova Scotia — $3,859, f.o.b. Edmonton.[1]

The Ottawa Car Company appeared to be extremely interested in furnishing this equipment to the ERR. Preston bid only $27 more per car on this group than it had for its successful bid on the previous group. Ottawa, however, came in some $801 less per car compared with its previous bid and undercut Preston's price for this third group by $525 per car. City Council accepted the Ottawa offer during October 1909. Specifications called for PAYE (pay-as-you-enter) cars which were very similar in size, appearance and design to the four Preston cars delivered earlier in the year. Traffic receipts had indicated that the four pay-as-you-enter cars already in service were consistently 3 1/2 to 4% ahead of those cars employing the former system, where a conductor passed through the car to collect fares.[2] In the latter system a passenger could disembark before being asked for his fare, and many fares were therefore never collected.

Delivery of these cars from Ottawa began with two in late June or early July 1910,[3] while two more arrived in August, just in time to be pressed into service for the heavy traffic to the new exhibition grounds in north-east Edmonton.[4] The final two were on the property by November.[5] Delivery of these new Ottawa-built trams, numbered 15, 17, 18, 19, 20 and 21, had been expected in March 1910 but the Ottawa car shops were very busy and Edmonton's order did not receive much priority because of the exceptionally low price of the cars.

New Brill 27-G-1 trucks arrived in Edmonton well ahead of the car bodies. These new trucks were placed under the cars in service, allowing shop crews the opportunity of replacing the well-worn iron wheels on those cars in service with new steel wheels, without removing the unit from service for a lengthy period of time.[6]

Early in 1910 City Council ordered a tower car from the Ottawa Car Company for $400. It was simply a four-wheeled wagon drawn by two horses and included an adjustable-height scaffold unit. Winter operation was facilitated with a set of runners. Since it did not have flanged railway wheels, it could be used to erect or service cross span wires at any point on the road. The tower car or wagon was lettered for the Edmonton Radial Railway and assigned the number 1. This new piece of equipment replaced a hand car with a scaffold mounted on it.[7]

Considerable controversy accompanied the laying out of the 1910 extension programme. The double tracking and paving of Namayo Avenue (97 Street) from the CNR tracks to Norwood Boulevard, then east to Syndicate (95 Street) posed no problem, as that project had been carried over from the 1909 program. The line into Inglewood via Jasper Avenue and Edward (124) Street to Albany (110) Avenue also received Council's quick acceptance.[8] The City Park line, however, which would also serve the new exhibition grounds, soon became a matter of controversy. Superintendent Taylor pressed for an eastward extension via Norwood Boulevard, but the Bulletin and the City Council both favoured an extension via Jasper Avenue East.[9] Finally Council directed that a single track line be built along Jasper Avenue and that a suitable wooden bridge be erected across the ravine to carry the car line to the park.[10] This route would also pass the penitentiary. Although a single track line, the construction of four passing sidings permitted acceptable service frequency.[11]

The fourth order for rolling stock — for another group of six double-truck trams — introduced the concept of single-end operation to the ERR. This car design did not affect the travelling public, but these cars had only one trolley pole (at the rear end) and the front vestibule was much shorter than the one at the rear. Therefore, these cars had to be turned at the end of each trip, so turning wyes or loops became a necessary feature of the system. They thus set a new pattern for the ERR, which gradually, over a long period of time, became predominantly a user of single-end cars.

In October 1910 the Ottawa Car Company received the $19,206 contract for these cars and their trucks. That worked out to $3,201 per car. This was a very favourable price compared to money paid for previous cars, considering that the trucks alone were valued at between $700 and $800 per pair. This contract price, moreover, covered the cost of installation of air brake and motor equipment at Ottawa. The new cars were to seat 37 passengers almost exclusively on transverse seats, and were to be numbered 8, 9, 11, 13, 22 and 23, thus filling in all the gaps in the car numbering system. These gaps had been first created with the numbering of the second group of cars which came to the ERR from Preston, and which had been only partially filled when road numbers were assigned to the third group of cars.

In January 1910, service on the interurban line began at 6:45 a.m. from the Strathcona car barns and at the same time from the CNR crossing on Namayo Avenue (97 Street). Cars operated every 45 minutes until 11:45 p.m. An additional car on the line left First (101) Street CNR/GTP station at 2:00 p.m. each afternoon. It laid over in Strathcona until 3:30 p.m., then returned to First Street. It left again at 4:15 p.m. for Strathcona operating every forty-five minutes from each terminal and making its final trip from Strathcona at 10:00 p.m.[12] The Edmonton-Strathcona schedule was speeded up effective Monday, March 14th 1910 with cars leaving the Strathcona terminal every thirty minutes from 6:30 a.m. to midnight and leaving the CNR Namayo Avenue crossing every thirty minutes between 6:10 a.m. and midnight.[13] It is not known how the afternoon extra fitted into the new schedule.

The new schedule was made possible by the opening of the second set of tracks on Whyte Avenue paving had been completed.[14] It appears that the trams simply could not maintain the faster schedule during the winter months. Since the system did not have any spare units, a slowdown in the running time of the cars meant that service frequency had to be extended from 30 to 45 minutes. Fairer weather allowed the speed to be increased again, resulting in the half-hour service being restored.

About this time a rash of mishaps on the Edmonton Radial drew harsh editorial comments from the Edmonton Bulletin. The Bulletin blamed these mishaps on the high operating speed of the street cars, and suggested that the speed bylaw limiting vehicles to 10 m.p.h. on city streets should be applied to street cars as well as other vehicles.[15] The speeding problem became so acute that police were using stop watches to justify levying fines to drivers exceeding 10 m.p.h.[16] No mention was made concerning street cars being stopped for speeding but drivers of automobiles and horse-drawn vehicles were often fined.

Charles E. Taylor resigned as superintendent of the Edmonton Radial Railway effective June 1st 1910. While somewhat of a controversial figure, he had apparently been highly regarded by his men, as they presented him with a suitcase, hand grip and a silver cigar case.[17] No reason was announced publicly for his departure but he had directed the building of the railway and then stayed on to operate it for the ensuing year and a half under an almost continuous handicap of lack of power — a matter which was entirely out of his control. When Taylor left, the system was operat-

ing at peak capacity and was in need of more rolling stock, both to keep up to passenger demand and to allow enough of a surplus so that cars could be cycled into the shop for much-needed repairs.

Commissioner Boullion, an aggressive, controversial administrator, temporarily took over the Superintendent's office until C.V. Biswanger's appointment as Superintendent, effective June 21st 1910.

Shortly after Biswanger assumed his duties, the long-awaited new street cars began to arrive. But the major problem of providing transit service to the new Exhibition Grounds lay squarely before him as well. Exhibition officials estimated they would lose a considerable sum because the new Jasper East extension would not be completed in time for the event. Biswanger, with four new cars on hand, had a total of fifteen cars available for service. He rearranged schedules so that approximately 1,000 people per hour could be taken to Exhibition Park via the Alberta (118) Avenue line.

Opposite page, left:

Car 11 takes on passengers from City Park (Borden Park) on a sunny summer day in 1913. Note that passengers are boarding at the rear door where a conductor is stationed to collect fares. Car 11 was among the first group of single-end cars delivered to the ERR. *(Glenbow Alberta Institute)*

Photo above:

The year is 1912 as ERR car 32 heads north on First (101) Street and is just about to cross the Grand Trunk Pacific and Canadian Northern Railway tracks. The engineer in GTP locomotive 1114 awaits a signal to take a morning train east. Several city slickers sit proudly in their automobile just ahead of a four-wheel wagon drawn by four oxen. The scene shows four modes of transportation, each utilizing a different method of power; an electric streetcar, a steam locomotive, a gasoline powered automobile and an ox cart.

(Glenbow Alberta Institute)

Effective August 23rd, twelve-minute service was available between Twenty-first (121) Street and Exhibition Park from 6:00 a.m. to midnight. Six cars operated on this route, going to the Park via Syndicate Avenue (95 Street) instead of Namayo Avenue (97 Street), with three additional cars assigned at peak periods. Strathcona service was modified from the usual twenty-minute service to half-hourly service to release a car for exhibition service. Two cars operated a fifteen-minute service between the Vermillion (106) Avenue terminus via First (101) Street, Jasper Avenue, Namayo Avenue (97 Street) to Sutherland and Syndicate (106 Avenue and 95 Street).[19] Edmonton Radial's fifteen street cars carried 15,216 passengers on Tuesday, August 23th 1910, 21,291 on the Wednesday, 24,630 on the Thursday,[20] and 21,371 on the Friday.[21] Street railway officials announced that 50,364 fares were collected on the Twenty-first (121) Street — Park line during the Fair period. This was estimated to represent some 20,000 return journeys to the Fair, as not all passengers on these cars went to that destination. In comparison Canadian Northern sold some 8,900 return tickets, while the Grand Trunk Pacific sold 11,900 return tickets.[22]

The only extension to go into service during the year 1910 was inaugurated on Saturday, November 19th[23] westward on Jasper Avenue as far as Twenty-fourth (124) Street. Service was later extended north on Twenty-fourth Street to McKenzie (104) Avenue. A new schedule providing Jasper Avenue with 7 1/2-minute service went into effect on Friday, November 18th 1910. One car left Twenty-fourth (124) Street and McKenzie (104) Avenue at 6:37 a.m. and every fifteen minutes thereafter to midnight. This car travelled to the northern terminus at Alberta (118) Avenue and Kirkness (95) Street via Namayo Avenue (97 Street) and Sutherland (106 Avenue). The next car began at the end of double track at Twenty-third (123) Street and Jasper Avenue at 6:30 a.m. and

33

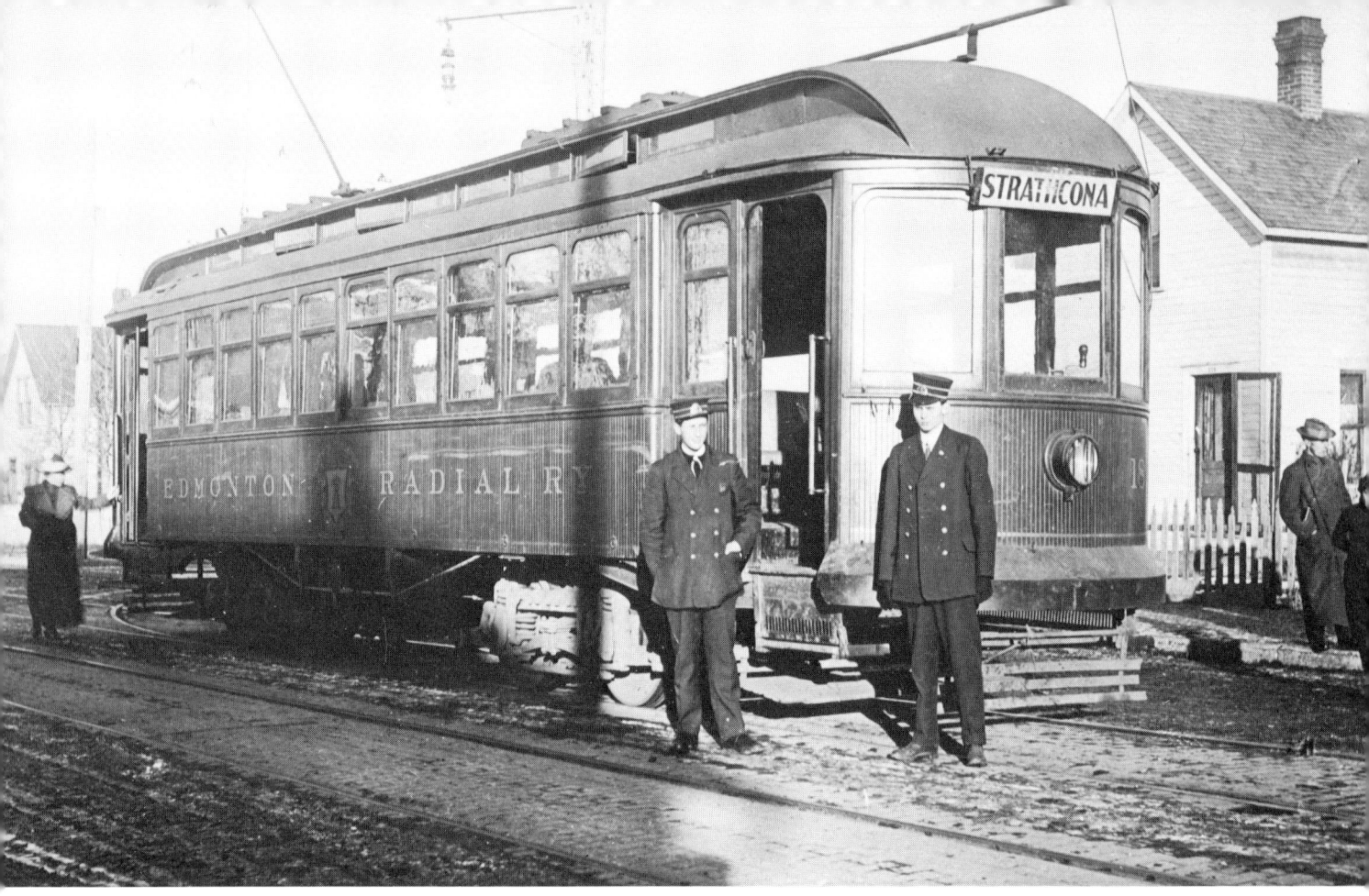

Photo above:

Motorman and conductor pose beside car 18 on Namayo Avenue (97 Street) at Sutherland (106) Avenue. The car has just completed its run from Strathcona and is about to embark on its return trip to the south side city. A cross-over just ahead of the car will lead it onto the right hand track. The scene dates back to 1911 — about one year after the car was delivered to the ERR, but before roof-mounted destination signs and route marker lights were applied. Note the storm windows on the car body windows. (Glenbow Alberta Institute)

every fifteen minutes thereafter till midnight. It operated to the same northern terminus via Jasper Avenue East and Syndicate Avenue (95 Street). The first car left the northern terminus at 6:00 a.m. and the last one at 11:30 p.m. The packing plant service from Kirkness and Alberta (95 Street and 118 Avenue) to North Edmonton operated every fifteen minutes until 9:00 a.m., then half-hourly until 4:30 p.m. when the quarter-hourly service was restored until 7:00 p.m. The Strathcona cars continued on a half-hourly schedule with "special" cars from Clark and Namayo at 7:30 a.m. to meet the 8:15 a.m. train and at 1:50 p.m. to meet the 3:00 p.m. train.[24] The new 7 1/2-minute schedule on Jasper Avenue required the building of a new siding on Kirkness (95) Street some three blocks north of Norwood Boulevard.[25] Shortly after being introduced, the operation of cars west of Twenty-third (123) Street on Jasper Avenue was curtailed due to power difficulties. Operation on the new 24th street section resumed on February 16th 1911 when power operations returned to normal.[26]

C.V. Biswanger's superintendency lasted only seven months, ending in January 1911 before all of the extensions and improvements proposed during 1910 could be completed. Robert Knight succeeded him as superintendent.[27] Knight inherited a system which was being used to its maximum and required continuous rehabilitation to keep it operating with any degree of reliability. The first annual report observed that track was difficult to maintain, as so much of the railway was built on non-gravelled roads. Water, therefore, did not drain away from the roadbed.[28] This concern was expressed again in the 1910 annual report, and for the first time Strathcona Hill was singled out as a particularly-difficult section of trackage to maintain, due to the heavy rains continuously undermining the ballast.[29] Open trackage was often allowed to become overgrown with grass which, retaining water in the roadbed, necessitated frequent maintenance.[30]

Some routes operated through very sparsely-settled areas. Cars on the packing plant line sometimes travelled for two miles or more without picking up a single passenger. Cost of operating this route was estimated at $55 per day while revenue amounted to only $40 per day. Similarly, the First (101) Street and Vermillion (106) Avenue line cost $35 per day to operate but brought in only $17 to $18 per day.[31] Track maintenance, particularly on the non-paved sections and the long stretches of track through unsettled areas, would continue to draw heavily upon the financial resources of the Edmonton Radial Railway.

The bitterly-cold winters of Edmonton affected street car operations considerably. Winter storms impeded the trams on many occasions, throwing scheduled operations aside. Sometimes a barn crew would neglect to fill the sandboxes in the course of their regular servicing: if that happened to an interurban line car it would take as long as fifteen minutes for the car to proceed just one block up one of the hills. Even on the downtown lines, cars might take a full block to resume speed without slipping after making a stop.[32] In addition to creating scheduling problems, this action drew tremendous amounts of electrical power, a commodity which cost the railway more each month than wages and salaries. Up to the winter of 1910-11 all of the cars were heated by electricity. On the First Street-Vermillion Avenue line, trolleys were changed every seven minutes, each time the car reversed direction, and the electric heaters did not get an opportunity to maintain an acceptable level of heat in the cars on this line. In January 1911, a sturdy coal stove called a Peter Smith heater was sent to Edmonton as a demonstrator unit and installed in one of the older cars normally assigned to the Strathcona run. An electrically-driven forced-air fan sent the heat through ducts along the side of the car at floor level. The Peter Smith heater boasted heating costs of 35-40¢ per day compared with $4-5 per day for the electric heaters.[33] The coal-burning demonstrator evidently prove itself efficient, as Superintendent Knight was instructed to proceed with the purchase and installation of this type of heater for all ERR cars. He had consulted with, and visited, Calgary, to observe these heaters and reported that the Calgary Municipal Railway was very pleased with the results of these stoves in its cars.[34] The smoke jack required by this type of heater became a hallmark of streetcars on Canada's prairie transit systems during winter months.

Strathcona residents had hailed the arrival of electric tram service in December 1908 but since that time had never been entirely satisfied with it. Early in 1909, airbrakes had been ordered for cars 1-6, which were usually assigned to the Strathcona route, but the air brakes had still not been installed as late as February 1911. No serious mishaps ever occurred on the hills as a result of cars operating without air brakes, but passengers were often concerned whenever a power failure caught a car on one of the hills and it started to roll slowly backwards. By simply leaving the controller in the forward position, the electric motors worked against the backward motion of the car, thus keeping it under control — but not stationary — if the hand brakes could not hold the car. The practice of collecting the extra fare at Cameron House at the south end of the Low Level Bridge had always been a bone of contention with Strathcona riders. In order to save time on the long ride west on Jasper Avenue and then back east on Saskatchewan (97) Avenue, Strathcona-bound passengers often walked down the steps at the foot of McDougall Street (100 Avenue) to the Low Level Bridge only a couple of blocks south of Jasper Avenue. They were required to pay a 5¢ fare if they boarded at this point and then another 5¢ at the south end of the bridge at Cameron House. Likewise Edmonton-bound passengers were required to pay a second 5¢ fare before the car moved across the bridge.

A Strathcona delegation met with the Edmonton Commissioners to present three suggestions: First, they pressed for the building of a shelter on the north side of the river to accommodate interurban passengers. Secondly, they demanded that cars on the Strathcona route be equipped with air brakes and finally, they requested a change in the fare system so that a passenger from Strathcona be carried to the north side of the bridge for a five cent fare.[35]

Edmonton agreed to all of these conditions but pointed out that passengers boarding at the north end of the bridge would continue to pay two fares. Only passengers from Strathcona could disembark at the north end before having to pay a second fare. Needless to say, Strathcona Council did not find favour with this solution, so Mayor Davies on behalf of Strathcona pressed to have the bridge made neutral territory. In that manner a passenger could board at either end of the bridge and would not be required to pay a fare until after the car had crossed the bridge. This new policy went into effect on April 29th 1911.[36]

The half-hourly car service led to crowded conditions, so complaints from Strathcona people finally led to an improvement when, on Monday April 3rd 1911, cars began to operate every twenty minutes. The first car left Edmonton at 5:50 a.m. and Strathcona at 6:10 a.m. The last car of the day left each terminal point at 11:30 p.m.[37] On Sundays between 8:30 a.m. and 1:50 p.m. cars operated every forty minutes. From 1:50 p.m. to 11:10 p.m. twenty minute service was in effect.

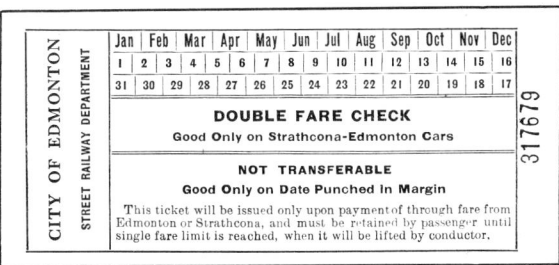

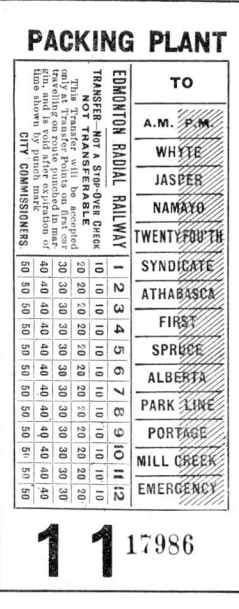

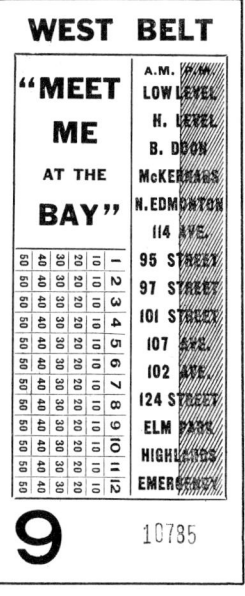

Photo above:

Motorman and conductor pose briefly after turning their brand-new Preston-built car at the 24th (124) Street and Athabasca (102) Avenue wye. Car 30 was delivered in 1911. The overhead Hunter roller sign has been installed on this car, but the roof-mounted route colour indicators have yet to appear.
(Glenbow Alberta Institute)

Opposite page, right:

Cars 5 and 20 travel westbound while car 18 travels eastbound on Jasper Avenue at First (101) Street in 1911. Edmontonians of the day appear to be very well dressed.
(Glenbow Alberta Institute)

Strathcona residents had better service in sight as the City of Edmonton had received permission to build a wye for turning single end cars at the western terminal of the Strathcona line at Sixth (110) Street west and Whyte Avenue.[38] Two of the new, single-end cars ordered the previous October arrived in Edmonton on April 3rd 1911.[39] By May 1st these cars were in service on the Strathcona route, just about the time the third and fourth cars in this group of six arrived in Edmonton from the builder.[40] Curiously, no mention is made of how these new cars turned at the Edmonton end of the line. It is possible that the wye at Namayo (97 Street) and Sutherland (106 Avenue) had been installed by then, but track on Namayo north of Sutherland did not go into service until the end of July 1911. There is also a possibility that these cars looped via Jasper, Syndicate (95 Street), Sutherland (106 Avenue), Namayo (97 Street) and back to Jasper Avenue again. Assignment of these cars to the interurban route answered Strathcona riders' requests for air-brake-equipped cars and no doubt further appeased riders on this line for they were the newest and finest cars on the Edmonton Radial Railway.

The controversial Jasper Avenue East extension went into service on Monday, May 29th. From 6:30 a.m. to 11:30 a.m. a car offered fifteen minute service from Eighth (108) Street and Vermillion (106) Avenue to the penitentiary bridge. Between 11:30 a.m. and 11:30 p.m., this route was extended to City Park, still offering fifteen-minute service.[41]

Steel work and paving had been completed during 1910 on Namayo Avenue (97 Street) north of Sutherland (106 Avenue) to Norwood Boulevard. However, special switch work for the intersections at Sutherland (106 Avenue) and Norwood and Syndicate (95 Street) had not arrived in time to connect up the new trackage. A cement base had to be laid under the connecting switches and the cold November weather did not permit that work to be carried out until the spring of 1911. At noon on Thursday, July 27th 1911 the first car operated over the Namayo Avenue (97 Street)-Norwood Boulevard section.[42] At some time between April and the end of July the extension north on 24th (124) Street to Albany (110) Avenue was completed. All street railway construction proposed for completion in 1910 had finally been completed by the summer of 1911.

June 1911 also saw the completion of deliveries from the Ottawa Car Company on the 1910 outstanding rolling stock order, bringing the number of cars on the system to a total of 23. The Ottawa Car Company had been successful bidders on three of the four contracts let out by the City of Edmonton for Edmonton Radial Railway passenger equipment. As it turned out, the Ottawa Car Company built a very fine car for the price, as evidenced by the fact that some of these cars were still operating in revenue passenger service when

the system dispensed with street car operations in 1951. But the Edmonton Radial Railway was growing very quickly and when it placed an order for cars it was usually in dire need of them as soon as possible. Unfortunately, the Ottawa Car Company had not been prompt in its delivery of cars to the ERR.

In October 1910 tenders had closed for a further group of eight single-end street cars. There followed considerable correspondence with both Preston and Ottawa, the two principal bidders.[43] The City of Edmonton expressed concern that Ottawa could not deliver in time for the 1911 exhibition. The City, therefore, turned to Preston, who had a reputation for delivering on time. Preston's bid was higher than Ottawa's, so the City Commissioners Office in Edmonton split the order for eight cars equally between Preston and Ottawa. At the same time both builders were requested to quote on the cost of increasing the length of these cars by one body window. Final prices for each car body were $3,031 from Preston[44] and 2,556 from Ottawa.[45] These prices included a $100 pay-as-you-enter royalty for each car as well as installation charges for air brake equipment and motors. Edmonton ordered all eight pairs of Brill 27-G-1 trucks with Schoen steel wheels through the Ottawa Car Company for $986 per pair,[46] in order to ensure uniformity of trucks under cars. Delivery of the cars with air brake and motor equipment installed indicated the need to have these cars pressed into service immediately upon their arrival in Edmonton. Two Preston cars arrived in Edmonton early in July 1911, while the final two arrived on Saturday, July 15th 1911. Preston lived up to its reputation for delivering on schedule. The interior layout of these cars, numbered 28 through 31, was similar to cars 8, 9, 11, 13, 22 and 23 except that a longitudinal seat was placed along one side at the conductor's end on the new cars. These Preston cars were the only cars on the Edmonton Radial Railway with arched or semi-elliptical upper window sash. All of the new single-end cars went into service as extras on the exhibition line via east Jasper Avenue. The large loop at the exhibition grounds made the turning back of these cars a very simple matter. The four Ottawa cars, numbered 24-27, arrived in September and October 1911.

Motormen, conductors and other staff of the Edmonton Radial Railway stand in front of the Syndicate Avenue (95 Street) car barns for a photographer in 1910 or 1911. Horace Stagg is immediately to the left of the gentleman smoking the pipe. Standing in the front row centre, thirteenth from the left, is Charles Wentworth. James Allen is standing beside the car on the extreme right. Starched collars, neckties, vests with pocket watch chains, suit coats, polished brass buttons and caps with badges illustrate the standard uniform fashion. Some of the men wear their uniform issue overcoats.
(Provincial Archives of Alberta)

The increased number of cars available for service resulted in a new schedule being published on September 14th 1911, as follows:

Namayo Avenue Every 10 minutes.	From Alberta Avenue 6:00 a.m. to 11:10 p.m. From Albany Avenue and 24 Street 6:40 a.m. to 11:50 p.m.
Strathcona Every 15 minutes.	From Jasper and Namayo 6:00 a.m. to 11:45 p.m. From Sixth Street west and Whyte Avenue Strathcona 6:15 a.m. to 12:00 midnight
Syndicate Every 10 minutes.	From Alberta Avenue 6:05 a.m. to 11:25 p.m. From Athabasca Avenue and 24 Street 6:40 a.m. to 12:00 midnight
Packing Plant Every 30 minutes.	From Alberta Avenue 6:35 a.m. to 11:45 p.m. From Norton Street and the Packing Plant 7:00 a.m. 12:00 midnight
Jasper Avenue East Every 15 minutes.	From Vermillion and Eighth Street 6:30 a.m. to 10:45 p.m. From City Park 6:52 a.m. to 11:07 p.m. Cars run to City Park from 6:30 to 9:15 a.m. and 12:30 noon to 10:45 p.m. Cars run to Penitentiary Bridge only from 9:30 a.m. to 12:15 noon.[47]

Finally, major maintenance work could now be carried out readily on some of the older street cars. A few of the first cars on the system received a complete overhaul and refinishing in the closing months of 1911. These cars had begun to look somewhat dilapidated, as most cars in the fleet had to be stored outside all year round. The barns could only accommodate eight or nine of the thirty-one cars on the roster at the time.[48]

Very little track expansion took place during 1911 with efforts being concentrated on completing the 1910 program and the building of turning facilities for single end cars. In Edmonton the paving and double tracking of a short piece of Namayo Avenue (97 Street) caused street car traffic to be rerouted along Syndicate Avenue (95 Street) for a few weeks. In Strathcona two construction projects were undertaken. Double-end cars returned to the Strathcona route in mid-September as transit service from Edmonton could not operate beyond Second (106) Street west while the paving and double tracking of Whyte Avenue to Fourth (108) Street west took place.[49] When construction crews began to double track and pave Whyte Avenue one block east from Fourth (100) Street east to Fifth (99) Street east in October, car service was disrupted again. Passengers simply transferred from one car to another, walking around the construction project.[50] By the end of 1911, double track car line in pavement extended along Whyte Avenue from Fifth (99) Street East to Fourth (108) Street West. The second Strathcona project involved an extension to the University of Alberta, one block beyond the western terminal on Whyte Avenue. The building of this extension was negotiated in connection with the Edmonton-Strathcona Amalgamation Act. Its specific location according to the Act was to have been worked out by the University and the City of Strathcona before amalgamation took place.[51] Commissioners were to have had the work started immediately,[52] but another month passed before grading and distribution of ties actually began.[53] Shortly after this, the interurban car service was apparently extended to the University, but on Thursday, December 26th 1911 the extended service was discontinued and Strathcona cars operated only every twenty minutes instead of the posted fifteen-minute service.[54] No announcement had been made to advise the travelling public of that decision. On Sunday, February 11th 1912 the cars began to operate on the University extension again,[55] but once more the service was short-lived and Superintendent Knight announced on February 29th 1912 that work on the University extension had been temporarily suspended as conditions did not warrant the heavy expense necessary to complete the trackage.[56] It is possible that reference to "completion" meant the building of turning facilities for the single-end cars. Double-end cars, therefore, continued to service the Strathcona route on a regular basis.

Motormen and conductors of the Edmonton Radial Railway organized themselves during 1911, and procured a charter from the Amalgamated Association of Street and Electric Railway Employees of America as Local Division No. 569 on August 22nd 1911. The first President was A.N. Elliott and T. Ferrier was the first Secretary. Mr. Ferrier later became Superintendent of the ERR. At the time the men organized, they sought a wage increase from 25¢ and 30¢ per hour to 30¢ and 35¢ per hour. The union also took issue with the ERR's practice of withholding $25 from each conductor as security for the value of street car tickets held by each of them.[57] The agreement requested by the street railwaymen covered several areas of concern. They sought a 9 1/2 hour day for conductors and motormen on regular cars. If they worked beyond that time but less than ten hours they requested a full ten hours' pay. Wage rates were to be established at 25 cents per hour for the first six months of service, 27 1/2 cents for the second six months and 30 cents per hour for the second and succeeding years. On holidays the conductors and motormen were to be paid at time and one half. Men in service for a period of six months were to receive a regulation uniform, paid half by the employee and half by the Company. Overcoats were to be purchased every two years on the same basis. Conductors on regular runs were to be furnished with tickets and change as follows: Namayo Avenue $30; Strathcona $35; Syndicate Avenue $30; Packing Plant $25; First Street — East End $25. They requested that all accidents and grievances be investigated and that employees not be held off the job more than three days. Evidence of all charges was to be taken up by a committee composed of two motormen and one conductor. No employee was to be disciplined until the investigation was completed. The agreement also gave the employee the right to appeal his case to the Commissioners.[58] By Tuesday, October 3rd 1911 Mayor G.S. Armstrong had signed the agreement with the street railwaymen.[59] The new union had successfully negotiated its first contract.

A number of interesting service features of the Edmonton Radial Railway presented themselves in the closing months of 1911. Special street car services were operated on many occasions, as the trams often provided the only means for citizens to get out to these events. Cars often ran in groups to City Park carrying church picnics. In September 1911 the Hospital Ball demanded late night services. Cars left Jasper and Second (102) Street for Strathcona, the East End and the West End at 1:00 a.m. A second series of departures for the East and West End left at 2:00 a.m. Fares were 10¢ in the City and 20¢ to Strathcona with no tickets accepted.[60] In the week immediately before Christmas in 1911, street cars operated for extended hours. Tuesday through Friday, December 19th-22nd, a night car left the north end terminal at 12:15 a.m., while the last car left Athabasca Avenue at 12:45 a.m. On Saturday, Sunday and Monday nights December 23rd-25th an all-night service operated hourly between 12:15 a.m. and 4:15 a.m. between the Athabasca (102 Avenue) and 24 (124) Street and the Alberta (118) Avenue and Kirkness (95) Street terminals via Namayo Avenue (97 Street).[61] No special fare structure was noted for this service. Edmontonians had the opportunity to visit friends and relatives at the other end of town, knowing that they had warm, comfortable transportation available for the trip back home again.

The Edmonton Radial Railway had 31 cars operating on six routes in the final months of 1911; but little had apparently been done to help passengers identify where the various cars were destined. A statement from the Edmonton Bulletin sums up the situation

> "Those who during the past few months have sighed disparingly at cars carrying no light or perplexed themselves with speculations as to the destination of a car carrying green or red lights will be relieved to learn that in the near future they will be able without difficulty to select the car which will carry them to their destination."[62]

The first step in that direction was the announcement that illuminated signs for the street cars were on order. These signs were to be mounted at the front, the rear and on each side of each car. White letters on black background, illuminated from behind, would indicate the car's destination day or night.[63] These were installed in 1912. Up to that time sign boards were carried over or below the front window of each car indicating its destination, but these were not illuminated. Early in 1912, Superintendent Knight announced that in addition, coloured route markers were being installed at the roof corners on the street cars. These markers indicated the car routes as follows:

- two blue — Namayo Avenue to Albany Avenue
- two red — Strathcona
- two green — Syndicate Avenue to Athabasca Avenue.[64]

A feature of Edmonton cars at this time was the practice of carrying an emergency lantern. If the electric power failed, leaving the vehicle in darkness, the lantern was to be lighted to signal an approaching street car in time to prevent a collision.[65]

In spite of precautions, however, it sometimes happened that cars met — headlight to headlight — on some piece of single track. Special runs, which operated frequently on the interurban line to meet CPR trains and in connection with other special events, complicated operations even further at these times.

Confusion existed even if cars remained in the sidings on the interurban line when they were unsure of where to meet oncoming cars. On one occasion a car waited nearly half an hour on the brewery switch — just north of the Low Level Bridge — while another waited at the top of the hill in Strathcona, each expecting the other to arrive. The motorman of the Strathcona bound car claimed he had not been told where to meet the northbound car from Strathcona. This tied up regular service on the line. In the meantime, the morning train from Calgary arrived at Strathcona. Fifteen minutes after its arrival a northbound car stopped at the CPR crossing and filled up very quickly with people from the train. The car could not take on any more passengers, so passed by potential passengers who had already been waiting for an unusually long time to board an Edmonton-bound car.[66] These types of delays and interruptions created unrest among regular passengers and the Edmonton Radial Railway was forced to make improvements to the line which would minimize such problems.

In the closing months of 1911 double ended cars operated on the interurban line to replace the single ended cars because the paving work on Whyte Avenue necessitated short turning cars where no turning facilities existed. Also the extended line into the University area did not have turning facilities. When these unscheduled meets did take place, passengers and crews simply changed cars. The crews reversed the trolley poles, the cars reversed their direction of travel and carried their new charges on to their respective destinations.[67]

December 1911 was not kind to the Railway. Street car number 13 derailed on Jasper Avenue at Queens Avenue (99 Street) on December 28th at 10:00 p.m. tieing up the whole system for almost an hour. The ERR was testing a new device which carried the street cars over fire hoses. Several cars apparently passed over the little bridge safely but unlucky car 13 jumped sideways onto the pavement as it went over. It appeared that measures to prevent tie-ups in emergency situations could not be taken without mishap.[67]

The year 1911 was not characterized by much track expansion, but was, however, a year when plans were laid and decisions made which were to lead the Edmonton Radial Railway into a period of tremendous and rapid growth.

Photo above:

Car 26, newly delivered from Ottawa Car Company, stands at 24 (124) Street and Athabasca (102) Avenue, ready to return to Syndicate Avenue (95 Street) in this 1911 scene. The electric fan on the Peter Smith coal heater can be seen through the front window. The lantern was carried as a safety precaution. It was to be lit if a car lost power and went into darkness in order to warn approaching vehicles of its presence. The route sign is carried below the headlight making it easy for the motorman to change the sign at each respective terminal point.
(Glenbow Alberta Institute)

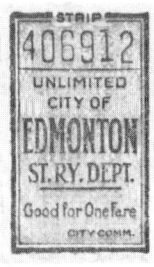  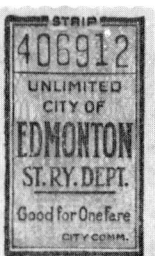

  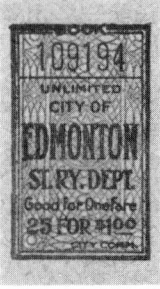

6

Plans Become Reality

THE EDMONTON STRATHCONA Amalgamation Act of the 1911-12 session of the Alberta Legislature had considerable significance on the development of the Edmonton Radial Railway in the 1912-13 period. This Act, negotiated throughout 1911 and assented to in the Legislature on December 20th 1911, provided the basis of agreement for the amalgamation of Edmonton and Strathcona into one municipality to be known as the City of Edmonton. It went into force on February 1st 1912 when amalgamation became a reality.[1] Several sections in the Act related specifically to the extension and operation of the Edmonton Radial Railway south of the North Saskatchewan River. The Act stated that the City of Edmonton was required to have a common basis for future extensions of its street railway system over the entire city and noted that all lines of the Edmonton municipal street railway, operating at the time the Act was negotiated, were to be maintained and operated.

The Act called for a total of four extensions to be completed as follows:

a) a line from Whyte Avenue to the University by November 1st 1911.[2]
b) east from the corner of Fifth (99) Street East and Whyte Avenue to or near the easterly boundary of Strathcona then north for a distance of eighteen hundred feet by December 31st 1912.[3]
c) south on Main (104) Street from Whtye Avenue to Sixth Avenue South by December 31st 1912.[4]
d) west from Main (104) Street and Sixth (76) Avenue South by February 1st 1914.[5]

The latter extension could be built to one of two proposals. One was a route which would have taken the line west then north west along University Avenue to Eighth (112) Street West then north to Whyte Avenue or another avenue north of Whyte Avenue, then east to connect with a line on Whyte Avenue or Fifth (109) Street West. The alternative suggested a route west on Sixth (76) Avenue South for a distance of about 2,960 feet and the choice of routes to be determined by the Superintendent of the street railway department.

The Act called for the operation of the street railway system on the line connecting Whyte Avenue and the Low Level Bridge along Fifth (99) Street East by cars running at intervals of not more than thirty minutes both north and south.[6] This clause ensured a reasonable level of car service to this area after the proposed opening of the line across the High Level Bridge via Fifth (109) Street West to the north side of the river.

The business district on Whyte Avenue received attention as well. "The City of Edmonton" shall furnish the best street car service to all parts of the city south of the Saskatchewan River that can be furnished consistent with the proper operation of the said system from a business standpoint, and in particular shall provide Whyte Avenue and other districts or centers on the south side of the river with good service, either by running all cars through or to such business districts or centers, or when necessary providing by transfer close connections therewith."[7]

Hearkening back to the 1909 encounters with former Superintendent Taylor of the ERR, Strathcona had one further stipulation written into the Act respecting the street railway. Part of that section read ". . . all poles used for the purpose of supporting trolley wires which shall be placed in the centre of the street shall be of iron, and iron poles shall be substituted for the wooden poles at present in use on the expiration of the lifetime thereof."[8] The steel or iron poles were eventually placed down the centre of Whyte Avenue. Strathcona residents also welcomed a uniform single fare structure on the ERR, as this, too, had been written into the Act.[9]

No mention was made of a street car line on Fifth (109) Street West in Strathcona to connect Whyte Avenue with Edmonton via the proposed High Level Bridge, as this had been negotiated separately between Edmonton and Strathcona when the latter city agreed to contribute some $50,000 toward the cost of the traffic and street railway decks on this project. These negotiations had been completed some time before amalgamation talks had commenced in earnest. The expansion of the

41

lines of the Edmonton Radial Railway south of the North Saskatchewan River had thus been projected and committed for some years to come.

The amalgamation of Edmonton and Strathcona was marked on January 31st 1912, when the street railway introduced the five-cent fare on the interurban line. The days of the double fare on the cross-river line had passed, a factor which no doubt affected the revenue position of the ERR. The spirit of amalgamation was celebrated further with a decorated and brightly illuminated car operating over the whole street railway system on Friday and Saturday nights, March 1st and 2nd, 1912, between 7:00 and 10:00 p.m. The words "Boost Greater Edmonton" were spelled out on each side of the car with electric lights. White lights dominated the dash at each end of the car but red lights among them spelled out *Strathcona* at one end and *Edmonton* at the other. The coat of arms and mottos of each city appeared on each side of the car outlined with lights. Lights surrounded each window frame, while the windows themselves carried paid advertisements.[10] This display car encouraged citizens to think of a new Greater Edmonton, while at the same time it brought revenue to the municipal railway. One of the original cars in the 1-6 series acted as the display car and was the first of a number of cars which ERR shop crews decorated from time to time to celebrate special events throughout the history of the system. References and inferences by the street railway suggesting that Edmonton and Strathcona were still separate municipalities, elicited frequent comment from the press. New signs were prepared, lettered *Jasper Avenue via Low Level Bridge* and *Whyte Avenue via Low Level Bridge,* but it took some time for these new signs to be installed.[11] The ERR was also criticized for placing a sign on a fence on Whyte Avenue near the CPR depot

Photo above:

One of the original cars on the Edmonton Radial Railway stands outside the Syndicate Avenue (95 Street) car barns in March 1912. The unidentified car was decorated to celebrate the amalgamation of the former south side City of Strathcona with Edmonton. The advertising undoubtedly provided a source of revenue as this brightly-illuminated tram travelled over the whole street railway system on March 1st and 2nd, 1912. (Les Corness)

which gave departure times for Edmonton. The newspaper felt that the sign left one with the impression that Whyte Avenue was not in Edmonton.[12]

The interurban line itself became known as the cross-river line, but the long stretches of single track and the heavy traffic continued to create many annoying delays. In mid-February 1912, there was a flood of complaints over crowded cars on the cross-river run. Would-be passengers were often left standing at Ninth (109) Street and Jasper Avenue, while between 6:00 and 7:00 p.m. most evenings, northbound passengers waiting at the Low Level Bridge experienced the same difficulty. Northbound passengers at the Legislature Building also found themselves left waiting as the packed cars passed by.[13]

Due to operating conditions, there was a tendency for the trams to become bunched in groups of three or four, making it difficult to pass at the passing sidings. Suggestions for installing a signal or telephone system along the cross-river route were commonplace, and it was suggested that telephones be placed at the regular passing points on the line at McKay Avenue (99 Avenue), the brewery switch just north of the Low Level Bridge and at the top of Strathcona hill.[14] A passing track had been installed on Ninth (109) Street at McKay (99) Avenue in the latter part of 1911 or early 1912 but services continued to be subject to delays throughout the spring and into the summer of 1912.

While amalgamation and the inadequate cross-river street car line shifted a lot of attention to the south side, that part of Greater Edmonton north of the river needed extended street car service as well. The Magrath Holgate Real Estate Company presented a proposal to build a street railway line into the Highlands area. Magrath-Holgate had considerable land holdings in this area east of the City Park and the exhibition grounds along the high bank of the North Saskatchewan River. The proposition was offered to City Council on August 29th 1911 and approved by Council on September 5th. Magrath-Holgate agreed to purchase the rail and fixtures as well as to cover costs of construction, which was to be carried out under the supervision of the city engineer. The Company also guaranteed any loss in the operation of the extension for a period of eighteen months. The portion of the car line covered by the Magrath-Holgate agreement began at the eastern boundary of City Park at Pine (112) Avenue and extended along Pine to Irwin (63) Street. The agreement placed the eastern terminal at Irwin Street (63 Avenue) but in fact the eastern terminal of the Highlands line was soon extended to 61 Avenue. Magrath-Holgate donated three blocks of land to the City to be used as parkland as part of the car line agreement.[15] The full cost of this extension was estimated to be some $20,000.[16] The City agreed to extend the car line from Agnes (79) Street across City Park to Pine (112) Avenue.

Photo below:

Double-ended St. Louis-built car 44 prepares to travel west-bound on Whyte Avenue from Main Street (104 Street) in south Edmonton toward Jasper Avenue via the High Level Bridge. The destination sign indicates the date of the photograph is August or September 1913 — after the opening of the car line across the High Level Bridge, but before the line south on Main (104) Street had been completed to McKernan's Lake. Overhead had yet to be installed into Main Street. Horse "tracks" are evident on the pavement in the foreground. (Provincial Archives of Alberta)

The population of Greater Edmonton grew by over 100% in the period between 1911 and 1913. ERR ridership, too, increased to a comparable degree. Figures for May 1911 indicated that 489,317 passengers rode on the nineteen cars then in service. In May 1912, the thirty-one car roster carried 990,585 passengers.[17] The steadily-increasing ridership trend had been well established and it was evident at the close of 1911 that more cars would be required. On February 9th 1912 the City signed a contract with the St. Louis Car Company of St. Louis, Missouri, for the provision of fifteen double-truck double-end street cars, each 45 feet in length. Car bodies were to cost $2,667 each while each pair of trucks cost $675. The original agreement called for Brill 27-G-1 trucks but the St. Louis carbuilder was very anxious to have its 47B truck "well represented in this region."[18] St. Louis agreed to reduce the contract price for the trucks by $800. if the City would agree to accept the St. Louis 47B trucks. In addition St. Louis agreed to provide the ERR with a spare truck of the 47B type.[19] Electrical equipment totalled $41,955 or $2,797 per car. Total cost of each car in this order worked out to about $6,085 excluding the air brake equipment. By June 8th 1912, eight of the new St. Louis cars in the series 32-46 had been delivered to the car barns. The motors and air brakes had to be installed on each car at the barns, a task estimated to take some ten days per unit.[20]

The first extension of 1912 went into service on June 7th of that year. The Magrath-Holgate line to the Highlands opened with half-hourly service when the first car left Sixteenth (116) Street and Jasper at 6:28 a.m. The last car of the day left downtown at 10:58 p.m., while the last car left Highlands for the barns at 11:28 p.m.[21] One of the new St. Louis cars made its debut on the Highlands line on Sunday, June 23rd 1912. Many Edmontonians rode the car as the hot weather drew crowds to City Park located on the Highlands line.[22]

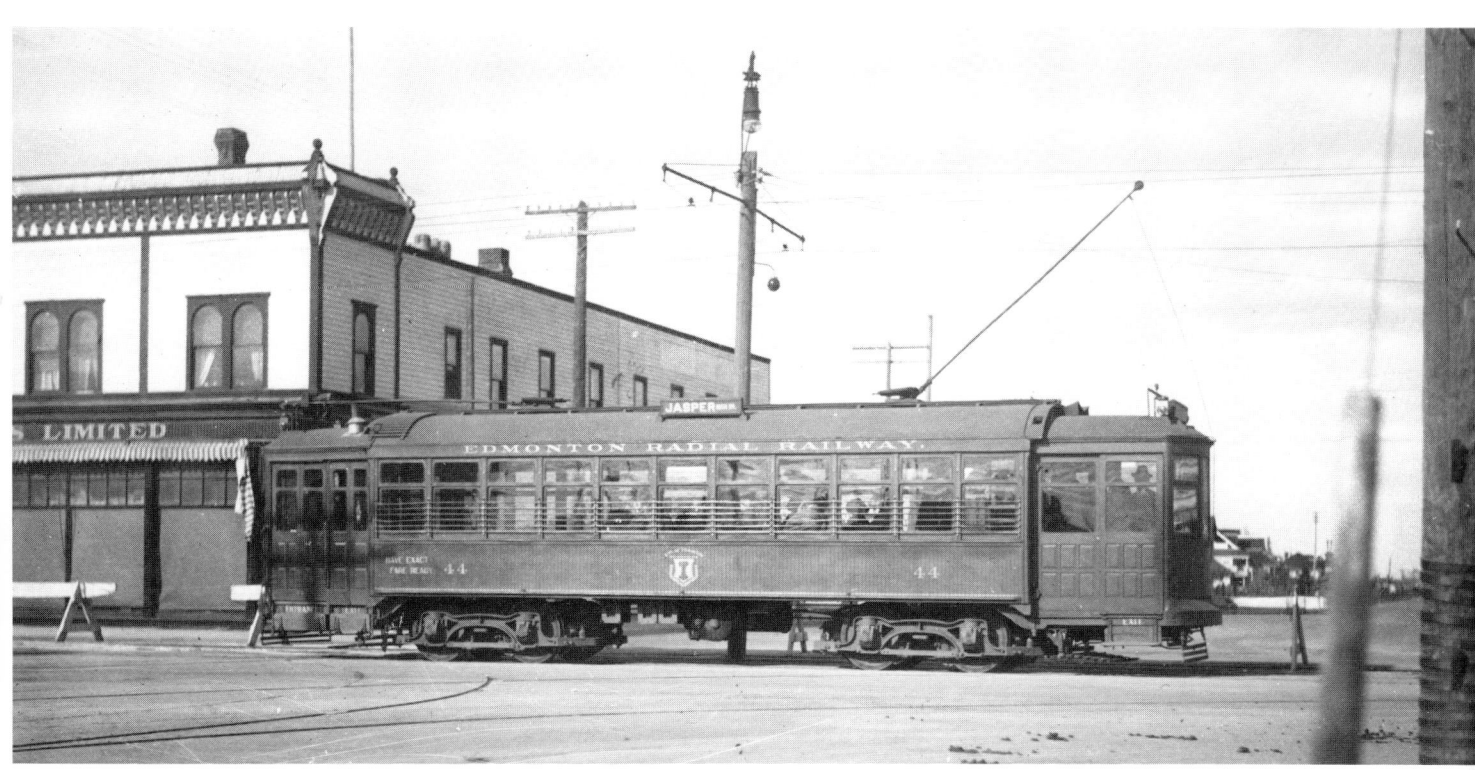

Photo above:

During the summer of 1913, car 2 was isolated on the Bonnie Doon line. Here at Whyte Avenue, looking east across Fifth (99) Street East, special work is about to be laid. This work was always done in stages to minimize disruption to regular car service. (Glenbow Alberta Institute)

Photo below:

Street railway construction work at the top of Scona Hill (99 Street) in 1913 goes on without interrupting service on the busy single-track southside car line. Track on the left is the original interurban line between Edmonton and Strathcona. Workers in the distance install overhead wiring using single truck passenger car 7. (Glenbow Alberta Institute)

Belt line routing found favour in Edmonton early in 1912. This concept took a street car line through a heavily populated area and into the downtown area in a circular routing formation as opposed to the "out-and-back" or radial concept which had been typical of Edmonton Radial Railway operations up to that time. Increased population density became apparent in the area east of Syndicate/Kirkness Avenues (95 Street) between Alberta (118) Avenue and Jasper Avenue. Buildings also sprang up west of First (101) Street to Twenty-fourth (124) Street along Vermillion (106) and Nelson (107) Avenues. Service into these areas with belt lines appealed to the ERR as street cars did not have to waste time standing at stub ends preparing for their return trip but could operate on a continuous route basis. Planners chose Spruce (114) Avenue as an appropriate right-of-way to introduce belt line service in the north east area and Nelson (107) Avenue in the west end.

Ever since the ERR began operations, the track on the unpaved roadways proved to be troublesome and expensive to maintain. The 1912 belt line program called for extensive double track in pavement. Consideration had been given to paving only the centre of some of the streets to contain the permanent double tracks,[23] while the paving on either side of the tracks could be completed at a later date when further funding became available. This arrangement apparently sparked considerable criticism, which resulted in the resignation of Robert Knight as Superintendent of the Edmonton Radial Railway. Superintendent Knight announced his resignation publicly in April[24] but remained on duty until his successor, W. T. Woodroofe, arrived on July 3rd 1912. During Knight's year-and-a-half term as Superintendent, the ERR earned its first monthly financial surplus,[25] and this happened in spite of the introduction of the single fare to the south side and amid all of the operating difficulties experienced on the single-track cross-river line.

The plan to take up the tracks on Vermillion (106) Avenue in favour of a line along Nelson (107) Avenue brought considerable reaction from Vermillion Avenue residents. Also at a mid-June public open-air meeting at the corner of Alberta (118) Avenue and Kinnaird (82) Street, the residents complained of the half-hourly service available to them at that time. They pressed for a twelve-or fifteen-minute service, and to this end the group passed a resolution and appointed a deputation to meet with the City Commissioners.[26] It appeared that this deputation must have had considerable influence, as extensive double tracking was completed on Kirkness (95 Street) and Alberta (118) Avenue and a large turning loop was installed at the packing plant in North Edmonton. The first phase to appease the Alberta Avenue residents came on Monday, July 22nd when through car service every 24 minutes was inaugurated from the packing plant in North Edmonton to Albany (110) Avenue at Twenty-fourth (124) Street via Namayo Avenue (97 Street) and Jasper Avenue.[27]

The Edmonton Radial Railway by this time had seriously outgrown the maintenance and storage facilities which were available at the Syndicate Avenue (95 Street) car barn. Several alternative sites had been suggested but it was not until late June when final approval for a new car barn site at Cromdale came through.[28] Superintendent Knight found himself dealing with all the problems typical of those experienced by a rapidly-growing system.

Very little was done toward establishing the belt line system during 1912. The only work completed was the laying of permanent double track on Jasper Avenue East from Syndicate Avenue (95 Street) to the penitentiary bridge across Rat Creek east of Government Avenue (92 Street); permanent double track north on Syndicate (95 Street) from Jasper Avenue East to Ross Street (108 A Avenue); and permanent double track on Whyte Avenue from Fifth (99) Street East to Seventh (97) Street East. All remaining trackage laid in 1912, with the exception of the Highlands line and the Whyte Avenue east line, simply allowed an improved car service on lines already in service at the time.[29]

W.T. Woodroofe, the ERR's fourth Superintendent, took up his duties on July 3rd 1912.[30] Three days later the railway announced a new south side service to take effect on Monday, July 8th 1912.[31] Between 5:45 a.m. and 1:30 p.m. cars were to operate every twelve minutes. After 1:30 p.m. and until 9:00 p.m. the long sought-after ten-minute service went into effect. Twelve-minute service was restored between 9:00 p.m. and midnight. On Saturdays, however, ten minute service was offered from 1:30 p.m. to midnight. The Edmonton Bulletin described conditions on the south side line in an editorial on July 10th headed "Improved Car Service":

> "The car service between the north and south sides of the river is to be made more frequent and extra cars will be run over to meet the CPR trains. Improvement in this service is called for. Cars either way at nearly every hour of the day are crowded, while at train times the accommodation is altogether insufficient. The service should be brought down to a five minute basis as soon as possible with plenty of extras for the crowd which every arriving train brings to the City . . ."[32]

Another editorial titled "Double Track Needed" appeared in the Bulletin on July 15th:

> "Those having occasion to use across the river cars complain of frequent delays in the service and of the "bunching" of cars. These things are unavoidable in the operation of a long stretch of single track. The line should be double tracked this summer if at all possible."[33]

While the double tracking did not happen that summer, improvements to the line were forthcoming.

While Edmonton Radial cars enjoyed some priority over the pedestrians and horse-drawn traffic of the day, there were occasional incidents that challenged the right-of-way of the electric vehicles. One such incident, which took place on a quiet Sunday morning in June 1912 at the corner of

Photo above:

Workers make final adjustments to the "grand union" intersection at Ninth (109) Street and Jasper Avenue in this 1913 view. A concrete base was first poured, then covered by a layer of sand; the special work was then assembled on standard railway ties. This was the only "grand union" on the ERR. It was never fully utilized as track was never extended north on 109 Street from Jasper Avenue.

(Provincial Archives of Alberta, E. Brown Collection)

Jasper Avenue and McDougall Avenue (100 Street), resulted in a streetcar with smashed windows and headlights, plus charges against ERR Inspector T. Ferrier and Motorman Arthur Elliott, of breaking the ranks of the parading 101st Regiment. The 101st Regiment, returning home from a week's encampment in Calgary, had disembarked from a CPR train at the south depot. It proceeded to parade in formation to the armoury on the north side. The band and part of the First Company had crossed Jasper Avenue when Colonel Carstairs noticed a street car approaching. The mounted Colonel spurred his horse and held his hand up as a warning to the motorman to stop. The Colonel apparently heard Inspector Ferrier, as he stood in the car vestibule, say "Go on". The motorman proceeded slowly; the Colonel's horse was nudged on the hip and shoved off the track. The car moved a second time, reportedly striking the Colonel on the leg. At that point, the Colonel and members of his Regiment began smashing the car windows and headlights.[34] The Motorman, Conductor and Inspector were pulled off the car and held by Colonel Carstairs' men. A city policeman persuaded the military to give up custody of the street railway men, who were instructed to appear before the Magistrate on Tuesday morning. After the crew was released the car completed its trip with its angry passengers.[34]

At the trial, Motorman Elliott swore that he had stopped his car as the militia crossed in front of him. When the band had passed, he observed a vacant space of some thirty feet in the ranks. He started his car and would have passed through had Colonel Carstairs not interfered. Motorman Elliott swore too that his car did not touch either horse or rider. When he received two bells from the conductor at the rear of the car, he proceeded about a car length, then noticed the Colonel's order to stop. Inspector Ferrier gave him orders to proceed. Then the trolley was pulled from the wire and the window-smashing occurred.[35]

Colonel Carstairs agreed that the car might have passed safely through the ranks had he not interfered, but seriously doubted the probability of it. The Colonel's concluding statement was: "I was a little angry and lost my temper. I have no special desire to make scape goats of these two men. I simply want the rights of His Majesty's servants with His Majesty's colours respected."[36] Three weeks later Magistrate Dyers charged Motorman Elliott and Inspector Ferrier with having obstructed His Majesty's militia and fined each one dollar and costs.[37] The militia apparently looked dimly upon being challenged by street railway cars.

An unfortunate mishap with serious, fatal consequences took place on another day in June 1912 — an accident that finally resulted in the elimination of the busy terminus at Kirkness (95) Street and Alberta (118) Avenue. Every six minutes a car wyed and every half-hour a connection was made with the packing plant car to North Edmonton. On the fateful day, one of the single-end cars struck a five-year-old child as the tram backed past the switch after turning into Alberta Avenue preparing to head south into Kirkness Street for its return trip.[38] The Conductor stationed himself on the rear platform, and when all appeared to be clear, he gave the four-bell signal to back up. He then moved to the step at the doorway of the rear platform to guide the trolley pole through the pans. A man on the sidewalk shouted at him to stop. The Conductor immediately stepped onto the rear platform and gave the motorman the emergency signal to stop, but the young child was seriously injured and died a few hours later. The motorman and conductor were exonerated of all blame, but the jury recommeded that a man be stationed at those streets where a wye was in operation for the protection of the public.[39] The City Commissioners announced that they would discontinue wying cars at Alberta Avenue and Kirkness in favour of a loop around the block.[40]

There is no record of a loop ever having been built at the Kirkness and Alberta Avenue terminal, but completion of a 1200-foot loop at the packing plant in North Edmonton allowed single-end cars to operate through to that terminal. Double tracking of the line on Kirkness Street and Alberta Avenue to James (81) Street made it possible for all cars to run past the Kirkness/Alberta intersection and at the same time provided the residents further east on Alberta Avenue with the increased car service they demanded. A turning wye at Douglas (78) Street and Alberta Avenue made it possible for single-end street cars to turn back in a much less-settled area. On Monday, August 19th

Photo below:

Edmonton Radial Railway trackage expanded very rapidly in 1913. Additional maintenance equipment was prepared at Cromdale to supplement line car L-1. The four-wheel track car holds the spool of copper trolley wire. Car 7 has been fitted with a roof-mounted platform to allow workers to secure the wire to the cross spans. Note that the cable going onto the drum is "hot" as the car is powered from the overhead line as it is being installed. This car is assisted by the ERR tower wagon. Line Foreman H. Gilbert Sorenson stands in the foreground, second from the left facing the camera and pointing to the car. (H. Gilbert Sorenson)

1912, the northern terminal at Kirkness and Alberta Avenue was abandoned and a new extensively-increased service along Alberta Avenue was introduced. New schedules were applied to all routes as follows:

Blue Lights   Packing Plant to Albany Avenue via Namayo Avenue.
Leaves Packing Plant at 6:06 a.m. and every twelve minutes to 12:18 a.m.
Leaves Albany Avenue and 24th Street at 6:12 a.m. and every twelve minutes to 11:48 p.m.

Green Lights   Douglas Street and Alberta Avenue to Athabasca Avenue and 24th Street via Syndicate Avenue.
Leaves Alberta Avenue and Kirkness Street at 6:00 a.m. and Alberta Avenue and Douglas Street at 6:48 a.m. and every twelve minutes until 11:54 p.m.
Leaves Athabasca Avenue and 24th Street at 6:36 a.m. and every twelve minutes until midnight.

Red Lights   South Side Line from the bridge on Jasper Avenue east to 7th Street West.
Leaves Namayo Avenue south at 5:55 a.m. and every ten minutes until midnight.
Leaves 7th Street West at 6:10 a.m. and every ten minutes until midnight.

White Lights   Highlands to Jasper and 16th Street.
Leaves 16th Street at 6:30 a.m. and every half hour to 11:00 p.m.
Leaves Highlands at 7:00 a.m. and every half hour to 11:00 p.m.

White Lights   First Street from Jasper Avenue to Vermillion Avenue and 8th Street.
Leaves Jasper and First Street at 6:20 a.m. and every eighteen minutes until 11:52 p.m.
Leaves Vermillion Avenue and 8th Street at 6:30 a.m. and every eighteen minutes until midnight.[41]

An "owl" car left Alberta (118) Avenue and Kirkness (95) Street at 11:48 p.m. via Namayo (97 Street) to Albany (110) Avenue and Twenty-fourth (124) Street. It left that point at 12:25 and travelled over the same route to arrive at Kirkness Street and Alberta Avenue at 1:00 a.m. Transfer passengers from other cars were required to pay 5 cents extra on boarding this car but this double-fare tariff was rescinded early in September.

The ten-minute service on the south side line had become more reliable with the installation of an extra passing track at the south end of the Low Level Bridge and signals at some of the sidings. The signal was simply a red light at the end of the siding. If the signal was lighted it indicated to the approaching car the presence of another car on the single track line ahead.[42] Emergency telephones had been installed at First (101) Street and Jasper Avenue, Ninth (109) Street and Jasper, the Low Level Bridge and at Whyte Avenue. Motormen and/or conductors could report delays or accidents with these telephones.[43] These improvements helped to alleviate the very frequent delays on the south side line. Completion of the second track on Jasper Avenue from the penitentiary bridge to the Exhibition Grounds via Kinnaird (82 Street), Pine (112 Avenue) and Agnes (79 Street) made possible the operation of two-minute

Photo below:

Canadian Pacific Railway's Strathcona station, Edmonton terminus for CP trains before completion of the famous High Level Bridge over the North Saskatchewan River in 1913. (Canadian Pacific)

service into the grounds during the mid-August exhibition week.⁴⁴ In preparation for the entry of the CPR into downtown Edmonton via the High Level Bridge, a temporary street car line diverted service from Jasper Avenue between 8th (108) Street and 11th (111) Street to a lane south of Jasper Avenue. The line apparently crossed private property at both 8th (108) Street and 11th (111) Street. On Monday, August 19th 1912 the first car operated over this temporary diversion. This diversion allowed excavation work to progress uninterrupted so that Jasper Avenue could pass beneath the CPR tracks.⁴⁵

On the south side, permanent track was laid on Whyte Avenue between Fifth (99) Street East and Seventh (97) Street East. Permanent single track was installed on Fifth Street East from Whyte Avenue to Seventh (89) Avenue North. This construction project drew complaints from residents living in the area as it blocked access to Whyte Avenue and to Fifth Street East.⁴⁶ Once the pro-

Photo above:

Four passengers step out into First (101) Street as car 37 signed "WHYTE AVENUE VIA LOW LEVEL BRIDGE" draws up to the stop at the Jasper Avenue intersection about 1912. A policeman directs traffic from the centre of the intersection, allowing free passage to the horse-drawn PDQ Messenger and Express wagon.

(Provincial Archives of Alberta, E. Brown Collection)

ject reached the completion stages, these difficulties ceased. When operation of the new service on Whyte Avenue east began on December 1st 1912 another problem arose, as residents along the new line discovered that ERR transfer policy dictated no more than one transfer be permitted with each fare. Passengers off the new Mill Creek line surrendered their transfer to the conductor on the cross-river line then had to pay another fare if they wished to continue their journey on a third car along Jasper Avenue. This raised considerable indignation which resulted in further representations to the ERR. The new Mill Creek service operated every half hour from Whyte Avenue and Fourth (108) Street West to the Rutherford school at Eleventh (91) Street East near Sixth (88) Avenue North. The introduction of this service fulfilled the second obligation of the Edmonton Radial Railway in the Edmonton/Strathcona Amalgamation Act. It also meant more cars had to be based at the south side car barn, necessitating an addition to this building for increased storage as well as facilities for light repairs and inspections.⁴⁷

 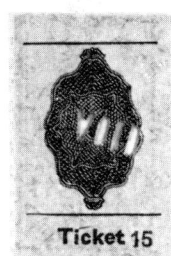 

Photo above:

The Alberta Legislature Building shortly after its completion in 1913. (Canadian Pacific)

A new schedule became effective on Sunday, November 3rd 1912 which featured two routing changes but no alterations in service frequency. On Sundays and during the week, cross-river cars operated north on First (101) Street to the Vermillion (106) Avenue and 8th (108) Street terminal, replacing the stub car service on that line. Residents along this line now benefitted from the south side's ten-minute car service. Monday through Saturday the Syndicate Avenue (95 Street) cars extended their west end trips to Albany (110) Avenue. On Sundays these cars turned back at Athabasca (102) Avenue.[48]

Freight service continued to grow in 1912. A motor-flat was added to handle switching duties, and a total of five sidings received cars via this street railway service. The C.F. Taylor Lumber Company located on the north side of Alberta (118) Avenue between Lorne (92) Street and Kennedy (93) Street was a typical example. This spur line was provided at a cost of $1,700 to the firm.[49] During the year 1912 receipts from freight switching amounted to $4,026.73.[50] This motor flat also carried rails and supplies to street railway construction sites.

The physical plant of the Edmonton Radial Railway did not experience tremendous growth during 1912. In the year ending October 31st 1912, the street cars carried 10,307,422[51] passengers, almost doubling the 5,748,157 figure published for the previous year end.[52] Car miles, however, rose to a figure of only 1,203,260[53] from 821,405.[54] In short the Edmonton Radial Railway operated at a higher level of efficiency during 1912, but expenses remained high. Power charges amounted to some 12¢ per car mile, compared to 2.5¢ to 3¢ per mile on other Canadian street railway systems. Operating expenses increased considerably too, due to a 16 percent wage increase to motormen, conductors and car barn staff during the year. Maintenance expenses fell compared to 1911, but the inordinate amount of unpaved trackage on the system[55] kept the costs of track maintenance higher than those experienced on other Canadian systems.

Passenger rolling stock at the close of 1912 stood at 45 units, all equipped for the pay-as-you-enter fare collection system. With an order for another thirty-five cars placed in November, it was evident that far superior storage and repair facilities were required. Approval was given and property purchased during 1912 for a large shop in northeast Edmonton. City Council also announced an extensive expansion of track mileage for 1913, most of it to be laid in pavement.

Photo above:

The crew of line car L-1 pauses briefly for a photograph as they install the wire over the east track on the High Level Bridge. The CPR track is in the immediate foreground. Fort Edmonton can be seen in the bottom right-hand corner while the Alberta Legislature Building is under construction, appearing to the left of the car. Line foreman H. Gilbert Sorenson is second from the left on the roof of the cab.

(H. Gilbert Sorenson)

Photo below:

Motor flatcar 4, often used as a locomotive, switches railway boxcars at the C.F. Taylor Lumber Company on Alberta (118) Avenue between Lorne (92) Street and Kennedy (93) Street. The tram line is double-tracked but the street is still not paved in this 1912 scene. The ERR switched boxcars over streetcar tracks from the steam railways to many industrial locations in Edmonton.

(Glenbow Alberta Institute)

Photo above:

A big southbound Preston is about to leave High Level Bridge in this late fall 1913 photograph. For a period of about five years, cars crossed the bridge with the door side opening off the edge. About 1918 crossovers were installed at each end of the bridge, allowing passengers to step out onto the centre of the bridge should a car stall. (Provincial Archives of Alberta)

Below:

Streetcars approaching the High Level Bridge from the south side headed down-grade from 109 Street to the bridge. On an early morning run, this northbound car carries a standing-room-only load of passengers from the south side to work on the north side. The streetcar trip across the river was not impeded by heavy automobile traffic. (W.C. Whittaker)

7

The High Level Bridge Opens

*P*RAIRIE CITIES experienced tremendous growth rates in the years leading up to 1913. Many erroneously anticipated this growth rate would be exceeded during 1913. The Edmonton Radial Railway could not be described as having been built beyond its means up to the end of 1912, as it experienced very heavy use of its cars throughout 1911 and 1912. There were, however, several Achilles' heels from a revenue-producing point of view.

An analysis of the system showed that all major routes carried a large number of passengers. Most of these, however, travelled long distances through sparsely-settled, low revenue-producing areas, such as the river valley on the cross river line, and the Hudson's Bay Reserve on the west end lines. The Dominion Government reserve along the City Park line and the unsettled land on the North Edmonton or packing plant line have already been discussed. The obligations incumbent upon the ERR through the Edmonton-Strathcona Amalgamation Act placed the railway in a situation where it became all but impossible for revenues ever to meet expenses. Many of these obligations were of a development rather than a service nature. The Highlands extension fell into the category of a development line as well, with operating deficits to be met by the Magrath-Holgate Real Estate Company until the end of 1913. All of these lines not only suffered from lack of short haul revenue, but they also tended to be a maintenance burden, because much of the track had not been laid in pavement. They therefore suffered from frequent misalignment and unevenness due to frost heaves in spring and heavy rains in summer. These conditions in turn slowed down the operation of cars and increased the need for rolling stock maintenance.

To keep the ERR abreast of the city's anticipated population growth, a long-range expansion program was announced late in November 1912. Commissioner Harrison, in presenting the plan to City Council, noted that the plan should do for the next fifty years, with the exception of a few possible extensions to outlying districts. Inspector Moir had prepared a very detailed map to illustrate the plan, which outlined fifteen belt line routes, signifying that the ERR preferred to adopt that concept of routing.[1] The 1913 track expansion program, which fitted into the overall plan presented by Commissioner Harrison and Inspector Moir, included the extensions not built under the previous years' programs. It supported the belt line routing concept adopted as a principle of operation in 1911 by providing major tracklaying projects on Nelson Avenue (107 Avenue) connecting First Street (101 Street) and 24th Street (124 Street); Spruce Avenue (114 Avenue) connecting City Park loop with Kirkness Street (95 Street) and First Street (101 Street) and Norwood Boulevard to provide an alternative route from Namayo Avenue (97 Street) and Norwood Boulevard to the city centre. The Athabasca Avenue (102 Avenue) line west of 24 Street (124 Street) did not fit into the short term belt line plan for the ERR, but conformed to the scheme for the long range program. On the south side of the river, two extensions beyond the then-existing trackage were built. One was the Fifth (109) Street West approach to the new High Level Bridge from Whyte Avenue and the other was the Main (104) Street — 6th (76) Avenue South line. The latter, which became popularly known as the McKernan Lake line, would complete the Edmonton Radial Railway's obligations under the Edmonton-Strathcona Amalgamation Act.

Rolling stock acquisitions at this time consisted of thirty-five large double-truck cars. The Preston Car and Coach Company was the successful bidder for the largest single order of street cars ever placed by the Edmonton Radial Railway. When delivered, the thirty-five cars in this lot would represent a 75% increase in the number of cars available for service on the Railway. The car bodies cost $5,375 each plus $65 per car to install the electrical equipment and $110 to install the air brakes. The 0-50 trucks from the Standard Motor Truck Company of Pittsburg, Pennsylvania cost $1,065 per pair.[2] The electric motors for this group of cars were divided between three contractors; Allis Chalmers provided three sets, Canadian General Electric ten sets and Westinghouse the remaining twenty-two sets. The Canadian General Electric contract for motors came in at $26,330[3] which worked out to some $2,633 per car. While no special price on air brakes was available, the arrangement for the ten sets of motors did include a contract for one set of air brake equipment which had been costed out to total $360. Using

A passenger boards blue-sign car No. 53 on 124 Street at Stony Plain Road just before the car bounces across the Canadian National Railways track in the summer of 1947. Note folding step arrangement installed in 1925-26.
(W.C. Whittaker)

the CGE prices as average, the total cost of each of these cars worked out therefore to some $9,608. In addition, the contract stipulated that the City of Edmonton would have to pay the freight on the motors and air brake equipment at a cost of $1.53 per 100 lbs.[4] Weight of the GE motors and controllers was some 12,280 lbs. per car[5] or an added $187.88 each, bringing the grand total price per car to approximately $9,800.

The "big Prestons", as they became commonly known among crews, were unique to the Edmonton Radial Railway. With the exception of two somewhat-similar cars delivered to the Toronto and York Radial Railway in 1914, no other street railway in Canada took delivery of cars of this type directly from the builder. Like most two-man, single-end cars, the rear platform was longer than the front platform. Their size, their broad uniform letter board extending all the way around both ends, arch roof and square-cut windows, gave them a very substantial look. The new Prestons had all-steel underframing and, like the St. Louis-built cars, side guards of 1 1/2" wrought iron pipe installed along the lower sides to act as protection against accidental blows from wagons.

Inside, the big Prestons were finished with bird's eye maple, with three-ply veneer ceilings. All interior finishings such as sash, doors and partitions were finished in cherry. Interior mouldings were inverse, plain and smooth. The car windows came equipped with wire netting 24" high extending the full length of the body on both sides. The motorman's mirror on the right outside front vestibule added a very modern touch to these cars as well. The exterior finishing of these cars was identical to those previously delivered (except cars 1-7) — with the main body of the car finished in the same shade as Harland's Coach Builders dark green and the area from the belt rail to the roof in the same shade as Harland's Birmingham Red. The lettering "Edmonton Radial" appeared in gold 3 3/4" high along the letterboard above the third to the tenth body windows on each side. The city crest was painted in gold on the centre of each side with the road numbers centered under the second from the end windows at each end on each side as well as on both sides of the front and rear bumpers. The words "PAY AS YOU ENTER" appeared in gold lettering under the rear window adjacent to the rear platform entrance. Gold striping extended all the way around the car (the doors excepted).[6] The arched roof was clean except for three shallow air ducts on each side, a center roof walk, the route number lights at each corner, the ladder to the trolley base and the drip guards over the front and rear entrances. Route destination signs appeared in the upper sash of the front and rear right platform windows, as well as in the upper sash of the sixth window on each side. Delivery of these cars, numbered in the 47-81 series, began with two on May 15th 1913[7] and concluded for 1913 in late September, when the final three of twenty-eight cars were delivered. Delivery of the last seven cars was held over to 1914 at the request of the City, as population growth figures were not up to those anticipated.[8]

The much-needed new car barns and repair facilities, known as the Cromdale Shops, were nearing completion in June 1913, when the ERR began, finally, to move into its new headquarters. The shops had been very carefully planned and provided space for fifty-one cars. Starting from the northwest corner of the building and working east, there were four storage tracks branching from a ladder track leading straight through the building to a similar ladder track at the south end. Inspection pits extended under these four storage tracks for most of the length of the building allowing access for underbody-inspection and maintenance. Timbers set upon concrete pillars supported the rails over these pits. Vestibules at each end of the car barns on these storage tracks minimized heat loss in winter and provided facilities for washing the cars.

The fifth track, in later years commonly called "the five track", led through the carpenter shop where street car body work took place; the armature and machine shop where electrical motor,

Photo above:

This is the south end of Cromdale car shop and shows the four storage tracks emerging to the south ladder track. The office building is to the left of the shop building. The two streetcars parked on the lead from the east storage yard were built in 1911 by Ottawa Car.

(Both photos this page: Glenbow Alberta Institute)

Photo below:

The storage tracks in Cromdale shop featured inspection pits, making regular car inspections a relatively easy task. Tracks, numbered from the left 1 through 4, ran all the way through the shop building. The "five" track on the far side was where the carbody hoist was located and where mechanical maintenance was carried out.

Photo above:

Streetcars receive attention in the paint shop at Cromdale. An unidentified Preston car stands to the left while St. Louis-built 39 stands on the right. *(Glenbow Alberta Institute)*

Photo below:

From 1908 until 1913, the ERR depended on the Canadian Northern Railway to do its wheel lathe and wheel press work. The opening of Cromdale shop with its wide range of machinery allowed the streetcar system to do more of its own work. Here a set of wheels is lowered for servicing beside the "five" track. *(Glenbow Alberta Institute)*

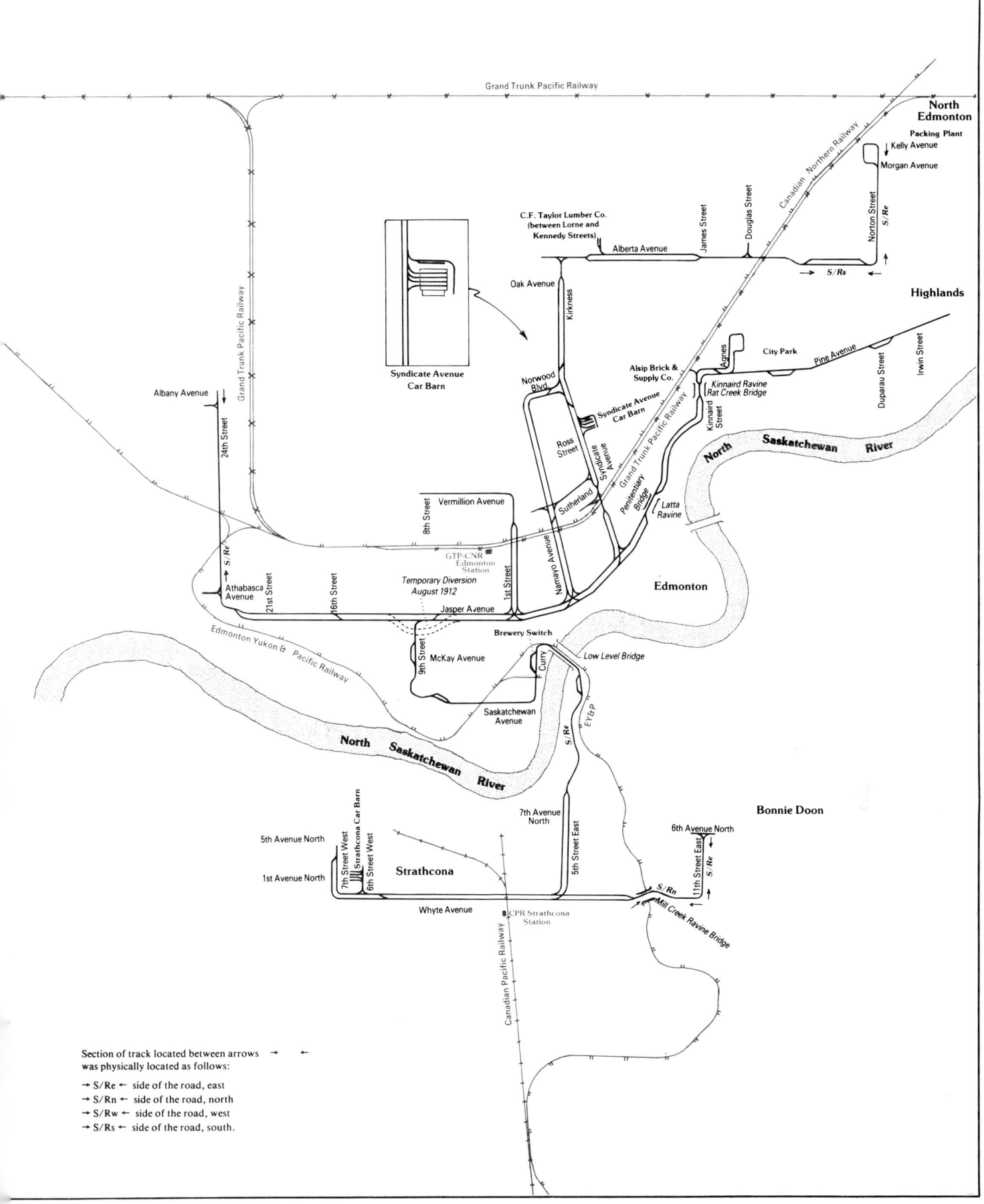

Edmonton Radial Railway Track Map 1912

wheel and axle repairs were made, and the blacksmith shop where major truck repairs could be carried out. The "five track" featured an electric motor-driven Columbia car body hoist and two three-ton jib cranes capable of lifting wheels and axles from the repair track to the various machines.

The sixth and seventh tracks led from the ladder track into the paint shop. Track six dead ended in the paint shop itself, where six cars could be accommodated at one time. Cars could be thoroughly washed and cleaned in the paint shop before painting began. A separate and specially-constructed fireproof room for storing and mixing paints stood adjacent to the paint shop.

The carpenter shop accommodated five carpenters' benches and could service two cars at once. The machine shop was equipped with the following tools: a 42-inch wheel truing lathe; a 24-inch engine lathe; a 14-inch automatic lathe; a 24-inch shaper; an emery wheel; a bolt threading machine; a 34-inch vertical drill press; a 250-ton wheel press and a forge for babbitt work. Many of these machines were driven by belts extending down from a system of overhead drive gears and pulleys.

The blacksmith shop adjacent to the "five track", where truck repairs were carried out, had two forges, a 200 lb. motor-driven hammer; a drill press, a bolt cutting machine and an emery wheel. The electrical shops contained a drying oven for coils, three large armature stands, three small armature stands, one controller repair outfit and the necessary equipment for rewinding armatures and rebuilding commutators. Facilities for testing armatures for short circuits and insulation resistance were also available in the electrical shops. Heating came from two systems: a low-pressure steam boiler provided steam to radiators located in the shops and vestibules, which looked after daytime heating needs. This same steam boiler fed a single-acting steam engine which drove a blower fan. At night when the street cars were in the barns the blower forced hot air through a series of galvanized iron pipes to the inspection pits. The hot air rose up under the standing cars to thaw them out and keep them warm until they were required for service.

The car building also had a sand storage room and a stores or stock room. The east and west exterior walls plus the interior walls were brick. The doors across the north and south ends of the building were wooden as were all the door support structures. The inner vestibule doors were all fireproof. Concrete made up much of the floor inside except for the wood block floor in the machine shop and the wood plank floor surrounding the inspection pits in the car storage area. The roof and most of the support poles within the building were of wood. Many large windows along the east wall made the shops very bright by day. Plenty of roof skylights let light into the car storage area and augmented the lighting within the shops too.[9]

East of the building was a materials storage yard and an interchange track with the Canadian Northern Railway. The interchange track at this location made it possible for the ERR to provide more efficient freight and switching services to the various sidings throughout the City. West of the building was the major outdoor storage yard for passenger cars. A separate building west of the shops housed the offices of the Railway.

The new Cromdale headquarters and shops for the Edmonton Radial Railway were, indeed, very up-to-date and far superior to the Syndicate Avenue facilities they replaced. The South Side car barn remained in service for a period of time following the opening of Cromdale, to provide storage and light servicing facilities for three or four cars assigned to southside runs, but eventually it, too, was removed from service, leaving Cromdale as the only home for cars on the ERR. The new barns provided the means to maintain the rolling stock in prime operating condition. In fact, within the first few weeks of occupying the shops, the ERR built its own overhead line maintenance car.

Although system improvements were underway, complaints about the service did not cease. An Edmonton Bulletin reporter interviewed a Winnipeg visitor who did not speak highly of Edmonton's street car service.[10] First of all the unhappy writer observed that there was no provision to meet the 6:30 p.m. train arriving at South Edmonton. In order to avoid the crowds, he was obliged to walk west on Whyte Avenue to catch an eastbound car. When the car did come, it already

Photo above:

The north end of Cromdale shop in 1913. The first four open doors lead tracks 1 through 4 into the shop. These four tracks were for storage, inspection and light repairs. The fifth door admits car to the "five" track and the mechanical shop area. The two closed doors lead to the paint and carpentry shop.
(Glenbow Alberta Institute)

Opposite page, left:

Car 47, a big Preston, is raised on the carbody hoist on the "five" track at Cromdale shop. (Glenbow Alberta Institute)

had a full load of passengers and of course got more crowded as it travelled along. He also noted that there were no straps for "standees" to grasp; the big Prestons were the only cars on the ERR to have these straps and the Railway had only just begun to receive the new trams. Finally the Winnipeg visitor complained that the car travelled very slowly. In his estimation the system needed a thorough reconstruction.

These kinds of complaints, plus concerns about the expenditures, led City Council to hire a consultant, E.W. Bowness, to bring in a report on how the Railway might improve its operations. Bowness suggested that $40,000 annually could be saved by speeding up the cars. He claimed that cars spent too long at stops and at passing switches — especially on the south side line; in the 24 (124) Street and Athabasca (102) Avenue area, as well as on the Highlands line. Superintendent Woodroofe reported that the average speed of cars when he took over was 7.3 miles per hour. He had attempted to raise the speed to 8.3 miles per hour but found that impossible due to the amount of single track. Average speed at the time had dropped back to 7.9 miles per hour.[11] Bowness further recommended that the railway should reduce its current order for thirty-five cars to eighteen cars and eight trailers. That, coupled with increasing speed of cars gradually over a period of time, would increase the efficiency of operations.[12]

Superintendent Woodroofe took issue with the report, declaring that trailers would slow down the service even more. Mr. Woodroofe also estimated that the ERR would be in need of at least sixty-five cars during August alone, to handle the estimated 70,000 people per day who were expected to ride the street cars.[13] Bowness recommended, too, that the ERR should attempt to build up the short-haul business rather than concentrate on operations over long branches.[14]

Bowness also recommended changes in the selling, registering and collection of fares. He proposed the selling of all but labourers' tickets at the car barns, at city offices and at stores throughout the City, and suggested that conductors register each fare and transfer. The Bowness report was heard in City Council in the final week of May 1913, and all recommendations were adopted except the one relating to the purchase of trailers.[15] It is not known whether, indeed, any of the Bowness recommendations were actually put into practice, as Edmonton cars never did carry fare registers, and the thirty-five Preston cars on order were all actually delivered. As late as mid-October the plan for selling tickets in retail outlets and not on board the cars had been held in abeyance.[16] It appears that Mr. Bowness was years ahead of the times, and this recommendation was never instituted.

Meanwhile the laying of track for the expanded system went ahead. A different method of setting trackage in pavement was adopted — called Concrete Slab Construction. Once the grade had been set, a concrete base was laid and a two-inch sand cushion went over the concrete. Standard railway wooden ties were set on the sand cushion at two-foot centers. The sand made the setting of ties easier and added some resilience. After being carefully aligned, the rails were spiked to the ties in standard railway fashion, and continuous rail joints were installed. The right-of-way was then concreted, leaving space for the addition of a pavement surface.[17]

Major efforts in the spring and early summer of 1913 went into the permanent track work on the south side line, Jasper Avenue under the new CPR overpass and between Jasper Avenue and Whyte Avenue on the north and south approaches to the almost-completed High Level Bridge.

Wooden ties are laid out atop the concrete base on Jasper Avenue at the western approach to the new CPR overpass. The streetcar is using temporary track in service for about one year between August 20th 1912 and August 1913, laid from Eighth (108) Street to Tenth (110) Street. This track diverted streetcar traffic south of Jasper Avenue to allow excavation and construction of the CPR overpass and installation of the "grand union" at Ninth (109) Street and Jasper Avenue.
(Glenbow Alberta Institute)

The new High Level Bridge accommodated its first CPR passenger train on Monday, June 2nd 1913. CPR class E5e 4-6-0 locomotive 2100, pulling seven coaches, left the Whyte Avenue station on the south side at 11:00 a.m. and reached the north side of the Bridge at 11:10 a.m. It backed across again a few minutes later after posing for photographs. The train order issued from the south side station read: "To engine 2100, operator and all northbound trains Strathcona to Edmonton and return to Strathcona. Engine 2100 run extra Strathcona, Edmonton and return to Strathcona with right over all trains. G. F. (dispatcher)."[18] Engineer Fuller piloted the train across the Bridge. Fuller had enjoyed a similar distinction thirty years earlier when he took the first train across the South Saskatchewan River at Medicine Hat in 1883. Much to the chagrin of Edmontonians, the CPR still referred to its south side station as Strathcona but by June of 1913, there was little other reference to the south side community by its former name.[19]

Almost three weeks passed before passenger trains began to make regular use of the new bridge. On Friday, June 20th 1913, a temporary depot was opened at the corner of Hardisty (98) Avenue and 9th (109) Street, just off the north end of the bridge. Passengers could ride between the north and south side stations for 10¢ one way or 15¢ return.[20] Fifteen minutes was added to train schedules as a result of this extension of the CPR Calgary-Edmonton main line. The press commented favourably about the new CPR service. "Instead of hanging by the strap in over crowded street cars, jolting over crossing and switches as a preliminary or termination of the railway journey, passengers will be able to get right into the cars of the CPR trains on Hardisty Avenue and make the journey across the river in comfort."[21] The trip by train was undoubtedly more comfortable, but the higher fare, less regular service (three trips per day each way) and distance from downtown Edmonton probably resulted in very few riders being wooed away from the street cars for the cross river journey. However, the opening of the temporary north side CPR station undoubtedly helped the crowded conditions on cross river street cars at train arrival and departure times. The temporary depot remained in service until September 1st 1913 when the permanent Edmonton CPR station booked its first departure.

Completion of the CPR overpass at Jasper Avenue just west of 9th (109) Street enabled street car service to be restored to Jasper Avenue between 8th (108) Street and 10th (110) Street after about eleven months of operation over temporary trackage south of Jasper Avenue between these streets. At the corner of Ninth (109) Street and Jasper Avenue, workmen had completed the assembly and laying of a complex piece of street railway special track work referred to as a "grand union". It was the only such piece of special work on the ERR. The "grand union" was a double-track crossover allowing a car travelling from any direction the choice of proceeding straight through the intersection or making a left or right hand turn. Since trackage never went further north on Ninth (109) Street than about one car length, the special work was never fully used. The new track at this intersection and under the railway overpass went into service on July 10th 1913.[22] By early August much of the permanent double track work on the south side line via the Low Level Bridge had been completed. The only portion of this route left as single track construction was on the bridge itself and up the hill from the bridge on the south side. This stretch never did achieve double track status.

Photo above:

The various stages of concrete slab construction are illustrated in this scene looking west on Jasper Avenue from 108 Street. Note the CPR station under construction just beyond the Jasper Cafe. (Glenbow Alberta Institute)

Photo below:

The new CPR station is open for business, and the new streetcar tracks on Jasper Avenue between 110 Street and 108 Street are in service in this 1913 scene. While the "grand union" trackage is in place, the overhead wiring at the Jasper Avenue and 109 Street intersection permits only limited use of the trackage. (Glenbow Alberta Institute)

Photo above:

Street railway overhead support poles were erected as the High Level Bridge was built. At this time the bridge had yet to reach out over the water of the North Saskatchewan River, but had been completed across the greater part of the valley on the south side. Fort Edmonton appears in the centre right of the photograph. The uncompleted dome of the Alberta Legislature Building dominates the sky line. The box cars at the left are parked on the Edmonton, Yukon and Pacific Railway line between Strathcona and Edmonton.

(Glenbow Alberta Institute)

Photo below:

Preston-built car 72 starts up the grade eastbound on Jasper Avenue from beneath the CPR overpass. The CPR station is on the right. The destination curtain carries the name "PACKING PT." indicating the car is on the blue line and heading for the packing plant at 66 Street and 124 Avenue in North Edmonton. The sign on the dash dates the photograph as the late summer of 1914. At that time, the cars began to carry these signs with the numbered street and avenue designations, to replace the named destinations on the roller curtain. The sign on Car 72 is partially illegible but clearly shows: 118 AVE., 101 AVE., 124 ST., INGLEWOOD. 101 Avenue was the seldom-used numbered designation for Jasper Avenue. Inglewood is the district surrounding the 118 Avenue and 124 Street terminal for blue sign cars. (Glenbow Alberta Institute)

Photo above:

A St. Louis-built double-ended car travels northbound across High Level Bridge on the west side of the structure. The roadway and the east (or down-river) track on the far side of the bridge have not yet been placed in service, indicating this scene illustrates one of the first streetcar trips over the bridge in August 1913. Regular service operated from Jasper Avenue and First (101) Street via Ninth (109) Street to Whyte Avenue and Sixth Street West (110 Street) and return until the car line across the bridge became fully serviceable a few weeks later.
(Provincial Archives of Alberta)

Photo below:

Edmontonians who travelled by streetcar across High Level Bridge always speak of it as an exciting experience. The experience was heightened for passengers on this southbound car when a decidedly larger Canadian Pacific passenger train stepped smartly past the cautiously treading streetcar. Canadian Pacific's G-2 type locomotive 2519 pulls its eight-car train toward its first stop at South Edmonton as it sets out on its trip to Calgary in June 1946. (W.C. Whittaker)

The High Level Bridge opened to street car service on Monday, August 11th 1913 at 11:00 a.m. Mayor Short, Commissioner Chalmers and Superintendent Woodroofe made the trip to the south side and return[23] on car 35. The Edmonton Journal described that first trip as many others have since described it. "From the street car one looks from a dizzy height down into the murky waters of the Saskatchewan without so much as a handrail to break the gaze into the abyssmal depths below. Many people will suffer that dizzy feeling as they look out of the street cars passing over the bridge. The cars run so near to the outer edge. The fact that doing so will not affect the safety of the car will not help relieve the shiver of apprehension the passengers will feel."[24] Superintendent Woodroofe announced that street cars would operate every fifteen minutes across the High Level Bridge between 6th (110) Street West at Whyte Avenue and Jasper (10) at First (101 Street). Only the west track on the bridge was in service at first as the overpass across the CPR tracks at the top of 5th (109) Street West on the south side had not been completed.[25] By early September 1913, however, the east track across the bridge had been placed in service.[26] The opening of this structure culminated many years of negotiating and construction. Its planning and building were not without controversy. The car line opening did end the controversy but it was taken as an occasion for the Journal to editorialize on the fact that the lower traffic deck had not been completed. The Journal suggested that the traffic deck should have been available for use when the upper deck received its first CPR train. An additional feature of the upper deck which had to be installed before the lower traffic deck could go into service was the placement of galvanized iron under the tracks to prevent cinders from the trains dropping through onto the traffic deck below.[27] Over the years the Edmonton Radial Railway became well known across the North American Continent because of the street car crossing over the North Saskatchewan River via the top deck of the High Level Bridge.

In the weeks leading up to the opening of the bridge, south side service was disrupted on several occasions. During May work proceeded on double tracking the Fifth (99) Street east line between Whyte Avenue and the top of the hill[28] and by early June this section had been completed. Construction then moved to Saskatchewan (97) Avenue on the north side.[29]

One Saturday afternoon in July, a crowded northbound car pulled into the siding in front of the Legislature Building on Saskatchewan (97) Avenue between 7th (107) and 8th (108) Streets. The signal indicated that the southbound car had not left Jasper Avenue, so the northbound car proceeded, only to meet an opposing car at Victoria (100) Avenue one block short of Jasper Avenue. Street railway rules apparently stated that Motorman Leslie on southbound car 43 should have backed up, as he was closest to a switch. The crews of each car got into a vociferous argument about the situation. The northbound crew finally relented and backed its car, crowded to the steps, the three blocks to Saskatchewan (97) Avenue, around the curve, and then down the grade to the switch another block further.[30]

Photo above:

The conductor, the motorman and two line workers pose on the deck of the line car on Whyte Avenue just west of 5th Street West (109 Street) about 1913. (H. Gilbert Sorenson)

One Wednesday evening a near accident occurred on the hill south of the Low Level Bridge. A citizen saw the inevitable about to happen and flagged a southbound car at the curve at the bottom of the hill. Two special cars — one of them part of a convoy of cars transporting 400 employees to the City Dairy picnic at east end City Park — had been ordered by an inspector to descend the hill. They were both coasting down the hill in the face of the southbound car starting up the hill under full power. The signal lights at each end of the single track stretch had failed and indicated the line clear at both ends. The cars stopped before a collision occurred, but again the crews could not agree on who held the right-of-way. The northbound cars claimed the rights of a regular car but they did finally relent and they backed up the hill "using some of the costly power which is blamed for the deficit of the street railway."[31] At the top of the hill five street cars and a water sprinkler awaited clearance. The inspector finally straightened out the problem.[32] The need for a double-tracked Low Level Bridge route to the south side in addition to the new High Level Bridge route became evident.

The opening of the 1913 exhibition coincided with the inauguration of the High Level Bridge line. Superintendent Woodroofe expected to have sixty-two cars on hand for service that week, in order to handle 100,000 passengers per day. Special cars were run from 9th Street (109) Street and Jasper Avenue to the exhibition grounds every five minutes. Difficulties were predicted in the east end as tracks on Kirkness (95 Street) and Alberta Avenue (118 Avenue) were being torn up, but new track had been laid down on Spruce Avenue (114 Avenue) through to the exhibition grounds from Kirkness (95 Street) via Spruce (114) Avenue, Kinnaird (82) Street, Oak (116) Avenue, John (80) Street and Alberta (118) Avenue.[33] As it turned out, the street cars never did carry anywhere near the projected 100,000 people per day during exhibition week. Some 70,344 people boarded the cars on the Thursday compared with a high of 65,400 on the corresponding day in the previous year's exhibition week. Throughout the week the street cars carried 364,863 people compared to 327,696 the previous year.[34]

As the month of August drew to a close permanent track work on Main (104) Street on the south side also drew near completion. South side residents expressed fear that the tearing up of pavement at the corner of Main Street and Whyte Avenue to accommodate the special track work would tie up the street car system and the roadway for as lengthy a period as had the special work installations at Fifth (109) Street West and 5th (99) Street East.[35] Actually the 5th Street West and Whyte Avenue special work was not completed until the end of September 1913.[36]

Workers started to lay the street car tracks along First (101) Street from the Canadian Northern Railway tracks north to Norwood Boulevard on Saturday, August 30th. The line on Norwood Boulevard connecting First Street with Syndicate (95) Avenue would be completed as a temporary double track line only. A property owner had filed suit against the City for thirty feet on the southern half of the boulevard. With the width of the boulevard an uncertainty, it was deemed advisable to construct the car line on a temporary basis until the issue had been settled. Apparently the property holder had already won his case but the City planned to appeal to the Supreme Court.[37]

Nelson (107) Avenue construction between First (101) Street and 12th (112) Street was almost complete at the end of August. The section from 12th Street to 24th (124) Street was laid down as temporary track as the trunk sewer along that part of Nelson Avenue had not settled satisfactorily. For some time, street railway officials spoke of the need for a line to connect First Street and Namayo Avenue (97 Street) via Sutherland (106 Avenue). When Namayo was paved in 1912, a crossing and turnouts were placed at Namayo and Sutherland to accommodate a connection. During 1912 rails were set out along Sutherland between First Street and Namayo Avenue only to be removed before

Photo below:

Workers pour the concrete base for permanent, paved streetcar tracks on Alberta (118) Avenue and John (80) Street in 1913 without disrupting car service.

(Glenbow Alberta Institute)

Photo above:

McKernan's Lake provided Edmontonians with a variety of winter outdoor activities.
(Provincial Archives of Alberta, E. Brown Collection)

Opposite page, right:

Differential Dump Car S-5, the only product of the Canadian Car and Foundry Company on the ERR roster, takes on a load of brick from the Alsip Brick and Supply Company in 1913. This spur was located at the corner of Pine (112) Avenue and Kinnaird (92) Street. Pallets and fork lifts are still in the future as eight men work to load the car.
(Glenbow Alberta Institute)

being placed upon ties. In September 1913 when First Street permanent track was being laid Superintendent Woodroofe arranged to place turnouts at First Street and Sutherland Avenue to accommodate the proposed line east on Sutherland. Commissioner Chalmers ordered them left out.[38]

In the northeast area, the north track on Alberta (118) Avenue had been completed as permanent track. Cars could use that track by the end of August. Pending completion of the special work and south track along Alberta Avenue cars used temporary tracks on Spruce (114) Avenue and Kinnaird (82) Street, Oak (116) Avenue and John (80) Street to Alberta Avenue. In the west end permanent double track work was progressing well on 24th (124) Street and Athabasca (102) Avenue.[39] Once the new Nelson (107) Avenue track had been placed in service, the line on Vermillion (106) Avenue was taken up. On September 6th Athabasca (102) Avenue was completed west from 24th (124) Street to 31st (131) Street. Cement foundation had been laid to 40th (140) Street but tracklaying had been delayed until completion of the bridges over the two ravines crossing Athabasca Avenue.[40]

Finally, during the first few days of October, car service began to operate on Nelson (107) Avenue every fifteen minutes from 10th (110) Street to the corner of First (101) Street and Jasper Avenue. This service would be extended to Curry (100) Street and McDougall Avenue at the north end of the Low Level Bridge as soon as Curry Street permanent track was completed. At this time the Alberta (118) Avenue permanent trackage opened to service as well.[41]

Main (104) Street south from Whyte Avenue received its first street car on Saturday, October 11th 1913. Crews strung up the cross wires, then the construction car secured the cable to the Whyte Avenue line and proceeded south setting up the energized overhead line as it went. The line at that date turned west onto 76th Avenue to the end of the paved permanent track.[42] By Sunday, November 9th the line had been completed to McKernan's Lake as service to the Lake began that day. Low Level Bridge cars extended their route to McKernan's Lake.[43] One week later, large crowds went skating to McKernan's Lake, arriving via the "red" car line across the Low Level Bridge, the special High Level Bridge cars to the Lake or the regular High Level Bridge cars to 109 Street and Whyte Avenue and walking to the Lake. Crowds were large enough to entice enterprising people to erect tents and shacks as parcel checking services for skaters.[44] Moonlit nights attracted many to the Lake but citizens still strongly suggested that the street railway install lights at the Lake. Lights were indeed installed and in fact a gala celebration with a band and fireworks took place at McKernan's Lake on New Year's Eve 1913.[45]

Passengers found it increasingly difficult to determine the routes of the street cars as more of the new extensions opened up. The fact that many cars were rerouted during various phases of track construction added to the confusion. Cars began to carry new coloured signs on each end below the right vestibule windows, the colours of which corresponded to the coloured lights carried on the

cars at night. These signs were a great help in identifying the car's destination, as the lettered signs on the roofs were hard to read by day when not illuminated from within. The new coloured signs were to display the streets upon which the car operated[46] in a fashion similar to that found on the Calgary Municipal Railway. The names of the streets were withheld from these boards for some time, however, as an injunction prevented the use of a new comprehensive street numbering system, which Edmonton had devised.

This system, applicable to both sides of the river would replace the use of street names with the exception of some major streets, notably Jasper Avenue and Whyte Avenue.[47] Street car roller signs would eventually have to be changed as well. At that time northbound High Level cars carried the sign "Syndicate", a sign which would have little meaning once the new street and avenue numbering became effective.

The proposed new schedules and routes required thirty-seven cars and allowed the schedules to be speeded up to an average of 9.25 m.p.h.[51] This improved speed was attributable to the good condition of the new permanent double track and because of the adoption of the belt line concept which kept more cars moving and eliminated the time formerly wasted at terminal stub end tracks.

Effective Saturday, November 15th 1913, the cars of the Edmonton Radial Railway began to operate over six routes. Route 1, the blue route, operated from a northwest terminal at 24th (124) Street and Alberta (118) Avenue to Jasper Avenue, east to Namayo (97 Street), north to Norwood Boulevard, east to Kirkness (95) Street north to Alberta Avenue and to 66th Street in North Edmonton at the packing plant. This route was 8.75 miles long, one way.

Route 2 began at Twelfth (116) Street West and Sixth (76) Avenue South on the south side along Sixth Avenue South to Main (104) Street, north to Whyte Avenue, east to Fifth (99) Street east down Strathcona Hill and across the Low Level Bridge to Curry (100) Street, south to Saskatchewan (97) Avenue, west to 9th (109) Street, north to Jasper Avenue, east to Syndicate Avenue (95 Street) and north to Norwood Boulevard, west to Namayo Avenue (97 Street) and south to Jasper then returning to the south side again via the same route. The length of this route was 8.89 miles, one way.

Route 3, the green line, also called the east end belt line began at First (101) Street and ran east on Jasper to Syndicate Avenue (95 Street) past Norwood Boulevard onto Kirkness (95) Street to Spruce (114) Avenue, then east to Kinnaird (82) Street north to Oak (116) Avenue east to John (80) Street and then north to Alberta (118) Avenue. From here the cars on the green line continued west to Kirkness (95) Street south to Norwood Boulevard, west to First (101) Street and south to Jasper Avenue. The green line was 6.70 miles in length. These three routes all enjoyed fifteen-minute service.

Route 4, the red-and-white line, began at 11th (91) Street East and Sixth (88) Avenue North, in the Bonnie Doon area, ran south to Whyte Avenue, west to Fifth (109) Street West, north across the High Level Bridge to 9th (109) Street and Jasper Avenue, then east to Namayo Avenue (97 Street) north to Sutherland (106 Avenue) east to Syndicate (95 Street) then south to Jasper Avenue. Cars operated every ten minutes over this route except that portion east of Fifth (99) Street east into Bonnie Doon where cars operated only every twenty minutes. Length of this route in total was 8.64 miles.

Route 5, the white line, served the east-west extremities of the system. In the west end it started out at 42 (142) Street and Athabasca (102) Avenue went east to 24 (124) Street south to Jasper Avenue, east to Kinnaird (82) Street north to Pine (112) Avenue, east to Knox (112) Avenue and further east to the Highlands terminal at 61st Street. This 6.54-mile line had thirty-minute service except at rush hours when extra cars were added.

Sprinkler car S2, with its three man crew, sprays water onto Jasper Avenue as it approaches 100 Avenue in this 1915 scene.
(Glenbow Alberta Institute)

Route 6, the blue-and-white line, or the west end belt line, offered ten-minute service via First (101) Street, Nelson (107) Avenue, 24 (124) Street and Jasper Avenue. Cars operated both ways on this 4.87-mile route.[48] For a period of time after this route system was inaugurated, the blue-and-white line cars were unable to complete their belt due to the fact that the diamond had not been installed at the Grand Trunk Pacific crossing about three blocks east of 24 (124) Street. During this time cars approached the crossing from either side and turned back again.[49] With the opening of the High Level Bridge, street car service into the University area via Whyte Avenue and Seventh (111) Street West (111 Street) was terminated by mid-September 1913. The City Commissioners deemed that the service along 5th (109) Street West was sufficient to serve that area considering the expense involved in operating a regular route along a parallel trackage only two blocks away. The City did construct a board walk into the main University area from 109 Street to accommodate street car passengers going to and from the University.[50] The introduction of these new routes and schedules marked the completion of some 23 miles of new trackage on the ERR, 18.63 miles of it laid permanently in pavement.

Special service cars in the form of line maintenance, sprinkler and gravel hauling cars, were added to the roster during the year 1913. Mention has already been made of the fact that a line car had been built entirely in the new ERR Cromdale shops, but the extensions required in 1913 were too much for this line car to handle on its own. ERR shop crews therefore built a platform on single truck passenger car 7, to allow it to be used as a line car to supplement the services of the new flat deck line car.

Car 7 pushed a hand car with a huge roll of overhead copper wire. This wire was fed from the roll over a simple support on car 7's front end to the crew on the roof platform who fastened it into place on the cross spans. The line crews first spliced the copper cable into an operating part of the street car line, so that the cable wrapped around the spool contained 600 volts direct current power. Once the initial section of line was secure, car 7's trolley pole went up to the wire and the unit moved ahead a few feet at a time under its own power. The same procedure was used with the big line car, but the spool of overhead wire was carried on the front deck of the car itself. The older horse-drawn platform car was used to fasten the cross spans to the poles along either side of the street.

A side dump car was delivered to the Edmonton Radial Railway from Canadian Car and Foundry in Montreal. This car hauled gravel for the construction of the street car lines, as well as general freight for line-side industries. Like the motor flat acquired in 1912, it too had standard railway-type couplers and air brake equipment, so that it could effectively switch railway cars from the interchange track, initially at the Syndicate Street Canadian Northern crossing and latterly at Cromdale car barns, to various sidings on the street railway system.

During 1913 a second sprinkler joined the rolling stock roster. It was a much heavier unit than the sprinkler then in service and came from McGuire-Cummings of Chicago, the manufacturer of the large double-truck sweeper which had been on the roster since 1909.

During 1913, the planned permanent track work and shop facilities had been completed as scheduled. All but seven of the thirty-five new cars were in service, and the completion of the Edmonton Interurban Railway, described in Chapter VIII, offered Edmonton-area residents as fine an urban and interurban rail transportation service as could be found in the West.

The Edmonton Interurban Railway

THE EDMONTON INTERURBAN RAILWAY completed its line to St. Albert during 1913, culminating several years of negotiating and planning. This company, and another line from Lacombe to Gull Lake, were the only interurban lines, of several incorporated in Alberta up to that date, actually to operate their own lines with their own equipment. The Edmonton Interurban Railway Company was incorporated by an act of the Alberta Legislature assented to on December 16th 1910.[1] Frederick de Sieyes, civil engineer; B. Shehyn Scott, contractor, and Raymond Brutinel, capitalist, were the sponsors of this Company with its head office located in Edmonton. It held rights to build and operate 4' 8 1/2''-gauge railway lines, utilizing any form of motive power other than steam, to several points from within or near Edmonton, St. Albert and/or Morinville. The Company had authority also to build either from Edmonton or Strathcona to Fort Saskatchewan; Pigeon Lake; Mewassin; Lac St. Anne and Beaver Lake. If a line was built beyond the south end of Beaver Lake, it was required to touch the town of Tofield; if it went beyond the north end of the same lake, its line had to touch the town of Vegreville.[2] It appeared that the St. Albert line was always regarded as a priority by the Company. The act gave the EIR power to "enter into an agreement with another company or companies for conveying or leasing to such company or companies the railway of the company hereby incorporated . . .'' provided that within one year of the date of the passing of the act to incorporate it, the EIR would construct its line from the foot of Pirron Street in St. Albert to the boundaries of the City of Edmonton.[3]

Another important aspect of the agreement provided for the City of Edmonton to take over any works of the EIR which fell within the boundaries of the City as a result of annexation or other expansion of the city boundaries. The EIR would be compensated only for the value of these works, without regard to franchise rights or earning powers. Such action could be taken by the city after giving six months' notice of its intention to do so.[4]

The Edmonton Interurban Railway in fact did not begin construction within the stipulated year. It is not surprising, then, that an Act to amend the original Act of incorporation was given assent on February 16th 1912; it gave the EIR authority to operate to a point at or near Namao post office in addition to the original points.[5] It also clarified the position of the Company with respect to the boundaries of the City of Edmonton under the new Edmonton-Strathcona Amalgamation Act. In the event of amalgamation with any other adjoining city, town or village, or by the extension of the city's boundaries to include an area not greater than one mile, not included within the limits of any city, town or village, the City of Edmonton or the city resulting from such amalgamation or extension of boundaries had the power to acquire and take over all the works of the EIR for the value of those works upon giving the railway six months' notice of its intention to do so. If the City annexed or acquired land more than one mile from its boundaries as defined in the Edmonton-Strathcona Amalgamation Act, then the EIR was to receive two years' notice of the City's intention to acquire the works of the EIR falling in that area.[6]

The Act to amend the original charter allowed the Directors an extension of the date by which the line had to be in operation. The EIR had made an agreement with the Town of St. Albert respecting operations, which would not be ratified and confirmed by the Act unless the EIR commenced construction of this line from the foot of Pirron Street in St. Albert to the City of Edmonton by October 1st 1912, and then had the line actually in operation by October 1st 1913.[7] Once again the challenge had been placed before the officers of the Edmonton Interurban Railway.

Grading did indeed get underway during October 1912.[8] The railway concluded land agreements with property holders along the line, some of whom apparently provided financing. The line followed a somewhat complicated pattern to reach St. Albert, in order to pass through land holdings of an associated real estate firm in what was to be known as Summerland. Once the right-of-way had

The only car on the Edmonton Interurban Railway waits at the end of track in St. Albert for its departure to Edmonton. This car built by the Drake Automotrice Company, could seat 44 people — 8 in a smoking section and 36 in the main section. One could speculate that the gentleman with the bow tie and coveralls, seated above the coupler, might be the conductor.
(Provincial Archives of Alberta)

been cleared, it was fenced in order to prevent cattle from wandering onto the track.[9] Then one contractor with twenty-one teams began to work from the operational headquarters of the EIR at Queen Mary Park westwards toward the Edmonton, Dunvegan and British Columbia Railway crossing. A second contractor worked from the west toward the same point. Steel had been ordered from the Carnegie company of Pittsburg, Pennsylvania, and it was expected that operation would begin as early as February 10th 1913, using five gas-electric cars. Shelters constructed of iron had been ordered from Glasgow, Scotland.[10]

The route of the EIR began at Brandon (127) Avenue and 124 Street in Calder. The line ran north from this point along 124 Street to Algonquin (137) Avenue. At the southwest corner of this intersection, grading was underway for the interurban line's shops, yards and operational headquarters in Queen Mary Park. From this point the line struck west on Algonquin Avenue for a half mile to about 131 Street. It then turned north for another half-mile before turning west once again and proceeding some 2 3/4 miles along the centre line of sections 25, 26 and 27 to the western boundary of the latter section. The line then turned sharply to the north in a slightly less than ninety-degree angle for the balance of the run into St. Albert.[11] At the point where the line turned north for its last lap into St. Albert, it was only two miles from Big Lake and it was thought probable that once the main line had been completed a branch would be carried west to the lake.[12] In fact two men from Victoria had already visited the area looking at the possibility of a park development at the lake.[13]

M. Kimpke, General Manager of the EIR at that time denied that he was demanding an extension of the Edmonton Radial Railway, but intimated that, had negotiations failed for an extension of the ERR to meet the EIR, passengers from the latter would be taken into Edmonton by auto bus.[14]

Track laying got underway early in June 1913. All of the track, frogs, ties and supplies had been delivered to the suburban railway's yards in Queen Mary Park.[15] It is not known how these materials were delivered, but it is probable that a connection was built with the Grand Trunk Pacific at Calder. The driving of a last spike in St. Albert on Friday, July 11th 1913 marked the completion of tracklaying for the main line of the Edmonton Interurban Railway.[16] With its road complete, the company waited for delivery of its rolling stock.

Apparently, four cars had been ordered to operate the service. Two were described as Hele-Shaw cars built in Belgium. These cars could reportedly seat 45 passengers and had the capability to haul up to ten trailer cars. The remaining two units, gas-electric cars, were expected from the Drake Automotrice Company of Chicago, and were capable of seating some 20 people.[17] The Hele-Shaw cars would contain a gasoline engine which provided power to the wheels by a hydraulic drive system.

The American-designed units were equipped also with a gasoline engine but it generated power for electric motors mounted on the axles which actually drove the car.[18] Single-end operation characterized all of these vehicles with the gasoline motor located in the front end. Smoking and non-smoking compartments made up the passenger section. The Company planned also to have a freight car placed in service with one half fitted up as a refrigerator in which garden produce, butter, eggs and cream could be transported into the Edmonton market on 101 Street.[19]

Car number 1, a Drake car, lettered for the Edmonton Interurban Railway, began trials on the line late in September 1913. On September 29th 1913, the Deputy Minister of Railways for the Province of Alberta accompanied EIR officials for the trip over the line to St. Albert in the new gas-electric car.[20] Permission was granted to operate the route and on Tuesday, September 30th, regular service began between Calder and St. Albert. The statutory deadline for providing service to St. Albert had been fulfilled by one day. The new car seated 44 people, 36 in the main portion and 8 in the smoking compartment. Its interior was finished in dark oak panelling and its seats upholstered in dark green plush. The gasoline generator developed 90 h.p. for the electric motors which propelled the car, which was capable of speeds up to 35 m.p.h.[21]

An advertisement appearing in the Edmonton Bulletin of Wednesday, October 1st 1913 indicated that the Edmonton Interurban Railway Company offered services on the Edmonton-St. Albert line effective September 29th 1913. The car left Brandon (127) Avenue and Edward (124) Street Monday through Friday at 9:30 a.m.; 1:30 p.m. and 4:30 p.m. The car returned from Pirron Street and St. Anne Street in St. Albert at 10:30 a.m.; 2:30 p.m. and 5:30 p.m. On Saturdays and Sundays four trips were made each way leaving Edmonton at 9:30 a.m., 11:30 a.m., 2:30 p.m. and 4:30 p.m. and St. Albert at 10:30 a.m., 1:30 p.m. 3:30 p.m. and 5:30 p.m. The advertisement carried the name of Felix Santallier, General Manager.[22] Some three hundred passengers rode the car on the first Sunday of operation. The EIR provided a bus to transport passengers from the end of the Edmonton Radial Railway at 24th (124) Street and Alberta (118) Avenue to the Interurban terminal in Calder.[23] The car made five stops on its seven-mile journey from Calder to St. Albert: at the car barns, in Summerland, at St. Albert Trail, at Government Road and at Hill Top. Summerland was a community being developed by EIR interests. The Company laid out a series of streets, set up an electric lighting system and built homes. It hoped to attract people to buy residences in the area, using the Interurban railway as a means of transportation. Large advertisements appeared in the Edmonton daily press promoting the virtues of country living in Summerland. The community was laid out at the curve where the Interurban line turned west about a half mile north of Alonquin (137) Avenue near the Edmonton Dunvegan and British Columbia crossing. At Hill Top a wire cable handled by a stationary donkey engine was attached to the car for safety purposes as it descended the steep grade into the Sturgeon River Valley to the Town of St. Albert. On the cars' return trip the cables were fastened again at the foot of the hill for the same purpose.[24]

The Edmonton Interurban Railway had over one hundred men working improving the roadbed, building the car barns, shops and offices, while at Summerland, a large force of workers were constructing houses and sidewalks.[25] The Edmonton Interurban Railway, now a reality, was indeed a prime example of a small development road based on optimism that St. Albert's population would grow and that the new community of Summerland would flourish.

A rail connection with the Edmonton Radial Railway now became an absolute necessity. Considerable pressure came from many quarters to help this step become a reality. Among others the Edmonton Board of Trade encouraged such a connection.[26] On November 7th 1913 the City of Edmonton signed an interim agreement with the Edmonton Interurban Railway Company, by which the EIR was given the power to lay a single-track temporary line under the direction of the City Engineer south from Brandon (127) Avenue and 27th (127) Street to Alberta (118) Avenue then east along Alberta Avenue to 24th (124) Street.

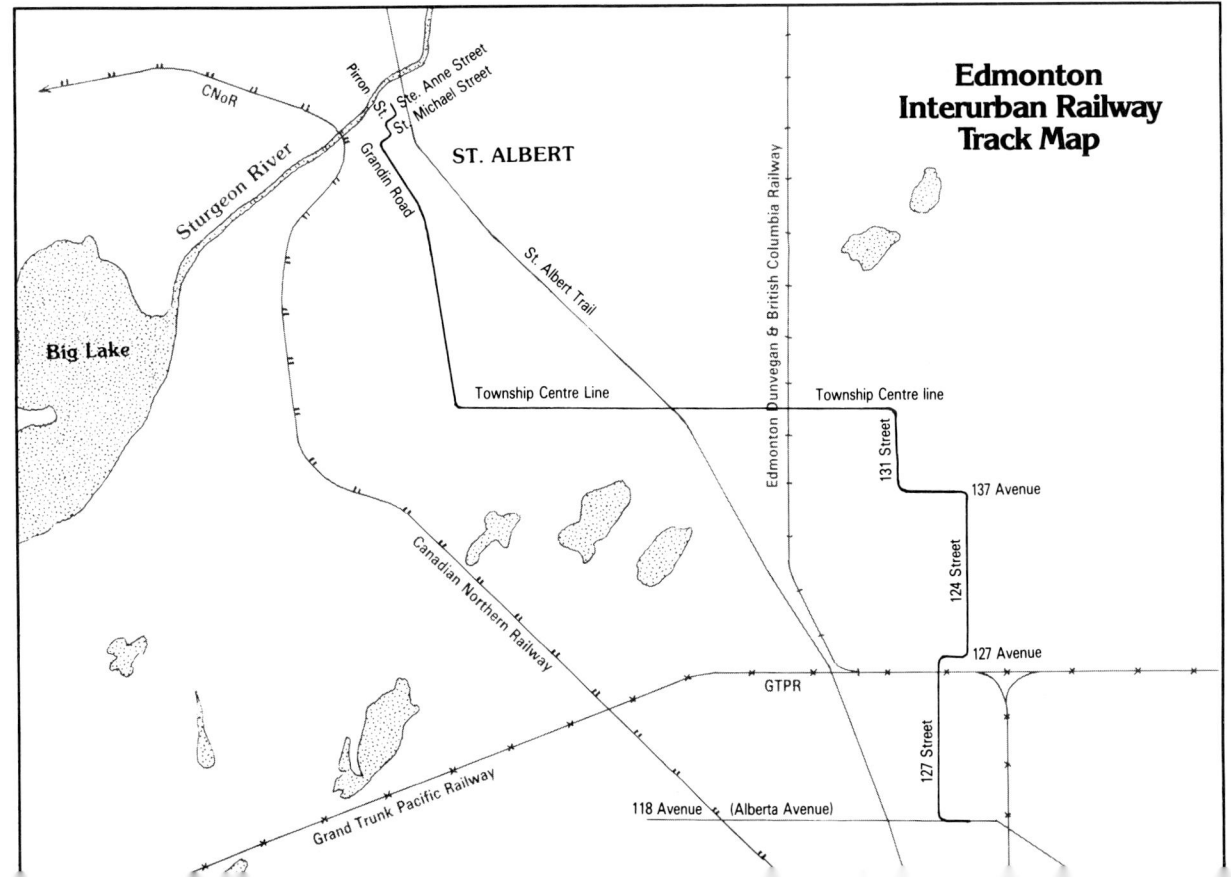

This line actually became part of the ERR for operating purposes, but ownership of the rails and ties remained in the hands of the interurban company. Trains of the EIR actually came under the direction of the Edmonton Radial Railway while operating within the city boundary. Passengers carried over this line within the city limits were thus required to pay the usual ERR fare which was collected by that company. The city agreed to extend its line on 24th (124) Street north to Alberta (118) Avenue to connect with the EIR line. A car or cars could be loaned to the Municipality (ERR) under the terms of the agreement; they could be brought in on their regular trips as far as necessary but not beyond Albany (110) Avenue, for interchange of traffic with the Edmonton Radial's cars. Each railway was to receive goods shipped by express or freight orginating at points on either system and consigned to points on the other. The charges were to be uniform. The agreement itself was to continue in force for a period of nine months. After that time the agreement could be terminated upon one week's notice by either party.[27]

The Interurban connection was virtually complete by the end of November with the only difficulty being the crossing of the Grand Trunk Pacific main line, where, by order of the Railway Commission, an interlocking device had to be installed. Since installation of such a device would take another six or eight weeks, the EIR sought permission from the Railway Commissioners to allow the posting of a flagman as a temporary measure. The Edmonton Radial Railway electrified trackage had been extended to Alberta (118) Avenue on 24 (124) Street with a wye to connect at that point with the Edmonton Interurban line.

The diamond for the Grand Trunk Pacific crossing arrived and was installed during the weekend of December 19th-21st, 1913,[28] and on Sunday, December 21st, the interurban car operated into Edmonton for the first time. It operated under its own power to Cromdale car barns where, at the expense of the EIR, some repairs were made.[29]

Regular service from 24th (124) Street and Alberta (118) Avenue began on Monday, December 22nd 1913.[30] An advertisement appeared in the local newspapers advising that the car would leave Edmonton — 24th Street and Alberta Avenue at 8:00 a.m., 10:00 a.m., 1:30 p.m., 2:30 p.m. and 4:30 p.m. It would leave for the return trip from Pirron and St. Anne Streets in St. Albert at 9:00 a.m., 11:00 a.m., 12:00 noon, 2:30 p.m. and 5:30 p.m. The ad noted that the cars connected at 24th Street and Alberta Avenue with City of Edmonton cars. Again, the name Felix Santallier, General Manager, appeared at the bottom of the ad. By early January 1914, the interlocking device at the ED&BC crossing had been installed and the GTP crossing interlocking device was being completed.[31]

At 2:30 a.m. on Wednesday, April 1st 1914 fire destroyed the Edmonton Interurban Railway car barns. Car number 1, standing in the barns at the time, was completely destroyed. Gasoline apparently exploded in the tanks of the car but no definite cause for the fire was determined. Total loss was estimated at $30,000, fortunately covered by insurance. Mr. Santallier estimated that service would be suspended for only a few days until two new cars on order from England were delivered, but the cars never did arrive. In mid-May, Bion Joseph Arnold, a traction expert from Chicago, visited the management of the Edmonton Interurban Railway. Apparently he was to advise about possible expansion to Fort Saskatchewan and about the most economical means of supplying power to the line. Until his report had been made to the board of directors, no steps were taken to operate the line to St. Albert.[31] As might be expected, the press carried little or no news of any further developments on the Edmonton Interurban Railway. It had a flourishing but short operating history.

In 1915 the Edmonton Radial Railway, under pressure from the residents of Calder, negotiated a lease of the trackage still intact within the boundaries of Edmonton. Later the City of Edmonton bought the EIR trackage in Calder itself and extended the ERR under electric trolley line into the area.

The Superintendent of the Edmonton Interurban Railway Company in Edmonton, M. Polet, prepared a report for the Board of Directors, dated September 14th 1917, about the feasibility of restoring operations on the line. The EIR had expected to haul coal from the St. Albert collieries but found it could not compete with the Canadian Northern which had a spur into the area and access with better grades to its freight yards in downtown Edmonton. The CNR hauled this coal at 30¢ per ton. The EIR could not compete as switching charges alone were 17¢ per ton. At the time the report was submitted the coal mine had closed and the CNR spur had been abandoned. The EIR had also hoped to gain revenue from the Acme Brick Company plant but experienced the same difficulties in hauling brick as it did in hauling coal. The Summerland housing subdivision had been abandoned with the last houses removed during the winter of 1916-17. This community was to have provided the EIR with a substantial passenger revenue. However, the old right-of-way had trepassed private property in several places, and it appeared that revival of the line over its former route was an impossibility.[33]

The report did suggest an alternate route into Edmonton, and the possible use of the unused ERR trackage on Portage Avenue. The new line would be six miles long compared with the former line which was eight-and-a-quarter miles long; the revived railway had the potential to pick-up traffic coming across the St. Albert bridge from Villeneuve, Ray, Riviere Qui Barre, Volmer, Cardiff and Morinville and taking it to market in Edmonton.[34] It was also thought that the company could pick up considerable passenger business, as evidenced by the fact that passenger traffic carried by the Edmonton Radial Railway over leased EIR trackage had quadrupled over a fifteen-month period from April 1916 to July 1917. The EIR might also pick up some of the dairy traffic then being handled by the CNR.[33] These eventualities, however, never occurred and the Edmonton Interurban Railway faded quietly away.

Photo above:
Residents and land promoters welcome the arrival of the Edmonton Interurban Railway car at the new community of Summerland. With the burning of the EIR car barn and the subsequent outbreak of World War I, Summerland quickly disappeared from the map. The community depended on the EIR for transportation and the demise of EIR service shattered the dreams of those who had invested in the new community. *(Glenbow Alberta Institute)*

Photo below:
Edmonton Interurban Railway's gasoline-electric car 1 appears to be a much heavier piece of equipment than the city cars of the Edmonton Radial Railway. The long wheelbase trucks and the massive wooden pilot attest to its service as an interurban unit. The knuckle coupler, airbrake hose and poling receptacle on the high front bumper indicate that it could be used also to switch steam railway cars. The absence of a pilot at the passenger end of the car suggests that the vehicle was turned at each end of the line. *(Glenbow Alberta Institute)*

Photo above:
Car 31, eastbound on Whyte Avenue, approaches 104 Street in this 1914 scene. *(Glenbow Alberta Institute)*

Photo below:
Passengers cluster to board at the rear door of car 73 on its eastbound trip along Jasper Avenue at 99 Street in this 1914 scene. *(Glenbow Alberta Institute)*

9 Economic Instability

By THE beginning of 1914, the overbuilding and overextension of services on the ERR demanded action, and during the month of January, street railway management made a careful assessment of the situation. By the end of the month, a new schedule and re-routing was announced to take effect on February 8th 1914.[1]

Route 1, carrying blue signs lettered "Packing Plant — 24th and Alberta via Namayo", operated from the packing plant in North Edmonton to 24th (124) Street and Alberta (118) Avenue via Norton (66) Street, Alberta Avenue, Kirkness (95) Street, Norwood Boulevard, Namayo (97) Avenue, Jasper Avenue and 24th (124) Street. Cars ran every fifteen minutes throughout the day until 10:00 p.m. After that hour, the service was every twenty minutes. On Sundays, the blue line offered twenty-minute service throughout the day.

Route 2 carried red signs lettered "Low Level" when running from Highlands to Whyte Avenue and Main Street and white signs lettered "Highlands" when running from Whyte Avenue to the Highlands. Its route began at Whyte Avenue and Main (104) Street, operating via Whyte Avenue, 5th (99) Street East, the Low Level Bridge, Curry (100) Street, west on Saskatchewan (97) Avenue to 109 Street, then north to Jasper Avenue, east to Kinnaird (82) Street, north to Pine (112) Avenue and east to the Highlands loop. This line had fifteen-minute service daily all day and evening. On Sundays, the fifteen-minute service was maintained until 10:00 p.m. when it was reduced to half-hourly.

Route 3 carried green signs, "Nelson, Spruce". Beginning at John (80) Street and Alberta (118) Avenue it ran south on John (80) Street, west on Oak (116) Avenue, south on Kinnaird (82) Street to Spruce (114) Avenue, west to Kirkness (95 Street), south to Syndicate (95 Street) and Jasper Avenue, then west to First (101) Street, north to Nelson (107) Avenue and west to Short (107) Avenue and 24th (124) Street. It turned back at Short (107) Avenue and 24th Street. The green line operated on an identical frequency of service as the blue line.

Route 4 carried red and white signs, "High Level Bridge". Its south side terminal was at 5th (99) Street East and Whyte Avenue. From this point its cars ran west on Whyte Avenue to 5th (109) Street West, north via the High Level Bridge to 9th (109) Street and Jasper Avenue, east to First (101) Street, north to Norwood Boulevard, east to Namayo (97) Street) and south to Jasper, whence they returned to the south side via the High Level Bridge. These cars ran every twelve minutes until 10:00 p.m. when service was cut back to a car every fifteen minutes. On Sundays these cars operated every fifteen minutes throughout the day and evening.

Route 5 carried blue and white signs "Athabasca" and "Syndicate". These cars began from Athabasca (102) Avenue and 42 (142) Street, and ran east on Athabasca to 24 (124) Street, south to Jasper Avenue, east to Syndicate (95 Street), north to Sutherland (106 Avenue), west to Namayo (97 Street), south to Jasper Avenue and return to its western terminal. These cars operated every twenty minutes Monday through Saturday. This route did not operate after 10:00 p.m. nor on Sundays.

Route 6 carried blue and red signs named "Bonnie Doon" and "McKernan's Lake". The route began in Bonnie Doon, ran south to Whyte Avenue, west to Main (104) Street, south to 6th (76) Avenue south and west to 12th (116) Street West, and returned by the same route. One car offered hourly service on this line, daily and Sundays, until midnight.

By the time the new schedules actually went into effect, a few minor changes had been made. The residents of Bonnie Doon expressed their displeasure at street car service being reduced from three times per hour to once per hour. Street railway officials promised better service would be offered if the traffic warranted it. In the short time before February 8th, enough Bonnie Doon residents used the cars to convince the ERR that Bonnie Doon should have twelve-minute service. The red-and-white sign High Level Bridge line was extended east of its intended terminus at 5th (99) Street East and Whyte Avenue into Bonnie Doon. This meant that the blue-and-red sign cars operated from Main (104) Street and Whyte Avenue to McKernan's Lake only. As a result, the Lake had car service every half hour. In addition High Level Bridge cars operated every six minutes between 4:00 p.m. and 8:00 p.m.[2] The new schedule did effect a considerable saving but was understandably not popular with the labour union as some thirty men were laid off.[3]

With approximately eighty trams available for service, a maximum of only 53 were being used each day on the average.[4] Ridership along Jasper Avenue was high. A special rush-hour car service along this thoroughfare, between Government Avenue (92 Street) and 16th (116) Street went into

75

effect on March 9th 1914. This special service operated every fifteen minutes between 5:00 p.m. and 6:30 p.m.[5] People travelling along Jasper Avenue within the boundaries of the special's route were encouraged to use it in order to relieve congestion on the longer distance cars.[6] The belt line concept of operation had certainly fallen into disfavour.

During the spring of 1914 the Edmonton Bulletin carried a series of short articles entitled "Street Railway News". These accounts explained delays, told of the number of cars operated, and the number of passengers carried. They usually concluded with a short message directed at speeding up the service. Messages to passengers, encouraging them to patronize the new Jasper Avenue rush hour service, appeared on a couple of occasions. Other messages cautioned riders not to expect a car to stop again once it had started up from a corner, since it cost more in electrical power to stop and start a car then it cost to run it for one block. People travelling with small children were encouraged to have the child vacate its seat when other passengers were standing, as small children were not fare-paying passengers. It concluded by stating that compliance with that rule would be much appreciated by the aged, weak and retired.[7]

J.H. Larmonth became the fifth Superintendent of the ERR, replacing W.T. Woodroofe, on April 1st 1914.[8] Mr. Larmonth took over a system which boasted a fine reputation as far as trackage facilities and equipment were concerned, but he was faced with the same difficulty his predecessor had — that of operating the system with considerable mileage through lightly populated areas. Estimates placed the costs of operating a car at approximately $40 per day. Receipts per car per day during the first week in April 1914 averaged out as follows: Packing Plant $57.50; Low Level (Red) and Highlands (White) $88.78; Nelson-Spruce (Green)

The June 1915 flood of the North Saskatchewan River inundated streets in low-lying areas of Edmonton adjacent to the river banks. At one point the Low Level Bridge — a major rail, transit and roadway link between north and south Edmonton — was threatened. A Canadian Northern switch locomotive and train were dispatched to the bridge to add weight to the structure to prevent it from being moved by the flood waters. (Glenbow Alberta Institute)

$40.87; High Level (Red and White) $52.47; Athabasca Avenue (Blue and White) $24.91; Sixth Avenue South (Blue and Red) $6.28.[9] A proposal to raise fares met with considerable controversy but on Sunday, May 17th 1914 the straight 5¢ fare became effective. Children's tickets at 10 for 25¢ and limited tickets available between 5:30 a.m. and 8:00 a.m. only at the rate of 8 for 25¢ were the only exceptions to the straight 5¢ fare structure.[10] Tickets could still be purchased but they sold for 5 for 25¢. Since no new rate structure had been posted in the cars, conductors were the targets of sharp criticism. One conductor became quite angry after being accused by a passenger of selling five tickets for 25¢ and pocketing the sixth ticket.[11] The railway did experience a small drop in ridership as a result of the new fares but revenues enjoyed a very decided increase. The following table shows receipts for the week ending May 28th 1914 compared with the final week in April 1914 (in parenthesis).[12]

	Total Receipts For Week	Average Receipts Per Car Per Day	Average Receipts Per Car Per Mile
124th Street-Packing Plant	$7013.65 (6061.92)	$57.87 (53.26)	$34.60 (36.12)
High Level Bridge	$3306.25 (2797.95)	$41.74 (50.87)	$33.23 (31.14)
Low Level-Highlands	$2341.00 (—)	$37.47 (34.38)	$27.49 (26.15)
Nelson-Spruce	$1211.63 (1093.00)	$44.87 (40.35)	$27.66 (24.94)
Athabasca-Syndicate	$ 114.14		
McKernan's Lake	$ 51.38		

The street railway's financial problems were not solved but the May 1914 fare increase did provide some much-needed additional revenue. This, coupled with the new routes introduced in January 1914, helped to place the ERR on a more solid financial base.

Street railway operations, however, were not devoid of interesting and unusual situations. Car 42, making a routine trip on the Packing Plant line at 7:30 p.m. on Friday evening, June 19th 1914, had its usual heavy complement of passengers for that time of day. As it approached Norwood Boulevard on its northbound trip, a lady returning home from work quietly went to Conductor Skillinton and whispered something in his ear. Skillinton blushed and assured the lady he would hurry the car along to her doctor's office near the corner of Alberta Avenue and Kirkness Street. The car plodded along too slowly, however, and when it reached Alberta and Kirkness, two women helped the lady and her newborn son off the car into the waiting room at the intersection. Her doctor was summoned from his office a block east only to declare that the newborn boy was as healthy a child as he had ever seen.[13] The Edmonton Radial Railway operated through into the year 1915 without any further significant newsworthy comment.

The outbreak of World War I inflicted a significant decline in ridership on the ERR. In the period January to April 1914, the railway carried some 4,897,008 passengers. Throughout the same period in 1915 only 3,724,023 passengers rode the cars.[14] About this time considerable concern was expressed that privately-owned jitneys were draining off the revenues of the street railway system by cruising along the street car routes, picking up passengers and taking them to their destinations. The Trades and Labour Council protested to City Council about the jitney service, claiming it was unsafe.[15] The jitney problem eventually disappeared but the revenues of the street railway continued to fall off.

During the summer of 1915, Mr. Larmonth left as Superintendent and his place was taken by Traffic Manager, J.H. Moir. Mr. Moir, in an attempt to bring the rising deficit under control, found it necessary to dismiss some employees. The street railwaymen's union and the Trades and Labour Council appeared before City Council to protest the dismissals,[16] but Mr. Moir stayed on to manage the new routes and schedules he had put into effect on September 20th 1915.

The new Superintendent had assisted in the preparation of the long-range routing plan in 1912. As we have seen in a previous chapter, this plan had embodied the belt line concept extensively, so it was not surprising to see this concept reintroduced in the 1915 route changes. Through service to downtown Edmonton was provided from McKernan's Lake and from 142 Street and 102 Avenue. That amenity was provided at the expense of service frequency, as cars now offered only hourly service on these two lines. These 1915 changes marked the removal of the roller signs from the car roofs, as they were outdated and practically useless. Street names appeared on these roller signs but by 1915 Edmonton had converted completely to a street number system and the names became redundant[17] (see page 12).

The new route plan set the whole system into three basic routes. Two of these routes contained a complexity of services. Route 1 consisted of all the services from the north east into and through the downtown area to the west and north west extremities of the system. The blue, blue-and-white, green and green-and-white sign cars all operated on Route 1. The blue sign cars signed *North Edmonton (via 97 Street)* north and eastbound and *124 Street and 118 Avenue (via 97 Street)* westbound formed the core of route 1 service. Cars on the blue line operated every fifteen minutes from the North Edmonton Packing Plant at 66 Street and 124 Avenue via 66 Street, 118 Avenue, 95 Street, Norwood Boulevard, 97 Street, Jasper Avenue and 124 Street to 118 Avenue. Cars carrying blue-and-white signs overlapped blue sign cars in both directions on the northeast section of route 1 and westbound on the west end of route 1 as far as 124 Street and 107 Avenue. Blue-and-white sign cars returned to downtown Edmonton via 107 Avenue and 101 Street thus forming a belt on the western part of their route. Blue-and-white sign cars carried westbound destination signs lettered *107 Avenue and 124 Street* and eastbound signs lettered *80 Street and 118 Avenue (via 97 Street)*.[18]

Still on route 1, green sign cars lettered *102 Avenue and 142 Street* travelled from that terminal into the downtown area every half hour during morning and evening rush periods and hourly throughout the remainder of the day. It is thought that these cars turned in the downtown area via Jasper 97 Street, 106 Avenue, 95 Street and back again via Jasper Avenue. Green sign cars travelled into northeast Edmonton via 97 Street, Norwood Boulevard, 95 Street, 114 Avenue, 82 Street, 116 Avenue, 80 Street and 118 Avenue. The cars, signed *114 Avenue (Spruce) (via 97 Street)*, operated every fifteen minutes in the morning rush hours and between 12:00 noon and 6:30 p.m. In the mid-morning and evening periods they operated every half hour.[19] Turnback location of these north east green sign cars in the downtown area is unknown.

A stub service ran from 124 Street and 118 Avenue to augment blue line car service up to 9:15 a.m. between 12:00 noon and 2:00 p.m. and between 5:30 p.m. and 6:30 p.m. It is known that this service operated to the downtown area[20] but its destination and route colour are not definitely known. It appears highly likely that these were green-and-white signed cars lettered *106 Avenue and 95 Street*.

On Sundays, blue and blue-and-white sign cars, each offered fifteen-minute service throughout the day, while the west-end green sign cars offered hourly service throughout the day. Between 2:00 p.m. and 9:00 p.m. service on route 1 eastbound and westbound from Jasper Avenue and 101 Street was stepped up, but no record is available as to which cars provided this augmented service.[21]

Route 2 was a very simple single route. White sign cars, carrying signs lettered *107 Avenue via 101 Street Belt (Nelson)*, originated at Highlands and travelled on 112 Avenue, 82 Street, Jasper Avenue north on 101 Street, west 107 Avenue, south on 124 Street and returned to Highlands via an easterly run along Jasper Avenue. These cars provided fifteen-minute service. They also provided service on the west end belt in the opposite direction to the blue-and-white sign cars. In the late evening after 9:00 p.m. and on Sundays up to approximately 1:00 p.m., cars on route 2 operated every twenty minutes.[22]

Route 3 covered all the south side tram services. Red sign cars carrying signs lettered *111 Avenue via 95 Street and Low Level* travelled every fifteen minutes from 111 Avenue via 95 Street, Jasper Avenue, 109 Street, 97 Avenue, 100 Street, the Low Level Bridge, Scona Hill, 99 Street to Whyte Avenue. These cars returned to the downtown area via Whyte Avenue, 109 Street, the High Level Bridge, Jasper Avenue, 101 Street and 111 Avenue. Red-and-white (diagonal) sign cars began their journeys, at fifteen-minute intervals, also at 111 Avenue but travelled via 101 Street, Jasper Avenue, 109 Street and the High Level Bridge to Whyte Avenue. They returned to 111 Avenue via the Low Level Bridge, 97 Avenue, 109 Street, Jasper Avenue and 95 Street. The red-and-white sign read *111 Avenue via 101 Street and Highlands*. Bonnie Doon cars carried red-and-white signs with the top half white and the lower half red. These cars crossed the High Level Bridge into downtown Edmonton via Jasper Avenue, 101 Street, 111 Avenue and back via 95 Street, Jasper Avenue and the High Level Bridge. Operating on a half-hourly schedule throughout the day and quarter-hourly at rush periods, they displayed route signs reading *111 Avenue via 95 Street and High Level to Bonnie Doon*. The fourth segment of route 3 was the blue-and-red route lettered *111 Avenue via 95 Street to McKernan's Lake*. These cars operated hourly from McKernan's Lake to Whyte Avenue and 104 Street, then into downtown Edmonton via the High Level Bridge, Jasper Avenue, 101 Street to 111 Avenue and back to the south side via 95 Street, Jasper Avenue, the High Level Bridge and Whyte Avenue. On Sunday mornings and late Sunday evenings red and red-and-white diagonal sign cars operated at twenty-minute intervals. Between 2:00 p.m. and 9:00 p.m. they stepped up to a fifteen-minute service. Red-and-blue (McKernan's Lake) and red-and-white (Bonnie Doon) sign cars offered service at forty minute intervals. At approximately 2:00 p.m. both of these areas received half-hourly service.[23]

As published in the local press, the new schedules and routes appeared to be very complicated for the average user to understand. It remained to be seen if the return to the belt line system was actually going to reduce operating expenses.

118 Avenue at 124 Street about 1942. Car 51, in the background, is on the wye which was extended the following year for the re-routed service to Calder and Elm Park. Norm Corness is operator of the two-wheeled vehicle in the foreground. (Les Corness)

Two Preston-built streetcars pass on Jasper Avenue at 107 Street about 1915. The brick building opposite the facing car is the MacLean Block which has been recently restored to house office and retail space.
(Provincial Archives of Alberta, E. Brown Collection)

An expansion of services seemed inconsistent with the new economy-minded schedule; nevertheless property owners in Elm Park and Calder petitioned the City of Edmonton for electric street railway service in November 1915. Both of these communities bordered upon 127 Avenue with Calder covering the area between 127 Street and 119 Street while Elm Park stretched east of 119 Street. The rail line was actually in place, as property owners had in mind the utilization of the idle tracks laid down in 1913 by the Edmonton Interurban Railway Company along 118 Avenue and 127 Street to the Grand Trunk Pacific crossing. The line required ballasting plus the installation of poles and overhead electric trolley wire.[24] Arrangements to lease the trackage from the Edmonton Interurban Railway were concluded. It was planned that cars would offer half-hourly service from 7:00 a.m. to 9:00 a.m., 2:00 p.m. to 8:00 p.m. and 10:00 p.m. to 11:00 p.m. between the Grand Trunk Pacific crossing and 118 Avenue and 124 Street.[25] Service on the new electric car line actually began in January 1916.

Five months later, Elm Park residents again petitioned Edmonton City Council to have the ERR cross the Grand Trunk Pacific tracks, to electrify the line on 127 Avenue and extend it to 119 Street. Council refused to move toward accepting the terms of this petition without support from the Village of Calder in the form of a guarantee to the city against losses on the operation of the line.[26] Either the City backed down on its request for a guarantee to meet the operating deficit, or the guarantee was agreed upon, as Mayor Henry attended a meeting in Elm Park on May 31st 1916. He explained that the Board of Railway Commissioners had to approve the installation of the level crossing over the Grand Trunk Pacific tracks, and that the Commissioners were to leave Ottawa on June 8th for a western tour; the case was to be presented when the Board sat in Edmonton.[26a] It appeared that the electrification was indeed extended across the Grand Trunk Pacific tracks to 127 Avenue, then east to 124 Street where the former EIR line turned north. The crossing at the Grand Trunk Pacific intersection was installed again to permit operation on this new segment. It is thought that this extension opened some time during July 1916. By that time the city was leasing 1.4 miles of EIR track[27] at a cost of $960 per year.[28] It is not known on what terms the city agreed to extend the line but a report shows a significant increase in car mileage and passengers carried in July 1916, pointing to the fact that this is possibly when the line was actually extended.[29] While the ERR seemed to be having considerable financial difficulties generally, the line to Elm Park continually met its expenses. A press account reported that revenue from the line for July 1916 was $590.91 while expenditures amounted to $351.04, leaving a surplus of $239.87. Expenditures included motormen and conductors' wages of $180.84; power charges of $100.95; track maintenance of $59.25 and interest on the capital expenditure of $20.00. It cost the city some $2,000 to install street railway facilities for service into the Elm Park area.[30]

Unfortunately, the optimism generated by operations on the Calder-Elm Park line did little to help negative attitudes toward the street railway system generally. Falling revenues, due to falling ridership blamed partly on privately-operated jitneys, continued to plague the system throughout 1916.

In what appeared to be an attempt to brighten up the scene, the city introduced a new yellow-and-brown paint scheme for the street cars in November 1915. Four cars appeared with bright yellow above the window sill and brown from the window sill to the bottom of the car body. The original red and green had not stood up well, so it was thought that the brown-and-yellow would weather for a longer period of time.[31] The four trams had been redecorated and were ready to enter service toward the end of November 1915.[32] The new paint scheme, however, did not enhance the attitude of the public toward the ERR. A news item from the Edmonton Journal of Wednesday, February 2nd 1916 entitled "City Automobiles Won't Need Sirens — May Be Painted Brown and Yellow" typified feelings toward the colours.

"The city's gaily decorated street cars, those brown and yellow painted vehicles which have been parading the streets lately, seem to have caused an infection for another little piece of funnyism is about to be negotiated.

Brown and yellow threaten to be the prevailing note of fashion till some administration tires of it and if these two contrasts, some people say they harmonize, are carried to many more extremes, it would be a wonder if the city itself did not have its houses decorated the same two colours.

The city's automobiles are to be painted brown and yellow!! Hereafter and whereas the city street cars are now painted brown and yellow, all city automobiles which need decorating or repairing will leave the city garage a different colour than when they went in. Instead of blue or black or grey or brown enamels like the cars are today, they will be the same colours as the street cars, and in future when citizens see these brown and yellow autos running through the city they can readily recognize their own property, and see whether it is being properly taken care of.

It is rumoured that all city employees are to be instructed to wear brown suits, brown shoes, yellow ties and brown hats with yellow bands, but the Commissioners this morning would not verify the accuracy of the rumour.

They did however acknowledge that the autos would undergo this change of colouring."[33]

Runaways on the hills leading into the North Saskatchewan River Valley were not unusual when hand-braking offered the only means of stopping a car. By 1916, however, all cars with the exception of number 7 featured air brakes, so runaways became very much an exception. One such exception, however, took place early in 1916. Cold damp air greeted car 23, one of the newly-painted trams, as it squealed out of Cromdale for its first run of the day on the Low Level Bridge route. It reached 109 Street and 97 Avenue without incident, but as it started down the long grade on 97 Avenue the motorman applied the brakes to check the speed. Nothing happened. Since the car thumped across the EY & P railway diamond in the middle of the grade at a pretty good clip, the conductor went forward to investigate. The brakes were indeed on but the car had gone into an uncontrollable skid. The conductor called back, warning passengers to lay on the floor. When number 23 hit the tight curve from 97 Avenue into 100 Street, its speed was so great that it turned onto its side. Fortunately no one was injured and, because of the early morning hours, few passengers were aboard for the wild ride over the rails coated with black ice. This was car 23's second mishap. In September 1913, as it made its way from the North Edmonton packing plant to downtown Edmonton, it was struck at the 118 Avenue crossing by a GTP switching train. One would have thought that car 23 was damaged beyond repair in the accident; in fact, Conductor Charles Wentworth was seriously injured in that altercation. Conductor Wentworth returned to the job after some lengthy absence and, apparently, so did car 23 for it ran into ill fame again with its January 1916 spill, new paint scheme and all. It is thought that this incident spelled "finis" for car 23, as it disappeared from the ERR roster at an early date.

Car 23 was wrecked at the Grand Trunk Pacific Railway crossing on Alberta (118) Avenue near Cromdale shop on September 13th 1913. (Glenbow Alberta Institute)

Conductor Wentworth experienced another injury at his post on the rear platform shortly after returning to work from car 23's first accident, when a car split a switch. Whether this accident precipitated Conductor Wentworth's move out of operations at this time is open to question, but when he did retire from the employ of the city in the 1940s, it was as the Street Railway Department's Storekeeper.

The year 1916 was a highly discouraging one for the railway. Car 77 followed in number 23's footsteps. It overturned early one morning late in April as it proceeded south on 101 Street. The motorman held the car at speed expecting to go straight through the intersection at 101 Street and 107 Avenue. Before he could check his speed, Car 77 had reached the intersection and lurched into 107 Avenue so intensely that the car turned over on its side. This being another early morning run, there were no passengers aboard and no injuries.[34] Car 77 was repaired and did go back into service again.

Passenger ridership continued to drop. March 1916 figures showed that the cars carried 982,674 passengers in that month compared with 1,081,451 in March 1915.[35] In a bid to reduce the deficit, Superintendent Moir announced that immediately following Fair Week in mid-July, schedules would be reduced, eliminating the need for ten cars per day. There were no route changes; only the number of cars servicing certain routes were cut back, including those for McKernan's Lake.[36] During Fair Week 72 street cars were in service compared with a normal operating schedule of 35 cars. When the new schedule became effective on Wednesday, July 19 it called for only 23 cars, and some forty street railway men found themselves without jobs.[37] Frequency of service on many lines was reduced, but no one-man cars went into service at that time.

The Edmonton Radial Railway had reached such a state of affairs in 1916 that petitions to lease or sell it became common place. The Edmonton Property Owners Association drew up a statement in July — "In the opinion of the majority of the property owners of the city the street railway cannot be operated as a municipal enterprise in as much as it has been a losing venture from its inception and the probabilities are that it will be a continual liability under municipal management in the future; and in the opinion of the property owners the time is now opportune for entering into negotiations for its disposal to outside interests."[38]

It appeared that the Association could not come to a firm decision over this statement.[39] The Utilities Committee discussed the issue and referred it to Council to decide upon the sale or lease of the system.[40]

Council bounced the issue about during a September meeting. One alderman blamed the carelessness of citizens in voting upon bylaws which had saddled Edmonton with an expensive street railway system. This same alderman, H.M. Martin, also pointed out that, while revenue per car mile in Edmonton was higher than in Calgary, the cost of maintenance and operation in Edmonton was much greater. Mayor Henry observed that the Edmonton Radial Railway faced higher power charges, higher depreciation charges and higher maintenance charges than Calgary's street railway system did; also that some of the Calgary Municipal Railway work was done at Calgary City Hall and not charged against the street railway. The Mayor also noted that the ERR was handling an average of over 40,000 passengers per day in 1913 and 1914 but by 1916 carried only 22,000-25,000 passengers. If the former level of fare-paying passengers could be reached without further extending the system, then it would solve the difficulty. Mayor Henry also underlined the fact that the street railway extensions in 1912 and 1913 had more than paid for themselves by the increased revenue taken into the civic coffers by the added assessment along the new car lines. Other aldermen stated that the deplorable service offered by the street cars with the reduced schedule really played into the hands of the jitney operators[41] who offered more frequent service at a price of 6 tickets for 25¢ compared to ERR tickets at the rate of 5 for 25¢.[42] The Board of Trade also encouraged Council to put the street railway system up to tender for leasing for a twenty year period.[43] It appeared that a decision to lease or sell the street railway never did materialize and the street cars continued to operate under municipal ownership and management.

The street railway workers, organized in 1911 as Local 569 of the Amalgamated Association of Street and Electric Railway Employees of America, began to get concerned about the expiration of their five-year contract with the City. The contract expired August 31st 1916. Its expiry came at an inopportune time for the men, as Council's energies were being diverted to the possible leasing or sale of the street railway system. Two major issues had come out of the discussions about the contract; one centered around overtime pay and the second around one-man cars.[44] In an effort to speed up negotiations for a new contract the street railway men appealed to the Deputy Minister of Labour to call for the appointment of a conciliation board.[45] Apparently negotiations did begin, but the city wanted to sign a contract with the Edmonton Street Railway Employees Society, a local organization, rather than with Local 569 which was a branch of a larger organization.[46] A one-year agreement with the Local finally passed through Council on October 17th 1916, retroactive to August 31st. Many features of this contract were similar to the previous one, providing for one weeks' holiday pay and an additional half hour for those who reported for duty in the early morning. The old agreement had stipulated the operation of cars by two men, but that clause had been dropped, leaving the way open for the introduction of one-man cars. The clause dealing with extra pay for overtime hours had also been removed. Wage rates remained unchanged, going up to a maximum of 34¢ per hour in the third year. Barn men and car repair men received the same settlement. Track men received 28.5¢ per hour. The agreement stated that in the event one-man cars were to go into service, operators of same would get 40¢ per hour.[47]

When the contract came up for renewal the following year, 1917, street railway men pressed for a 20% general increase in wages plus special conditions for operators of one-man cars. The union asked for 55¢ for one-man car operators and an eight-hour day with a period of no longer than six hours without relief.[48] When no steps toward settlement appeared to be in sight on August 31st when the agreement expired, the street railway men called a meeting for that evening. They requested a range from 30¢ to 40¢ per hour with 45¢ to be paid to operators of one-man cars. Following the meeting the street railway men failed to report to work and by Saturday, September 1st 1917, some 172 men were on strike.[49]

The strikers were ordered to return their cash and uniforms, and Superintendent Moir was instructed to hire on as he saw fit in order to keep a basic service going.[50] Fifteen-minute service on Jasper Avenue to the south side was expected to be effected on September 4th 1917.[51] Only on September 6th, however, did cars begin operating to the south side and over one west end route.[52] The following day, the men were given a final opportunity to return to work or they faced losing seniority. Enough men were available to offer half-hourly service on 124 Street and the packing plant line in addition to those routes opened up the previous day.[53] By Tuesday, September 11th, the street railway strike was over and men were being recalled apparently on the city's terms.[54] No agreement was signed until the following year in August 1918, at which time pay for one-man operators was established at 50¢ per hour. Since the system had been converted to one-man cars by that time, new men started at 45¢ per hour for the first six months, 47.5¢ per hour for the second six months and 50¢ per hour at the end of the first year. While the wage rates had not reached those demanded a year earlier, the contract was signed before it expired.[55] With the system apparently on a more stable basis and the one-man car issue well settled, negotiations between the ERR and its employees seemed to be more content.

The jitney operators continued to provide competition to the street cars during 1916. Jitneys were motor vehicles rebuilt with a larger body so that they could carry up to about ten people. They operated along the street car routes picking up fare-paying passengers as they went. At one Utilities Committee meeting, Superintendent Moir reported that he had observed passengers at a street car stop on 124 Street and 110 Avenue allow a street car to pass and board a jitney following behind the car. As previously noted, the fare for riding the jitney was less than that for the street car and often the service was better. Commissioner Harrison proposed an amendment to the charter, giving the city an exclusive right to operate jitneys in addition to street cars.[56] In an effort to encourage the public to use the street cars the following advertisement was placed in the daily press in February 1917.

" Edmonton Municipal Railway
Did you ever stop to think as you jolt along in a jitney that the streets, the roadbed over which the competitor of the street railway is travelling are maintained by the tax receipts?
When the jitneys "go broke" you will have to fall back on the street cars. What if the street railways operation is then not so efficient as it formerly was? Will it not react against your personal comfort?
If not as a matter of justice at least give it consideration as a matter of your own personal convenience."[57]

Superintendent Moir went to a meeting of the residents of Jasper Place and Westgrove on the 102 Avenue line early in 1917. As a result of this meeting the 9:35 a.m. car from 142 Street and 102 Avenue was dropped in favour of one at 10:35 a.m. An additional car left the terminal at 3:35 p.m. He also promised that the switches would receive more attention thus ensuring better service in cold weather.[58] Superintendent Moir responded to a general request for better west end service by having a passenger count on all eastbound cars at three points in the west end. Apparently there was not sufficient demand for an increase in service, and west end residents retaliated by circulating a petition to all homes in the area objecting to the proposed charter amendment allowing city to deal with jitneys.[59] It appears that residents along the 107 Avenue strip were most concerned about the west end street car service, as they had only white line cars offering service westbound on 107 Avenue. The reduced schedule introduced in July 1916 took the blue-and-white sign cars off the eastbound loop along 107 Avenue, thus removing all regular eastbound service on 107 Avenue. After July 1916 the blue-and-white sign cars terminated their westbound journey at 107 Avenue and 124 Street but returned to the downtown area via Jasper Avenue and then proceeded as previously into northeast Edmonton to 80 Street and 118 Avenue. This move was no doubt made to assist with handling heavier traffic demand along the 124 Street and Jasper Avenue section.

Superintendent Moir guided the Edmonton Radial Railway through a very turbulent period. The deficit position of the ERR made it unpopular with the taxpayers, and attempts to deal with the deficit by raising fares and cutting back services did nothing to enhance the citizen's feelings toward the railway. Mr. Moir had serious labour difficulties with which to contend, and he was often put into the difficult position of laying off men due to decreased services. Council tended to be slow and undecided about approving contracts with the street railway men and Superintendent Moir also came under criticism from the Returned Soldiers Bureau for the 1916 exhibition services because he was allegedly taking on extra men who were not returned soldiers.[60] Being Superintendent of the Edmonton Radial Railway in 1916 was no easy job. Mr. Moir did stand behind his conviction that the belt line system of operation was an effective system from a service and financial point of that the belt line system of operation was an effective system from a service and financial point of view, and the year end report for 1916 supported his contention. The deficit position of the ERR was reduced at the end of 1916 to $120,000 as contrasted to $135,000 at the close of 1915. The reduction could not be attributed solely to the belt line mode of operation, but that change, coupled with Mr. Moir's management competence under severe restraint conditions, helped to keep the street cars operating.

The fabled street car line on Portage Avenue (Kingsway) was constructed during this turbulent period of time. Construction of this trackage was the most notable example of a development line on the ERR not paying off. It never earned a penny as no electric street car ever turned a wheel on it. The City of Edmonton entered into an agreement with the Hudson's Bay Company, owners of the land over which Portage Avenue crossed, to pave and lay a permanent double track car line from 101 Street at about 108 Avenue in a northwesterly direction to a point intersecting with an extension of 118 Avenue just east of the GTP tracks near an extension of 122 Street. Part of the avenue was completed in 1915[61] with the balance completed in 1916. The 100' wide pavement and permanent double track street car line extended a distance of 1 3/4 miles over barren unsettled prairie and cost some $415,000.[62] Needless to say the street railway department did not jump at the opportunity to place the line into service and electric wire was never strung up over the double

Photo above:

A wide band of pavement with streetcar tracks down the centre stretched across the unsettled prairie on the Hudson's Bay Reserve. Streetcars never operated over these tracks on Portage Avenue. The thoroughfare adjacent to the Edmonton Airport was later named Kingsway.

(Glenbow Alberta Institute)

track Portage Avenue line, which, in fact was never connected physically with the rest of the system.

An economy for which the Edmonton Radial Railway had been quietly preparing was the introduction of the one-man car. During the early months of 1917 shop crews transformed a couple of the cars to offer this service, and in March the ERR began training men to play the dual role of motorman and conductor. On April 18th 1917 the Edmonton Bulletin reported a one-man car in service on the Spruce Avenue (114 Avenue) line. This same report indicated that the city had received approval from the Board of Railway Transport Commissioners to operate these cars provided flagmen were available to flag one-man cars over railway crossings.[63] On Wednesday, April 18th 1917 another one-man car went into service on the Calder line.[64] Operators on the one-man cars received 40¢ per hour.[65]

The ERR entered very cautiously into the realm of one-man operations and it remained unresolved whether the experimental services on the Calder and Spruce Avenue lines could be carried to the busier lines in the centre of the city. The Highlands line was identified as the next possible experimental project for the one-man car. The Street Railway Department anticipated savings of $6,500 per year on this line alone, and suggested that if the one-man car scheme became popular on most routes, a reduction in fares or other concessions to the travelling public might be possible.[66]

Little more appeared in the press about the one-man cars until early June, when car 16 carrying Mayor Henry, Deputy Mayor Wilson, the aldermen, and Commissioner Harrison travelled through the city on Friday afternoon, June 8th 1917 to demonstrate a car rebuilt for one-man operation.[67] Passenger entrance and exit was located on the front platform to the right of the motorman. The fare box faced the entry door and was in full view of everyone. A press report described the car as follows: "Its general makeup is similar to that of the one-man cars in Calgary, but there is nothing of its kind in Calgary, or anywhere else, it is believed that makes a better appearance or fills the bill for economical transit more effectively."[68] Upon entry, a partitioning bar guided the passenger past the fare box while those leaving the car passed on the other side of the bar and stepped down to the road through an adjacent door. A mirror allowed the motorman to see passengers in the car. The rear vestibule was partitioned off so that it could be used as a smoking compartment.

A circular seat ran around the circumference of the rear vestibule. An emergency exit on the rear platform was controlled by a lever at the front of the car which operated a cable running down the side of the car. When the lever was pulled, a portion of the circular seat flipped up and a door opened allowing access to the street."[69]

The demonstrator car ran out to 124 Street, and on the return trip eastbound, picked up passengers who naturally gravitated to the rear of the car to board it. Again it was suggested that the car would be placed on the Highlands/107 Avenue and 124 Street line in order to experiment with this system on the main thoroughfares.[70] Car 16's platforms had apparently been entirely rebuilt and in this rebuilding the broad Preston-style letterboards over the platforms narrowed as was typical of Ottawa-built cars. The car also became single-ended at this time. It appears likely that Ottawa-built car 15 became a one-man, single-ended car about this time as well.

Street railway employees predicted failure for the one-man cars and a delegation met with Commissioners and the Utilities Committee on June 11th 1917 to express that view. Motorman A.R. Mason spoke on behalf of the group, stating that there would be less room for baby buggies in the vestibules, a slower operating schedule and higher power consumption. Superintendent Moir and Chairman Bush of the Utilities Committee indicated that one-man operation was only experimental, and while that system had been successfully adopted for Calgary, it would not be applied completely to Edmonton until a thorough trial had been made.[71] The street railway men also advanced the argument that the one-man cars could never operate across the High Level Bridge, as any child could operate the lever which opened the emergency exit. Finally, the street railway men stated that the St. Louis-built group of cars chosen for this conversion were the coldest cars on the system.[72] Thus, conversion would perpetuate use of cars disliked by motormen and passengers alike.

The latter argument appeared to be a good one as Edmonton's Commissioner Harrison had wired Manager Fleming of the Toronto Railway Company only six months earlier in January 1917 offering to sell the fifteen St. Louis-built double-ended cars. The TSR had lost a number of cars in a car barn fire but no cars left Edmonton for Toronto at that time.[73] That sale never did materialize and the argument did not deter plans to continue experimenting with one-man car operations. The Edmonton Radial Railway did negotiate a sale of two cars, Prestons 80 and 81 to the Oshawa Street Railway. The sale was actually completed on July 6th 1917 and expedited by D.M. Campbell, the late manager of the Preston Car and Coach Company. The cars which had been purchased in 1912 for $9,800 each were sold for a sum of $14,000. Since that time $255 had been allowed for depreciation and the cars had earned an estimated $250 each. The Preston Cars were chosen for this sale as they seemed to be the least adapted for conversion to one-man operation.[74]

Another car was removed from the roster about three weeks prior to the sale of cars 80 and 81. At 8:20 p.m. on Wednesday, June 13th 1917, car 22 proceeded south on 109 Street. A broken trolley wire at 99 Avenue dropped onto the car and apparently shorted out on the smoke jacket atop the roof of the front platform. The wire could not be removed and the continuous arcing set fire to the roof. Before the fire apparatus arrived, the car burned totally except for the trucks and steel underframe. Street car traffic was held up for three quarters of an hour. The car was pushed over to the south side barns but never returned to service. There were no injuries.[75]

Throughout the summer of 1917 only the two stub lines, Calder and Spruce Avenue (114 Avenue) operated with one-man cars. Tram 16, specially built for one-man car service, had been slated for service on the Highlands (white sign) route but instead operated as a two-man car.[76] Apparently Superintendent Moir felt a route had to be completely serviced by one-man cars in order to avoid service tieups.

On Wednesday, October 17th 1917 one-man street cars went into general use on at least two major street car routes. Seventeen cars had been fitted up to provide this service, some permanently and some only temporarily.[77] It is thought that car 15, car 16 and the fifteen St. Louis-built units (32-46) made up the initial group of one-man cars. Apparently 15 and 16 became single-ended when altered for one-man service, while the St. Louis group continued to operate as double-ended cars. The double-ended cars were conducive to the conversion as the long platforms made it possible to have an entry and an exit door on the forward platform. Apparently the practice of having paired doors on the forward platform was dropped, as all cars — both single and double ended — eventually reverted to the single doorway through which passengers both embarked and disembarked.

New routes and schedules became effective on Wednesday, October 17th 1917. Route 1 from North Edmonton to 118 Avenue and 124 Street offered fifteen-minute service. It was identified by blue signs and spotlights. Extra cars operated on route 1 between 80 Street and 118 Avenue and 118 Avenue and 124 Street every fifteen minutes giving a 7 1/2-minute service over that portion of route 1 between 7:00 a.m. and 9:00 a.m. and from 12:00 noon to 8:00 p.m.[78] While not designated as such in the newspaper advertisement it is thought these cars carried blue-and-white signs. Route 2 offered twenty-minute service from Bonnie Doon via the High Level Bridge to the Highlands. Route 2 cars carried white signs and white spotlights.[79] One-man cars operated on the Bonnie Doon-Highlands route.[80]

Route 3 consisted of the two major south side services. Red sign cars, instead of turning via a belt line on the north side, simply ran north on 101 Street and turned back at 107 Avenue. Red sign cars operated every twenty minues going to the south side via the Low Level Bridge and returning via the High Level Bridge. Red-and-white sign cars offered twenty-minute service from 106 Avenue and 97 Street via Jasper Avenue, 109 Street and to the south side via the High Level Bridge returning to the north side (106 Avenue and 97 Street) via the Low Level Bridge, 97 Avenue, 109 Street and Jasper Avenue.[81] With the combined services of route 2 and route 3, ten-minute service was available in both directions across the High Level Bridge.

Route 4, referred to as the "Figure 8 Route", carried green-and-white signs. A total of eight one-man cars (four in each direction) provided the fifteen-minute service on this line.[82] Cars in one direction began at 111 Avenue and 95 Street, ran west on 111 Avenue, south on 101 Street, west on Jasper, north on 124 Street, east on 107 Avenue, south on 101 Street again, east on Jasper Avenue and north on 95 Street to 111 Avenue. Cars in the other direction on the route began at 111 Avenue and 95 Street, turned south on 95 Street, west on Jasper, north on 101 Street, west on 107 Avenue, south on 124 Street, east on Jasper, north on 101 Street and east on 111

Avenue to 95 Street.[83] This new "Figure 8 Route" restored regular eastbound service to 107 Avenue for the first time since the July 1916 service reductions some fifteen months earlier. Mr. Moir noted that this restoration of service had been made possible by the economics offered by one-man cars.[84] This new route also provided the north side belt line service formerly provided by the south side cars.

With the introduction of this new schedule, the ERR added the McKernan's Lake line and the 102 Avenue line to 142 Street to its stub operations. These routes brought to four the total number of stub routes on the system, Spruce Avenue (114 Avenue) and Calder being the previous such services. The Calder and 142 Street stubs both received improved services. Calder had a car every thirty minutes to 124 Street and 118 Avenue throughout the day while a car left the 142 Street and 102 Avenue terminus for 124 Street every thirty minutes from 6:30 a.m. to 10:30 p.m. and from 12:30 noon to 11:30 p.m.[85] The 102 Avenue to 142 Street line lost its direct service to downtown but received a more frequent service throughout longer periods each day.

The 114 Avenue (Spruce) stub car maintained fifteen-minute service from 95 Street and 114 Avenue east every fifteen minutes between 12:15 noon and 3:00 p.m. and from 5:00 p.m. to 10:45 p.m. McKernan's Lake suffered a general loss in service. A through car to downtown operated at 7:15 a.m. and at 8:15 a.m. Then half-hourly stub service to Whtye Avenue and 104 Street began at 1:15 p.m. until 2:45 p.m. and then again from 5:15 p.m. to 11:15 p.m.[86]

One-man car service had expanded from the Calder and the 114 Avenue local routes to encompass a new total of six routes. Route 2 (Highlands to Bonnie Doon) route 4 "The Figure 8 Route", McKernan's Lake and 102 Avenue to 142 Street became part of the one-man street car network on October 17th 1917.

The year 1917 closed with a $91,298 surplus over operating expenses. The system had a deficit of $150,480 once the capital charges were added. The cars carried some 10,086,283 passengers during 1917, a decrease of 583,162 from 1916. Superintendent Moir attributed the reduced passenger carryings to the absence of the battalions stationed at the exhibition grounds during 1916. He also reported that the one-man cars had reduced operating costs from 75¢ per hour per car to 65¢ per hour per car. Clearly, in light of the above facts, the improved services implemented in October 1917 were due to the reduced costs attributable to one-man car operation.[87]

Opposite page, left:

Robert Farrants (left) and Fred Sear (right) pose in this 1916 scene in front of car first 81 on the McKernan's Lake line. The two-colour dash-mounted destination sign replaced the roller curtain in the upper sash from 1914 until the early 1920s, when roller curtains were changed to designate the numbered streets and avenues. This car and first 80 were sold to the Oshawa Railway in July 1917. (Robert Farrants)

Photo below:

The turning loop at the end of the Highlands line, across 112 Avenue at 61 Street. This view, showing car 73 approaching the loop, was taken in 1945, shortly before the road was paved and the trams replaced by trolley coaches. (Bob Walker)

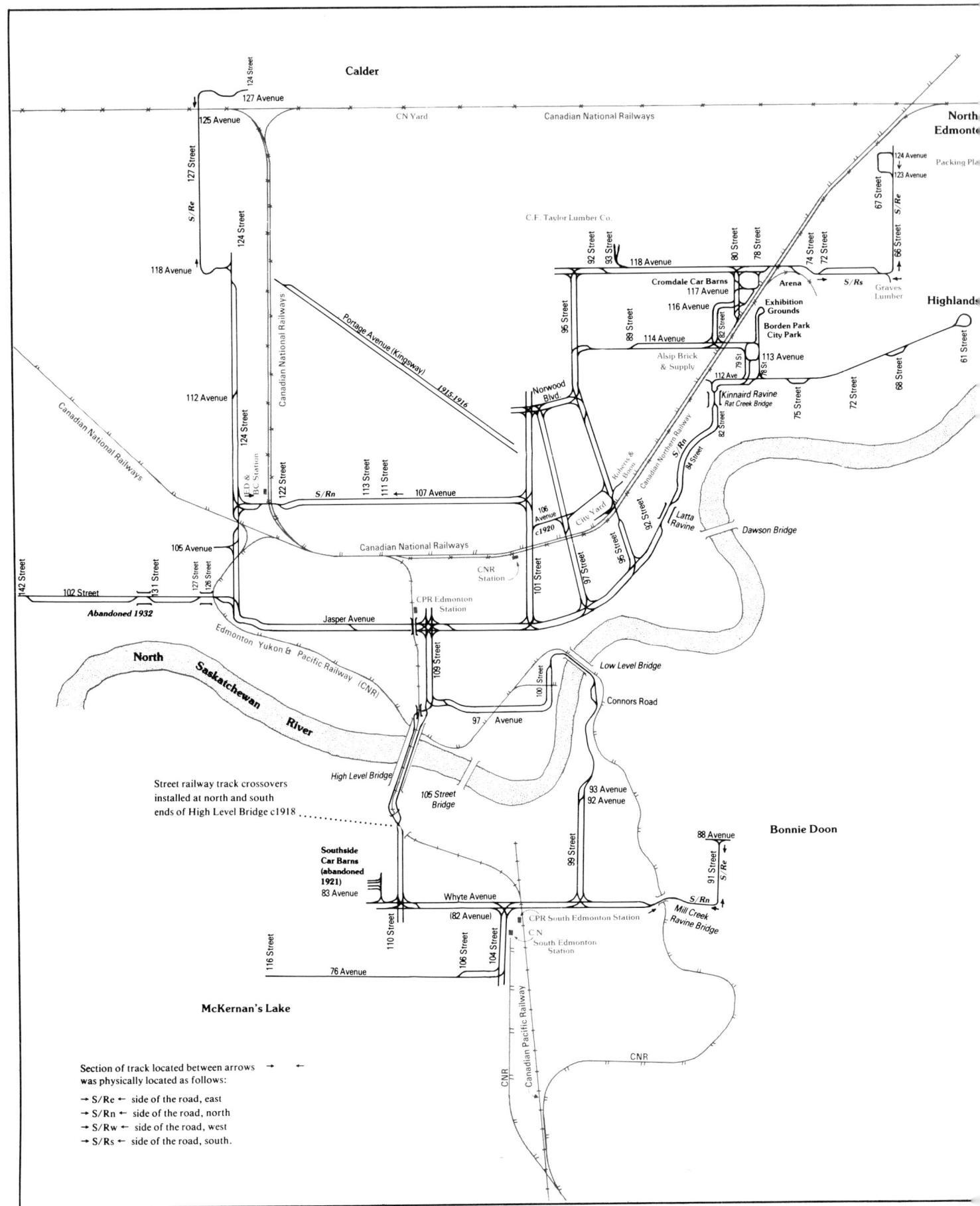

City of Edmonton Street Railway Department
Track Map
1924

10

Stability Returns

THE YEAR 1918 got off to a flying start as the ERR played its part in assisting in Edmonton's first arrest of the New Year. On January 1 an automobile narrowly avoided a collision with a street car at Jasper Avenue and 121 Street. Apparently Police Constable Foster ordered the automobile to stop, but the driver disregarded the order and continued on his way. Undaunted, Constable Foster commandeered the street car and the great street railway chase began, the constable and the motorman disregarding the protests of passengers who wished to alight. At 114 Avenue the policeman jumped from the street car and overtook the motor car, whose driver was under the influence of liquor. However, a passenger in the auto was sober and able to drive to the police station where a charge of illegal possession of liquor was laid against the auto driver.[1] Obviously liquor prohibition had not put a complete damper on the New Year's Eve revelry of the day, but an Edmonton street car played its part in chasing down one who had celebrated too much.

Unfortunately, 1918 brought no improvement in the financial position of the railway. The second fare increase in the ERR's history went into effect on May 1 of that year, despite the economies of one-man cars, when single cash fares rose from 5¢ to 7¢. Passengers could still purchase tickets at the former rate of 5 tickets for 25¢ but these had to be obtained from depots or retail outlets in various parts of the city. Passengers buying tickets from street car operators paid a premium price of four tickets for 25¢[2] This appeared to be an effort to ease the work of the motormen on one-man cars and speed up service. The new fare structure did not provide for any workmen's tickets. Children under the age of six years continued to travel free, children under 15 years of age and high school students with certificates could purchase tickets at half fare — 10 tickets for 25¢. Passengers riding after 11:00 p.m. carried the brunt of the fare increase, as they paid a premium fare of 10¢ cash or two tickets. Juveniles travelling after 11:00 p.m. paid 5¢ cash or two juvenile tickets. Passengers carrying large parcels were levied 5¢ for each such package. Finally, between the hours of 5:00 and 6:30 p.m. there was a charge of 5¢ for baby carriages transported on the street cars.[3]

A further route change became effective on Sunday, July 21st 1918, to divide up traffic between east and west end cars for one-man operation. North Edmonton (blue sign) cars began to operate south on 101 Street, then turned back to North Edmonton by turning east onto Jasper Avenue and north on 97 Street. Service frequency remained at fifteen minutes. The "Figure 8" car which operated south on 101 Street changed its route to run south on 97 Street from 111 Avenue. The 124 Street and 118 Avenue green sign car turned back from 106 Avenue at 97 Street on the same schedule. Blue-and-white sign cars continued to operate without change from 80 Street and 118 Avenue to 124 Street and 118 Avenue via 97 Street. On Sundays, the 142 Street cars left that terminus at 10:00 a.m. and every half hour until 11:30 p.m. Despite these alterations, passenger ridership remained low on the ERR.[4]

During the summer of 1918 the city received an offer from the Toronto and York Radial Railway to purchase two cars. Cars 50 and 58 were selected from the fleet and sent off to that city. By this time, from the total of 81 cars, four had been sold (50, 58, 80 and 81), one burned (22) and one scrapped (23). This left the ERR with a total of 75 serviceable units.

Two proposals to utilize the unused permanent track on Portage Avenue (Kingsway) were presented during 1917 and 1918. In 1917 the Edmonton Interurban Railway gave consideration to re-opening its railway service to St. Albert, using the St. Albert Trail to 118 Avenue, then east on 118 Avenue to Portage Avenue, then southeast to 101 Street and finally to the market at 101 Street and 103 Avenue.[5] This proposal never went beyond the planning stages. In 1918, the Edmonton, Dunvegan and British Columbia Railway made application to the city for running rights from Armstrong Avenue and 127 Street to 118 Avenue, along 118 Avenue to Portage Avenue, then via Portage to the 101 Street market. The City would be expected to construct a permanent curve at the junction of 101 Street and Portage Avenue and supply switches on loan to the ED & BC, who at its own cost would do all other construction necessary.[6] The ED & BC proposal went so far as to state the terms of payment to the city for transporting cream cans, passengers and other freight and express. Since it called for operation over Edmonton Interurban trackage on lease to the Edmonton Radial Railway for the Calder line, the city had to negotiate with the EIR.[7] The ED & BC wished to operate a three-times-weekly service from Westlock into the city market with the gasoline car.[8]

Photo above:

Additional revenue for the Edmonton Radial Railway was earned by hiring out cars for advertising. It would appear that tram No. 14 has been converted to one-man operation, as it features a folding front step and the front bulkhead has been removed. The fixed rear step, however, is still in place, as is the staunchion pole in the centre of the rear doorway. At an early date, car 14 apparently suffered collision damage and the front platform was rebuilt with the narrow Ottawa Car Company style letterboard. The rear letterboard is a wide one; a feature common to Preston-built cars. The motorman in uniform is thought to be Dan McKilligan. The two gentlemen beside the car are unidentified. *(Glenbow Alberta Institute)*

Photo below:

Jasper Avenue at 101 Street in the 1920s. Compare with similar view on Page 2. Improved street lighting and modified overhead wire brackets have accompanied the gradual change-over from horse power to automobile transportation, while considerable building activity is evidenced, especially on the south side of the Avenue. *(Canadian Pacific)*

Opposite page:

This archway on Jasper Avenue at 109 Street welcomed the Prince of Wales (later King Edward VIII) who visited Edmonton on September 12th and 13th 1919. The Prince's train arrived at the CPR station just west of the archway. The poles down the centre of Jasper Avenue are decked with bunting and a second arch is visible in the next block. Both streetcars are in the 1916 brown-and-yellow paint scheme. The condition of the small Preston car in the foreground, which appears to have been partially converted to single-end operation, is in sharp contrast to the recently-outshopped big Preston approaching. The white and red sign on the approaching car is lettered "MAIN ST. and WHYTE AV."

(Glenbow Alberta Institute)

The Portage Avenue proposal with the ED & BC never materialized owing to the difficulty of obtaining the necessary material to connect with Portage Avenue.⁹ The material for crossing the GTP line at 118 Avenue possibly also held up this project. In lieu of the Portage Avenue line the ED & BC received running rights over the GTP to 121 Street and 107 Avenue where it requested permission to erect a platform to entrain and detrain passengers.¹⁰ Permission was apparently granted and the ED & BC offered to improve its facilities at this point if the city agreed to construct a boardwalk on 107 Avenue from 124 Street to 107 Avenue and place the road between these points in suitable condition for heavy traffic.¹¹ Thus, Edmonton received another railway station to accommodate Edmonton, Dunvegan and British Columbia Railway trains. The Edmonton Radial Railway apparently dispatched special cars to meet these trains but, much to Superintendent Moir's chagrin, the railway trains often arrived late. When the service was resumed again in the spring of 1919 the ERR via City Council informed the ED & BC that a 25¢ fare would be charged to passengers arriving after 12:00 midnight instead of the regular 10¢ late night fare. Apparently ERR cars had occasionally waited hours at the station for trains to arrive. Car crews had to be paid during the waiting period and the five cent fare did not provide sufficient revenue to cover these costs.¹²

During 1919 ridership began to increase again as large numbers of World War I veterans returned home. The early months of that year were months of labor unrest all across Canada, and the ERR experienced a minor work stoppage during this period. In order to keep up with rising costs, another fare increase became effective on April 21st 1919. With this increase tickets could be purchased on the cars again without penalty, and the rate was 4 tickets for 25¢. Passengers could use yellow/buff tickets at the rate of 5 for 25¢ before 8:30 a.m. The former seven-cent cash fare remained in force and children's green ticket prices also remained unaffected at 10 for 25¢. Under the former fare structure, the premium late evening fare became effective at 11:00 p.m. Coincident with the ticket price increase, the premium fare of 10¢ cash or two adult tickets (children, 5¢ cash or two children's tickets) did not become effective until 12:30 a.m. Cars did operate from downtown to the west end, south side and east side at 12:30 a.m.¹³ Just before the fare increase became effective fares were being collected in the following proportions: 66% at 5 for 25¢ tickets; 18% red tickets at 4 for 25¢ available from motormen on board the cars; 9% children's tickets and 7% in cash fares. South side residents protested the new fare structure as they claimed that the agreement set out between the former City of Strathcona and the Strathcona Radial Tramway Company stated that cash fares were levied at 5¢ and tickets at 6 for 25¢. The City of Edmonton quickly pointed out that Section 39 of the 1918 Charter amendments gave the city full authority to change fares or tolls provided there was uniformity throughout the city.¹⁴

During the 1919 exhibition week Superintendent Moir pressed every car into service and carried 334,624 passengers compared to 278,482 in 1918. He reported that the cars could have carried even more passengers during the week.¹⁵ July 1919 also turned out to be a banner month for the railway as it showed a profit during that month for the first time since July 1912. The 1919 surplus was $2,200.¹⁶ The railway did not see an annual sur-

Photo above:

Car 21 tumbled off the bridge on 102 Avenue at 132 Street at 7 a.m. on Monday, October 27th 1919. A heavy, unseasonable snowfall resulted in a build-up of ice between the rails and in the flange ways. The car derailed and flipped over into the ravine. This was the most serious of about a dozen derailments on the streetcar system that day. Car 21 was eastbound with four passengers and a motorman. Only the motorman suffered serious injury. The single-track car line crossed the ravine, a practice common to all ravine crossings in Edmonton in the early years. (Glenbow Alberta Foundation)

Photo below:

Edmonton Radial Railway's observation car stands on 109 Street just south of 97 Avenue, with the Alberta Legislature Building forming the background. The crossover, to enable cars to cross High Level Bridge with doors opening to the centre of the span, is immediately in front of the car. Bill Gordon was the Motorman and Dave Ghormley the Conductor of the car. The fare schedule hanging over each doorway indicates that adults paid 25 cents and children paid 15 cents.

(Alan Manly)

Workers attempt to clear snow and ice away from the track across the bridge on 102 Avenue at the scene of an accident involving car 21, October 27th 1919. (Glenbow Alberta Institute)

plus for some time to come but July 1919 offered some hope that the ERR would return to the passenger loads it experienced in 1913 and 1914 — a load level for which the line was designed.

Considering the number of level crossings between the ERR and the steam railways, it is not surprising that several altercations between steam trains and street cars took place. Late one afternoon in August 1919, car 39, travelling south, moved up to the shared track with the CNR at the north side of the Low Level Bridge. Just one hundred feet away on the bridge and travelling toward the street car was the mixed train from Alliance. Hurriedly the motorman stopped car 39 and threw it into reverse, but the train struck the front of car 39 as it backed away. Car passengers were shaken up but no serious injuries resulted. Possibly the most spectacular (and miraculous) mishap in the ERR's history occurred about 7:00 a.m. on the morning of Wednesday, October 22nd 1919.[17] Edmonton had experienced an early freeze and snowfall. Car 21, eastbound on 102 Avenue from 142 Street, approached the wooden bridge across the ravine near 132 Street cautiously as usual as the double track narrowed to a single track. The car approached with power off and in a slight skid as brakes were applied. The skidding wheels pushed ice and snow along in front of the flanges, causing the wheels to mount the ice and snow thus lifting the front truck off the track.[18] The front of the car veered to the right and crashed through the wooden railings. The front truck dropped over the side of the bridge and the car body tumbled after, landing on its roof in the ravine twenty feet below. The rear truck remained on the track.[19] Motorman McLennan and five passengers crawled out of the wreckage alive. One unidentified, uninjured passenger helped the others to safety to a nearby home and remained until medical aid arrived; he then glanced at his watch, then simply said "Goodbye, I have to get to work".[20] Car 21 had been regularly assigned to the run for about one year. Motorman McLennan was commended in a resolution put forth by the 142nd Street Community League. The League formally complained to city authorities who had not responded to complaints of poor track conditions at that point.[21] The city engineer noted, however, that there were a dozen derailments on the street railway that same day due to the unusual freezing conditions. Service had been disrupted for several days along 118 Avenue between 95 Street and 80 Street due to rails and pavement heaving from the frost.[22] Car 21 was never rebuilt after this mishap leaving a total of seven cars removed from the roster.

On a more positive note, the ERR further expanded its line into Calder during the closing months of 1919. A council resolution stated "that the extension of the street railway system be made on Brandon Avenue for such distance not less than five blocks and not exceeding nine according to material the street railway department is in a position to allow. The distance to be governed by the material now on hand and also the engineering conditions. Further that the work be undertaken for completion this fall."[23] The line was actually extended from 124 Street to 119 Street.

Further optimism about the future of the ERR was shown when the ground work for a new service was laid during the closing months of 1919. Car barn craftsmen under the direction of its designer, J. Longworth, began work on an observation car for Edmonton. By the end of June 1920 the car neared completion.[24] The new car, thought to have been constructed on the frame of car 22, was painted white, with six gold panels on each side. Each panel was outlined in red; the frames over the panels featured neatly-rounded corners. Panels increased in height progressively from front to rear. An 18-inch-high balustrade topped each panel. On the right side a metal rail paralled the top of the balustrade. On the left side, wire screening, approximately to head level at each seat, was placed on the top of the balustrade. The front platform featured a contoured dash and window sash from the top of the dash to the roof. A balustrade enclosed the end of the rear platform as well as the left side of each platform. Entry could be gained from the right side at both the front and rear platforms. The observation car required two crewmen — a motorman and a conductor. The project, exclusive of trucks and electrical equipment, cost some $2,500. Forty-two passengers could be seated on the wood slat seats arranged in transverse formation rising in tiers

from the front to the rear of the car. A permanent wooden roof protected riders from showers but the open sides and tiered seating offered a fine view of the municipal scenery.[25] Edmonton now ranked with Quebec, Montreal, Calgary and Vancouver in that it, too, offered an amenity for seeing Edmonton's scenic highlights — the wide Jasper Avenue, the North Saskatchewan River Valley and the spectacular view from the High Level Bridge — from a street railway observation car. Adult passengers paid a 25¢ fare while children rode for 15¢.[26]

The observation car began service on Dominion Day, Thursday, July 1, 1920. By the following day the car operated on a schedule from 101 Street and Jasper Avenue as follows:[27]

    2 p.m. to west end and south side.
    3 p.m. to east end and packing plant.
    4 p.m. to west end and south side.
    5 p.m. to east end and packing plant.
    8 p.m. to west end and south side.
    9 p.m. to Highlands and east end park.

The observation car offered summer tour service for a total of six seasons, making its final run at the conclusion of the 1925 season. In February 1926, the announcement was made that the observation car would not operate that year as revenue did not offset the expense of operating the car. In addition, the announcement noted that the car could not be loaded conveniently at Jasper Avenue and 101 Street. It appeared that there was no place where the car could wait without interfering with regular car traffic through this busy intersection.[28] The observation car went into permanent storage at Cromdale in a lean-to type shed against the southwest wall of the shop. It remained under cover in that shed until 1945 when preparation for construction of the trolley coach garage began. At that time, it was moved to the east side of the shop and supported, off trucks, on railway ties. It was apparently burned for scrap.

A new system-wide schedule and route change became effective Sunday, May 23rd 1920. At that time, route 1 blue sign cars from North Edmonton returned to their pre-1917 routing via 97 Street, Jasper Avenue and 124 Street to 118 Avenue, offering a fifteen-minute service daily and Sunday. Route 1a, blue-and-white sign cars, offered service at the same frequency daily between 118 Avenue and 80 Street and 118 Avenue and 124 Street via 97 Street, Jasper Avenue and 124 Street. On Sundays, the blue-and-white sign cars operated every twenty minutes. Route 2, white sign cars continued to offer twenty minute service daily and Sunday from Highlands to Bonnie Doon via the

High Level Bridge. Route 3, red sign cars operated to the south side via the Low Level Bridge from Jasper Avenue and 101 Street every twenty minutes. The red-and-white sign cars offered the same service via the High Level Bridge.

Route 4, the "Figure 8" Belt cars carried green-and-white signs. These cars reverted to their pre-1917 routing as well, using 101 Street instead of 97 Street. These cars provided a fifteen-minute service to the west end via 107 Avenue, 124 Street, Jasper Avenue and 101 Street and the north central area via 101 Street, 111 Avenue, 95 Street and Jasper Avenue. On Sundays between 8:30 a.m. and 1:00 p.m. these cars operated half hourly. Between 1:00 p.m. and 11:30 p.m. Belt cars operated quarter hourly. Route 5, carrying green signs, provided through car service from 142 Street and 102 Avenue in Westgrove to 101 Street and Jasper Avenue. On Sundays, green sign car service was intermittent. The first car left the 142 Street terminal at 10:00 a.m. on Sunday morning, the next at 10:30 a.m. and then hourly only until 2:30 p.m. Half-hourly service became available at that time until 11:30 p.m. when the last car for the day left for downtown.[29]

Three stub services were offered. The 114 Avenue (Spruce) stub provided twenty-minute service between 95 Street and 114 Avenue and 82 Street and 115 Avenue. The 114 Avenue stub car operated on Sundays providing the same frequency of service between 10:00 a.m. and 10:00 p.m. The Calder stub car left from 118 Avenue and 124 Street every half hour from 6:35 a.m. to 10:00 a.m. and from 10:45 a.m. to 11:45 p.m. On Sundays Calder cars left 124 Street and 118 Avenue every half hour from 10:00 a.m. to 11:30 p.m. The 76th Avenue stub (McKernan's Lake) left 104 Street and 82 Avenue at 7:00 a.m. and every half hour till 10:00 a.m. Between 12:00 noon and 11:00 p.m. half-hourly service continued. On Sundays only four trips were made. These trips originated at 101 Street and Jasper Avenue at 9:56 a.m., 12:28 p.m., 6:25 p.m. and 9:00 p.m.[30]

The schedule offered more direct service on several routes with fewer stops and transfer points. It also allowed motormen more time to make their runs. These concessions obviously were made to accommodate one-man operations more readily. A number of the downtown stops were changed or eliminated due to the increase in vehicular traffic on Edmonton streets. Also cars westbound on Jasper Avenue stopped west of 101 Street, cars eastbound on Jasper stopped east of 101 Street and northbound cars made their stop for 101 Street and Jasper Avenue on 101 Street only.[31]

By 1920 the conversion to one-man operation had been officially completed, although it appears that by late 1918 or early 1919, all regularly-assigned cars on the ERR were operated by one man. At some time in 1917 or 1918 the wooden trestle carrying 109 Street traffic over the CPR tracks at the south approach to the High Level Bridge was removed in favour of a concrete structure. At that time, the street railway tracks were arranged so that the double track line on 109 Street crossed over itself just before reaching the approaches at each end of the bridge. This meant that southbound cars crossed over to travel on the downstream side of the bridge while northbound cars travelled on the upstream side of the bridge. As thus arranged, if a car became stranded on the bridge, passengers could step out of the car onto the CPR tracks on the centre of the bridge. This safety precaution was necessary for single-end cars, as the doorways were on the right side only. It seems likely that one man car operations precipitated the change. South siders became concerned when operators approached the bridge too fast from the south side. At this point the approach led downgrade to the bridge. Superintendent Moir issued a standing order that all cars had to come to a complete halt before setting out across the bridge. Another order stated that a motorman must not leave the controller while the car was travelling across the bridge. Failure to follow this rule would result in immediate dismissal.

The physical conversion of Edmonton cars to one-man operation was simple and inexpensive. On the double-ended St. Louis-built cars, the large rear entrance/exit doors were moved to the front of the car, and the smaller door plus panelling were re-installed at the rear. The same procedure appeared to be followed for all of the other double-ended cars on the system except for cars 15 and 16 which were converted to single-end operation. The doors on the left side were panelled in and a double door installed to the right of the motorman. The rear platform had a single emergency exit. The rear platform on these two cars was closed off, the floor raised to the level of the car body floor and seating installed around the circumference of the platform. As the smaller single ended cars came into the shop for conversion, the rear platform arrangement was patterned after that of cars 15 and 16. The front platform remained the same except that a folding step was installed and a portion of the front bulkhead removed to give easier access to the front entrance way. The single ended cars (Nos. 15 and 16 excepted) always had a single front entrance. The big Prestons (Nos. 47-79) received the same treatment as the smaller single-enders except that the front bulkhead was moved back a foot or two giving more room on the front platform and slightly altering the exterior appearance on the left side of these cars. Moving the bulkhead back made it necessary to place an additional partition in the centre of the first window on the left side of the car. Since the bulkhead did not extend all the way across the width of the car, the right side window arrangement remained unchanged. Thus, the completion of the first twelve years of street car service in Edmonton was met with an air of optimism.

Opposite page, upper:

Edmonton Radial Railway Car 72 from rear of southbound car on High Level Bridge in October 1950. This illustrates the left side running described above. (O. Lavallée)

Opposite page, lower:

A big southbound Preston car passes under the CPR track on the north approach to High Level Bridge. The streetcar tracks in this circa 1914 scene do not cross each other on 109 Street, and the car's doors will face the open, or river, side of the bridge. About 1918, crossovers were installed both at this point and at the south end of the bridge. Left side running over the bridge resulted in doors opening onto the centre of the structure, enabling passengers to more safely disembark from a car which happened to stall or become disabled on the bridge. (Provincial Archives of Alberta, E. Brown Collection)

11 | The Twenties and Thirties

$\mathcal{D}$URING 1920, while ridership increased, Moir stepped down as Superintendent of the Edmonton Radial Railway. W.J. Brunlees took on the job for a few months but he relinquished the duties to Superintendent R. Colwell in 1921. A new city administration and the new Superintendent immediately began to look to ways of minimizing costs with the least effect on service to various areas of the city. Expenses climbed sharply about this time and jitney operators continued to compete for passengers.

A new street car schedule introduced as an economy move became effective on May 3rd 1921.[1] The new schedule drifted away from the belt line concept of routing which since 1914 had been regarded as the most economical form of providing Edmonton with car service. Double-ended cars became prominent in the downtown area as well as serving on the stub lines. Route numbers superimposed on the colour signs supplemented the colour route identification so typical of the ERR up to that time. The blue sign cars (route 1), blue-and-white sign cars (route 1A) and the white sign cars (route 2) did not change routes or frequency of service. The "figure 8" belt line was dropped entirely. The 107 Avenue and 101 Street leg of its route was replaced by an extension of the red sign cars (route 4). Red sign cars travelled to the south side via the Low Level Bridge returning to downtown Edmonton via the High Level Bridge, 109 Street, Jasper Avenue and 101 Street. Under the new schedule red sign cars continued north on 101 Street to 107 Avenue, then west to the CNR crossing near 121 Street. At the crossing, the red sign cars turned back to downtown Edmonton over the same route and then onto the south side. Since the red sign cars stopped short of the railway tracks on 107 Avenue, the system was able to eliminate a flagman at the crossing. The other south side route, the red-and-white sign cars (route 3) continued to run south via the High Level Bridge and back to downtown across the Low Level Bridge, 97 Avenue, 109 Street, Jasper Avenue, then into east Edmonton via 95 Street and 114 Avenue to 82 Street. It returned to the downtown area over the same route. The red-and-white sign cars operated every twenty minutes. These cars also served part of the old "Figure 8" belt line route as well as taking in the area formerly served by the 114 Avenue (Spruce Avenue) stub car. This left 101 Street north of 107 Avenue and 111 Avenue to 97 Street without regular street car service. Service to Calder, to 142 Street via 102 Avenue and to McKernan's Lake remained unchanged.[2] The new schedule called for 29 cars in regular service compared to 33 formerly and 36 cars in rush-hour service compared to 46 formerly.[3]

The south side car barn was closed as a further economy measure with the introduction of the May 3rd 1921 schedule. W.J. Brunlees and Superintendent Colwell both supported Commissioner Yorath's recommendation to close that facility. All cars on the new schedule ran in and out of Cromdale, a move which cost approximately $4,000 annually due to extra running time but the cost of maintaining the south side barn was estimated to cost some $5,100.[4]

The May 1921 schedule did reduce costs considerably but the reduced streetcar service only encouraged the expansion of the unauthorized and competing jitney service. Consequently the Edmonton Radial Railway announced a further route and schedule change to take effect immediately following exhibition week on Sunday July 17th 1921.[4a] The July 1921 routes were destined to be the most stable in the history of the railway, remaining in effect with only minor variations until May 1933.

Calder residents benefitted from direct service into downtown Edmonton for the first time effective with the July 1921 schedule change. The new Calder schedule offered half hourly service from 127 Avenue and 124 Street via 127 Avenue, 127 Street, 118 Avenue, 124 Street, 107 Avenue, 101 Street, Jasper Avenue and 95 Street to 105 Avenue Short turn cars operating from 118 Avenue and 124 Street to 95 Street and 105 Avenue over the same route brought the headway along 107 Avenue to a car every fifteen minutes. The route colour designation for the new Calder route does not appear to have been announced in the press, but it was possibly green and white, the colour reportedly carried by Calder cars in 1926.

Service to 101 Street north of 107 Avenue was also reinstated in July 1921. Red sign cars from the south side operated north on 95 Street to 111 Avenue then west to 101 Street and south to Jasper Avenue. The red-and-white sign cars travelled north on 101 Street to 111 Avenue, east to 95 Street then north to their north east terminal while the southbound red-and-white sign cars travelled south on 95 Street to Jasper Avenue and on to the south side.

A rebuilt roof, a new red and cream paint scheme, conversion back to its original configuration as a double-end car, and set once again on its original Bemis trucks, car 12 poses with motorman Bob Chambers on 102 Avenue just west of 124 Street. Motorman Chambers is about to take the tram on its westbound trip along 102 Avenue to 142 Street. Note the route sign displaying an abbreviated form for Athabasca Avenue, the former name for 102 Avenue. Note too the re-railer carried on the bumper below the headlight. The road number on the letterboard over the centre-end window was typical of the red and cream paint scheme until the mid 1930s, when road numbers again began to appear on the dash. Date of this scene is May 1929. (Glenbow Alberta Institute)

Service frequency increased on the white sign car line to a car every fifteen minutes. Base blue and blue-and-white sign car service remained unchanged but at rush hours the blue-and-white sign cars extended their westbound run from 107 Avenue and 124 Street to 118 Avenue and 124 Street. Base service for the July 1921 schedule called for 34 cars from the total roster of 72 cars.

This stepped up service preceded the introduction of a bylaw in August 1921 which was designed to control jitney service by outlining the restricted routes upon which the jitneys could operate.[5] An incentive fare structure introduced in the closing months of 1921 helped to attract more riders onto the streetcars. A passenger could purchase a book of 50 tickets for $3, offering a discount over the regular fare structure of 4 tickets for 25 cents.[6] All of the above measures apparently combined to disperse the jitney threat, as ridership on the streetcars increased in the following months and years. Sometime during the mid 1920s a wye was installed at 124 Street and 112 Avenue. At that time blue and blue-and-white sign cars made this point their western-terminal.

The need for grade separations where the CNR line intersected major downtown roads had become more evident as road traffic increased. The 101 Street underpass construction got under way late in 1924 and was completed in 1925. This underpass permitted more reliable service on the street car line as the trams were no longer subjected to long waits as CNR trains arrived at and departed from the station just west of 101 Street. Diverted street car trackage crossed the CNR line temporarily at about 100 Street while subway construction was under way.

Throughout the 1920s Edmonton's population slowly began to recover from the sharp decline experienced following the outbreak of war in 1914. The Hudson's Bay Company reserve, bounded by 101 Street on the east and the CNR tracks on the west, and approximately north of 107 Avenue to the CNR Calder yard, lay largely undeveloped except for the Royal Alexandra Hospital near Portage Avenue and 101 Street. It will be recalled that the Hudson's Bay Company had the city pave and lay car tracks along Portage Avenue in 1915 and 1916, cutting a curbed swath diagonally from southeast to northwest across the centre of the reserve. In an attempt to attract buyers into the area, the HBC encouraged City Council on several occasions in 1924 and 1925 to activate the car line. In February 1925, however, a new ERR Superintendent, W.J. Cunningham, reported to Council that radial tramway operation on Portage Avenue (Kingsway) was not feasible. He estimated that 1,361 fares had to be generated daily to cover the cost of operating the line.[7] As a result, Council decided against activating the tram trackage on Portage Avenue.

Car 37, decorated with over 1,000 lights, flags and photographs, standing on the north side of Cromdale shop. On July 1st 1927, it toured the system, celebrating the 60th Anniversary of Canadian Confederation.
(Alberta Pioneer Railway Association, Holden Swift)

About 1921 the sprinkler cars were withdrawn from service. The tanks became surplus but the frames and trucks were utilized to build at least one service car for the system. In 1925, shop crews built an arched roofed body on the steel frame of the big McGuire-Cummings sprinkler. With the experience gained in rebuilding the work car and the observation car, the shop men at Cromdale were prepared to do considerable rehabilitative work to make improvements to the passenger cars in the closing years of the "Roaring Twenties". One report noted that twelve passenger cars had been rebuilt in 1928 alone, in addition to the repair, rebuilding and painting of the three sweepers. Thirty sets of trucks received new axles, new steel wheels and helical gears and pinions. Motor and control equipment for these cars received a complete overhaul as well.[11]

The craftsmen at Cromdale took great pride in their work. In May 1927, a committee of car barn employees headed by A.J. Brass, Barn Foreman as Chairman and Charles H. Wentworth as Secretary, presented a proposal to Mr. A.R. Robertson, Acting Superintendent to decorate a street car for the Diamond Jubilee Pageant in honour of the 60th Anniversary of Confederation. Their proposal called for a sum of $263.89 to be expended. It required the purchase of 1,000 lamp receptacles and 1,000 ten-watt coloured lamps, but the committee reported that the Canadian General Electric Company had agreed to take back 500 receptacles and 500 lamps. Also required were 2,500 feet of No. 14 wire which was of the same standard used in car repair work and could therefore be placed back in stock. When all the employees volunteered to assist with the project without remuneration,[12] the City Commissioners agreed.[13] The car barn employees, with the help of J. Longworth, Foreman of the carpenters and painting department and H. (Bert) Ward, Foreman of the electrical department, began work. They selected car 37, a St. Louis-built double-ender, at that time in the shop for major repairs. The car was refurbished and when decorated with the 1,000 lights, flags and bunting, was a fine sight indeed. On Friday, July 1st 1927, Canada's 60th Birthday, the car toured the city. In the evening, it moved slowly across the High Level Bridge and halted for a few moments on the bridge so that citizens at the huge civic bonfire could view the colourful spectacle.[14] The car was a fine contribution to the Jubilee Pageant and illustrated the esprit de corps and pride in workmanship among the employees of the Edmonton Radial Railway.

Businessmen on the south side had often attempted to encourage street car patrons to shop in the stores along Whyte Avenue. The belt line system of routing on the south side took passengers from the western section of south side destinations right past these shops on Whyte Avenue to destinations in downtown Edmonton. Passengers who chose to break their journeys to or from downtown Edmonton to shop along Whyte Avenue were penalized by the additional fare required to complete their journeys. At one time, south side merchants suggested to the ERR that all cars be terminated at Whyte Avenue and 104 Street so that it would become a major transfer point. Passengers might then be enticed to shop in the area while waiting for the transfer car. Such a scheme was neither encouraged nor accepted by the ERR, but in 1925, South Side Business Men's Association did negotiate a system of stopover transfers for street car patrons,[8] which allowed the rider a limited amount of time to stop anywhere between 99 Street and 109 Street along Whyte Avenue. Passengers boarding a street car at any of these points on Whyte Avenue and surrendering a valid stopover transfer did not have to pay an extra fare to complete the journey.

By the mid 1920s, the Edmonton street car system began to feel the effects of its age. Cars looked decrepit and track work had become rough in many locations.

In 1926, the Edmonton Radial Railway adopted a new paint scheme for its cars. The brown-and-yellow treatment which had drawn such comment ten years earlier gave way to a smart, crisp-looking, red-and-cream, with a black roof replacing the former white roof. Car 77 paraded through town on Wednesday, May 31st 1926, sporting the

The motorman watches the road ahead while another crewman carefully adjusts the water-spraying apparatus as the Preston-built sprinkler works its way off 101 Street onto Jasper Avenue about 1915. (Glenbow Alberta Institute)

new colours.[9] However, passengers complained of the high single step required to gain entry to some of the cars. When the big Prestons and the smaller Ottawa- and Preston-built single end cars were converted for one man operation, they were equipped with two steps. When the motorman opened the door, the step dropped down, exposing an intermediate step which simplified entry onto the car. By early 1926, 44 of the cars in the ERR's fleet of 72 cars had been equipped with this folding step arrangement. In November 1926, the first St. Louis-built double ended car had been shopped to receive a single front entry door and a folding step, apparently the first of the double ended cars to receive this feature. It appears to have been successful as all cars on the system were subsequently equipped with the same arrangement.[10]

As the one-man car became popular across Canada, a means of circulating the movement of passengers was studied. Passengers entering a one-man car at the front could leave via a rear door equipped with a treadle exit mechanism. Edmonton installed a treadle rear exit on car 74 with the intention of using it in rush hour service to determine if passenger movement could be speeded up. Since the operation of the rear door was coordinated with the car's braking system, it was a completely safe operation. If a passenger stood on the treadle the door would not open until the car came to a stop and the motorman set the door motor in motion. On the other hand the motorman could not close the door or move the car until the treadle and the outer step were clear of passengers.[15] This arrangement, with minor variations, was adopted by most North American transit systems, but no other street cars were converted to use the treadle exit on the ERR.

The system also experimented with a K-35 controller on car 56. The car so equipped, went into regular service on November 14th 1929,[16] and was highly regarded by the motormen because it responded very well and was very fast, making it easy to keep on schedule or make up lost time.

The extensive car repair program begun in 1926 put most of the fleet in top operating condition by the close of the decade, but even with the rolling stock in good shape, the street cars were hard pressed to keep pace with the traffic demand. At this time the railway was faced with the choice of some major track rehabilitation and purchasing new rolling stock, or of moving toward the use of the bus as an alterate means of public transportation. Up to the latter part of 1930 the ERR had used the electric tram exclusively, but reports of utilizing a bus service to replace or supplement the cars began to circulate.

In a report presented to Council in March 1930 Superintendent W.J. Cunningham pointed out that the system should immediately order six new street cars. He noted that summer traffic was generally light but winter traffic was much heavier. On several occasions during the winter of 1929-30, every car on the system was in service. Overcrowding occurred and more cars could have been used but there were no spares available. Superintendent Cunningham cautioned against moving quickly into using the motor bus to replace the radial car, but noted that the bus could be coordinated with the street railway system to advantage. He cited, as an example, the University of Alberta Board of Governors' request that city live up to its agreement to furnish public transportation facilities to the University. A bus would be a logical alternative to building a car line to the area, although Superintendent Cunningham pointed out that a bus line to the University would not in itself be a paying proposition if it was used as a feeder to the car line where passengers were charged a uniform fare.[17]

With the proposed building of a subway under the CNR tracks at 97 Street, consideration was given to taking the cars off 97 Street and routing blue and blue-and-white sign cars on 101 Street.[18] Such a move would save a considerable sum compared with the cost of laying street car tracks through the new subway. The residents of 97 Street however protested the discontinuance of car service on that street in favour of buses as proposed in Superintendent Cunningham's report,[19] and Council

at a special meeting on Wednesday, May 7th 1930 therefore decided to retain the street car line on 97 Street and include tracks in the new railway underpass.[20] At the same meeting City Council further committed itself to the continued use of street cars by agreeing to the immediate purchase of five new cars from the Ottawa Car Manufacturing Company at $23,000 each.[21]

Track rehabilitation work started in 1928 when some 2,479 feet of 103 lb. girder grooved rail was laid on 101 Street and 2,921 feet of the same type of rail was laid on 97 Street. In 1929 the special work at 101 Street and Jasper and 97 Street and Jasper was replaced. About the same time the curve at Jasper and 99 Street was replaced as well. During 1930 the length of Jasper Avenue from 97 Street to 109 Street was completely renewed as was some trackage on Whyte Avenue. Work continued until 1932 when it had to be curtailed for economic reasons, but by that time the special work at Jasper and 95 Street, 95 Street and 111 Avenue, 97 Street and 111 Avenue, 95 Street and 114 Avenue had all been renewed. Most of the trackage on 97 Street, 111 Avenue, 95 Street, and 118 Avenue up to the 80th Street intersection had been replaced with the 103 lb. girder grooved rail as well.

The opening of the 97 Street underpass with street railway tracks included, established this thoroughfare as the main tram route through that part of Edmonton. Marginal 60 lb. trackage and the single track across the CNR line made 95 Street undesireable as a main transit line. Residents on 95 Street between 111 Avenue and Jasper Avenue petitioned on several occasions for increased through car service. The first of these petitions came while they enjoyed the frequent car service on 95 Street occasioned by the re-routing of the blue and blue-and-white sign cars during construction of the 97 Street underpass in the latter half of 1930. Up to and following that time, they were limited to a red sign car northbound every fifteen minutes and a similar frequency of southbound service from the red-and-white sign cars. Residents near 106 Avenue had the advantage of additional service to and from downtown as the red-and-green sign Calder car turned back at 106 Avenue and 95 Street. Repeated attempts to have alternate blue sign cars or blue-and-white sign street cars operate along 95 Street were turned down. Superintendent Cunningham noted that it would be impossible to keep the cars on the blue or blue-and-white line coordinated, if some were operating on good track on 97 Street *without* being delayed by trains while others operated on 95 Street, a slightly longer run with poor track and subject to railway crossing delays. Superintendent Cunningham refused to run the red-and-green sign Calder cars further north on 95 Street as the wye at 106 Avenue constructed in 1930 to accommodate single-end cars on that run had been set in place at the furthest point north where single open track was available. Construction of a wye further north would have necessitated setting trackage in pavement — an expense regarded as unwarranted. He refused to turn the cars at the 111 Avenue wye as traffic conditions precluded the turning of one-man cars safely.[22]

Calder benefited from improved tram service in late 1930. At that time the line in Calder was extended one block further east on 127 Avenue from 119 Street to a point directly across from the CNR roundhouse. At the same time construction of a wye at the Calder terminus[23] and re-installation of the wye at 95 Street and 106 Avenue took place. Single-end cars could now be assigned to the red-and-green sign Calder service. It is thought that all of the St. Louis-built cars were rebuilt to single end operation about this time. All major routes of the Edmonton Radial Railway could now accommodate the single-end car with this construction of turning facilities at each end of the red-and-green car line.

One of the passenger amenities afforded by the introduction of the one-man car was the smoking compartment on the rear platform. As early as 1926 Calder residents had pressed City Council to build a loop at Calder so that cars assigned to that service could be operated with the smoking compartment continuously at the rear end of the car.[24] At the time a $6,000 cost estimate for a wye at both Calder and at 95 Street and 105 Avenue ruled out the possibility of providing this service.[25] In order to deal with the immediate problem it was agreed that the vestibules on the Calder cars should be swept out regularly to minimize the smoking nuisance.[26] Complaints about smoking on the cars continued over the years, specifically related to the Calder cars. No seating was available in the vestibule of double-ended cars so passengers often smoked in the rear of the main

body of the car. By 1930 Superintendent Cunningham had engaged the police to help enforce violations of Bylaw 22 passed in 1920, prohibiting smoking on the street cars except in the smoking area. He explained that it was difficult for the operator of the one-man car to enforce the bylaw since there was a tendency for the smokers to encroach upon the rear seats in the main body of the car, particularly the recently remodelled cars.[27] He also noted that he would be pleased if all smoking on street cars were prohibited, a ruling which would result in a cleaner vehicle. Extended smoking privileges had been granted to the Calder shopmen on the Calder street cars by the City Commissioners in October 1924, allowing them to smoke anywhere on the extra cars at certain times and between certain stops. In a letter from Thomas Ferrier, Acting Superintendent to the City Commissioners dated June 3rd 1936, it was noted that no complaints had been received about smoking on the cars in the five years previous.

Opposite page, upper:

Ottawa Car Manufacturing Company built five steel cars for the City of Edmonton Street Railway Department in 1930. These very fine cars represented the most modern development of the streetcar in Edmonton. They were very practical in handling large crowds quickly, as passengers could embark and disembark simultaneously. Car 82 is shown here on 124 Street. *(W.C. Whittaker)*

Opposite page, lower:

An interior view towards the rear of Car 81, illustrating the seating arrangement. These trams were amongst the most comfortable in North America. *(A. Clegg)*

Photo above:

Northbound blue-and-white sign car 81 is about to pass under the CPR track as it completes its descent from the upper deck of High Level Bridge to street level at the north end of the bridge. The photograph was taken July 8th 1949.
(Foster M. Palmer)

This indicated perhaps that the single end car with seating space in the rear smoking area made smokers and non-smokers alike happier.

Almost coincident with the opening of the 97 Street underpass was the delivery of the five new steel cars from the Ottawa Car Manufacturing Company of Ottawa, Ontario. The design and appearance of these cars was unique to Edmonton. (The only other cars bearing any resemblance to them were the heavier interurban motor and trailer cars built by Ottawa about the same time for service on the Windsor Essex and Lake Shore Railway in the Windsor, Ontario area.) These new Edmonton Radial Railway cars could seat 51 passengers and featured double entrance exit front doors and a single centre exit. They were numbered 80 through 84 inclusive, and were referred to by crews as "the 80 cars". They embodied all of the latest in operating equipment. The motorman's controller handle had a safety feature in that it had to be pressed down at all times to keep the car operating. Should the operator become incapacitated and his grip released, the controller handle sprung up. When this happened, the power was cut off, brakes were applied, sanders operated and car doors opened. The front doors were pneumatically-operated by the motorman while the centre exit door responded to a passenger standing on the pneumatic treadle, provided that the car was stopped and the motorman's pneumatic control switch was in the "open" position. As long as any car door was open, the brakes would not release nor could power be applied to the motors. Seating included one longitudinal three-passenger seat on each side at the front of the car body; one just behind the centre exit; seventeen transverse seats in the balance of the car body; and longitudinal seating around the outer edge of the rear platform area. All seats were upholstered in leather, with individual backs on the double transverse seats. On arrival in Edmonton, the new cars began service on the blue-and-white sign route and never strayed from that assignment.

Repair work in May 1931 to the south end of the High Level Bridge necessitated its closure to street railway traffic for over a month. Consequently, the ERR maintained service with four 26-passenger buses rented from Brewster Transportation Company of Banff. Effective Tuesday, April 28th 1931, the buses commenced service: starting at 100 Street and Jasper Avenue, the buses ran south to McDougall Hill across the 105 Street Bridge to 88 Avenue and 109 Street, then south to Whyte Avenue. They returned to the downtown area via the same route to the post office at 100 Street, west on 101 A. Avenue to 100 A. Street, south to Jasper Avenue, then east to 100 Street and south again. Regular street car fare was charged, transfers to and from street cars at 109 Street and Whyte Avenue and at 100 Street and Jasper Avenue were issued. Transfer privileges were available from buses to westbound cars only at 103 Street and 97 Avenue and from eastbound cars only at the same point.[28]

Needless to say, the ERR watched the bus operation very carefully, as the advent of regular rubber-tired service on the system was close at hand. This was not the first time that buses had been used on the ERR. Between December 15th and 20th 1930, a demonstrator bus had been loaned to the City to provide experimental service on the 102 Avenue route west of 124 Street. The bus replaced the regular streetcar service on the route and extended the service seven blocks further west to 149 Street.[29] West end residents responded very positively toward the new mode of public transportation. The bus began to make its impact on the Edmonton Radial Railway in 1930.[30]

During this time, route 2 white sign cars operated from Highlands to 109 Street and Whyte Avenue via the Low Level Bridge both ways. Red-and-white sign cars operated from 82 Street and 115 Avenue via the Low Level Bridge both ways to 82 Avenue and 109 Street. A stub car operated from Bonnie Doon to 99 Street and Whyte Avenue.[31]

Regular street car service across the High Level Bridge resumed on Thursday, June 4th 1931. The bridge had been closed to allow workers to reduce the approach curve on the traffic deck from a 45-degree angle to a 19-degree angle. CPR service was suspended on Sunday, May 24th, with the ERR providing bus service from Whyte Avenue to the downtown station for train arrivals and departures on that day only.[32] During the time that car service was suspended, the opportunity was taken to replace ties on the street car right-of-way.[33]

Bridge repairs at two other locations disrupted street car services early in 1932. Wooden bridges on 102 Avenue at 131 Street, and on the Jasper Avenue East line over Rat Creek at 82 Street had to be replaced. The 102 Avenue Bridge work spelled the end of street car service on that thoroughfare between 124 Street and 142 Street. At 6:18 a.m. on Monday, January 25th 1932, the first permanent Edmonton bus service became effective.

Photo above:

A big Preston streetcar travels south across High Level Bridge in September 1936. (Provincial Archives of Alberta)

Opposite page, upper:

Edmonton Radial Railway No. 84 approaching High Level Bridge from the north in October 1950. The upper view on Page 99 was taken at the opposite side of the elevated CP tracks. (Omer Lavallée)

Opposite page, lower:

The five new steel lightweight cars ordered from Ottawa Car Manufacturing Company added to the changing scene in downtown Edmonton. Here, two of the new cars, assigned to the blue-and-white sign route, travel along Jasper Avenue at 101 Street. Automobiles are becoming more evident, and Liggett's Drug Store has replaced the Bank of Nova Scotia on the ground floor of the Empire Block.
(Provincial Archives of Alberta)

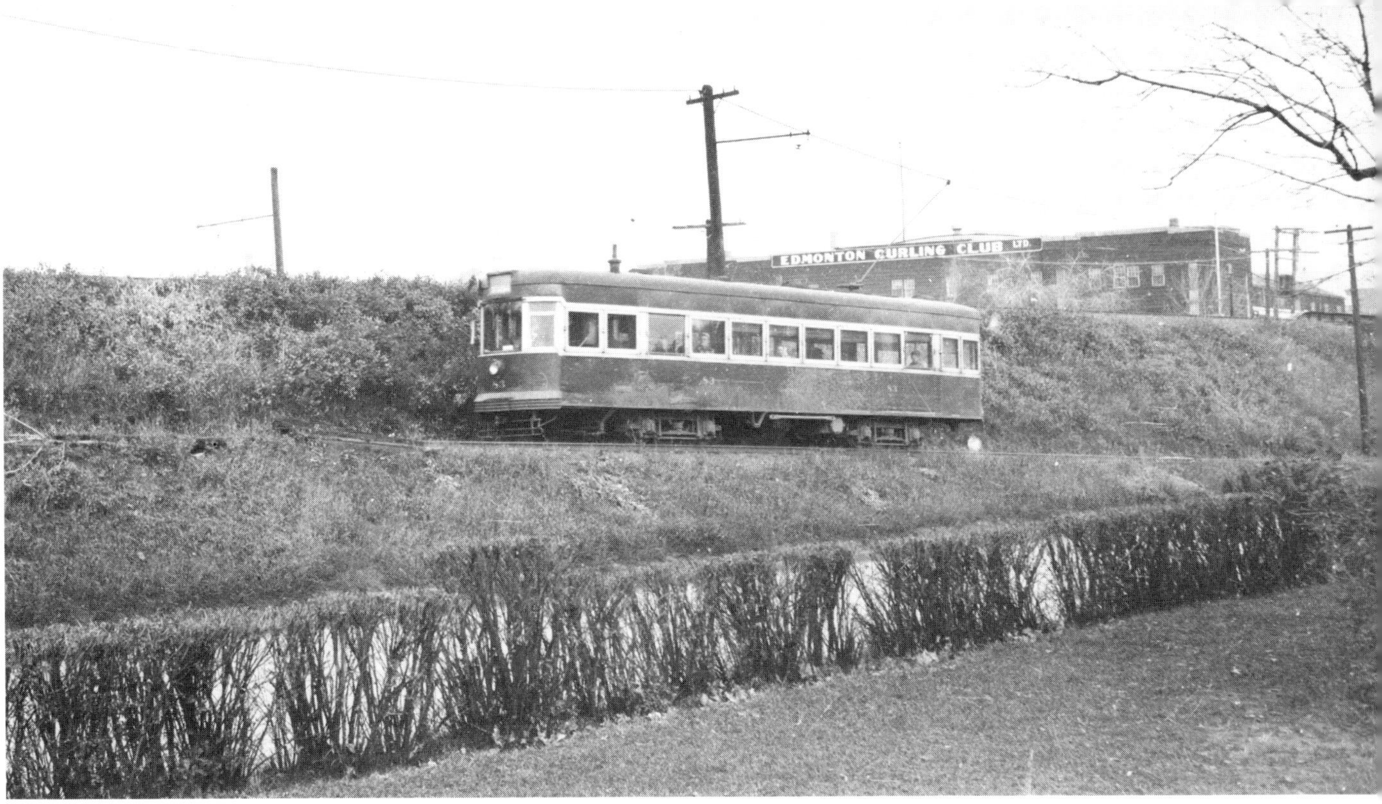
EDMONTON CURLING CLUB LTD.

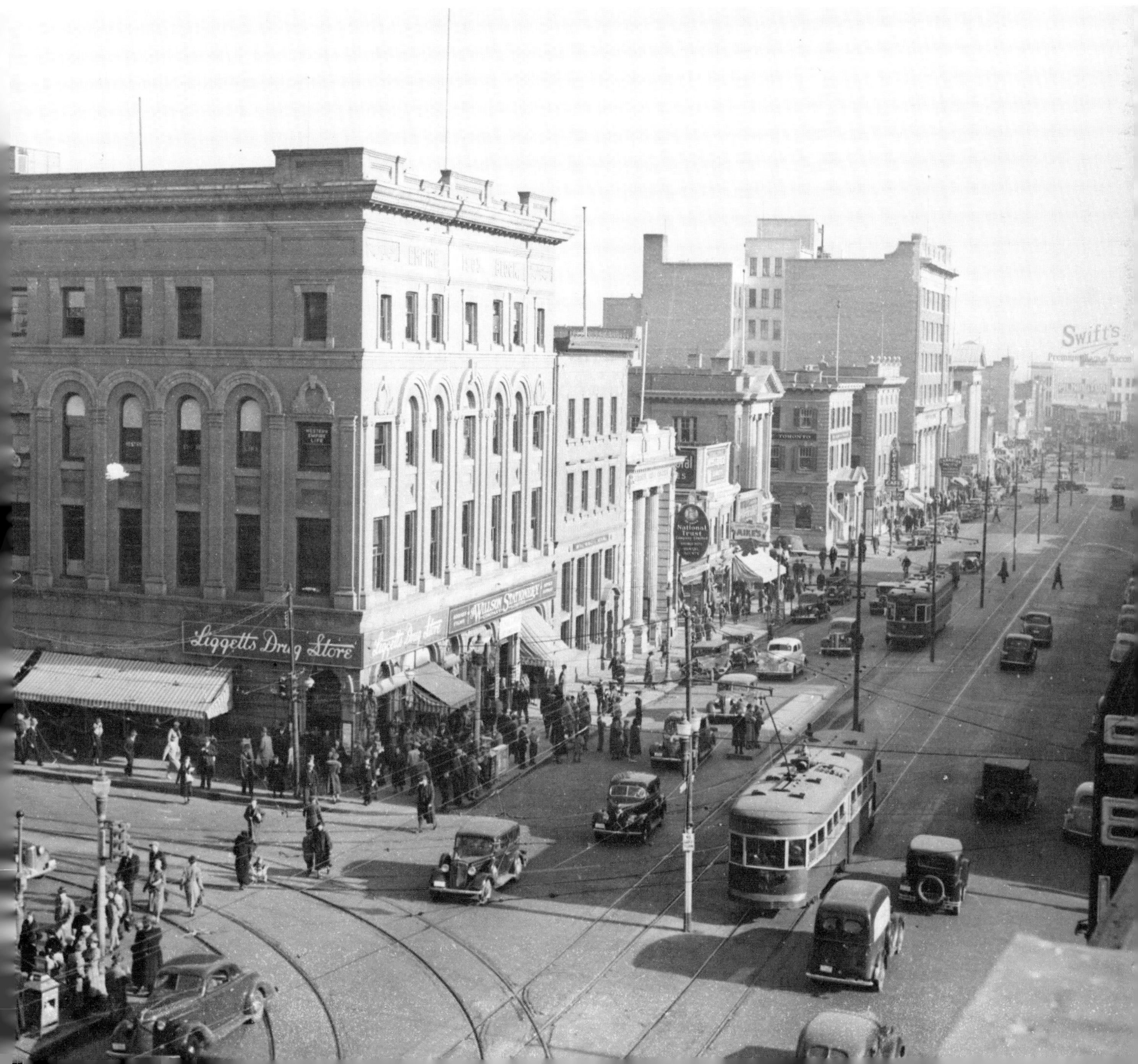
Liggetts Drug Store
Willson Stationery
National Trust
TORONTO
Swift's

The route began at 124 Street, operated west on 102 Avenue to 130 Street north to 104 Avenue, west to 132 Street, then south again to 102 Avenue and on out to 149 Street. The bus was scheduled to operate every twenty minutes, but if that schedule proved impossible, would only go as far as 145 Street while the bridge was out.[34] Initially the 102 Avenue bus route used a rented vehicle, but late in January, City Council ordered the purchase of three units: a White 25-passenger bus for $8,377; a slightly-used 21-passenger Leyland demonstrator; and a GMC chassis at $4,238. Fane Auto Works of Edmonton was awarded the contract to construct a 25-passenger bus body for the GMC chassis.[35] As Superintendent Cunningham had reported to Council that the 21-passenger Leyland bus on the 102 Avenue line had been giving good service,[36] it is presumed that this was the same coach which Council had agreed to purchase. The other two buses were ordered to provide service to the University of Alberta every fifteen minutes.[37] By April 1932 one bus was being tested on the University route beginning at 88 Avenue and 109 Street, west along 88 Avenue to 112 Street then north to the University buildings. From here the bus ran south on 112 Street making its way back to 109 Street, south on 109 Street to 82 Avenue, then north on 109 Street to 88 Avenue. Initially service was provided between 7:00 a.m. and 8:30 p.m.[38]

Street car service was restored to the Jasper Avenue east line but while the 82 Street bridge was out of service, the white sign car from Bonnie Boon travelled only to the south approach of the bridge. The Highlands was served by an extension of the red-and-white sign cars via 95 Street, 114 Avenue and the exhibition grounds loop.[39]

However, the motor bus era had come to the Edmonton Radial Railway. On one route it replaced the street cars, while in the case of the service to the University of Alberta it became a new feeder service to the south side street car line.

The year of the bus in Edmonton was also the year when the extensive track renovation project had to be curtailed due to declining revenue caused by a sagging economy. Edmonton's public transportation did not experience as severe a decrease in revenue as was the case with many other systems across the nation, but it certainly was affected, and it attempted to reduce operating expenses by a realignment of routes. Effective Sunday, May 28th 1933, an economy route realignment left 101 Street between 107 Avenue and 111 Avenue without regular street car service. The red sign cars came off 95 Street so that they could turn north at 101 Street and proceed to Calder via 107 Avenue and 124 Street. Red-and-green sign cars disappeared completely. Calder thus received the benefit of fifteen-minute rush and twenty-minute regular service instead of the former twenty-and thirty-minute service respectively. Red-and-white sign cars travelled both ways on 95 Street to and from their northern terminus at 114 Avenue and 82 Street. The blue, blue-and-white and white sign car routes remained unchanged.[40] Merchants north of 107 Avenue on 101 Street soon got together to petition City Council about their dissatisfaction at losing car service. Superintendent Cunningham was asked to revise the schedule to accommodate the petition. Under the alternative plan which actually went into effect on Saturday, June 24th 1933, the red-and-white sign cars turned north on 101 Street, and after reaching their terminus at 114 Avenue and 82 Street, returned south via 95 Street. Two additional cars carrying red signs provided service from Jasper Avenue and 101 Street via Jasper, 95 Street, 111 Avenue and 101 Street. Cars to Calder did not change their route but carried green-and-red signs again.[41] This general routing remained in effect until the 1939 introduction of trolley coaches to the system.

Fares, too, were adjusted in the mid-1930s. Superintendent Cunningham resisted reducing the car fare to a straight 5¢ as the ERR had the lowest fares in Canada for cities of comparable size. Passengers could purchase strip tickets at the rate of 4 for 25¢ which gave them a 6 1/4¢ ride, a book of 50 tickets for $3.00 offering a 6¢ ride, or a 10¢ cash fare. Children could purchase 10 tickets for 25¢ or pay a 5¢ cash fare.[42] Superintendent Cunningham proposed the trial sale of a book of tickets offering 20 rides for $1.00 and withdrawing the sale of the book of 50 tickets for $3.00 during this period of trial.[43]

On Monday, December 18th 1933, the new blue book tickets (20 for $1.00) went on sale.[44] Initially the sale of these tickets was to conclude in January 1934 but the experiment continued through until the end of February as passenger ridership in January 1934 rose 5.21% over the same month in 1933.[45] During January 1934, receipts were in the following proportions: cash fares, 1.31%; 20 for $1.00 tickets, 62.26%; 4 for 25¢ tickets, 24.46%; children's 10 for 25¢ tickets, 11.66%; adult $3.00 book tickets, .31%.[46] Another evaluation at the end of February 1934 resulted in the experimental fares continuing another two months until April 30th[47] and then again until June 30th. At the conclusion of May 1934 passenger ridership had increased 5.18% over the same period in 1933 which amounted to an actual gain of 266,953 passengers. Revenue had fallen, however, from $297,306 in 1933 to $269,894 in 1934. The net surplus to May 31st 1933 amounted to $15,497 while it came in at $14,082 at the end of the same period in 1934. Superintendent Ferrier noted that if the straight 5¢ fare or 5 tickets for 25¢ had gone into effect the Street Railway Department could have experienced a loss of $17,000 to the end of May or $40,000 over the whole year. Up to that time, 76.6% of the adult fare revenue was being paid with the 20 for $1.00 blue tickets while 23.4% was generated from the sale of the 4 for 25¢ strip tickets.[48] At the end of June, Council decided to continue with the 20 tickets for $1.00 fare system for an indefinite period; however, the straight 5¢ fare or 5 tickets for 25¢ scheme did not pass unforgotten.

The 1935 civic election saw the 5 tickets for 25¢ scheme as a plank in the platform for mayorality candidate J.A. Clarke. Clarke won that election and he gained enough support from the new Council to push that scheme through in the face of opposition from city administrators, particularly Thomas Ferrier, acting Superintendent of the Street Railway Department. The scheme passed through Council on November 25th 1935, giving Edmonton (along with Regina, San Francisco and a Rhode Island system) the lowest street railway fares in North America. The average street railway fare at the time in Canada was 6.20 cents while Edmonton's average fare with the introduction of the 5 tickets for 25¢ program dropped to 4.971 cents.[49] The new 5-for-25¢ tickets finally went on sale on Sunday, December 22nd 1935.[50] The cash fare remained at 10 cents. Ridership to the end of 1935 had climbed to 13.2 million from a low slump of 11.3 million in 1933[51] without the incentive of the 5 tickets for 25 cents program but with the enticement of the popular 20 tickets for $1.00 program. As expected, ridership did continue to grow with the lower fare structure but it became more difficult to show a surplus, even though many of the street railway debentures had been paid off by this time.

Another of Mayor Clarke's programs which had a slight effect on the Street Railway Department was the closure of the Latta Ravine bridge on Jasper Avenue near 92 Street. When the wooden structure was declared unsafe, road and streetcar traffic was detoured around the head of the ravine only a few yards north of Jasper Avenue. The new steel bridge did not have street car tracks built on it, so the trams on Jasper Avenue east continued to be diverted around the ravine.[52]

Photo above:

When the new steel and concrete bridge on Jasper Avenue was constructed across the Latta Ravine in 1935, the streetcar tracks were simply routed around the head of the ravine instead of across the bridge. (Bob Walker)

 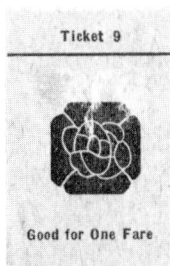 

Photo below:

Jasper Avenue looking east from 102 Street is quite deserted in this dusk scene. The effect of the coloured-light route-indicators can be clearly seen on the front and rear letterboards of the four streetcars. Car 39 in the foreground carries its road number on the centre of the letterboard at the front of the car, a practice common in the late 1920s to the mid 1930s. (Provincial Archives of Alberta)

Gradually short portions of single track on the ERR became doubled as track improvements took place in the 1930s. Some $50,000 was appropriated by Council in June 1934 to double track 124 Street between 104 Avenue and 107 Avenue, to reconstruct all the line on Norwood Boulevard and to replace part of the Bonnie Doon line on Whyte Avenue.[53] The Jasper Avenue east line received more attention in 1938 as the double track line was extended about 300 feet to 84 Street.[54]

Since its inception, the Edmonton Radial Railway had provided special street car service to various events in the city. The annual exhibition was always a time when every available car went into service, but by 1938 some passenger cars were being withdrawn from service and stored unserviceable in Cromdale yards. Among these was the observation car which had a special wooden shed built over and around it on the south west corner of the car house. Single truck car 7 was completely stripped to the frame; in 1938 the ERR built an open rail grinding car from it for a total of $1,400. It consisted of an abrasive carbonundum brick mounted on each side between the wheels.[55] The brick under heavy pressure from the springs smoothed out the rough corrugations in the rails. The grinder carried a tank the full length of the body of the car and had open platforms at each end for the operator. Three other passenger cars (10, 14 and 16) were stored, apparently unserviceable, in Cromdale yards in 1938. These retirements reduced the passenger-carrying fleet in 1938 to 74 cars.

Photo above:

Car 41 performs the honours to celebrate the Coronation of King George VI on May 12th 1937. As was the case ten years earlier, carbarn employees, superintended by H. (Bert) Ward, decorated the car for the occasion. (Edmonton Transit)

Photo below:

A revision to the Coronation decorations on car 41 resulted in a travelling billboard for the City of Edmonton's Telephone and Transportation services. It is believed that the decorated car participated in a parade during July 1937. (A. Clegg)

104

Cars are lined up on 97 Avenue in the foreground and on 109 Street in the background, having transported Edmontonians to the Legislature Grounds for special ceremonies celebrating the Coronation of King George VI on May 12th 1937.
(Provincial Archives of Alberta)

This fleet, plus three buses, went into full service during the Royal Visit to Edmonton on Friday, June 2nd 1939. Special schedules had to be set up for the day, as cars could not cross the level crossings at 107 Avenue or 127 Street for a period of three quarters of an hour before the Royal Train arrived from the west. Likewise street car traffic could not cross 95 Street or 118 Avenue for the same period of time before the departure of the eastbound Royal Train from Edmonton that evening. Car service to various parts of the city had to be curtailed at varying times to allow for the passage of the Royal Parade.[56] One alderman had inquired about the possibility of offering free street car transportation on the day of the Royal Visit but Superintendent Ferrier recommended against this proposal because the cost of operating 74 cars and three buses was estimated to be $2,100 to $2,500. He stated that about 75,000 riders would bring in approximately $3,700. He was also concerned about providing the best service at the prime rush periods, as well as on all regular routes. He felt that provision of free service would create more demand for service throughout the day, which would create accident hazards and interfere with the usual safe operation of the cars.[57] The Commissioners and Council concurred with Ferrier's recommendations to carry passengers at the regular schedule of fares during the Royal Visit.

Through the final years of the 1930s, passenger riding continued to rise on the street cars. Automobile traffic, too, became more dense, particularly at the Jasper Avenue and 101 Street intersection. Pressure was put on the street railway department to change car routes to avoid the need for red-and-green and red-and-white sign street cars to make lefthand turns at this busy intersection. Superintendent Ferrier opposed this proposal because the street railway department would be faced with considerable route changes which would not be in the best interests of providing good car service. He also drew attention to the objection by 101 Street businessmen when some cars were taken off that street in 1933. The suggested solution to the problem was to allow eastbound street cars to make the lefthand turn onto 101 Street against a red light to minimize having to cross the heavy streams of traffic westbound on Jasper Avenue. The City Police Department approved and gave Superintendent Ferrier permission to allow eastbound trams on Jasper to turn left at 101 Street on a red light.[58]

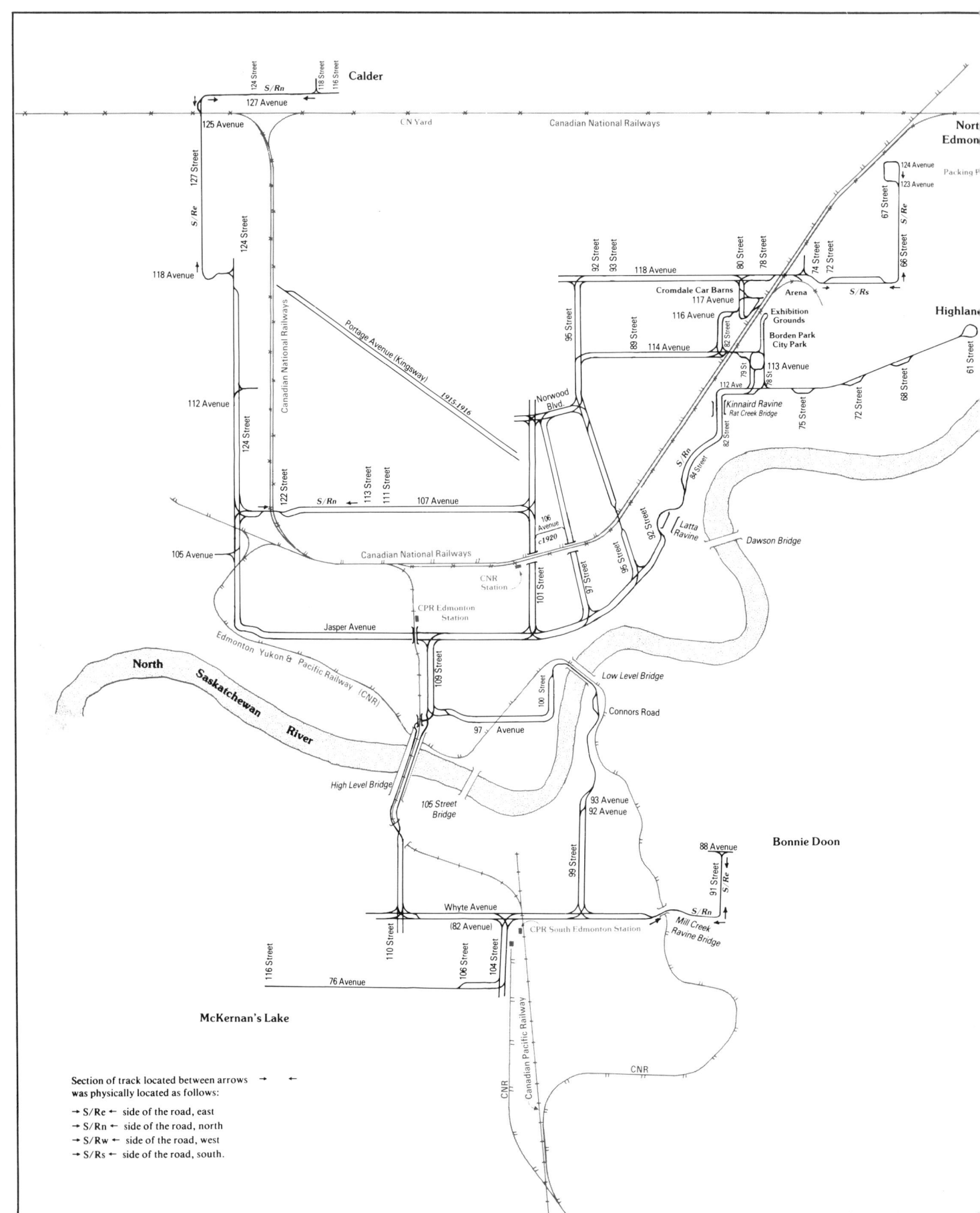

City of Edmonton Street Railway Department
Track Map
1938

The North Saskatchewan River, the Low Level Bridge and the community of Strathcona, as viewed from the Macdonald Hotel gardens before the proliferation of the automobile eliminated the gardens and changed the pattern of roads and bridges. (CP photo)

The second abandonment of an Edmonton tram line began when the Low Level Bridge was closed to street car traffic on Wednesday, July 26th 1939. Regular belt line service between downtown Edmonton and Whyte Avenue via the High Level Bridge and Low Level Bridge, which had been established back in 1914, ceased permanently with closure of the bridge. The street car tracks were removed, leaving only the CNR tracks to be enclosed in a new concrete decking to enable smooth operation for the new trolley coaches. Effective that date, the red-and-green sign cars operated to and from 99 Street and Whyte Avenue via the High Level Bridge and red-and-white sign cars ran between 82 Street and 114 Avenue and downtown via 95 Street southbound and 101 Street northbound. A stub car operated from 99 Street and Whyte Avenue to the Low Level Bridge and from 109 Street and 97 Avenue down 97 Avenue to the north side of the Low Level Bridge.[59] When the Low Level Bridge reopened to traffic on September 1st 1939, two motor buses hired from Central Canadian Greyhound provided service from 99 Street and Whyte Avenue via Scona Hill, Low Level Bridge and McDougall Hill to 100 Street and Jasper Avenue where they turned back for the return trip.[60]

Almost 31 years after its inception the first street car service to the south side via the Low Level Bridge had been terminated to make way for installation of trolley coach services. All street car service to south Edmonton now travelled by way of the spectacular High Level Bridge.

One of Edmonton's most distinctive engineering features is the spectacular High Level Bridge between the north and south sectors of the Alberta Capital. On June 25th, 1948, a southbound ETS car occupies the left-hand track, contrary to the "rule of the road" in North America. The double track was transposed on the bridge so that, in an emergency, the transit car's occupants could be unloaded safely onto the centre of the structure. (A. Clegg)

Photo above:

A southbound red-and-green sign car bound for Whyte Avenue via the Low Level Bridge boards passengers on 101 Street at 101A Avenue. The scene dates back to the mid 1930s. This routing for Calder cars carrying red-and-green signs went into effect on Saturday June 24th 1933. (McDermid Collection)

Photo below:

On June 1st 1939, Jasper Avenue was decorated to mark the royal visit of King George VI and Queen Elizabeth. Car No. 72, travelling westbound on the blue-and-white-sign route to 124 Street and 112 Avenue, takes on a load of passengers at 101 Street. (Bob Walker)

12 Streetcar Service Declines

THE INTRODUCTION of trolley coach operations terminated tram services on 95 Street, the Low Level Bridge, Scona Hill and 99 Street. Only one car route — the two cars on the red sign route — ceased operation. This fact, plus the increasing demand for public transportation, continued to keep all 74 units in service on the remaining rail system. In 1939 ridership came very close to equalling the previous high established in 1914. In 1940, this figure increased by about 900,000 over the 1939 one, pushing the total number of passengers carried to an all-time high of 16 million.[1]

The new south side trolley coach line, originally scheduled to run to the centre of the south side business district at 82 Avenue and 104 Street, terminated instead at 99 Street and Whyte Avenue. This terminal was apparently chosen as a temporary move to allow the Street Railway Department time to assess trolley coach and tram ridership patterns. Had the extended trolley coach line gone into service, one of the tracks on Whyte Avenue east of 104 Street was to have been lifted, as the only tram service expected there was the service to Bonnie Doon.

The longer tram run on the south side resulted in some changes in routing. The Calder red-and-green sign cars returned to their former southbound run along 97 Avenue, serving the Rossdale area, and turned back on a new loop constructed north of the Low Level Bridge. The red-and-white sign cars from 114 Avenue and 82 Street extended their southbound run across the High Level Bridge to the south side terminal at 99 Street and Whyte Avenue and returned again via the High Level Bridge.

Repairs to the Mill Creek ravine bridge deck brought an end to Bonnie Doon car service in 1940. During previous bridge repair interruptions, a street car was isolated on the east end of the line in stub service between Bonnie Doon terminal and the bridge, where passengers walked across to board the through tram which came east on Whyte Avenue as far as the bridge. The 1940 redecking program did not call for replacement of the street car tracks, so a diesel-driven bus served Bonnie Doon via Connors Road. Late in May 1940, the last tram left the Bonnie Doon loop at 88 Avenue and 91 Street and on Sunday, June 9th, the bus began to provide fifteen-minute service over the old tram route from the terminal at 91 Street and 88 Avenue to Whyte Avenue and 99 Street.[2] The latter intersection thus became the terminal point for three different modes of municipal transportation: a motor bus from Bonnie Doon; the white sign and red-and-white sign street cars; and the Low Level Bridge trackless trolleys. The track into the Bonnie Doon area was lifted; instead of paving the street car right-of-way on Whyte Avenue between the bridge and 99 Street, the strip formed the centre of an attractive tree-lined boulevard.

Declaration of war on the European front almost a year earlier had quite a different effect on the Street Railway Department than the same action had in 1914. During the 1914-18 period ridership fell drastically as the city's populaton fell. Street car services were reduced and one-man cars appeared as an economy measure. Street cars went into storage and some were even sold.

In 1939, Edmonton was a larger city and, as the gateway for traffic into Canada's north country, air services had become an important ingredient in the city's economy. Wartime restraints on gasoline and tires forced many people to move out of their autos and make greater use of the street cars and buses. The city's population grew during World War II as opposed to the sharp decline during World War I, and the Street Railway Department suddenly found itself attempting to handle an increasingly larger number of passengers on its vehicles in the face of severe restraints on the availability of public transportation vehicles of all types.

When the United States entered the war arena in December 1941, an influx of United States service men came into Edmonton by virtue of its strategic position as a supply base for the north, particularly Alaska. The US services established a large community called Camp 550 along the west side of the city airport, north of 118 Avenue and along 127 Street. This base contributed positively in many ways to community life in Edmonton. In November 1942, soon after the arrival of US forces, Edmonton experienced one of its worst snow storms; as the storm reached its peak, street cars began to derail, particularly in outlying areas. One motorman on a Calder car stopped at the railway crossing at 127 Street to inquire if another car had gone into Calder. The flagman, whose duty it was to open the derail to allow the street cars to cross the CNR main line west, advised that he hadn't seen a street car for an hour. The car proceeded and found another car derailed on the switch at the terminal. The two motormen (using a rerailer carried as standard equipment on all Edmonton street cars) got the car back on the track and the two vehicles then started back through the storm toward downtown Edmonton. The car which had derailed at Calder went off the track again at 118 Avenue and 124 Street, tieing up the Calder line for the duration of the storm.[3]

Photo above:

In November 1942 a heavy snowstorm tied up transportation in Edmonton for several days. Car 34 derailed on its southbound trip from Calder on 118 Avenue at 124 Street. At this point, the track on 118 Avenue crossed from the south side to the north side in order to get a wide curve into 124 Street. This alignment was apparently initiated by the Edmonton Interurban Railway for ease in operating their own long-wheelbase car. When the Edmonton Radial Railway leased, and later purchased, the EIR right-of-way for its access to Calder, the original alignment remained. In 1943, this 118 Avenue section (from 124 Street to 127 Street and north to 125 Avenue) was abandoned in favour of the line on 124 Street to 125 Avenue and west to 127 Street. (Les Corness)

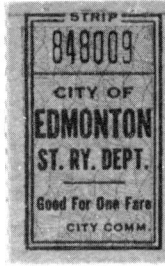  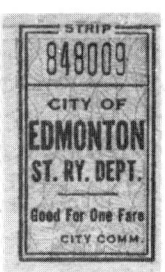

Photo below:

Edmonton Transit System No. 45, at the diamond crossing with the double track CN main line at Calder, June 25th 1948. The switchtender, seen behind the tram, holds the spring derail closed to allow the streetcar to cross the CN tracks in safety. (A. Clegg)

When Edmontonians awoke the following morning, they found the streets buried under heavy snowdrifts. The US service men with the heavy equipment they had on hand cleared the street car lines first, then helped to get auto traffic moving as well.

Late in 1941, the question of street railway service to the Aircraft Repair and Assembly Plant area arose. The City had contracted in 1940 with the Checker Taxi Cab Company Ltd. to operate a bus service from the city centre to the Airport and the aircraft repair shops at 125 Avenue east of 127 Street. The two buses carried 500 to 550 passengers per day. It appeared that the bus service could not handle the required traffic volume so alternate street railway services to the area were considered. Superintendent Ferrier suggested three possible routes. One was an extension of the existing car line up 124 Street to a spur east on 125 Avenue to serve the plant. The track could also run west on 125 Avenue to 127 Street to connect with the Calder line making it possible to abandon the track on 118 Avenue and 127 Street to 125 Avenue. An alternative would utilize the paved trackage on Kingsway with a connecting link at 101 Street and 111 Avenue or Kingsway at 101 Street and an extension northerly from Kingsway to 125 Avenue along the east side of the CNR tracks. This plan would add more street railway mileage but would offer better service to employees going downtown or living in the east end. A third option would have been to build an entirely new route from 95 Street and 118 Avenue via 95 Street, 122 Avenue, 104 Street, 124 Avenue, 107 Street and 125 Avenue to the plant gates.

It was not until the Federal Transit Controller visited the city in October 1942 and recommended that Ferrier's first proposal be carried out that work actually got underway. On February 21st 1943 all regular cars to Calder began using the new line north on 124 Street and salvage work to remove the track on 118 Avenue and 127 Street to 125 Avenue began immediately. The following week, the spur track east on 125 Avenue to the CNR crossing near the aircraft repair depot went into service.[4] The Street Railway Department dispatched special cars to carry workers to and from the crossing, a few hundred yards from the repair depot.

Photo above:
A little girl walks beside the car tracks on 118 Avenue near the corner of 66 Street, as Edmonton Transit No. 56 returns from the North Edmonton terminus. It was a cold and frosty Thursday, January 18th 1951. Wonder where the little girl is today!
(A. Clegg)

Photo below:
A Canadian National 0-6-0 switcher crosses 107 Avenue as a westbound Calder streetcar waits its turn to proceed. Streetcar service over this section of track terminated on August 8th 1948.
(Les Corness)

Above:

The Edmonton Street Railway Department rebuilt car 14 for service as a Library Car in 1941. It is pictured here on July 8th 1949 at the end-of-track on the north side of 127 Avenue in Calder. *(Foster M. Palmer)*

Below, left:

Jack Fearon, librarian, suggests some good reading to a young visitor while two youngsters keep a friendly dog occupied.
(Foster M. Palmer)

Below, right:

It is almost 8:10 in the evening of July 7th 1949 when the photographer recorded two young people taking advantage of the Library Car's visit to the Sherbrooke area on 127 Street, just south of 125 Avenue. *(Foster M. Palmer)*

This is the interior of Edmonton's unique library car. The librarian, seated at his desk at the left in this photograph, advises a youthful reader about one of the tram's many volumes, as the car waits on a siding near Calder, June 25th 1948.

(A. Clegg)

During 1941 the Edmonton Street Railway Department embarked upon a unique cooperative project with the Edmonton Public Library. Shop crews rebuilt car 14 (which had been retired from passenger service in May 1938) to enter service as a travelling library. The idea for the tram library came from Edmonton Librarian Hugh C. Gourlay who conceived the idea based upon buses serving as mobile libraries operating in other North American cities. As far as the author knows, the tram library idea was unique to Edmonton. The Edmonton Public Library provided the books and the staff to operate the library service, while the Edmonton Street Railway Department provided the labour to rebuild the car for that purpose and render it serviceable for operation under its own power. The transit system also provided the crew to take the car to its various locations and to return it to the barns again once it had closed for the day.

On Friday, October 10th 1941 the completed cream-and-blue car moved to a short display track at the southwest corner of 101 Street and Jasper Avenue. At 8:15 p.m. that evening Mayor Fry presided at the official opening ceremony.[5] By Tuesday, October 14th, 9,000 people had visited the tram library. The display was extended for an extra day at 101 Street and Jasper Avenue. On Wednesday, October 15th it went on display at 109 Street and Whyte Avenue.[6]

Shelves on either side of the main body of the car had space for 1,500 books but the library had purchased 3,000 new books specifically for service from the tram. The schedule initially called for a visit to North Edmonton on Wednesdays and Calder on Fridays. Neither of these areas had paved roads and both were some distance from the central library facilities in downtown Edmonton, so the use of the tram to bring reading services to the area was congruent to the initial concept of using street cars to provide passenger services to these areas where paved roads did not exist. A bus simply could not negotiate the unpaved roads.

On its first trip on October 17th 1941, the pioneer rolling library went to new siding tracks constructed specifically for that purpose at 127 Avenue opposite the CNR Calder shops. Approximately 700 Calder residents visited the library between 3:00 p.m. and 9:00 p.m. that day. Half of the borrowers were new clients; 75% were children.[7] The library tram was equally popular on its first trip to North Edmonton on Wednesday, October 22nd, attracting 424 newcomers including 348 children and 76 adults. A total of 576 people from the area visited the library that day.[8]

The library tram continued in service until 1949 when street car service to the Calder area was terminated. When the Calder street car line was physically isolated from the rest of the rail system in 1948, the library car was stationed at 124 Street and 118 Avenue. During its final year of operation on this line, it also served Sherbrooke from a short stub siding at 127 Street and 125 Avenue.

The Edmonton Street Railway had the good fortune to be able to obtain several additional pieces of public transit equipment during the war years in the form of trolley coaches and buses. Acquisition of this additional equipment allowed the Street Railway Department to increase frequency on heavily-patronized trolley coach lines and to

Photo above:

Edmonton tram No. 60 pauses for additional passengers on 118 Avenue near 95 Street on August 15th 1951. (Les Corness)

Photo below:

Car 1 on the blue-and-white sign route stands at the wye on 124 Street and 112 Avenue, ready to begin its journey to downtown Edmonton and then on to its northeast terminal at 80 Street and 118 Avenue. The "V" in the front window below the destination sign indicates that passengers may board via the rear door. From 1943 to 1946, cars on heavily-travelled routes carried a "conductorette" whose task it was to collect fares and distribute transfers at the rear door. Her presence helped to speed loading and unloading of passengers so that cars could run on a faster schedule and thus collectively handle more passengers during these very busy years. For this photograph, the "conductorette" poses at the front entrance of Car No. 1. (City of Edmonton)

Opposite page, upper:

Car No. 39 climbs up out of the Canadian National Railways overpass on 101 Street, bringing a few passengers from Calder into downtown Edmonton on an early morning run. An abundance of express shipments waits to be loaded aboard cars of the Northern Alberta Railways, whose trains used the CNR station in downtown Edmonton. (W.C. Whittaker)

Opposite page, lower:

In the late 1940s the Edmonton Street Railway Department streetcar maintenance crew gathers for a photographer beside car No. 83 at Cromdale Shop. In the back row left to right are: Charlie Chambers, Kenny Orr, George Hollands, Harold Johnson, Morris Beaugard, Harry Griffin and Ted Mayhew. In the front row from left to right are: Joe Potter, Jimmy Conlan, Bill Emblem and Arch Clarke. (A. Clarke)

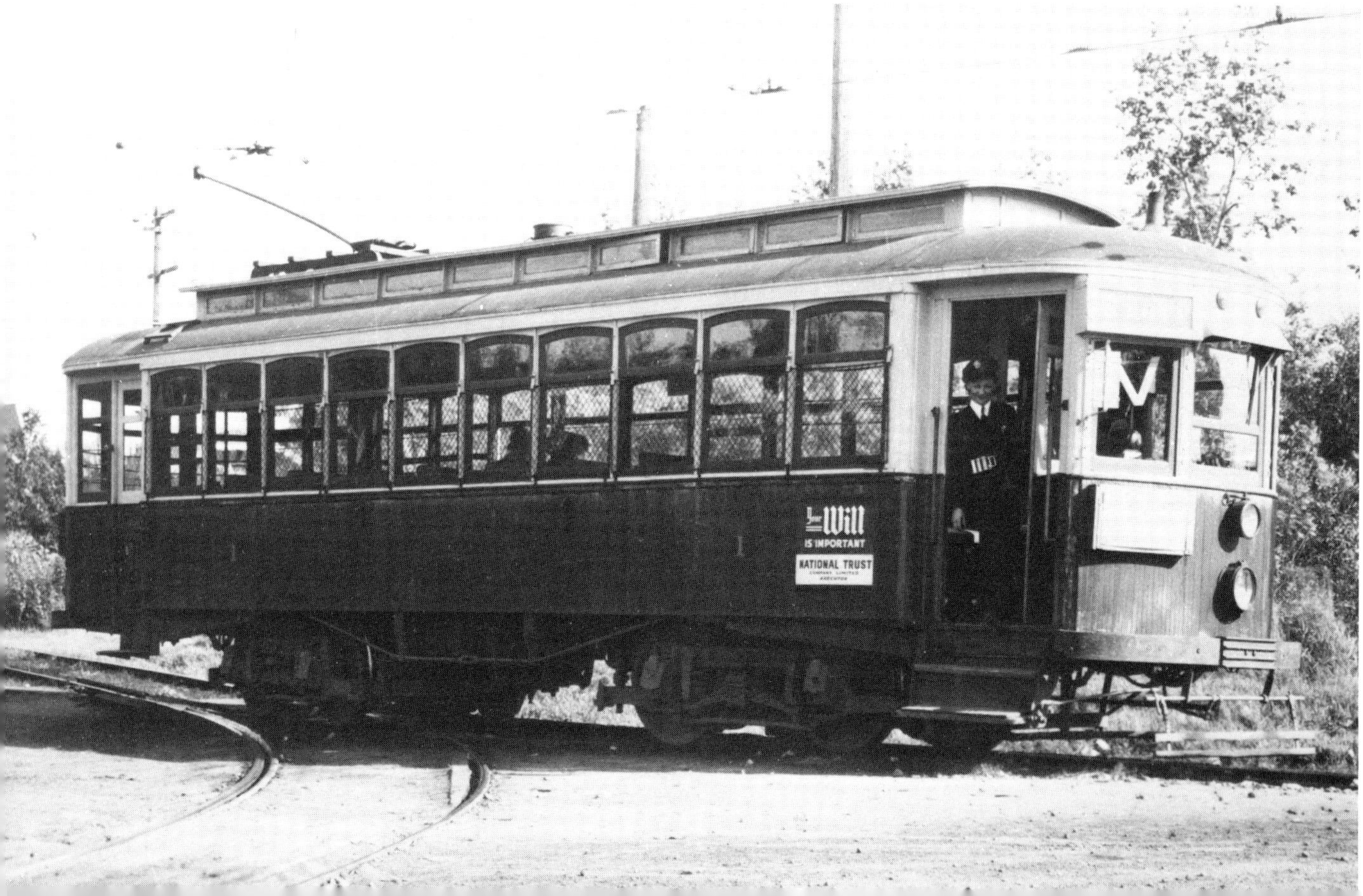

extend service to growing areas of the city such as Forest Heights, never before serviced by public transportation. As more electric and motor buses arrived, consideration was given to curtailing tram services in certain areas. This allowed the Department to assign more trams to the heavily-used main line services and to rotate trams through Cromdale shops for more frequent regular maintenance. Throughout this period of heavy activity the Edmonton trams always appeared trim, clean and well-maintained.

South side businessman had long complained that the south side Low Level Bridge trolley coach service stopped short of the centre of the Whyte Avenue business district around 104 Street. During August 1944 the Street Railway Department finally extended the south side trolley coach line on Whyte Avenue from 99 Street to 104 Street. White sign and red-and-white sign trams made their final trips east of 104 Street along Whyte Avenue on Saturday, August 10, 1944. Termination of tram services on this section permitted the abandonment of the street railway grade crossing with the CPR on Whyte Avenue. Ironically, on the final day of street car operation east on 104 Street, car 70 skidded on wet rails into the side of a moving CPR train occupying the crossing. The impact demolished the front platform. The motorman, realizing that the inevitable was about to happen, jumped back into the passenger compartment to avoid injury, and fortunately, there were no other casualties.[9] Effective Sunday, August 13th 1944, white sign and red-and-white sign cars terminated their trips on the south side at Whyte Avenue and 104 Street. The Low Level Bridge trolley coaches extended their trips west on Whyte Avenue to 104 Street to service the abandoned five-block tram line between that point and 99 Street. Trolley coaches and street cars maintained a five-minute base service from the new south side terminus.[10]

In December of the same year, the Street Railway Department achieved a further reduction in street car route mileage. Red-and-white sign car service from 95 Street and 114 Avenue to 82 Street and 115 Avenue was withdrawn except during peak hours with the idea of placing the trolley coach line into Cromdale along 115 Avenue into revenue service. Consequently red-and-white sign trams travelled northbound on 101 Street and southbound on 97 Street. Blue sign trams provided service in the opposite direction on each respective street. This alteration lasted about four days[11] after which time the red-and-white sign cars took up their regular daily service again on 114 Avenue using 101 Street in both directions and allowing the blue sign cars to return to 97 Street for their trips in both directions.[12]

Increasing demand for passenger service forced the Department to consider ways to better utilize the trams. First of all, City Council passed a bylaw in October 1943 to abolish the practice of allowing passengers to smoke in the rear of the streetcars.[13] About the same time the Street Railway Department introduced women as conductors on the rear platform of some of the cars, particularly during the rush hours. They collected tickets and let passengers on and off the cars in a manner very similar

to that employed during the two-man car operation days some 25 years earlier. Rear doors were altered to allow easier opening and closing, and railings to guide passengers were installed.[14] The "conductorettes" started work during the first week of October 1943, and helped to speed the loading and unloading of passengers, allowing cars to cover the route in a shorter period of time.[15] The practice continued for the duration of the wartime period, being expanded as necessary. As late as November 1945, two-man cars, employing ex-servicemen as conductors, were utilized on the blue-and-white sign routes.[16] The railway also hired men and women to turn the track switches to the appropriate direction for approaching cars, there being no electrically-activated automatic switches on the system.

The first major street car route abandonment occurred on Sunday, July 22nd 1945. Highlands white sign cars operated for the last time on the previous day. With the abandonment of the Highlands route, Calder red-and-green sign cars operated on a twelve-minute base schedule to 104 Street and 82 Avenue on the south side again via the High Level Bridge. This left Rossdale to be served with a stub car from 109 Street and 97 Avenue.[17] Rossdale residents were not happy with the stub car service[18] and by early October 1945 the car line down 97 Avenue into Rossdale was abandoned in favour of motor bus service.[19]

Very gradually and almost unobtrusively the street car lines in Edmonton were disappearing. It had

Above, left:

Car 31, an afternoon peak-hour extra on the red-and-white sign route, approaches the stop on Jasper Avenue at 109 Street on June 5th 1946. Here a female switch-tender has lined the switch, thus enabling the motorman of car 31 to make the turn onto 109 Street without wasting precious moments stopping to turn the switch himself. (F.M. Palmer)

Above, right:

Charlie Wentworth, storekeeper at Cromdale in this 1943 photograph, began working on the Edmonton Radial Railway in the early years. He was the conductor on car 23 in its 1913 accident at the GTP crossing on Alberta (118) Avenue. Mr. Wentworth was active in the Street Railwaymen's Union and was also involved in decorating streetcars for special events.
(Eric M. Smith)

started in 1932 with the abandonment of the 102 Avenue line to 142 Street. The 95 Street and Low Level Bridge, Scona Hill lines followed in 1939. The Bonnie Doon service ceased in 1940, Whyte Avenue from 104 Street to 99 Street succumbed in 1944, while the long run out to the Highlands closed in 1945 and the Rossdale stub later that same year. By that time the war was over, but people still depended upon the Edmonton Street Railway for local transportation within the city. As the car lines were taken up more trolley and motor buses appeared on the streets, but the number of trams on the roster remained constant.

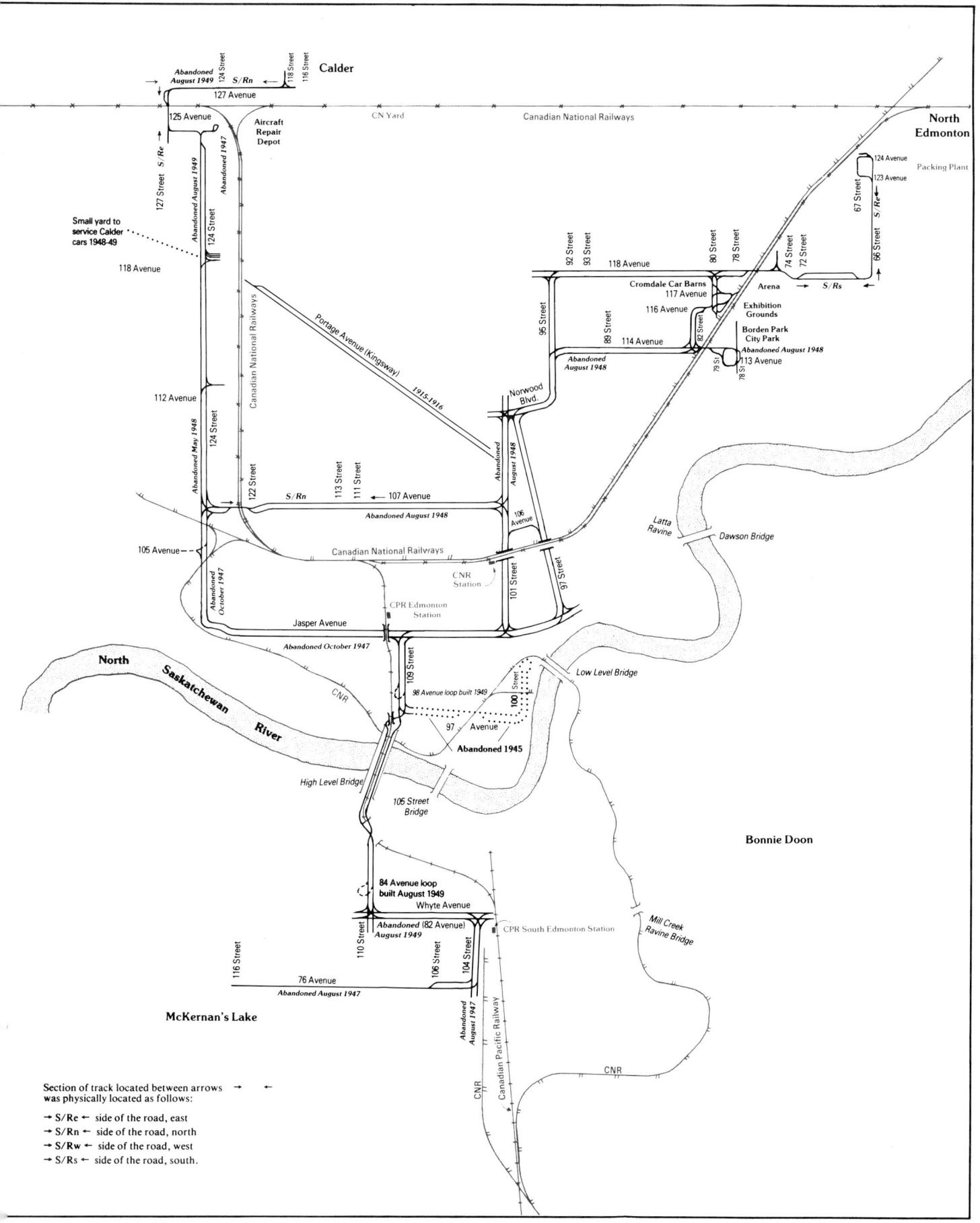

Edmonton Transit System
Track Map
1950

117

Inevitably, accidents occurred on the busy system. Rear end collisions, upsets, a derailment resulting in a side swipe and crossing accidents with trains, kept Cromdale shopmen constantly busy with car body work. Throughout the 1940s Edmonton Street Railway cars always appeared well-kept. One morning in March 1943 car 28 suffered severe damage as fire caused by overheating of the coal stove in the forward end of the car, gutted its interior and most of the forward part of the car body above the window sills. Meanwhile, Car 16 had been stored for some years in the yards out of service. An examination disclosed that this car could be made serviceable more readily than could car 28, so it went through a complete refit, emerging with both end platforms completely rebuilt, with the original wide Preston letterboard all the way around, replacing the narrower Ottawa style letterboard installed during its 1916 refit. The Edmonton Street Railway still maintained 74 serviceable cars on the system.

The need for more trams to serve the shrinking mileage continued on into 1946. For about three years, the partially-burned shell of car 28 reposed in Cromdale yard. Finally the shell was pushed into the shop and the Cromdale coach builders began a rebuilding job. In 1946 a new car 28 rolled out the shop looking strikingly similar to the big Prestons on the system, its railroad-style roof replaced by an arched roof and its upper semi-elliptical window sash replaced with standard square cut window sash. Its passengers, however, had the dubious honour of sitting on the uncomfortable wood slat seats removed from the observation car body.

As the trolley car mileage shrank and bus services increased the name Edmonton Street Railway became a misnomer. The system did have 75 serviceable street cars in 1946 but it also possessed 30 trolley coaches and 28 motor buses at that time. On July 16, 1946 the system became officially known as the Edmonton Transportation System.[20] A scant few months later, on April 29th 1947, it became known as the Edmonton Transit System.[21] In keeping with the name change, street car trackage was further reduced when the storied McKernan's Lake "toonerville trolley" made its last run on Saturday night, August 9th 1947.[22]

For almost 35 years the McKernan's Lake tram dipped, dived and rolled over the marginal skeleton track laid down along a muddy 76 Avenue to the 116 Street terminus. In the early days the cars

Above, left:

The victim of an untended, overheated stove in 1943, car 28 reposed for three years in this condition at the back of Cromdale shop. (Railway Negative Exchange, C.K. Hatcher)

Above, right:

When car 28 was rebuilt in 1946 after being destroyed by fire, its seats were replaced by the wooden seats from the observation car. (Eric M. Smith)

Below:

Car 28 returned to service again on April 1st 1946. Here the newly-refurbished car travels south on 124 Street at 118 Avenue, as an extra on the red-and-green sign route. (Les Corness)

Heavy traffic to Calder and the Aircraft Repair Depot called for double-tracking of the Edmonton Transit line on 124 Street between 118 Avenue and 125 Avenue in 1946. Here, line car No. S-5 is being used to instal the overhead on this newly-relocated section of the system. (Les Corness)

provided through service to downtown Edmonton and turned on a loop at the Lake. Once the Lake had been drained, the loop was taken up and a double-ended stub car provided service along the line from 104 Street and 82 Avenue. Over the years cars 1, 3, 10 and 20 acted as the "Toonerville Trolley". During the 1920s, experiments in scheduling were carried out to have the single tram on the line give the best frequency of service to the most people, sparsely scattered and thinly straddling the route. The small thriving community of Allendale had perpetuated a 1921 schedule which called for a trip to the end of the line from 104 Street and 82 Avenue on the hour and twenty-four minutes past the hour. The third trip at forty-eight minutes past the hour went only as far as 109 Street and 76 Avenue.[23] The track must have been in good shape for one car to maintain that schedule. It is highly unlikely that the storied Scottish tram operator, Bob Chambers, who reportedly used to recite the poetry of Robert Burns, had much opportunity to sit at the end of the line and memorize the works of his favorite poet during that period of time. Most of the time the schedule called for a more leisurely trip over the full length of the line every half hour.

The McKernan's Lake line had become as much an Edmonton legend as the High Level Bridge. Motormen often ran errands for folk along the line — picking up odds and ends of groceries such as a loaf of bread, a pound of butter or a quart of milk and dropping them off to a housewife waiting at lineside on the next trip past. Folk often asked the motorman to deliver items to a friend further down the line.[24] Pranksters abounded along the way too. A lamp pole with a cluster of five light bulbs marked the end of track. Neighbourhood youngsters were known to shoot out the bulbs, leaving the end of the line in complete darkness. Motormen, groping their car through the darkness without the aid of street lamps or a terminal light and depending entirely on the somewhat dull yellow glow of the tram's head lamp, periodically overshot their mark and ran the car right off the end of the line.[25] The "toonerville trolley" to McKernan's Lake was indeed a real community affair.

Superintendent Ferrier estimated that the Lake route had accumulated an operating deficit of some $350,000 over its total operating history. It could not be taken off, as some form of public transportation service had to be provided through the terms of the Strathcona-Edmonton Amalgamation agreement.[26] After Saturday night, August 9th 1947 the tram at Whyte Avenue and 104 Street no longer waited to pick up its handful of passengers every half hour, as the new Edmonton Transit System had two brand-new buses, one operating from 82 Avenue and 109 Street to 76 Avenue and 116 Street and another from 84 Avenue and 104 Street serving that end of 76 Avenue.[27]

Another street car line abandonment occurred on October 5th 1947 when tram service on Jasper Avenue west of 109 Street to 124 Street and north to 107 Avenue ended. Blue sign cars from North Edmonton travelled south on 101 Street then turned east on Jasper and north again on 97 Street. Blue-and-white sign cars from 118 Avenue and 80 Street looped through downtown Edmonton southbound on 97 Street and northbound on 101 Street. Red-and-white sign cars from 114 Avenue and 82 Street travelled both ways on 97 Street to and from their south side terminals.[28]

Lower photo:

The Calder car line has been isolated from the rest of the system in this July 8th 1949 scene. Car 45 acts as a waiting room for passengers transferring between buses and trams. Car 35 has just completed a southbound trip from Calder to the terminus on 124 Street at 118 Avenue. It is about to back into the wye which crosses in front of car 45 and leads into the small yard at the right. *(Foster M. Palmer)*

Upper photo:

Car 45 southbound on 127 Street turns into 125 Avenue on its trip from Calder to 118 Avenue and 124 Street. At this time the line has been isolated from the balance of the system and paving work on 127 Street indicates the end is near for the Calder streetcars. It is the summer of 1949. The stub track in the foreground accommodates the library car on its regular visit to the Sherbrooke area of Edmonton. Prior to 1943, Calder cars continued south from this point to 118 Avenue before turning east. *(N.F. Corness)*

As tram service gradually gave way to motor and trolley coach services, ridership began to decline. The automobile had more appeal as a means of getting around a growing city than the spanking new trolley coaches. As monthly operating deficits appeared in 1947, fare increase proposals became more common. On September 1st 1947, the 5 tickets for 25¢ fare introduced in 1935 was superseded by the pre-1935, 4 tickets for 25¢ structure.[29] Riders could purchase 17 tickets for $1.00. For the first time in many years, the closure of tram lines left a surplus of street cars on the roster. Eight cars were declared surplus in September 1947[30] leaving 68 units to provide service to a greatly-reduced rail network. Once armatures, gears and electrical wiring had been removed, the car bodies were sold off to local farmers, who found a variety of uses for them. During this period the long-familiar line of overhead support poles along the centre of Jasper Avenue disappeared, so that trolley coach overhead could be located independently of the street car overhead, allowing the coaches to stop at the curb rather than in the centre of the Avenue on the street car right-of-way.

The rail system experienced little or no change over the winter of 1947-48, but paving operations on 124 Street began early in the spring of 1948. While this work proceeded, the Edmonton Transit System cleared an area at the north-east corner of 118 Avenue and 124 Street and laid out a small temporary four-track street car yard with a turning wye. Seven street cars (17, 35, 36, 38, 40, 41, 45, the single truck sweeper and the library car) were assigned to this yard and placed there before final paving work began on 124 Street between 118 Avenue and 107 Avenue. Then on May 2nd

Upper photo:

Three passenger cars and a sweeper occupy the storage tracks on 124 Street just north of 118 Avenue. The terminal was constructed in 1948 to accommodate cars assigned to the Calder service when this section of the line was isolated from the rest of the system. (Foster M. Palmer)

Lower photo:

Another view of the storage yard for Calder cars. Note the Library Car at the end of the wye track. (N.F. Corness)

1948, red-and-green sign cars short-turned back downtown and to the south side on the wye at 107 Avenue and 124 Street.[31] Buses provided a transfer service from this point to 118 Avenue and 124 Street where Calder-bound passengers caught the street car for the balance of the trip. The Calder car line had become completely isolated from the remaining street car system. There being no paved roads in the area, the library car continued to serve the Sherbrooke neighbourhood from a short spur on 127 Street just south of 125 Avenue, and the

Photo above:

Streetcar No. 43 at 82 Avenue and 104 Street on July 8th, 1949, a few months before abandonment of the Whyte Avenue line. Note the switchman at the rear. Tram service ended on August 21st and the trolley coaches started operating at the end of the month. (Foster M. Palmer)

Photo below:

Car 1 is on the blue-and-white sign route on July 7th 1949. The car appears to be in fine shape, in spite of its 41 years of service, as it travels east on Jasper Avenue between 100 Street and 99 Street. (Foster M. Palmer)

Streetcars of the Edmonton Street Railway Department line up on the tracks west of the shop building at Cromdale as their day's work is completed. Photo taken summer of 1944: trolley coach shops were built on this site, c1946.   (Bob Walker)

Calder area from the end of the north leg of the turning wye on 118 Street. Calder residents enjoyed twelve-minute service, and a ten-minute rush hour service. While the Calder stub was in service, one of the cars, either 38 or 45, proivided a comfortable shelter with heat, light and plenty of seating space for passengers transferring to and from the Calder cars. One of these two cars was always spotted at the southernmost extremity of the line adjacent to the trolley bus turning loop.

All car service to the west end, except for the Calder stub, ceased in midsummer of 1948. At that time paving work on 107 Avenue had reached the point where car tracks had to be removed from the street. Effective Sunday, August 8th 1948 red-and-green sign cars terminated operations on 101 Street and 107 Avenue. From the south side they proceeded across the High Level Bridge to Jasper Avenue, then east to 97 Street where they wyed for the return trip to Whyte Avenue.[32] The extra street cars operating from 114 Avenue to the south side began using 97 Street instead of 101 Street at this time.[33] For the remainder of the month of August 1948, five street car routes served Edmonton. In addition to the two just noted, the blue and blue-and-white sign cars operated from North Edmonton to downtown, and 80 Street and 118 Avenue to downtown as they had since October 1947, and the Calder stub line was still in service.

Edmontonians soon found themselves with only three street car routes, for in the early morning hours of Sunday, August 29th 1948 street cars made their final trips on 114 Avenue and on 101 Street.[34] Blue sign cars from North Edmonton and blue-and-white sign cars from 80 Street and 118 Avenue operated along 118 Avenue, 95 Street, 111 Avenue, 97 Street, Jasper Avenue, 109 Street across the High Level Bridge to Whyte Avenue and the south side terminal at 104 Street. The Calder cars continued to operate on the self-contained line from 118 Avenue north on 124 Street.

Since much of the track through downtown Edmonton had been rehabilitated extensively and the ties across the High Level Bridge had been replaced and the rails relaid about a year earlier, street cars offered a smooth fast ride through the city. The Calder stub line, comprising all open or skeleton track, didn't offer any opportunity for motormen to break any speed records. However, it certainly offered smoother, more reliable service than could be provided by any other means of transportation over the unpaved roads. In order to offer maximum transit services to the Government center, the Edmonton Transit System constructed a short turn loop at 98 Avenue west off 109 Street.

Street car services remained stable in Edmonton for almost a year. In spite of steadily increasing ridership over the whole system deficits were creeping in. City Council voted 6-5 in favour of a raise in fares to stave off the deficit, and so the Transit System introduced a new fare schedule on February 22nd 1949, the second one in an eighteen-month period. Riders paid 10 cents cash or had the option to purchase tickets at the rate of 3 for 25¢ or 14 for $1.00. Passengers using the owl service after midnight paid a premium fare of 15 cents cash or two tickets. Children's tickets remained at 10 tickets for 25 cents.[35] During the first seven months of 1949, ridership began to fall slightly behind figures for the comparable period in a previous year[36] for the first time since 1934. Apparently the High Level tram line also experienced a significant drop in ridership over the first seven months of 1949.[37]

Early Sunday morning, August 21st 1949 the last tram operated on Whyte Avenue removing street car service completely from a major thoroughfare which had seen trams for almost 41 years. The blue and blue-and-white sign cars travelled only as far as a new loop constructed at 84 Avenue just off 109 Street. Blue and blue-and-white sign cars offered a six-minute off-peak service and a four-minute service on Saturdays between the south side and 80 Street and 118 Avenue. Blue sign cars continued on to North Edmonton providing a twelve-minute service over that portion of the route.[38]

Photo above:

All is ready for the official last run of streetcars in Edmonton on September 1st 1951 at 8:00 p.m. Car 1 stands on the north approach track at Cromdale, ready to be dispatched for its final trip. (Edmonton Parks and Recreation Archives)

Below:

Early in the morning of September 2nd 1951, Motorman George Evans poses beside car 52 at the south side loop off 109 Street at 84 Avenue. He prepares to take the last streetcar in regular service from the loop to Cromdale car barns.

(N.F. Corness)

Mileage and Passenger Statistics

Year	Total Mileage Operated (millions)	Route Mileage Rail	Route Mileage Trolley	Route Mileage Motor Bus	Total Passengers Carried (millions)	Edmonton's Population (thousands)
1908	0.03	12.0	0	0	0.13	
1909	0.30	12.0	0	0	2.2	27.0
1910	0.56	19.5	0	0	3.7	31.1
1911	0.64	19.4	0	0	4.7	
1912	0.95	28.0	0	0	8.4	
1913	1.7	30.7	0	0	13.8	
1914	2.0	52.6	0	0	15.3	
1915	2.0	53.9	0	0	11.9	59.4
1916	2.1	53.9	0	0	10.9	
1917	1.9	53.9	0	0	10.1	
1918	1.8	54.1	0	0	10.2	
1919	2.1	54.1	0	0	11.8	
1920	2.0	56.2	0	0	12.4	61.0
1921	2.1	56.2	0	0	12.8	
1922	2.3	56.2	0	0	12.9	
1923	2.3	56.2	0	0	12.3	
1924	2.4	56.2	0	0	12.3	
1925	2.4	56.0	0	0	12.6	63.4
1926	2.4	56.0	0	0	12.4	
1927	2.4	56.0	0	0	12.9	
1928	2.4	56.0	0	0	13.3	
1929	2.5	56.0	0	0	14.1	
1930	2.5	56.0	0	0	13.7	77.6
1931	2.4	56.0	0	0	12.2	
1932	2.3	54.0	0	3.7	12.2	
1933	2.4	54.0	0	3.7	11.3	
1934	2.4	54.0	0	3.7	12.1	
1935	2.4	54.0	0	3.7	13.2	82.6
1936	2.5	54.0	0	3.7	13.9	
1937	2.5	54.0	0	3.7	14.0	
1938	2.5	54.0	0	3.7	14.2	
1939	2.6	49.6	4.5+	3.7+	15.2	
1940	2.7	48.0	6.0+	3.7+	16.0	91.7
1941	2.7	48.0	6.0+	3.7+	17.1	
1942	3.0	48.0			21.4	
1943	3.6	48.3			30.7	
1944	3.7	48.4	NO RECORDS		32.1	
1945	3.9	43.4	AVAILABLE		34.0	111.7
1946	4.3	43.4			36.6	
1947	4.9	34.3			36.4	
1948	5.1	20.0			36.9	
1949	5.1	17.0			36.8	
1950	5.3	17.0	37.4	54.4	37.0	148.9
1951	5.3	0	46.9	73.4	36.3	
1952	5.1	0			36.2	
1953	5.1	0			35.9	
1954	5.1	0			35.9	
1955	5.2	0	55.6	99.6	34.7	209.4
1956	5.5				34.5	
1957	5.6				34.1	
1958	5.7				31.6	
1959	5.8				29.1	
1960	5.7	0	60.59	153.8	28.2	269.3
1961	5.7				27.2	
1962	6.2				27.9	
1963	6.6				27.0	
1964	7.0	0	74.0	366.0	28.0	357.6

Calder saw its last street car early Sunday morning, August 28th 1949.[39] Abandonment of this service left the blue and blue-and-white sign cars to offer the only remaining tram service in Edmonton. Cars assigned to the Calder stub operation were stripped of all electrical and mechanical components at the temporary 124 Street and 118 Avenue yard, and the car bodies were offered for sale and removed from that site. Abandonment of this service not only spelled finis to the line popularly referred to as the northernmost street car line in North America, but also to the final existing portions of the old Edmonton Interurban Railway.

Photo above:

At the southern terminus of Edmonton's last remaining tram route. An unidentified car is shown at the turning loop near the Strathcona end of the High Level Bridge, January 19th, 1951. (A. Clegg)

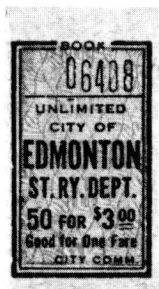  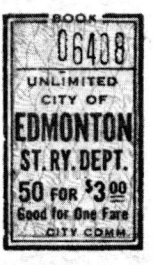

For two more years the street cars operated from North Edmonton to 84 Avenue and 109 Street. Then early on the Sunday morning of September 2nd 1951 car 52 made a final trip from the south side loop across the High Level Bridge through downtown Edmonton to Cromdale shops. Motorman George Evans took that last return trip with a group of interested citizens aboard. A few hours earlier, at 8:00 p.m. on Saturday, September 1st 1951, car 1 carrying a banner on its side reading "1908 OLD FAITHFUL 1951" made a ceremonial last run from 97 Street and Jasper Avenue with a group of special guests aboard including Mayor Parsons and some of the aldermen. William Innis, retired Assistant Chief Inspector of the Edmonton Transit System, took the car on the first part of its last run. On the way to the south side Mayor Parsons; Municipal Affairs Minister C.E. Gerhart; Albert E. Miller, one of the first motormen on the system, and Lieutenant Governor J.J. Bowlen each took a turn at the controls. The Lieutenant-Governor had been a tram operator for the West End Street Railway in Bostom from 1895 to 1900 and observers noted that he had not lost his touch. Superintendent Thomas Ferrier operated the car over the High Level Bridge.[40]

A large crowd greeted the car on its arrival at 84 Avenue and 109 Street. Guests bade farewell to car No. 1 and to street car service in Edmonton, then boarded bus No. 74 to be taken to the official opening ceremonies for the new $500,000 Strathcona bus garage.[41]

How to Rebuild a Streetcar

Photo above:
After retirement and ten years of outside storage, car 1 suffers from extensive weathering and vandalism. The weeds grow high over the rails at Cromdale yard in September 1961. The body of car 29 rests to the right of the photograph while the body of car 61 sits behind car 1. (Eric M. Smith)

Photo left:
Interior restoration work begins on car 1. The duct along the right side of the car carries hot forced air from the Peter Smith coal stove at the front of the car. (Eric M. Smith)

Opposite page, upper:
The trucks have been removed from under the car and car-body restoration begins. (Eric M. Smith)

Opposite page, lower:
Exterior body restoration has been virtually completed by the members of the Canadian Railroad Historical Association (Rocky Mountain Branch) and Edmonton Transit System employees. The car sits on streetcar tracks still in place at Cromdale shop. (Eric M. Smith)

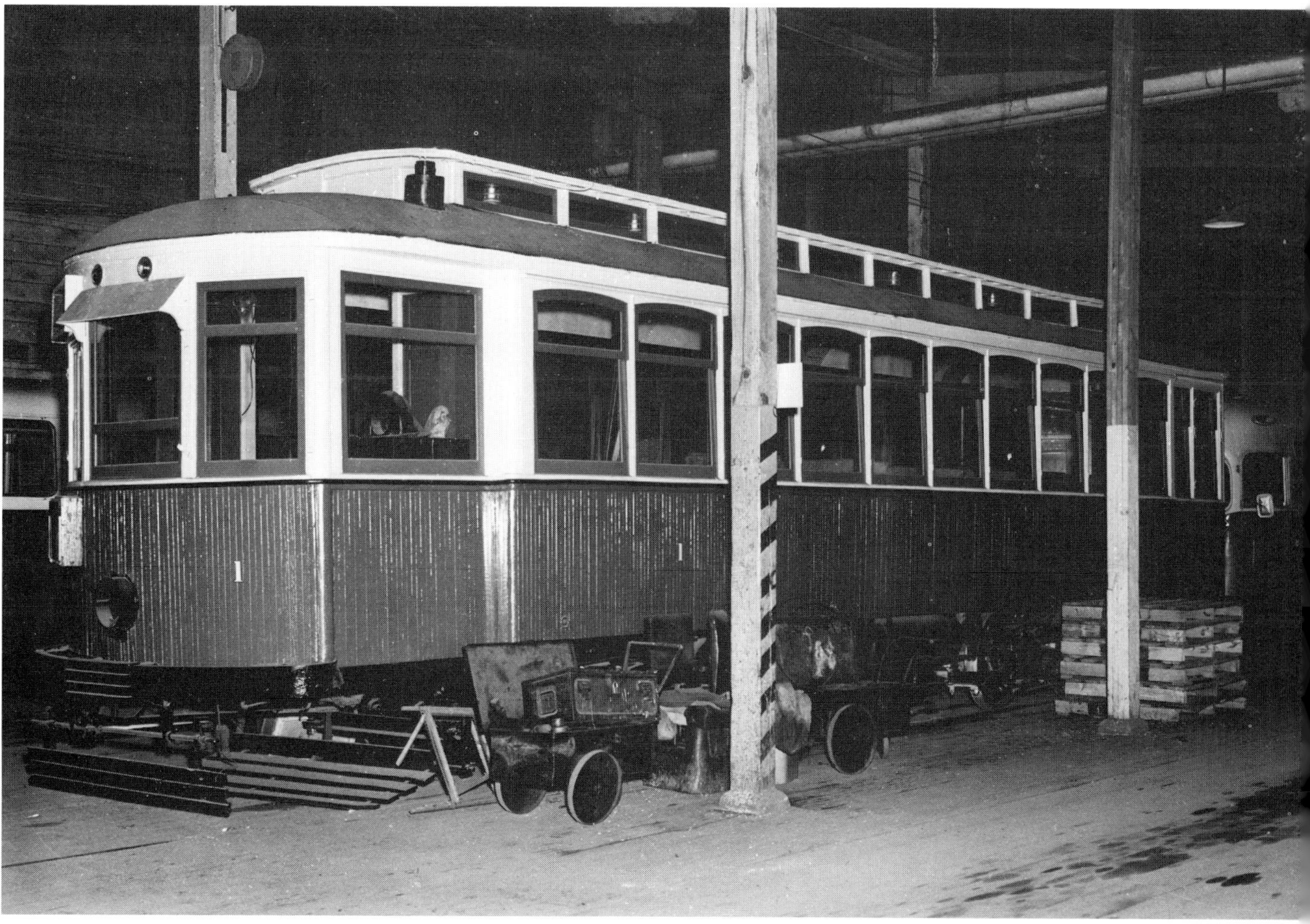

13 Streetcar Epilogue

FOR SOME YEARS after its ceremonial last run on September 1st 1951, street car 1 sat in the Cromdale yard, exposed to the elements in a line up with the five steel cars. By late 1954 all of these cars were indeed in a badly-deteriorated state. Sometime between 1954 and 1959 number 1 became a loner in the back yard at Cromdale.

Eleven years after its last run, car 1 stood on that track suffering from the effects of weather and vandalism. Its body was bleached white from the sun. Its roof had gaping holes, and the torn roof canvass lay draped over the sides in wind blown fragments. All of the window glass had been broken, its seats torn by vandals, and the grass grew long around its trucks. At this time, members of the fledgling Rocky Mountain Branch of the Canadian Railroad Historical Association and some interested Edmonton Transit System employees decided to restore car 1. In 1962, space was allocated inside Cromdale barn for that purpose.

By 1967, restoration of the body had been completed. The car was mounted on a float, without its trucks, and once again passed through downtown Edmonton in the Centennial observance of Edmonton's Klondike Days Parade. After this brief showing, it returned to a dark corner in Cromdale where orders were given that no further work was to be done on the car; a sign was hung on it saying "Held for Archives".

In 1979 Edmonton celebrated the 75th Anniversary of its incorporation as a City. Several events were planned to celebrate the Anniversary during the weekend of October 6th, 7th and 8th 1979.

The 75th Anniversary Committee, supported by Edmonton Transit employees and others interested in the project, began work on restoring street car 1 to operating condition. It was to run back and forth across the High Level Bridge as part of the celebrations.

For some months, volunteers, some of whom had driven street cars in Edmonton, worked to get car 1 operational. As the event drew near, weekly work parties turned into daily sessions, often extending into the early hours of the morning.

A local heavy-equipment dealer, R. Angus (Alberta) Ltd., provided a diesel generator which was mounted on a frame supported by two four-wheeled railway handcars. The diesel generator would supply 600 volts of electrical current to street car 1's electric motors in the absence of overhead wire. Arrangements were concluded with CP Rail to use its track from Jasper Avenue and 109 Street to the south end of the high level bridge. Several branches of the Toronto-Dominion Bank sold the 5,000 5¢ streetcar tickets in a period of some three hours on the first day they went on sale, a few weeks before the event.

Car 1 successfully completed trial runs with its own power plant in tow one evening on the LRT line, It then operated under its own power from Cromdale over CN Rail lines to the CP Rail interchange at 109 Street.

After a twenty-eight year absence from operations on the bridge, car 1 ventured across the High Level Bridge on Saturday morning October 6th 1979 at about 8:30 a.m. For the rest of the three-day weekend, the streetcar crossing the Bridge drew many onlookers and a full load of passengers on each trip.

Currently, the car reposes, fully restored, on its own piece of track inside its old home at Cromdale barn. It is destined eventually for regular museum service at the City's Fort Edmonton Park.

Opposite:

Car 1 crosses the High Level Bridge, looking just as it did in the first half of the century. However, this photograph — which was actually taken on October 8th 1979 — has been carefully retouched to eliminate the power generator that trailed behind the streetcar. (Colin K. Hatcher)

Left:

Car 1 disembarks passengers via the front door at the site of the CP Rail station on Jasper Avenue at 109 Street. Embarking passengers are to use the rear door. It is the weekend of October 6th 1979, when Edmonton is celebrating its 75th anniversary as a city. (Colin K. Hatcher)

Photo above:
Fully restored to operating condition, Car 1 pauses on one of its trips on the CP Rail right-of-way just south of the Jasper Avenue overpass. Date is October 8th 1979.
(Colin K. Hatcher)

Opposite page:
Fall colours frame Car 1 and a fast-growing Edmonton skyline provides a backdrop for a trip to the south side of the High Level Bridge on Monday, October 8th 1979.
(Colin K. Hatcher)

Photo below:
Don Bearham, retired Edmonton Transit operator and president of Edmonton Radial Railway Society since its inception, is at the controls of Car 1 en route over the High Level Bridge in October 1979.
(Colin K. Hatcher)

The temperature was hovering around 25° below zero on January 19th 1951, as one of Edmonton's steel, 80-class trams was photographed leaving the south end of the High Level Bridge. (A. Clegg)

Photo below:

Edmonton Transit Brill trolley coach 130 heads north across 105 Street Bridge. (Colin K. Hatcher)

Photo above:

Edmonton Transit System car 64 is shown travelling eastbound on 118 Avenue near 66 Street, North Edmonton, January 18th 1951. (A. Clegg)

Photo below:

Edmonton Transit Flyer trolley coach 241 is turning at 111 Street and 54 Avenue. The trip on Route 9 is taking place on Saturday, October 9th 1976. (Colin K. Hatcher)

Below, left:

Edmonton Transit LRT line looking south from 92 Street on Saturday April 30th 1977. Handcars are loaded with ribbon rail for the tunnel section. *(Colin K. Hatcher)*

Below, right:

Edmonton Transit Central Station. Note tube tunnel looking toward Churchill Station on September 1st 1977. The bare concrete floor is ready to receive a rubber mat and crushed rock ballast before track is laid. *(Colin K. Hatcher)*

Photo above:

A panoramic view of the construction of Edmonton's LRT underground transit line. The photograph, looking eastward from the 24th floor of the CN Tower, shows the backfill covering the cut and cover tunnel extending from the lower right-hand corner. In the centre, with CN tracks on both sides, is the LRT line's exit ramp from tunnel to surface. Transit and CN trains then share the same right-of-way to the edge of the photograph at the top left. *(A. Clegg)*

14 | Return to the Rails

*E*DMONTON GREW very rapidly in the decade following the abandonment of its streetcar system. Its 1951 population of 159,631 increased to 289,027 by 1961.[1] The communities of Jasper Place, immediately west of the city boundary, and Beverly, immediately east of the city limits, grew considerably as well, and the combined population of these communities brought the 1961 Edmonton area population up to 337,568.[2] The population increase naturally brought with it a need for improved transportation.

By 1961, passenger ridership on the Edmonton Transit System had fallen off. Residents, no different from those in other communities, favoured their private automobiles and it became difficult for the bus system to attract more patrons. Moreover, the buses became involved in the same rush hour tangles as those which plagued the automobiles. City Council began to look at a number of transportation alternatives for Edmonton area residents. Extensive expansion of the roadway system alone would be very costly; financially, socially and, in the case of the river valley, ecologically. Rail public transportation, designed to attract riders and relieve congestion on an expanded roadway system, offered a second option. Edmonton was not alone among North American cities with its growing traffic congestion problems. Most other cities sought solutions to the same problem.

Only a very few North American cities had, however, retained and modernized their streetcar systems. In those cities, automobiles were prohibited from impeding the centre of the road streetcar rights-of-way, allowing fast efficient operation of the streetcars. Toronto retained its streetcars and initiated the operation of a four-mile subway system in 1954; both became an integral part of Toronto's public transportation network. During the same period, many European cities had developed a network of efficient light rail operations which utilized tunnels, private rights-of-way and street running, and combinations of all three. Montreal had abandoned its street car operations in 1959, only to embark on subway construction in the early 1960s. Edmonton began to plan for future transportation solutions with some of these ideas in mind.

In December 1962 the City of Edmonton commissioned Canadian Bechtel Limited to develop a plan for a rapid transit system for Edmonton as it would exist about 1980 and beyond. The objective of the Bechtel study was "to define a concept of a rapid transit type facility to which a high percentage of peak period travellers will be attracted and to insure the continued orderly growth of Edmonton about a strong central core".[4] The resulting report noted that "the system described herein is a modern, efficient, and compact high-performance electrified railway, operating on an exclusive grade separated right of way. Quick, convenient service is provided over six branches which converge and pass through the heart of the Central Business District (CBD) in a twin tube subway."[5] The Bechtel report created considerable interest among Edmonton Transit System officials but the only immediate result of the study was further extensive research into the possible acquisition of, and/or sharing of railway rights-of-way in the city.

In the meantime Edmonton Transit System did embark upon an extensive program to encourage better patronage of the existing bus system. Rush hour express bus routes were introduced. More buses were purchased and headways on the main lines were increased. The timed transfer concept, introduced with the opening of the Jasper Place transit centre, where collector routes fed into a main line route, spread out to other parts of the system. Bus-only traffic lanes went into service. The monthly bus pass was introduced with a small discount over the regular fare to encourage more people to take the bus to and from work. Services into the University area from all parts of the city were vastly improved. An effort was also made to offer direct service between major community areas such as shopping centres, so that for the first time Edmontonians could travel from certain suburban areas of the city to another without having to travel first into the downtown area. These measures were successful in bringing riders back to the buses, establishing Edmonton Transit among the highest per capita ridership transit systems in Canada.

Roadways continued to become crowded as the population grew, in spite of extensive road expansion and increased transit riding. In 1970 The City of Edmonton introduced its "Edmonton General Plan". The transportation section of this plan called for an extensive roadway expansion with minor emphasis on rapid transit. The Northwest-Northeast Rapid Transit Feasibility Study and the University Line Rapid Transit Feasibility Study, both by Deleuw Cather, followed in November 1970 and January 1971 respectively. A University of Alberta Practicum introduced an extensively-researched proposal in 1972, encouraging the use of a European-style light rail transit mode. In the Edmonton model it encouraged combined use of private rights-of-way and tunnelling proposed in the earlier Bechtel report, with the addition of considerable street running. The University Practicum

(Paul McGee)

encouraged planners to place transit centres with a full range of business, cultural, social and transportation services at the core of new communities. From this centre, fast, quiet, efficient, non-polluting transportation via light rail transit would be available into the downtown area.[6]

After considerable debate, approval for the construction of the Northeast Rapid Transit Line came from City Council in 1973. D.L. MacDonald, Superintendent of the Edmonton Transit System, became the project co-ordinator. He had been assistant to Thomas Ferrier when streetcars terminated in 1951. Thus, as public transportation in Edmonton turned full cycle, after having phased out streetcar operation in the city, he found himself in the unique position of re-introducing the rail mode of public transportation to Edmonton nearly a quarter of a century later.

On September 30th 1974 construction of the new 7.2 km (4.5 mile) system actually began at 95 Street near 106 Avenue, very close to the yard where Edmonton's first streetcars were delivered to the Edmonton Radial Railway. At this point work began on tunnelling in a southwesterly direction toward the city centre. Northeast of this point the new system would utilize the unused portion of the Canadian National right-of-way for most of the distance to the northeast terminal at Belvedere. The total project budget was $65 million.

The 1.6 km (1 mile) subway section utilized two construction methods common to subway building. The two underground stations, Central Station under Jasper Avenue between 101 Street and 100 Street and Churchill station under 99 Street between 103 Avenue and 102 Avenue were both cut-and-cover projects. This necessitated Jasper Avenue, Edmonton's main thoroughfare, being closed to automobile traffic for some four months in the summer of 1975. Many merchants along Jasper Avenue in the vicinity of the closed-off area between 100 Street and 102 Street formed the Downtown Area Rapid Transit committee (DART). This group sponsored special sidewalk events and special sales promotions intended to attract shoppers into the downtown area, particularly on Saturdays, while the construction progressed. Even though automobile traffic was taken off this section of Jasper Avenue and, for a time, buses also had to be rerouted, it was still business as usual for the merchants as the sidewalks never did close. The construction project also attracted the usual share of sidewalk superintendents. Many marvelled at the fact that the streetcar tracks which had been buried in the pavement appeared again and had to be removed to prepare the way for the new set of rails to go into service eventually under Jasper Avenue and 101 Street.

Once work on the mezzanine level at Central station had been sufficiently advanced to allow further excavation to continue under cover, the project was covered over and road traffic restored. Further work, on the mezzanine and track levels, continued after Jasper Avenue was opened to traffic again and the spoil removed via ramps which led into side streets. With the restoration of traffic to Jasper Avenue, work began on the Churchill station under 99 Street. Some traffic disruption occurred at that point, but it was not as critical since 99 Street was not a major traffic artery.

The second subway construction method was carried out by Edmonton Water and Sanitation Department's sewer construction section. The sewer department had considerable experience tunnelling huge trunk sewers, so its crews mined out the twin tube tunnels between Central and Churchill stations, with a huge mechanical mole. These twin tunnels, one 230 metres and the other 220 metres long (about 750 feet and 715 feet respectively) take the track from an east-west direction to a north-south direction.

Upon leaving Churchill Station the tunnel curves again to a northeasterly direction. At the approach to this curve provision has been made for future extension of the system into northwest Edmonton. Most of the tunnel work northeast of Churchill was cut-and-cover.

The tracks are laid in two fashions in the tunnel. At the stations a thick rubber mat was laid on the concrete floor to reduce noise levels. Ballast was spread over the mat. The rail itself is set on standard wooden railway ties. This same method has been used to lay the track at the end of the twin tube section near Churchill Station, where a double crossover is located, and continues through Churchill Station for some distance into the tunnel northeast. In the twin tunnel section and at the northeast end of the tunnel where the tunnel rises to ground level, the rails are fixed directly to the concrete floor. Rails in the tunnel are fastened down with Pandrol clips while standard railway spikes are used to hold rails to ties on the surface section.

The balance of the system is on a 5.6 km (3.5 mile) surface private right-of-way. All the surface track is laid on wooden ties in ballast using 50 kg/metre (110 lb./yard) continuous rail. On the north side

of the LRT is the CN line to North Battleford and on the south side is the CN line to Wainwright. The North Battleford track is largely a service track for the industries in the area, while the Wainwright track handles the daily transcontinental and local Drumheller passenger train service to and from downtown Edmonton. At the 66 Street crossing the line begins to drop below grade to cross under the CN main line into Calder freight yards and returns to grade again before crossing 129 Avenue and entering the northern terminal, Belvedere station.

Immediately after emerging from the tunnel the LRT crosses the first of nine level crossings. Automobile traffic signals in the vicinity of these level crossings are computer-controlled to prevent traffic back ups due to the frequent passage of the LRT trains.

The surface stations, like the underground stations, have centre high level loading platforms. The first surface station called Stadium is adjacent to the 42,000-seat Commonwealth Stadium immediately south of the 112 Avenue level crossing. It is a simply-designed structure with a transparent plexiglass arched roof extending the length of the platform. The tracks are covered by a flat roof and the sides of the structure are transparent. The next station in succession heading northeast is Coliseum. It serves the coliseum, Northlands Park horse racing track and the exhibition grounds, and utilizes the overpass at 118 Avenue. Its design is similar to Stadium station except that the roof over the tracks is arched. A transparent plexiglass roof over the platforms is also arched. These two surface stations and the two underground stations feature escalators and elevators to accommodate handicapped travellers. The last station on the line is at Belvedere immediately north of 129 Avenue. It is a simple open platform with the track along the west side only. All three of the surface stations have feeder bus service transfer facilities immediately adjacent to them. Surface exits and entrances at the two subway stations enable passengers to transfer to or from buses to all parts of the city.

The fourteen Light Rail Vehicle RTE 1 cars came from DuWag of Dusseldorf, Germany. Electrical components were built and installed by Siemens AG, Germany and Siemens Canada Ltd. Final assembly of the cars and installation of the electrical equipment was completed at the former trolley coach servicing building at Cromdale which is immediately adjacent to the old streetcar shop. The car body is a lightweight welded steel design. Cable and air ducts, equipment boxes, longitudinal, articulation and end members are welded together in a solid body underframe. Roof and side wall frames, fabricated of rolled and bent profiles and welded together with the side wall sheet and the body underframe, provide a self supporting tube, offering maximum safety to the passengers. The car ends are made of reinforced fibreglass, fitted tightly to the car body end rib. Fibreglass is used as it is lightweight, has good shaping qualities, is corrosion-resistant and can be readily replaced in case of collision damage.[7]

Photo above:

Edmonton Transit LRT 1012 is northbound at 91 Street. This cold New Year's Day 1979 is quickly giving way to evening, and Edmonton's "blue cold" is caught in this dramatic photograph. (Colin K. Hatcher)

Opposite page:

Edmonton Power workers adjust overhead wire installations on the LRT line on the northbound track south of Coliseum Station. A four-wheel handcar similar to those found in the yards of the Edmonton Radial Railway, a Fairmont speeder, a scissors platform and a tool car — all part of the LRT work roster — are illustrated in this March 1978 scene.

137

Upper photo:

The Cal-Trac switcher handles the spool car which carries both sets of wire for the overhead catenary system. The upper support wire is referred to as the messenger wire while the lower wire, from which the car collects power via the pantograph, is called the contact wire. (Paul McGee)

Photo centre, right:

Edmonton Transit LRT car interior. Taken at Cromdale September 1st 1977. (Colin K. Hatcher)

Photo, lower left:

Edmonton Transit LRT Coliseum Station, looking south on Saturday May 20th 1978. Note arched roof over tracks. (Colin K. Hatcher)

1012 is northbound leaving Stadium Station May 13th 1978. Stadium Station features a clear plexiglass arch over the platform and a flat roof over each track. (Colin K. Hatcher)

The cars are all articulated (two bodies on three trucks) and the articulation is built to a European design which has proven itself in long-term city service. Passengers can pass safely from one section of the car to the other through the articulated section. As the cars are double-ended, all seats are arranged compartmentwise; i.e., transverse and facing one another with fixed backs. They are upholstered with a very colourful striped heavy weave cloth. The aisle side of the seats is supported by grab irons fixed to the ceiling. The floor is 16 mm plywood covered with carpet. The cars are heated from underfloor braking and starting resistance grids with air passing over them from intakes through the side skirting. Heated air is controlled by thermostats. During summer the air simply bypasses the resistance grids thereby providing ventilation for the cars. The ventilation system includes a roof fan in each compartment and the system has the capacity to exchange the air about thirty times per hour. In addition the upper sash in each main carbody window can be opened.

The double-panel, double-width folding doors are opened individually by the passenger after the train has come to a full stop. The operator selects from his control panel, the side on which the doors may be individually opened by boarding and disembarking passengers. This system minimizes heat loss from the car in cold weather. Once the doorway is clear the doors close automatically. Photo electric cells and pressure sensitive door edges ensure passenger safety. The train cannot proceed until all doors have been tightly closed. The operator has the option of opening and closing all doors from the control panel when the train is standing.[8]

Each car has three trucks. The two end trucks are each powered by a Siemens self-ventilated, 4-pole compensated series wound traction motor. The motor is longitudinally mounted between the two axles and drives both axles of each powered truck. The operator uses a motor driven controller with double cam switches for series/parallel starting of the traction motors with change over diode in twenty steps including two field weakening steps and for self-excited rheostatic braking in seventeen steps. The self-excited double circuit rheostatic brake with pre-excitation from a 24-volt battery is independent from the 600-volt overhead contact wire voltage.[9] The rheostatic braking will decrease car speed to about 5 kilometres per hour. A mechanical spring brake actuator on each motor truck in turn operates a disc brake on each motored axle bringing the car to a full stop. An electromagnetic brake is mounted on both powered trucks and the centre idler truck.[10] This third braking system is also operative from the 24-volt battery power supply and, like the other two components of the braking system, will operate in the event of overhead line power failure. The electromagnetic brake is used for emergency stopping and can be activated by the operator pulling back on his controller to an extra notch below the "off" position. The electro-magnetic brake is automatically applied when the "dead man" control feature is activated.

A semi-automatic electronic SIMATIC unit in each car controls motoring and braking functions and provides train control for multiple unit running. Other functions of the SIMATIC unit include

Photo above, left:

Edmonton Transit LRT car 1012 control panel.
(Colin K. Hatcher)

Above, right:

Trucks for Edmonton Transit LRT car at Cromdale, September 1st 1977. *(Colin K. Hatcher)*

Photo below:

Edmonton Transit LRT cars 1015, 1016 and 1017 being completed at the ET Cromdale Carbarn in Edmonton on September 16th 1979. *(Colin K. Hatcher)*

jerk limitation, current control, wheel slip and spin protection, zero voltage monitoring, cam-controller position monitoring, braking current monitoring and motor control for positioning drive and power supply.[11] Solenoid-operated and heated sanders deliver sand to the rails in front of each motor truck when conditions warrant.

Each car is double-ended with complete control equipment at each end in an enclosed operator's compartment. The control console houses controls for many of the simple functions one would find on an automobile dashboard such as lighting, windshield wipers, defroster, heater, odometer and the more railway-oriented functions such as pantograph raising and lowering, door opening selector for activating passenger push buttons on the left or right side of the car and the public address system. The control panel also has a number of functions in it related to the computerized train control signal system which is controlled from the transit control centre at Churchill station. It is fully automated and will stop a train very abruptly if any aspect is disregarded by an operator. The transit control centre is in voice contact at all times with operators on the line. A bank of TV screens monitors all the LRT station platforms and passenger access areas. The train operator can communicate to passengers in his cars via a public address system and uses this means to announce all station stops to the riders. The operator can also communicate to people outside the car through roof-mounted speakers. The external speakers are sometimes used to warn persons standing too close to an approaching train at station platforms or to admonish pedestrians at level crossings who fail to heed the crossing gate signals of the "bleep" sound (most associated with the horn of a well-known automobile of German manufacture) which is the LRT cars' only warning signal.

The automatic couplers carry all braking and electrical functions. An electric motor engages or disengages the couplers. A lone operator can control a train of up to five cars in length. Two-car trains are used for regularly scheduled service, but for major special events such as during exhibition time, the Commonwealth Games and football games three-car trains have been used.

Each car can seat 64 passengers and accommodate an additional 161 standing persons for a total carrying capacity of 225 people. Passengers pay their fares or present their transfers at the gate of the station where they board. There are no fare collection facilities on the cars. Passengers may transfer from ET buses to the Edmonton Transit's LRT train and vice versa, as the LRT is an integral part of the total ET network.

In the years following the initial green light from City Council for construction of the system, work progressed in small contracts in an orderly manner. As the last of the subway sections neared completion, surface grading began, followed by the laying of track. Then overhead wire support poles appeared. Edmonton Power, a City of Edmonton-owned utility, outfitted a truck with flanged wheels to begin stringing the catenary, which work was underway by mid-1977. On Monday, April 11th 1977 the first cars arrived in

Photo above:

An Edmonton Power vehicle, fitted for track work, is used to make final adjustments to the overhead line on the southbound track, south of Coliseum Station in March 1978.
(Paul McGee)

the CP Rail's South Edmonton yards, having been delivered by ship to Vancouver a few days before. The scheduled opening date for the system was still one year away, but the car shells had to be finished inside and the electrical equipment had yet to be installed before testing could begin. Car 1001, the unit used for testing in Europe before being shipped to Edmonton, made its debut in Edmonton on Friday, September 30th 1977. The unit was taken from Cromdale and slowly pushed along the right-of-way by a trackmobile and into the almost-completed Central station. That day car 1001 was shown to the DART committee.

Completed overhead catenary began to appear in the area south of Cromdale depot. The afternoon of Monday, October 17th 1977 saw the first test run of an LRT car in Edmonton. Initially, car 1003 with its pantograph raised was pushed back and forth across 115 Avenue by a trackmobile. This movement tested the overhead crossing between the LRT catenary and the trolley coach overhead line. Later the same day car 1003 was operating under its own power. Subsequently, cars regularly operated on that short piece of track between Cromdale depot and 112 Avenue. Very soon after the initial tests were completed, the trolley coach overhead crossing at 115 Avenue was removed and replaced with a simpler-looking, apparently more successful, design. With the regular appearance of cars on the line for testing, interest in the new system heightened.

April 23rd 1978 was slated as opening day for Edmonton's Light Rail Transit. The final countdown began on Monday, April 17th, when the cars officially carried passengers — ET personnel and their families — for the first time. On Tuesday, Wednesday and Thursday, April 18th-20th, between 9 a.m. and 3 p.m. Edmontonians had the first opportunity to "Take a Look at LRT — Ride Free". Large crowds turned out to ride. Many technicalities were ironed out in these "shake down" tests. On Friday, April 21st the cars operated all day without passengers, providing one last opportunity to work out problems before the official opening. All that week, downtown businesses, which had promoted special events and sales during the construction days banded together and were joined by other downtown merchants to offer special "On Track" sales celebrating the opening of the new Light Rail Transit line.

Shortly after 10:00 a.m. on Saturday, April 22nd 1978, Dr. H.M. Horner, Deputy Premier and Minister of Transportation of the Province of Alberta and Edmonton Mayor C.J. Purves, cut the ribbon at Central station platform and the Northeast Light Rail Transit line officially opened. The Province of Alberta had provided funding for the line to the extent of $45 million. The occasion called for an official tour and two three-car train sets carried official guests over the line. The first train to leave

Photo above:

Edmonton Transit LRT car 1004 is northbound at 111 Avenue, on a cold, blustery winter day. The train is leaving Stadium Station on December 9th 1979. (Colin K. Hatcher)

Photo below:

Edmonton Transit's Central Station is a bee-hive of activity on this July 15th 1979 summer day. LRT 1009 is collecting passengers for the outbound trip. (Colin K. Hatcher)

Photo above:

Cars 1005, 1004 and 1003 arrive from Vancouver on flat cars in CP Rail's South Edmonton yard on May 7th 1977. Trucks and electrical equipment arrived in separate containers.
(Colin K. Hatcher)

Below:

Edmonton Transit LRT car 1004 getting finishing touches at Cromdale on September 1st 1977. (Colin K. Hatcher)

Central station with its guests following the official opening ceremony included cars 1003, 1004 and 1012. A second train consisted of cars 1011, 1007 and 1008.

Finally, on Sunday, April 23rd 1978, Edmonton's new LRT was "on track" carrying revenue passengers. Several days passed before operators became accustomed to the extremely sensitive automatic signals which indeed stopped trains very abruptly for exceeding the speed limit or passing a red signal. One of the notices in the cars advises passengers that they are riding high performance vehicles and that standing passengers should hold the handrails tightly at all times. Although many riders experienced high performance starting and stopping characteristics during the initial days of operation, passengers travelling with a seasoned operator experience a very fast, smooth and quiet ride.

The route is designated LRT 101. Service is offered every five minutes during peak hours and every ten minutes through the day. Ten-minute service is offered all day Saturday until 6:15 p.m. when fifteen-minute service is available. Fifteen-minute service is offered all day Sunday and on holidays. During the week, cars begin their runs at 5:22 a.m. and continue until 1:03 a.m. On Saturdays the first car leaves Coliseum northbound at 5:42 a.m. with the last run from Central at 1:03 a.m. Sunday service begins at 5:51 a.m. from Coliseum northbound and the last train for the day leaves Central at 12:03 a.m. In addition to well-timed transfers to and from the buses at all stations, passengers may park their cars free at Stadium and Belvedere stations and ride the LRT into downtown Edmonton.

The line, capable of carrying 5,000 to 6,000 passengers per hour, has far exceeded expectations. Officials originally anticipated handling an average of 12,000 passengers per day but figures approaching 18,000 passengers per average working day have been common. During the 1978 Exhibition and the 1978 Commonwealth Games, the LRT handled crowds of up to 60,000 per day on several occasions and on one record day approached the 64,000 mark.

Opening day of the Commonwealth Games, Thursday, August 3rd 1978 sees Edmonton Transit LRT 1002 ferrying passengers to and from the special event. (Colin K. Hatcher)

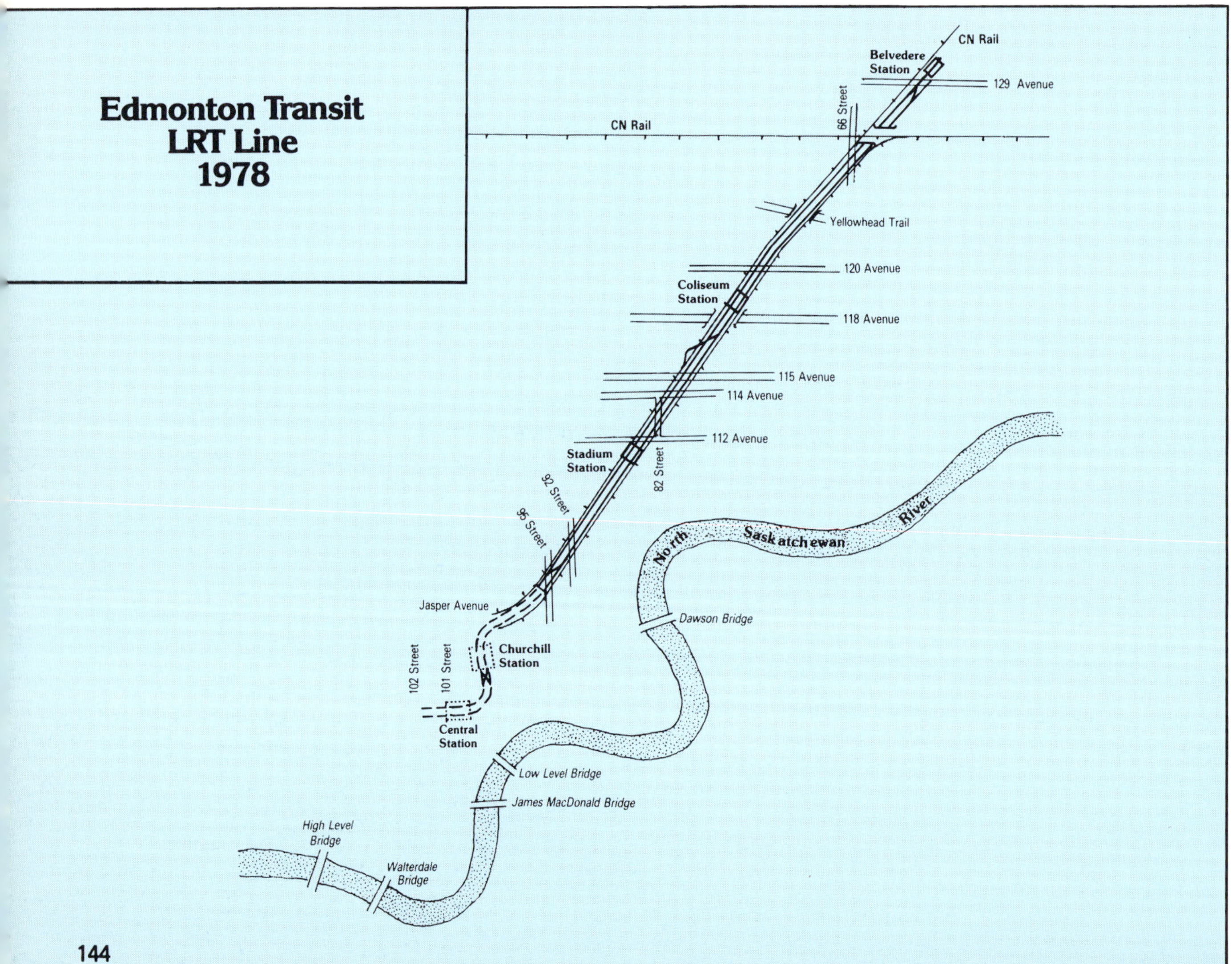

Edmonton Transit LRT Line 1978

The LRT line, as it exists, embodies some of the terms of reference referred to in the 1962 Bechtel study, particularly concerning underground and surface private right-of-way operation. It also echoes the versatile light rail equipment concept encouraged by the 1972 University of Alberta Practicum. Similarities also exist between the new LRT and the old Edmonton Radial Railway. First, it is serving a heavily-populated northeast Edmonton as the first streetcar line in Edmonton did. Secondly, an extension into Clareview is being considered and City officials will require private developers to assist financially, a concept which bears some similarities to the McGrath-Holgate proposal respecting the Highlands streetcar line constructed in 1912. To meet the anticipated equipment needs of the 2 km (1.25 mile) extension, Edmonton Transit has already ordered three additional cars identical to those in service, these to be constructed along with an order for somewhat similar cars for Calgary Transit. Finally, studies are under way for a leg of the LRT line to serve the growing transportation needs south of the North Saskatchewan River into the University of Alberta and reaching even further south to the heavily populated Mill Woods area. This extension could restore urban rail transportation to the former street car right-of-way on the upper deck of the High Level bridge.

Urban rail and electric transit in Edmonton has grown with the city and indeed has helped Edmonton to grow. The future for rail and electric transit to continue enhancing Edmonton's growth appears optimistic. Edmonton's transit history has turned full cycle. In doing so it has introduced a proven light rail transit concept to North America.

Edmonton's LRT with Nos. 1006 to 1012 is northbound at Coliseum Station, 118th Avenue, on September 7th 1978. Note crossover track permitting access to yards at right.

(John F. Humiston)

One of the English trolley buses moves smoothly through the curve on Edmonton's first trolley bus route, approaching McDougall Hill.
(McGregor Telephone & Power Construction Co. Ltd. Courtesy B.E. Jacquest)

Below:

Leyland coach No. 106 unloads passengers on Scona Hill at Connors Road during its southbound trip of May 4th 1940.
(Alberta Provincial Archives)

15 The Trolley Bus

THE CLANG OF streetcar bells and the screech of wheels on the rails drifted through the window on a warm summer day in 1938. The sounds were a constant reminder to two men, seated at a table, of decisions that had to be made.

Thomas Ferrier, Edmonton Radial Railway Superintendent, and City Commissioner Robert J. Gibb looked at the material spread out in front of them, material gathered on a recent trip across Canada and the USA to attend a transit convention in Quebec City. The brochures and notes were grouped into three subjects: streetcars, motor buses and the new electric bus or trolley bus. The Edmonton streetcar system was in bad shape and something had to be done. Would they rehabilitate the lines, extend them and replace the ageing fleet with the new PCC car? Were motor buses with their smaller capacity but increased mobility the answer? Or was the hybrid electric bus the best solution? It used the existing technology and investment in electric transit, but didn't rely on costly rails. It had a larger carrying capacity than the motor bus, but a limited mobility to manoeuvre around obstacles. Finally, roadways could be paved more economically if the rails were removed.

But the public liked the trams. There had been a great outcry when the subway under the CNR tracks crossing 97 Street was constructed. Plans had included the removal of the streetcar tracks, but the ERR had been forced to replace them when construction was complete. If it tried to introduce the same kind of rubber-tired vehicles as were running in Montreal and were soon to be operating in Winnipeg, would it get the same opposition even if the new vehicles were smoother and quieter than the streetcars?

Questions went back and forth for hours. The advantages and disadvantages of each vehicle were carefully weighed. A consultants' report the previous April had strongly recommended that the street railway system be replaced by trolley buses on a gradual basis. City Council had tabled that report and asked the Commissioners and the Superintendent to forward their recommendations as a basis for a decision.

After much deliberation, Ferrier and Gibb arrived at a decision. They would recommend to the City Council that an experimental route be strung with double overhead wires to accommodate new trolley buses. This experiment could relieve a troublesome situation on Scona Hill where the track shifted in the unpaved roadway during every rain. It would retire some of the worst downtown track, that on 95 Street, and hopefully provide a fast, quiet and clean service that the public would accept. If all went well, Edmonton would be, by early 1939, the third Canadian city to use the modern trolley bus. Trolley buses had been tried in Toronto in the 1920s using crude vehicles and the experiment was subsequently dropped). This was to be the start of the longest-lived continuous trolley bus service in Canada.

Let us review the steps that led up to this decision. As early as 1930, Edmonton Radial Railway had been receiving literature on trolley buses. Information had been also solicited on motor buses and some companies had even sent demonstrator vehicles. The main drawback of the motor bus however, was its small size, typically 25 to 29 seats capacity. By 1937 the transit situation had become critical, with the tram system limping along. Due to the steep inclines on either side of the North Saskatchewan River, one streetcar crossing was limited to a very circuitous route down the slopes and over the Low Level Bridge. A trolley bus could climb the steep hills more directly and shorten this route considerably. The 1937 report on the Street Railway recommended that for 1938 either trolley or motor buses be used between the (Cromdale) car barns and Whyte Avenue via 95 Street and McDougall Hill. This report favoured trolley buses over the motor buses, but left the decision open.[1] When trolley bus suppliers became aware of this report through the papers they rushed to forward literature favoring their particular products.

At a City Council meeting on February 28th 1938, a motion was passed to retain Wilson & Bunnell, engineering consultants of Toronto, to make a report on the state of the transit system in Edmonton with attendant recommendations.[2] They subsequently accepted this offer and dispatched Norman Wilson to Edmonton to study the situation.

The street railway in the meantime queried Portland, Oregon for information on its trolley bus system, influenced, no doubt by the fact that conditions there were similar to Edmonton's. A trolley bus network in Montreal had started to function, using English-built buses, and its progress was also being carefully followed.

Wilson tendered his report to Council on April 30th 1938. In it he recommended against further street railway extensions; instead, a trolley bus system should be started to "ultimately eliminate streetcar service". The first route he proposed was to extend from Whyte Avenue and 104 Street via 99 Street and McDougall Hill to a downtown loop via 100 Street, 102 Avenue, 102 Street and Jasper Avenue and thence by 95 Street, 111 Avenue and 86 Street to 115 Avenue at 85 Street. Six buses were to service this route. He also drew attention to the possible legal implications involving the Edmonton-Strathcona Amalgamation Agreement, resulting from using vehicles other than trams. However, he noted that the Statutes of Alberta gave the City the right to use other types of vehicles to give the same service to Strathcona without violating the Amalgamation Act. Since Edmonton's weather and terrain conditions were not the same as Montreal's, he suggested that if British-built buses were chosen they should be specially designed for Edmonton's severe weather conditions.[3]

In his report, Wilson referred specifically to British buses although there were several US trolley bus builders active at this time. He felt that the British had more experience building trolley coaches as they were supplying, besides the many networks in the UK, other Empire countries as well. In addition, there were no tariff barriers when importing from within the Empire, whereas US-built buses would be subject to duty and tax. Loyalty to the Mother Country had economic advantages as well as emotional ones.

Following the tendering of this report, Superintendent Ferrier and Commissioner Gibb headed across Canada to the Canadian Transit Convention at Quebec City. This afforded them the opportunity of visiting, along the way, the Winnipeg transit system which was preparing to put trolley buses into operation; Associated Electric Co. of Montreal, agents for the Associated Equipment Co. of England (trolley bus manufacturers); Ohio Brass Co., Niagara Falls (makers of overhead); Wilson & Bunnell; and the Montreal Tramways' trolley bus operation. They also toured trolley bus installations in Milwaukee and Duluth as well as the Pullman and Ford bus manufacturing plants, and the General Electric Company's trolley motor manufacturing facility in Chicago.

As a result of their observations during this trip, Commissioner Gibb submitted their report on June 20th recommending the installation of a trolley bus line. Some cost figures presented showed the anticipated economies of this conversion:

Cost to convert to 40-passenger trolley buses:
6 buses and spare parts	$120,000
overhead	70,636
paving	73,190
	$263,826

Cost to convert to 25-passenger motor buses:
9 buses and spare parts	$ 90,000
paving	73,190
garage	27,000
	$190,190

However, operating 40-seat trolley buses amounted to 12,000 vehicle miles per day, whereas running the 25-seat motor buses would mean 17,000 vehicle miles per day; at 16¢ a mile operating costs, the city would save $17,000 each year on mileage alone using the trolleys. Moreover, the trolleys would not need a new garage: their motors were immune to cold weather starting problems, and these buses could be stored outside if need be. Gibb and Ferrier had been especially impressed with the smooth ride of Montreal's English Electric three-axle buses, and recommended that similar equipment be considered.[4] However, City Council wanted more time to consider this proposal and deferred its decision for the time being.

Early in July, Commissioner Gibb appeared before Council again stating that, judging from answers to enquiries made to other transit companies, electric trolley coaches were definitely past the experimental stage. Finally, on July 13th 1938 the City Council of Edmonton passed the recommendation of the City Commissioners regarding Street Railway Rehabilitation which included the installation and operation of a trolley bus route. Council upheld the consultants' recommendation that British manufacturers should be favoured with the bid.

Tenders were called for six 38- to 44-passenger buses. They were to have the ability to negotiate a gradient of 9.8 percent maximum on a 133-foot radius at 22 mph up the north hill, and 30 mph up the south hill. The buses were to handle a peak load of 80 people and have an average speed of 12 mph with seven stops per mile. An unusual feature specified was equipment to discharge coarse sand by air pressure in front of each driving wheel and, as well, in an emergency, to discharge it behind these wheels. The low speed points were to be controlled by the motorman to facilitate starting on ice. There were three brakes specified: regenerative, emergency and air. Storm sashes were required on the windows to cope with Edmonton's notorious winter cold. This practice has continued right up until the end of the Brill Trolleys. The buses were to have a centre exit for one-man operation as opposed to the British practice of rear exits and two-man operation. The recommendation added that "the attention of British manufacturers is drawn to the fact that the drive is on the opposite side from English practice".

Although Council favoured British manufacturers, this specification was sent to fifteen firms in both the British Isles and the United States. Notable among them were: the English Electric Co. (EEC)*, Sunbeam, Guy, Leyland, Pullman, Ransomme Simms, Canadian Car, General Motors, St. Louis Car and Mack. Two electrical equipment suppliers were also included.[5]

---

*In the early 1930s, the Associated Equipment Co. Ltd. and the English Electric Co. Ltd., foremost manufacturers of gas and electric buses respectively, collaborated in producing a line of trolley buses. AEC manufactured the chassis and components, while the bus bodies were manufactured (usually by a subcontractor) by EEC as was the electrical equipment and motors. AEC and EEC are often referred to by one or the other's name and the names have been wrongly used interchangeably in correspondence. The bus crests carried both companies' names. Reference here to EEC implies the consortium of EEC/AEC.

A Pullman trolley coach is sandwiched between English buses and streetcars on a crowded Jasper Avenue. The view is looking east toward 101 Street, after a parade. The date is November 5th 1945. (Provincial Archives of Alberta)

While the bids were being solicited, details such as battery-powered manoeuvring capability during power interruptions and the advantages of three axles over two were weighed. The Brill Company, at that time one of the foremost builders of trolley buses in the US, replied offering an off-the-shelf bus, feeling probably that it was uneconomical to build only six buses to the special requirements of the Edmonton specification. After the bids had been awarded for steel poles, overhead and fittings, General Motors asked the ERR to reconsider using motor buses. Commissioner Gibb replied that planning for trolley coach operation had advanced to the point where Edmonton was fully committed to that mode.

Twin, Pullman, Brill, GM, St. Louis and Mack all sent in proposals and the UK firms of Ransomme, Karrier, Sunbeam, EEC/AEC and Leyland also submitted bids. Based on these tenders, the Commissioners tabled their report to Council. "The American firms make only two axle buses while British manufacturers turn out both two and three axle jobs. Supt. Ferrier as a result of his visit to United States points and Montreal was of the definite opinion that the three axle job gives better riding quality. . . . In view of their recommendation we finally eliminated all bids except those of the English Electric Company and the Leyland Company. . . . However in view of the fact that both Mr. Ferrier and Mr. Watson have actually examined the English Electric Company's buses in Montreal, your Commissioners agree with them in recommending that the bid . . . for English Electric buses be accepted at a price of $17,053.00 per bus." This price was for an EEC body as there were several body options.[6] On October 11th Council passed the recommendation "That if the Leyland Company can advance delivery date satisfactory to Commissioners and provided the English Electric Company will undertake to put in a stock on consignment to be paid for as the parts are put into the buses — and provided satisfactory arrangements can be made by Commissioner Gibb for a uniform body by both firms — we award a contract for three English Electric and three Leyland buses."[7]

Additional features requested on the EEC buses were resistance heaters, 38-passenger capacity, extra heaters and insulation and Ohio Brass (US) trolley pole retrievers as well as battery-powered manoeuvring and a 115 hp traction motor. The battery-powered manoeuvring capability previously discussed was specified only for the EEC buses and was to be sufficient to be able to get them off the railway tracks on the Low Level Bridge. The Leyland buses were to have 135 hp motors and Ohio Brass harps and shoes. Both buses were to have Park Royal bodies. EEC had quoted on this body option at a higher price, but presumably it accepted the change at the bid price.

Interior notices specified "No Smoking" front and rear, "Watch Your Step" and "Step on Treadle to Open Door" at the centre exit. The upholstery was in a tasteful green matching the paint of the interior panels.[8]

The colour scheme specified was:

> Exterior:
> Roof — Aluminum
> Above Waist — Vitrolite Railway Cream Enamel
> Below Waist — Vitrolite Railway Red Enamel
> Waist 7-8" — Orange with Black beading along both edges
> Between Cream & Aluminum — Black beading
> Sashes — Natural, polished or satin
> Between windows — Cream
>
> Interior:
> Ceiling — Cream Rexine
> Rear — Green Rexine
> Panels — Green Rexine to match the seats
> Stanchions & Mouldings — Blue

The bus numerals on the exterior were to be orange-edged in black and were also to be displayed in bold letters at the interior front. The EEC buses were assigned numbers 101-103, and the Leyland buses numbers 104-106.

There were no side destination boards. Front destination sign names, white on black, were:

> 104 St : 82 Ave.
> 99 St : 82 Ave
> 95 St : 111 Ave
> 115 Ave : 82 St
> Exhibition
> Arena
> Centre Loop
> Car Shops
> Special[9]

Wire was to be strung from 104 Street and 82 Avenue (including a South Side loop via 104 Street, 83 Avenue, 103 Street), via 82 Avenue, 99 Street, Scona Hill, Low Level Bridge, McDougall Hill, 100 Street, and a downtown loop via 100 Street, 102 Avenue, 102 Street and Jasper; thence via Jasper and 95 Street to 115 Avenue and 80 Street, and from there to the barns, as well as a small loop at 95 Street and 111 Avenue. This was a change from the recommended route in that the "jog" at 111 Avenue was eliminated in favour of the 95 Street/115 Avenue routing.[10]

After the contract had been awarded, some consideration was given by Council towards the purchasing of an extra bus, but a decision on this was delayed until service had started when the need for extra buses could be evaluated. If a proposal to extend the passenger-carrying route to 82 Street along the car barns wire was to be put into effect, then more than one additional bus would be required.

Arrangements for procuring and constructing the overhead line concluded early in 1939. The Northern Electric Co. and Canadian General Electric provided the wire; the contract for erecting it went to McGregor Telephone & Power Co. Ltd. In April of that year, Commissioner Gibb somewhat prophetically expressed the hope in a letter, that "Mr. Hitler wouldn't start something before their buses were shipped".[11] In May he told the Edmonton Journal that Britain's rearmament race had caused a delay of at least two months, setting the arrival date back from July or early August to September or October.[12] Finally on June 28th, EEC informed the City that it would ship its three buses on the *S.S. Lochkatrine* bound for Vancouver. Shipping restrictions at the time, however, delayed loading and space on another ship was procured.

On September 4th 1939, a German submarine torpedoed the passenger vessel *RMS Athenia,* Montreal-bound from Great Britain. This action, a scant seven hours after Britain had declared war on Germany, killed six and sent 1,400 persons into lifeboats after the torpedo struck without warning.[13] Edmonton's Leyland buses were supposed to have been loaded on this vessel, but fate intervened and space had been found for two of them on another ship, the *Beaverford,* leaving on August 25th for Eastern Canada. This area of entry was considered a quicker passage, and EEC had also revised its shipping plans, having sent its buses as well as the remaining Leyland bus on September 1st and 3rd to Montreal. Edmonton Radial Railway wasn't the only one grateful for this turn of events. An irate passenger was informed on sailing day that his space on the *Athenia* had already been taken and that he would have to take the next ship. The author's father calmed down when he read the next day of the ship's fate, and he cheerfully accepted the later, but safer, crossing to Canada. Had things worked out differently, Edmonton's first trolley coaches and the writer of this account might not have arrived.

On Tuesday, September 12th, buses 101 and 102 arrived by train in Edmonton. Two more were in Montreal being unloaded and the third pair was expected to dock soon "unless the boat carrying them has been torpedoed" said the Edmonton Journal.[14] The second shipment of buses had the distinction of carrying Edmonton's first trolley bus passengers. Two hoboes named Hughie and Walter had taken a ride in bus 103 from Toronto to Edmonton where they apparently had a speedy and forced evacuation, leaving behind half a loaf of bread and a pound of bologna. They had the audacity or perhaps the good grace, to write to Mr. Ferrier from "Jungles Ltd.", the transient settlement near the Calder railway yards, to thank him for the shelter. They apologized for not asking his permission for the ride, and asked for the return of their food. Mr. Ferrier insisted to the press that the letter was genuine and said that he had found the food in the coach, but had given it to children playing nearby.[15]

On September 22nd and 23rd, trial runs were made with the new trolleys on the North side over the newly-completed wiring. The northern terminus was the loop at 95 Street and 111 Avenue. The remainder of the overhead was service-only wire. The south side wire was to be completed a week later.[16] On Sunday, September 24th, the north side service was officially placed in operation with three buses[17] and the public was encouraged to "take a ride and see how you like them". The regular fare, ten cents cash or five tickets for a quarter, applied even for this first day. The South Edmonton Weekly News,[18] the Edmonton Journal[19] and the Bulletin all heralded this start of a fifteen-year program of modernization of the Street Railway system. This program was to cost $1,500,000 and involved purchasing a total of 45 trolley buses. The Journal gave its readers some cost comparison figures for the various transit modes.

Vehicle	Vehicle Cost	Operating Cost	Top Speed	Operating Speed
Trolley Bus	$17-18,000	18¢/mile	40 mph	11 mph
Streetcar	$22,000	21¢/mile	25 mph	9 1/2 mph
Diesel Bus	$17,000	19¢/mile	—	—
Gas Bus	$14,000	23¢/mile	—	—

Public response showed a wholehearted acceptance of the new buses; the motormen, James Billingsley and Thomas McWhirter, twenty-year tram veterans, and four younger men, Harry Humpish, Gordon Murray, Lionel Fouracre and Edward Hillary were kept busy all day Sunday. All six drivers said that they liked the new buses better than the trams.[20]

By mid-October, partial paving on the south side was complete[21] and on October 11th, the buses started running over the Low Level Bridge to a terminus at 99 Street and 85 Avenue. Paving on 99 Street as far as Whyte Avenue was to be completed by the weekend and the buses were then to run via 99 Street to Whyte Avenue and 104 Street where they were to be turned.[22]

Within a week, ridership pushed the system to its peak capacity and on October 18th, Mr. Ferrier asked Council for more buses. In the meantime, the route was terminated at 99 Street and Whyte Avenue until traffic conditions on Whyte could be studied more carefully. A wye had been built at this intersection and this was used to turn the buses.

The new service was not without problems. There was a heavy snowfall on October 23rd and some delays were experienced before adequate cindering of the hills kept the buses moving. Another delay occured when a CNR locomotive, unable to get a grip on the icy rails on the Low Level Bridge, stalled and blocked traffic.

Opposite, upper:

Leyland trolley coach No. 109 sits outside Cromdale circa 1948. This is a 1942-built unit with the protruding side destination sign. A newly-arrived Brill sits in the background, ready to displace the tired English expatriate, but the old-timer has a few months of service left yet. (N.F. Corness)

Opposite, lower:

Interior of one of the A.E.C./E.E.C. trolley coaches Nos. 101 to 103. Leather seats provided a comfortable ride, and passengers sitting in the raised areas felt like kings as they swept silently through town. (Collection of Colin K. Hatcher)

The headway of this route had been doubled over that of the trams and, as a result, the number of passengers carried also doubled. Still, ridership over the route increased dramatically and motor buses were needed in the peak hours to help.[23] By early November, Council asked both of the bus suppliers to quote on two more buses as "patronage had exceeded expectations". At this time the two portions of the route were treated as two separate routes, probably to allow better balancing of passenger flow from and to the south side. On November 27th, the purchase of three more buses was approved, one for each route and one spare, for a total cost of $54,000. These were to be ordered from Britain, again because of the tariff costs on buses from the US. Even though delivery time from Great Britain was longer, it was argued that the savings realized and the contribution to the war effort made this a wise decision.[24] This decision was to be regretted often during the next months.

The order was split, one bus to Leyland and two to EEC. Heavier springs, improved (non-dragging) brakes, traffic turn indicators, better dust protection for the equipment and passengers, and stronger rear bumpers, better able to withstand the frequent impacts of Edmonton's drivers, were specified.[25] On December 13th, EEC regretfully informed the city that due to the war it had been instructed by the British Government to discontinue the manufacturing of buses. Accordingly its order was transferred to Leyland. As the year closed and the war clouds darkened, Council optimistically asked for estimates to be prepared for several trolley bus extensions.

Early in 1940, several more estimates were prepared for proposed routes, as well as for lifting of the Bonnie Doon streetcar stub from 99 Street to the originally-proposed trolley terminus at 104 Street. City engineers were also looking at replacing the streetcar line over the High Level Bridge with trolley buses, either on the upper or lower decks, to serve a belt line running along 109 Street.

It had been suggested that trolley bus service be extended through Norwood from 111 Avenue and 95 Street via 111 Avenue east to 91 Street thence north to 115 Avenue, thence east over what was now service wire to 85 Street and the Fort Trail. This was as recommended in the original Wilson & Bunnell report. This line, however, was never built but service from 95 Street and 111 Avenue to a loop at 115 Avenue and 82 Street was probably put into effect along the former service wire.

In the meantime, small design problems in the first order of buses were being rectified and turn indicators were being installed to lessen the occurrence of impacts with Edmonton motorists. Ridership increased 25 percent due to the new buses, and at peak hours was estimated to have increased from 50 to 100 percent. In June the city asked Brill (Chicago) if there were two trolley buses available for delivery in November. Brill would have been happy to supply them, but investigation showed that there would be a ten percent duty imposed; therefore, the City reluctantly decided to wait for the British buses to arrive and risk possibly-impaired winter service. Commissioner Gibb all the while was pushing the British Trade Commissioner to speed up the shipment of the Leyland buses. Steel shortages and quotas in Great Britain were delaying the fabrication of the chassis, and the manufacturer was reluctant to have the bodies or motors fabricated in a time of intense shortages

Photo below:
Leyland trolley bus turning onto Jasper Avenue in front of The Bay at 102 Street, on March 20th 1946.   (Les Corness)

Photo above:

Trams and trolley-coaches shared the centre-of-the-road overhead on Jasper Avenue during the early years of trolley-bus operations. *(CP photo)*

until the whole bus could be assembled. Edmonton argued that special consideration should be given this order because it not only supplied much needed foreign exchange to Britain, but also the route that the buses were to be used on served Canadian war industries. Volumes of correspondence were exchanged between Edmonton and the British Trade Commissioner in Vancouver, and between Vancouver and England, but all to no avail. The quota systems were so complex and restrictive that any pleas fell on deaf or at least immovable ears.[26] The best that Leyland was able to do was offer some 80 hp diesel buses built for Canton and undeliverable due to the hostilities. They were very anxious to get rid of them, but Edmonton felt that they were underpowered for climbing the hills and that gas rationing would render them useless. Moreover, they would have no value at the war's conclusion. By the end of 1941, Leyland advised that the trolley bus chasses were finally completed. Early in 1942, Edmonton's new Leyland trolley buses were still only partly fabricated in England. A considerable exchange of letters ensued and the City retained a Consultant Engineer in England to supervise Leyland's progress and to push where necessary.

The first of these Leyland buses was finally shipped in June 1942 and arrived in Edmonton by the end of July. But the troubles were not over. The second bus was broken into enroute, and despite careful supervision by the Associated Equipment Co. of Montreal during the unloading, the third bus had some of its panels damaged. This added one more delay to a frustrating wait, but finally all three buses were safely housed in the Cromdale barns. These units, numbered 107-109, were supposed to be used to augment service on the 95 Street line but were instead used on the south side line. Leyland regretfully informed the city that this shipment of export buses was the last it would be allowed to produce for the duration of the war. A curious fact was that all the Leyland buses lacked a builder's crest. This omission might have gone unnoticed, except that in July, Leyland shipped twelve crests to Edmonton and asked that two be affixed to each of its last export order of buses. These were, in fact, the last overseas-manufactured trolley buses shipped to Canada by any manufacturer.

Photo above:

Pullman No. 115 at The Bay, Jasper and 102 Street, March 20th 1946. (Les Corness)

Photo below:

Leyland coach No. 105 already sports a few dents as it takes on passengers on Jasper Avenue eastbound at 101 Street. It would appear that the coaches sat very high, making the first step a real stretch. (Alberta Provincial Archives)

16

The War Years and Beyond

*I*N AUGUST 1941, the Canadian government had established the position of Transit Controller in the Department of Munitions and Supply, a post which was responsible for the administration of urban and interurban transportation vehicles. Indirectly, as shortages of tires, gasoline and equipment increased, it became responsible for all civilian vehicles. Local committees assessed the needs of the community and requested vehicles or service accordingly. All purchases of equipment were placed by the Controller and equipment was allotted on a need basis by him. A thorough study in 1941 of transit needs and speedy ordering of equipment led to the majority of Canadian orders being filled in the United States before the US War Production Board terminated export production in July 1942. The Transit Controller passed orders forbidding charter buses except as a direct contribution to the war effort. Interurban bus lines were consolidated, terminated or shortened to maximize utilization of available resources. Few vehicles were scrapped and most modernization programs were shelved. Taxis were restricted and so eventually were private cars, except where pooled to drive workers to war industries. Even then the riders were assigned by the Board. All this placed a severe load on public transit systems. Even with staggered work hours and advertising imploring the housewife to shop in off-peak hours, the buses and trams were packed. The farsightedness of the Board, however, resulted in more new vehicles being available to transit systems than might otherwise have been the case, but every request for additional vehicles involved a fight to convince the board that Edmonton's need was greater than another city's. George S. Gray, the Controller, had an excellent relationship with Edmonton, one that helped propel Edmonton, after the war, into the front ranks of Canadian transit systems and established it as a leader in trolley and motor bus networks.[1]

In May 1942, the Transit Controller approved a tentative Edmonton order for three more trolley buses to be the same as those ordered by Winnipeg. These were to be 40-seat Mack buses to be built in the US. Meanwhile service was suffering because of the supplemental diesel buses' inability to handle McDougall Hill. Accordingly trolley bus service was withdrawn from the northeastern extension and these buses used on the Low Level Route instead.

On May 21st 1942 the order for Mack buses was confirmed by the Transit Controller. The order was allowed only because Winnipeg had already ordered some Macks and the Edmonton order could be tacked on.[2] These buses were to be numbered 110-112. Their paint scheme as ordered was:

Exterior :	Victory Model — War Production Board regulations Khaki No. 3
Main Panels :	Vitrolite Railway Red Enamel below belt line
Waist (or belt) :	Vitrolite Railway Cream Enamel
Window frames :	Vitrolite Railway Cream Enamel

The earlier bus paint scheme was revised here to eliminate the orange belt rail. The buses were to be equipped with storm sashes and the seats were Victory Type No. V-630 made by the Art Rattan Company. Despite the Company's name the seats were genuine leather as were those in the English buses. Destination signs were to read:

High Level Bridge
Low Level Bridge
104 St: 82 Ave
 99 St: 82 Ave
 95 St: 111 Ave
115 Ave: 82 St
Exhibition
Arena
Centre Loop
Car Shops
Special
No Passengers[3]

The Mack order dragged through an expected December delivery date and then a January one. Finally on February 10th 1943 the buses arrived and were placed in service the following week on the 95 Street route.[4]

A request was received in September 1942 asking for the south side service to be extended to the University of Alberta Hospital. The shortage of buses forced this request to be placed in abeyance.

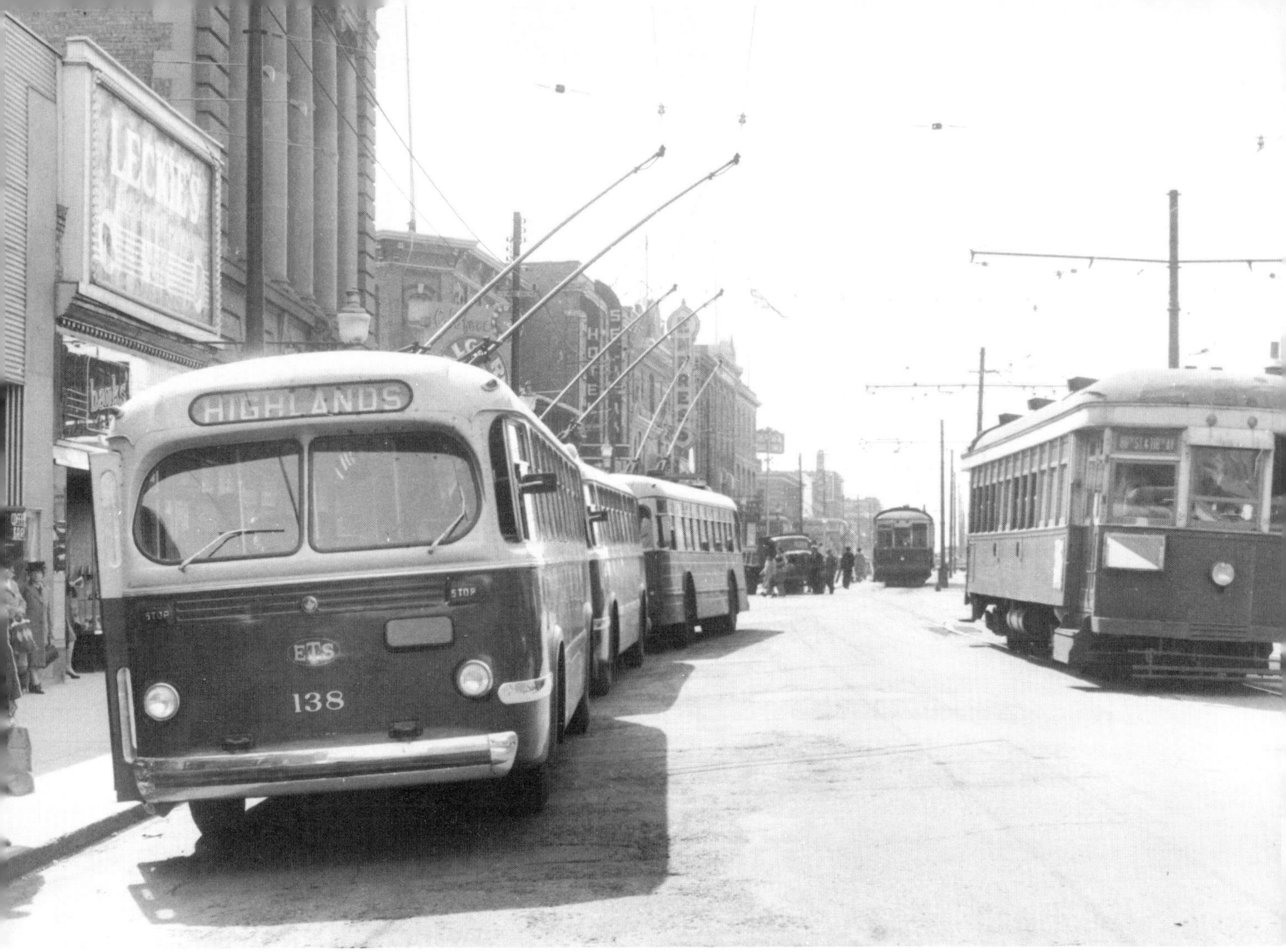
LECKIE'S
HIGHLANDS
STOP
STOP
ETS
138

104TH ST. 82 AVE.
104TH ST. 82 AVE
114

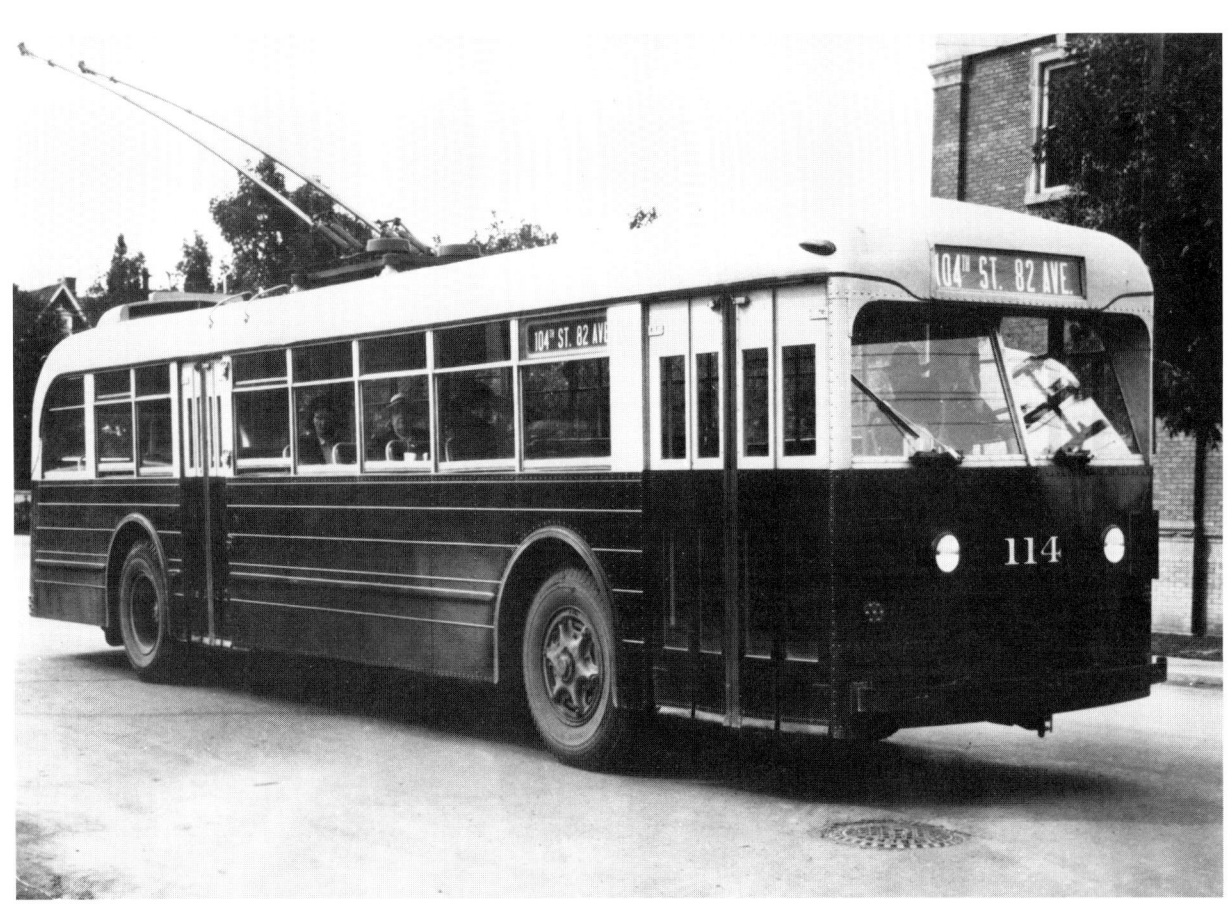

Ridership had mounted steadily, 2,463,071 in February 1943 compared with 1,762,490 for the same period in 1942. The arrival of the three Mack buses permitted increasing service on the Low Level route and allowed the English buses to be overhauled, a much-needed chore. The EEC buses were giving the city problems due to severe passenger overloading, thus straining the smaller motors. The situation would have been graver, however, had Edmonton accepted the standard 80 hp motors on these buses instead of specifying heavier ones.

The northeastern extension was probably not re-opened when the Macks arrived as the number of vehicles in service was still inadequate. Immediately on receipt of the Mack units the City asked the Transit Controller for permission to order three more. However, the US Dept. of Defense curtailed production of Mack buses and the order was denied. It was suggested that Edmonton try instead to get Pullman trolleys. In August 1943 an order to the Pullman Standard Car Co. of Worcester, Mass. for eight 44-seat trolley buses at a cost of $21,000 each was approved by the Dominion Transit Controller.[5] Completion of this order would give Edmonton one of the largest fleets of electric buses in Canada and would release six streetcars for other service. Trolley bus service was to be extended to 104 Street and 82 Avenue on the South Side, probably using the original loop proposed by Wilson and Bunnell. On 115 Avenue, an extension was proposed through to the Exhibition Grounds. The Pullman buses were scheduled to arrive in December;[6] however, fabrication did not commence immediately as a shortage of axles delayed the start of construction until the following April.

Optimism replaced pessimism in the latter part of 1943. In October, City Council approved planning for the post-war modernization of the transit system. Extension of trolley coach service to Highlands was recommended, as well as the conversion of the south side tram loop. The new trolley coach belt line would tap the existing line on Whyte Avenue, running along Whyte to 109 Street; it would return to the North side via the High Level

Photo opposite, upper:

The transfer of trolley coach overhead from the centre of Jasper Avenue to both sides of the avenue permits two brand-new Brills and a wartime-built Pullman to pull into a new curbside stop on Jasper Avenue at 101 Street on May 27th 1947. Car No. 76, a sturdy 33-year veteran on Jasper Avenue, and an unidentified 35-year-old St. Louis-built car, travel freely along their traditional position in the centre of the road. In this view, steel poles erected along both sides of Jasper Avenue support span wires stretching across the thoroughfare, from which both the trolley coach and streetcar overhead systems are suspended. Removal of the brackets and support poles from the centre of Jasper Avenue was completed later.
(Provincial Archives of Alberta)

Opposite, lower:

An obviously new Pullman (No 114) has its picture taken while the operator waits patiently. The unusual air scoop at the rear of the roof was an as-delivered feature, but was removed during rebuilds that also reshaped the rear-side windows. *(Colin K. Hatcher Collection)*

Photo above:

Interior shot of a Pullman trolley coach. The advertising cards indicate that this was during the war years; note especially the one depicting the woman volunteer. *(Colin K. Hatcher)*

Bridge to Jasper and link with the existing route at 102 Street. The run over the High Level was proposed to be on the top deck, then occupied by streetcars, using steel plate decking and substantial concrete wheel guards acting like a guideway.[7]

In February 1944, the City requested eight additional trolley buses to help keep up with the increasing demand, but this request was turned down by the Transit Controller in April of that year. This decision was reversed in May[8] and the order confirmed in June.[9] The English buses were showing signs of wear and the war prevented a good supply of spare parts from being available. The public liked the Mack buses better than the English ones, and the feeling was that Edmonton Radial Railway should stay with North American buses when the conflict was over. In the early fall the first eight Pullman buses, ordered in August 1943, finally arrived and were immediately put into service, probably on August 12th 1944 as tram service on Whyte Avenue to 104 Street ceased that day. At this same time the terminus was finally extended to the originally proposed-location at 104 Street. In December, the 95 Street trolley coach route was extended again in the northeast to run via 95 Street and 115 Avenue to 82 Street and 115 Avenue. "Red-and-white" trams cars ran along Spruce Avenue only in the early morning and evening rush hours. This service change lasted about four days before lack of trolley buses forced restoration of all-day streetcar service and withdrawal of the 115 Avenue line from service for the second time.[10]

The service was still badly pressed; the Street Railway Department asked later that month for an additional two trolleys, and indicated that the system might need as many as four more buses. In January 1945, the Transit Controller, Mr. Gray, wrote a confidential letter to Commissioner Gibb in which he revealed that Canadian Car & Foundry (CCF) was planning to produce, under license, the ACF (American Car & Foundry) Brill trolley bus. He offered Edmonton the choice either of two more Pullmans or two ACF-Brills. He stated that he hoped that he would be able to get the opinion of one of Canada's most progressive transit operations on the proposed Canadian trolley bus. He also asked that the ERR keep the streetcars running on 114 (Spruce) Avenue until the spring when he could then get eight more Pullman buses for Edmonton.[11] In a later official letter he asked if the City would like to try the new ACF-Brill trolley buses.

Commissioner Gibb replied that they would like to have the Brills instead of Pullmans because of the many favorable reports they had heard about them.[12]

On March 16th 1945, ACF submitted a quote on two Standard Model TC-44-1945 trolley buses, complete except for the tires, for US$13,650 each net. The tires were excluded due to high tariffs on rubber goods and would be bought locally. This quote was less than the list price of $14,600, but the order had been tacked on to a US order and the saving passed on to Edmonton. The buses were to feature aluminum sheathing, sloped front windshields, a centre control cabinet and protected control rods, a feature needed in the severe weather and not found on any previous buses. The buses were 102 inches wide, 36 feet, 10 inches long and had a short turn radius.[13]

The order was duly placed through Canadian Car & Foundry Co. Ltd., for two ACF-Brill trolley buses to be delivered in the spring of 1946. These were said to be for use on the University (Hospital) extension that Gibb implied had already been strung with wire.[14] Such does not seem to have been the case, as this extension was not effected until ten years later. CCF also advised the City that it expected to start manufacture of the Brill trolley bus under license in 1946, and in March of that year (1945) announced officially the signing of an agreement to build the ACF-Brill buses under the name "Canadian Car-Brill". This trademark was to grace nearly all Canadian trolley buses from that time until 1954 when CCF ceased trolley bus production.[15]

The City stated that it would definitely buy Canadian-made trolley buses when they became available, but it still asked for two additional Pullmans to add to the eight expected in May.[16] This request was turned down by the Transit Controller's office on the grounds that Edmonton had been favoured in the past and many cities were worse off.[17]

CCF promised to start production of coaches in the third and fourth quarter of 1946. Selling price was estimated to be $15,500 each. Given the import duties on the US buses, this was a saving between $4,000 and $5,000 per unit. The City accordingly placed a tentative order for twenty coaches for 1946 delivery.[18]

With an additional eight Pullman buses on order and two ACF-Brills expected in September, the Transportation Committee was asked to consider building a downtown trolley bus depot. At an estimated cost of $200,000 it would have facilities for washing, inspection and running repairs of buses, offices, a motormen's room, ticket office, battery room and lunch room. It was proposed that some of the materials come from buildings at the Exhibition Grounds. The site chosen was that of the old Bitulithic Paving Plant on the flats near the river bank between the Low Level Bridge and the Brewery. This location, right on the proposed Belt Line and only half a mile from the Jasper Avenue routes, would save many miles of deadhauling.[19] However, in September 1945, the Department of Munitions & Supply, which controlled the distribution of vital materials, denied the request for bricks for the depot and the idea was allowed to die.[20]

The planning for a trolley bus route over the High Level Bridge went ahead, but there was considerable public fear expressed about the possibility of a bus going off the deck and plunging 150 feet to the river below. On the other hand, the public also objected to the concept of using the lower deck for fear of dewired trolleys fouling up traffic. Public opinion favored some form of transit across the bridge, however, and the Street Railway Department was hard put to plan around these conflicting preferences. In February 1946, a growing concern by the public about the safety of the High Level route, forced the Commissioners to seek reapproval of the decision made by them the previous August to go ahead with the High Level plan. Council showed their confidence in the Commissioners by reaffirming this decision.[21]

A concerned citizen of the Walterdale area asked the City in a letter if the public would be better served by having the proposed High Level route go instead over the 105 Street Bridge. This would serve residents who had no service instead of those who already had, in her opinion, adequate service.[22] In his reply the Commissioner stated that the High Level Bridge route was the best to serve the needs of the public, as a 105 Street route would antagonize the west-end residents and Provincial Government employees.[23] Council concurred with the Commissioner, but the public-spirited citizen was prophetically right. Some time, however, was to pass before this was borne out.

Pullman sent word that delivery of its buses would be delayed till mid-June. In mid-July 1945, with still no sign of the Pullman buses, Commissioner Gibbs' patience was wearing thin. He complained to the Transit Controller that he was most anxious to get the buses by September. Pullman promised delivery early in July, then late in July or early August. Pullman finally promised partial shipments through the month of August.

The Commissioners had recommended to the Transportation Committee that a new Highlands trolley bus line replace the remains of the "White" car line. This was a secondary streetcar line with long stretches of single open track. Where track was paved, it was in very bad condition. Reconstruction would have cost over $230,000. New pavement could also be laid when the open track was lifted, giving a new roadway into the area. While not a heavy residential area, it was growing, and the trolley bus line would also serve the Exhibition Grounds, and Borden Park with its zoo and open swimming pool, as well as a hockey arena.[24] The trolley coaches could be run downtown, they suggested, in an opposite direction to the South side and 95 Street routes. The buses would go west on Jasper, north on 102 Street, east on 102 Avenue, and south on 100 Street to avoid congestion at Jasper Avenue and 101 Street and continue from there along Jasper to 112 Avenue and 61 Street. This meant doubling the overhead in the downtown loop but the new set of wires would go on the existing overhead spans and cost only $7,000. Council concurred.[25]

On July 22nd 1945 the "White" (Highlands) car line ceased operation. In the meantime, rapid progress was being made on the new trolley wire along this route.[26] Trolley buses replaced the trams in

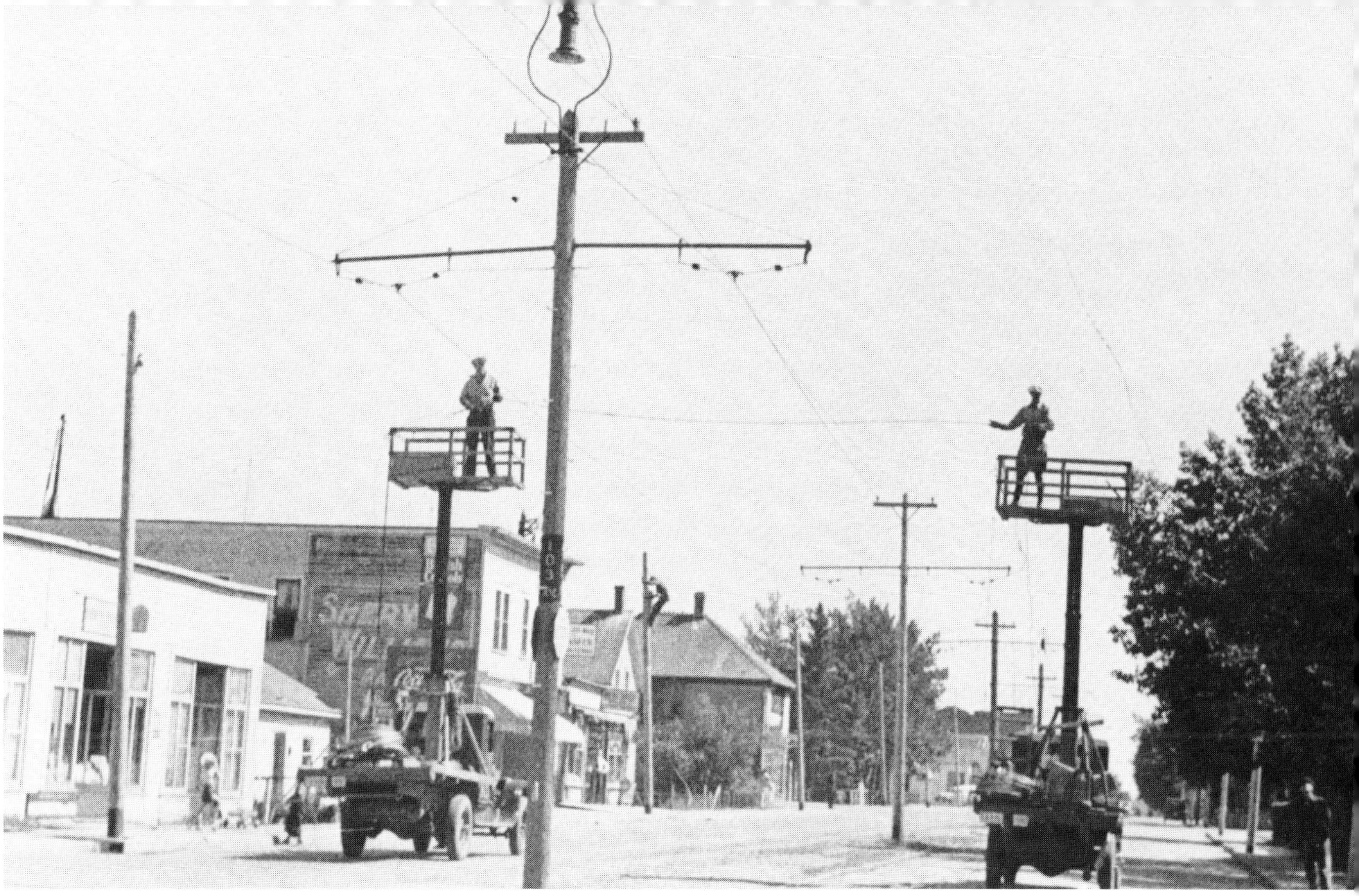

Photo above:

Stringing the wire on 95 Street in 1947. Employees of McGregor Telephone and Telegraph stretch span wire over the centre-of-the-street tram wires. The trolley lines will later be attached to the span wires and the old streetcar overhead brackets removed.
(McGregor Telephone & Power Construction Co. Ltd. Courtesy of B.E. Jacquest)

Right:

A McGregor T&T worker installs insulators on the overhead for the new trolley buses that are soon to run on Edmonton streets. (McGregor Telephone & Power Construction Co. Ltd. Courtesy of B.E. Jacquest)

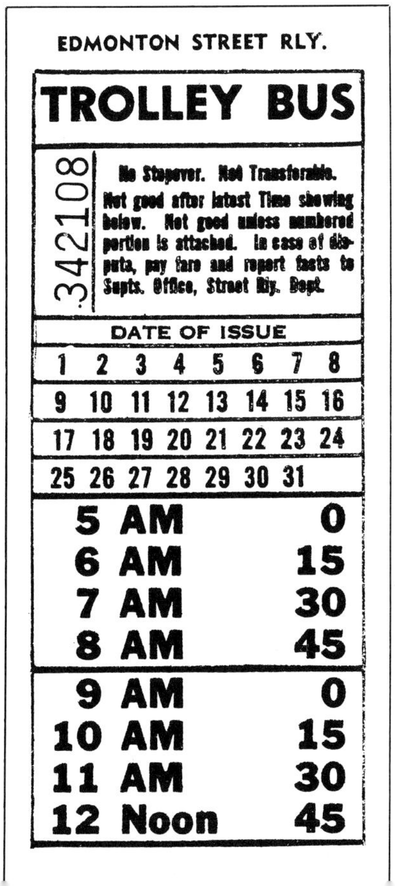
EDMONTON STREET RLY.

TROLLEY BUS

342108

No Stopover. Not Transferable. Not good after latest Time showing below. Not good unless numbered portion is attached. In case of dispute, pay fare and report facts to Supts. Office, Street Rly. Dept.

DATE OF ISSUE

1	2	3	4	5	6	7	8
9	10	11	12	13	14	15	16
17	18	19	20	21	22	23	24
25	26	27	28	29	30	31	

5 AM	0
6 AM	15
7 AM	30
8 AM	45
9 AM	0
10 AM	15
11 AM	30
12 Noon	45

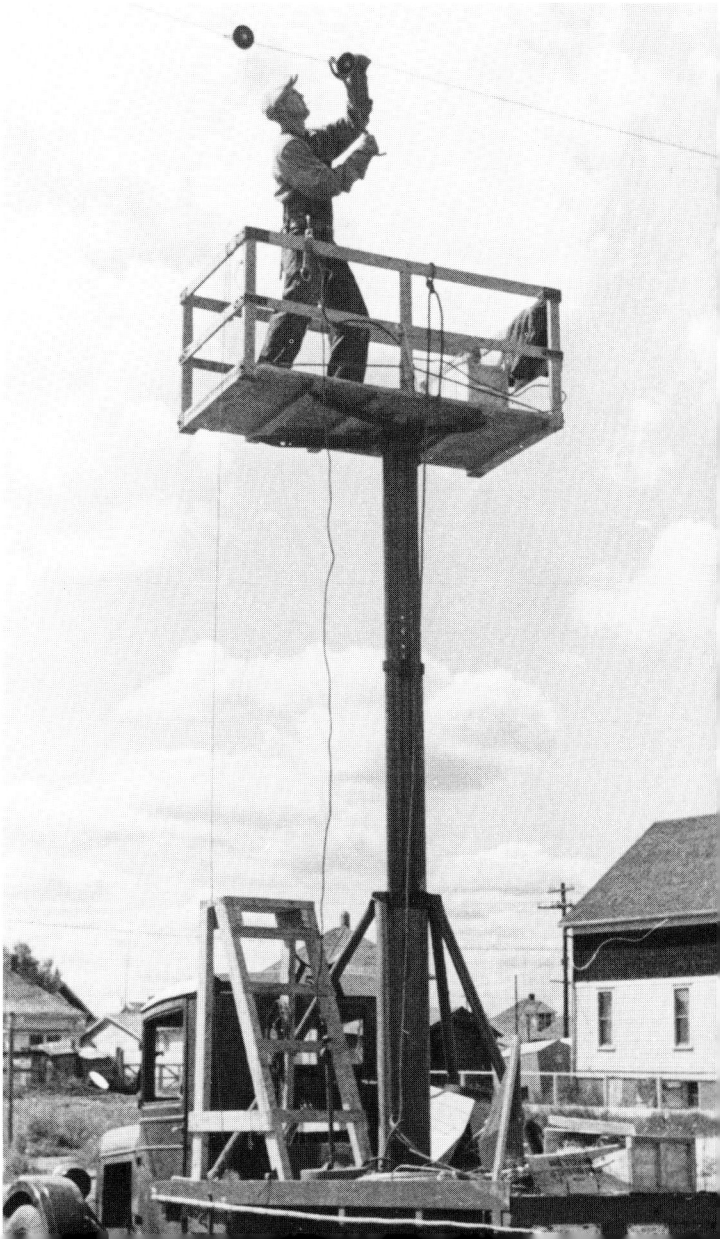

Photo above:
CCF/Brill No. 158 waits to go into service in front of Cromdale barns. (N.F. Corness)

Opposite page:
The route number was carried in an outside holder as shown here, and at the rear below the rear window on the same side. Side window bottom halves slid sideways to admit fresh air.
(N.F. Corness)

September after the open track along Borden Park was lifted and the street paved. The route ran from an off-street loop at 112 Avenue and 61 Street, via 112 Avenue, 82 Street and Jasper Avenue to the downtown loop where it followed the existing single wire in the same direction as the other routes, and not on the double wire as recommended.[27]

On September 30th 1945 control of transit by the Transit Controller was withdrawn. This allowed the City to place whatever bus orders it felt necessary to meet its post-war expansion plans. To fill 1946 requirements for trolley buses, bids were requested from Pullman, Twin, Mack, Motor Coach Industries (Winnipeg) and Canadian Car and Foundry for twenty 44-seat coaches.[28] CCF bid $15,500,[29] Mack was not ready for production,[30] Twin wasn't sure about re-entering the field[31] and Pullman felt that it couldn't compete with tax and duty on imports.[32] Its poor delivery on the last order probably didn't help. MCI, which had built one Mack-type trolley bus as a prototype for Winnipeg, bid $19,660 and so ended its chance of being a second Canadian trolley coach manufacturer.[33]

Accordingly, on October 10th 1945, a firm order was placed with CCF for 22 trolley coaches.[34] In a letter to Twin Coach, which was now promising the imminent arrival of "the best trolley bus ever,"[35] and in another to Mack,[36] the City said that they could risk waiting no longer. This removed the last US contenders from Edmonton's market; it was CCF all the way. Even with a rise in price of the ACF-Brill, to be delivered in November,[37] from $13,776.50 to $14,465.32, the City still felt that the Brill bus was the way to go. Another Canadian venture, Hayes Manufacturing Co. Ltd. of Vancouver, belatedly offered a 100% Canadian-built trolley bus, but Edmonton's order had already been awarded by Council.

This first order for CanCar-Brill T-44 trolley coaches had the following destination signs:

```
HIGH LEVEL BRIDGE
LOW LEVEL BRIDGE
104th ST      82 AVE
99th ST       82 AVE
95th ST      111 AVE
115th AVE     82 ST
79th ST      112 AVE
HIGHLANDS
ARENA
EXHIBITION
CENTRE LOOP
CAR SHOPS
SPECIAL
NO PASSENGERS
118th AVE     80 ST
112th AVE    124 ST
107th AVE    124 ST
118th AVE    124 ST
NORTH EDMONTON
```

Side signs were the same as used on motor buses and read:

2	HIGHLANDS	124 ST
5	95 ST	EAST END
6	LOW LEVEL	
7	GLENORA	115 AVENUE
1	105 STREET	BRIDGE
4	CALDER	
8	BONNIE	DOON
9	FORT	TRAIL
10	DAWSON BRIDGE	BRIDGE
11	BELGRAVIA	82 AVE
12	CALGARY TRAIL	RITCHIE
13	NORTH	EDMONTON
14	111 AVE	
	101 STREET & JASPER	
	EXHIBITION GROUNDS	
	SPECIAL	
	CHARTERED	
	GARAGE[38]	

The City's enthusiasm for trolley buses was somewhat ambivalent at times. The Canadian Department of Transport, when it wanted to lower the strectlights and poles at the airport on Kingsway Avenue, asked about the mode of transit to be used in the future on this route. The City Engineer specified diesel buses but the Commissioner said that trolleys would be used. DOT took its chances and lowered the light standards. The Commissioner's proposed trolley bus subway along Kingsway never materialized, but statistics bore out the popularity of the trolley bus routes elsewhere. 1945 ended with the Street Railway Department again planning many ambitious trolley routes.

In January 1946, the 95 Street route northeast extension was recommended for the third time. Also planned was an extension of the trolley route west on Jasper from 101 Street to 124 Street then north on 124 Street with turning loops at 112 and 118 Avenues. Another route was to be established on 107 Avenue from 101 Street and Jasper, north on 101 Street, west on 107 Avenue, south on 124 Street, east on Jasper and the same route in reverse.[39] This line was not, however, run as a separate route as proposed but was, as we shall see, absorbed into an existing route.

On March 20th 1946, 25 more trolley buses were ordered from CCF for the third and fourth quarters of 1947.[40] Special service during the Exhibition was advertised that year. Ten-minute service from the centre of the city to the Main Gate via "the most direct route from 102nd and Jasper" was provided by the quiet, fast trolley coaches.[41]

Changes were made in the trolley bus overhead, in March of 1947, from the streetcar wire that was being used at that time, probably to the grooved wire the characterizes trolley bus operation

today. During this conversion the practice of centre street running was changed in favour of curb-side running.[42] The centre street bracket arm poles that had been installed for streetcar overhead were removed on Jasper from 109 to 124 Streets as they were replaced with curbside poles and span wire. The streetcar rails were also removed on 124 Street from 102 to 107 Avenues and the track allowance paved. Paving was continued to 108 Avenue where the turning loop for the trolley buses was constructed.

Buses 153 through 177 were delivered in September 1947.[43] Twenty-two Brills had been received in January and February and twelve of those were then immediately put into service; the rest were held until paving programs were complete.[44]

The new west service went into operation starting Sunday, October 5th, with twenty trolley buses serving a route from 111 Avenue and 95 Street south on that street to Jasper Avenue, then west to 124 Street and north to 108 Avenue and return. Introduction of this new trolley coach service terminated streetcar service on Jasper Avenue west of 109 Street.[45]

An Edmonton Journal headline of October 4th 1947 read "Trolley buses take on route numbers". These were shown in an outside holder at the right rear of the bus. Officials felt that the front roller names were sufficient without numbers. The west end route was numbered 5, the Highlands route numbered 2 and the Low Level route numbered 6. For a time previous to this, the routes had been referred to by number even to the point where the English buses displayed route numbers. The English buses were delivered with route indicator windows in the front, but they weren't used in the beginning. The Pullmans and Brills did not have separate route number windows so the outside signs were necessary.[46] By March 1947, the three AEC trolleys were operating only occasionally but were scheduled for regular service in the summer after extensive overhauling.[47]

Ten more Brill T44 trolley buses were ordered in March 1948, bringing the total fleet up to 78.[48] By late April of that year overhead had been strung on 124 Street to 118 Avenue. On Sunday May 2nd, service on the 95 Street (No. 5) line was extended on 124 Street from 108 Avenue to 118 Avenue except for rush hours when extras turned short at the 112 Avenue loop. Red-and-green streetcars westbound on 107 Avenue wyed at 107 Avenue and 124 Street and then left this point operating over the same route to the south side as before. A stub service operated into Calder from 124 Street and 118 Avenue.[49]

Street car service on 114 (Spruce) Avenue and also on 101 Street was discontinued on Sunday, August 29th. The 95 Street west end trolley bus route (No. 5) was extended as recommended in January 1946 to serve 115 Avenue for the third and final time. It ran as follows: from 82 Street and 115 Avenue west on 115 Avenue to 95 Street, south on 95 Street to Jasper Avenue, west on Jasper to 124 Street, north on 124 Street to 112 Avenue and return. Extra coaches were operated from 111 Avenue and 95 Street to 108 Avenue and 124 Street only. The Highlands (No. 2) trolley coach route was also extended to run to 118 Avenue and 124 Street as follows: from 61 Street and 112 Avenue, west on 112 Avenue to 82 Street, south to Jasper Avenue, west to 101 Street, north to 107 Avenue, west to 124 Street, north to 118 Avenue and return. This routing finally used the 107 Avenue section that was proposed as a separate route in 1946 but was never used as such. The sign carried on the westbound leg was "118th Ave. & 124 St." and on the eastbound run "Highlands".[50]

On January 23rd 1949, a disastrous fire in Regina destroyed the car barns of the Regina Transit System. Included in the loss were many new CCF/Brill trolley buses stored there awaiting the conversion of the Regina street railway system to trolley bus; many of these had never seen service. The fire so crippled the Regina system that Edmonton's Mayor H.D. Ainlay sent a telegram offering to lend six of Edmonton's trolley coaches.[51] This offer was graciously declined, but Edmonton, which had nine buses on order, waived its place in the CCF order schedule so that Regina could get its desperately-needed buses more quickly. (Several other Canadian companies did likewise.) Because of this the three AEC and six Leyland buses were given a reprieve from scrapping and were used as short haul peak-hour extras. To reduce the maintenance problems associated with the twin rear axles, one set of the dual axle drives was removed.[52]

Norman D. Wilson returned to Edmonton in 1949 to give a report on the system's future. He expressed the opinion that the 115 Avenue trolley line, which had been originally strung as a necessity to reach the car house, should be abandoned in favor of a north/south line on 95 Street. To solve immediate problems, Council approved an extension of the 115 Avenue trolley coach line west to 102 Street, south on that street to Kingsway Avenue and thence to 101 Street. This was to overcome duplication of service on 95 Street and bring mainline service into the growing area north of the Royal Alexandra Hospital. This line was, however, never built. The ultimate extension of this proposed 101 Street line south was to be via a descent to the 105 Street bridge and up Walterdale Hill to 109 Street and 82 (and eventually 72) Avenue. This was planned to be put into effect before the High Level Bridge could be closed for reconstruction.[53] Extension of trolley coach service over the former 102 Avenue and Bonnie Doon car lines was also approved. A problem with the proposed 102 Avenue line was that it would provide service to an urban area outside the city limits, the Town of Jasper Place. The city fathers felt that for a self-sustaining transit system no discrimination should be made as regards suburban residents and so they recommended that the line terminate at the city limits either by an around-the-block loop (149 Street and 103 Avenue) or by an off-street loop. It was further suggested that looping arrangements be made at 123 Street to permit the 102 Avenue line to be operated as a stub service at offpeak hours. Overhead was also to be constructed to permit trolley coaches to be routed to and from the carhouse from the 102 Avenue line via 107 Avenue and 115 Avenue without having to go through downtown.

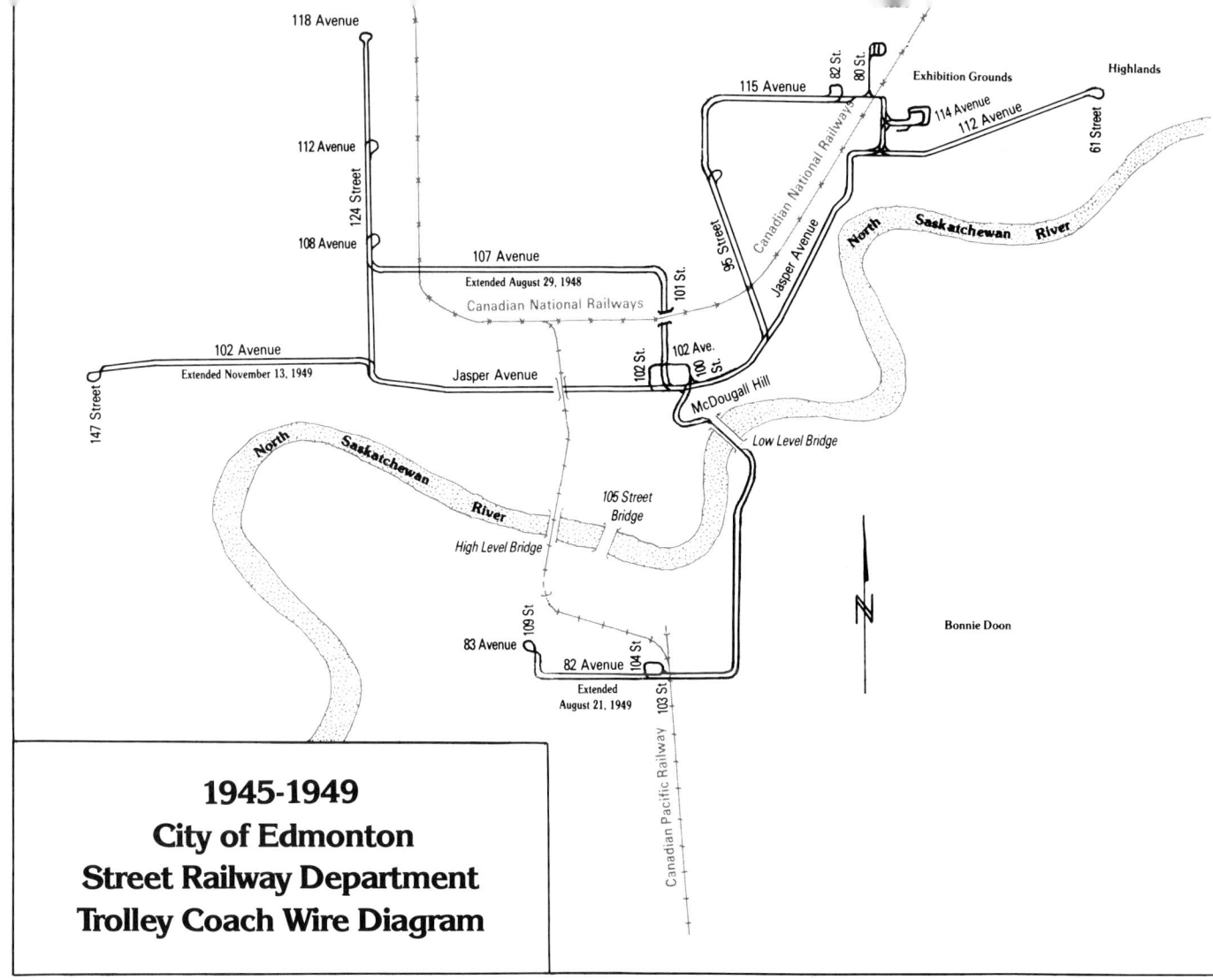

1945-1949 City of Edmonton Street Railway Department Trolley Coach Wire Diagram

This was approved in principle except for the western terminus of the 102 Street line which was to be considered further.[54]

Projected Bonnie Doon trolley coaches were to operate via 109 Street and 82 Avenue to provide a cross-town service on 82 Avenue. The line was to follow the same route as the tram line did, except that it would loop downtown or be temporarily linked to the 101 Street - 118 Avenue line via 101A Avenue. The question was raised of having the line go up a new road near Connors Road instead of up the hill in Cloverdale. The Cloverdale route was, however, agreed upon.[55] The Bonnie Doon extension was not built, as, in 1951, the feasibility of this cross-town service on Whyte Avenue was discounted due to the great length of this branch, compared with the King Edward Park (99 Street) branch. It was felt that this would result in irregular service over the common route to the North side.[56]

Some further studies were suggested in 1949 on downtown loops and crosstown service[57] as well as a change from Calder streetcars to trolley buses and extensions to the 95 Street and Highlands trolley routes.[58] Council could only agree to locate the 102 Avenue loop of the west end line on the south side of that Avenue between 147 and 148 Streets.[59]

In May, Brill buses 188 through 192 were ordered with delivery for late November and early December.[60] A noticeable change in these and subsequent orders was that the side windows lifted in a manner similar to a house window instead of the lower sash sliding as it did on the previous models. Improvements in control cables and operating parts were also introduced at this time to better cope with winter icing conditions. Probably at this point the destination signs had "GLENORA — 115 AVE 7" added to them.

On August 21st 1949, streetcar service on Whyte Avenue ceased and was replaced by trolley buses. Route 6 trolley coaches continued west of 104 Street along Whyte to 109 Street where they looped off-street at 83 Avenue to connect with the streetcars. Motor buses served the extension until paving was completed[61] at the end of August when the trolleys then took over.[62] On November 13th, the 102 Avenue west end motor bus service was converted to trolley bus as route 7. The route was from the off-street loop at 102 Avenue and 147 Street, downtown via 102 Avenue, 124 Street and Jasper Avenue. Return was by way of 97 Street, 102 Avenue, 102 Street and then via Jasper and as above.[63]

This new west end service called for additional power. Late delivery of equipment to increase the capacity of the west end power substation in 1950 led to a severe drain on power resources early that year. This necessitated spacing of trolleys and trams during the rush hours and corresponding service impairment.[64]

Photo above:

Edmonton Transit Flyer Coach No. 224 approaching the 105 Street traffic circle on its southbound trip across the 105 Street Bridge. This view of the trolley-coach features the new paint scheme, new route signs, rebuilt rear roof line. April 25th 1979.
(Colin K. Hatcher)

Photo below:

Brill No. 127 gets ready to load passengers at the Exhibition loop and head downtown. During special events at the Exhibition grounds, and during the horse racing season, Route 3 was extended into the grounds. *(J.A. Kernahan)*

17 | The Not-So-Final Years

IN 1951, THE FINAL conversion from street railway to bus operation was outlined. The premise in 1939 had been for a basic electric coach network with motor feeder buses. The war and the attendant material restrictions that continued afterward had given rise to transit operating deficits. Over this period Edmonton had expanded rapidly, putting an additional strain on the system. However as the following comparisons show, the trolley coach was still the most economical vehicle to operate; next came the streetcar and last the motor coach.[1]

	Mileage	Expenses	Revenue	Profit or Loss/Mile
1947-trolley	1,365,246	$ 625,843	$ 564,384	-$.04
-tram	2,552,895	$1,030,110	$1,092,809	+$.02
-bus	960,357	$ 413,326	$ 258,339	-$.17
1949-trolley	2,573,574	$1,207,031	$1,333,785	+$.05
-tram	1,282,388	$ 710,783	$ 734,932	+$.02
-bus	1,265,249	$ 633,495	$ 476,960	-$.13
1950-trolley	2,946,063	$1,404,886	$1,538,839	+$.05
-tram	972,472	$ 568,272	$ 585,120	+$.02
-bus	1,332,762	$ 703,351	$ 529,835	-$.13 [2]

For example, in January 1951, streetcar and motor bus operation lost $16,401 while the trolleys made $13,262 profit. Cost of running a trolley bus was 46.1 cents per mile while it earned 51.05 cents per mile. Motor buses cost 55.1 cents per mile and earned only 42.03 cents per mile. Streetcars cost 62.8 cents per mile and earned 61.2 cents per mile. In the light of these figures, the original policy of using the trolleys on the main routes was upheld.

A new $500,000 south side Strathcona ("Scona") garage was opened in July 1951, and trolley bus servicing for the buses used on the south side runs was moved there from the Cromdale Barns. The Pullman buses were used mostly on the south side route 6 and were based out of Scona garage as were their replacement Brills, which were acquired second-hand from Regina in 1966.

A money bylaw to provide funds for conversion of the upper deck of the High Level Bridge to a four-lane street had been defeated in the previous November's election. This was a blow to the High Level trolley bus belt line proposals. However an alternative north/south route was urgently needed, and while the planning went ahead, a motor bus shuttle was instituted across the lower deck.

Ritchie service was started directly to the north side with gas buses but conversion to trolleys was forecast. New housing around the shopping centre in Belgravia demanded bus service and again motor buses were to be used with eventual replacement by trolleys.[4]

Routes 2, 5, 6 and 7 were suggested for restructuring in a report by the consulting firm of Stevenson and Kellogg. It was also felt that the use of a downtown loop on a regular basis should be eliminated.[5] One alternative suggestion was to move it so that it ran; north on 100 Street to 102 Avenue, east to 97 Street, north on it to 111 Avenue and thence by 95 Street to 118 Avenue and east to 80 Street and return.[6]

The trolley bus, soon to be the only electric transit in Edmonton, had brushed up its service on August 29th with a switch in routes. *"It will be noticed"* the Edmonton Journal said, *"that the east end of the Number 5 Route which formerly went from 95th St. and 115th Ave. to 82nd St. and 115th Ave. has been re-routed to go up 95th St. to 118th Ave. and along 118th Ave. to 80th St. The Number 7 Route which at present is looped downtown will service 97th St. and 115 Ave. from 95th St. to 82nd St."* This route ran in the northeast, north from Jasper Avenue on 97 Street to 111 Avenue, east on it to 95 Street, north on 95 Street to 115 Avenue, and along it to 82 Street.[7]

On September 2nd 1951 the last streetcar ran on Edmonton streets and the trams became just a nostalgic memory.[8] Where the steel wheel on steel rail had jostled and swayed with its clickety-clack, now there was just the muffled whine of the trolley buses' motors as they moved deftly in and out of traffic. The public was enthralled with its quietness and comfort. But the tram had died prematurely and the Seventies would see its rebirth.

After over a decade of hard service, the last of the English-built buses were retired and scrapped. There was an attempt to sell them in June to the Montreal Transit System which had been the first post-World War I trolley network.[9] The MTC had also used English buses in the beginning but it wasn't interested in them now. Leyland trolley bus 104 had been equipped with a streetcar air whistle at one time in its life and its scrapping ended many an innocent citizen's bewilderment at hearing a tram coming along trackless pavement.

In 1952 a study was undertaken on the costs and possibilities of operation by trolley coaches on a 105 Street bridge route. When the new Bellamy Hill road was paved in the spring a more direct motor bus route from Westwood to Parkallen and Belgravia was instituted. The motor bus route prior to this time detoured west to 109 Street and then back east on Jasper. This resulted in low ridership but the Hill route was expected to increase passenger loads to the point where electrification was economical. This route would allow a decrease in running time from 82 Avenue and 109 Street to 101 Street and Jasper Avenue to twelve minutes from the 21 minutes that a trolley coach would take over the High Level Bridge. This, along with the adverse public reaction over the years, sounded the death knell for the High Level Bridge trolley coach proposal.[10]

The following operating statistics for the first 11 months of 1952 were probably compiled to show the economy that could be achieved by trolley buses on routes such as that of Bellamy Hill/105th Street bridge.

	Trolley Coach	Motor Coach
Maint. of way	$ 28,451.13 = 1.04¢/mi	$ 8,744.93 = 0.45¢/mi
Shop & garage expense	76,083.40 = 2.79¢/mi	53,741.10 = 2.76¢/mi
Maint. of revenue equip.	153,528.78 = 5.62¢/mi	151,859.92 = 7.79¢/mi
Service of revenue equip.	72,749.61 = 2.66¢/mi	71,588.58 = 3.68¢/mi
Total	$330,866.92 = 12.11¢/mi	$285,934.53 = 14.68¢/mi
Mileage	2,733,418	1,947,928
Power (fuel)	$ 85,280.80 = 3.12¢/mi	$85,182.47 = 4.38¢/mi [11]

During 1952, Edmonton ordered four T48A Brill trolley buses. These bigger buses seated 48 passengers and were equipped with independently opening, double-width, front doors. These could be opened separately or together to facilitate passenger loading and unloading, while keeping the minimum amount of cold air from entering.[12] In 1953 the only expansion in the trolley network was on route 2. It was extended in the west end to the Groat Road traffic circle along 118 Avenue.[13]

In August, 1954 Council approved the purchase, at a cost of $24,706 each, of six more T48A trolley buses.[14] This was the last order for such vehicles, as in that year Canadian Car ceased production of trolley buses, ending a remarkable manufacturing career in this electric vehicle field.[15] These larger buses were purchased to meet a steady increase in passenger traffic which had not been budgeted for. Fortunately funds were made available from reserves.[16]

In 1954 the original span of the Low Level Bridge was raised and a new span built beside it. After both spans opened, the north span was only used for northbound travel and the new span for southbound traffic.[17] The route 6 trolley wire was altered accordingly. In that same year ETS pioneered the use of fibreglass panels on buses by installing curved panels at the rear between the back wheels and at the front from the door to the opposite wheel. These were made in its own shops.[18]

Photo below:

Regina Transit System Trolley Coach 125 at Regina, being shipped to Edmonton March 1966. This unit became No. 125 on ETS.   *(Colin K. Hatcher)*

Brill No 170 used the service wire on 102A Avenue in front of City Hall. This piece of overhead was used during LRT construction to route trolleys around a torn-up Jasper Avenue.
(J.A. Kernahan)

In 1955 Parkallen residents fought the battle of the petitions for and against a trolley bus route on 65 Avenue. The "cons" were against the sight of poles along their tree-lined street, however they were outnumbered 512 to 45.[19] The next year the original 1951 proposal for Belgravia was implemented and that part of the motor bus line moved from 72 Avenue to 76 Avenue and south on 118 Street to loop at 73 Street. This was in preparation for the final electrification stage of this line which served both Parkallen and Belgravia.[20] Route 6 was extended on the south side to the University Hospital looping via 82 Avenue, 114 Street, 83 Avenue, 112 Street and return via 82 Avenue eastbound. This was announced on November 27th 1955 and went into service shortly afterwards when wire stringing was complete.[21]

On October 13th 1956, Route 1 was changed from propane buses* to trolleys. It went north on 101 Street to 118 Avenue and the motor bus section from there to 122 Avenue was dropped and covered by other routes. Trolley wires had been installed on 76 Avenue in Parkallen and 65 Avenue in Belgravia and a roundabout constructed to connect Princess Elizabeth Avenue, 101 Street and 118 Avenue at the north end of the route. The switch from propane to trolley was a matter of economics as electricity was cheaper. This completed the long-range plan of electrifying this Bellamy Hill/105 Street bridge route as patronage increased. Availability of buses, however, was a concern as the extension had cost $25,000 per mile over four miles.[22]

"Patrons are advised that during the next few weeks they will not see the familiar trolley coaches on this (the No. 6) route. Construction work at the north end of the Low Level Bridge requires the substitution by motor buses. Schedules and service will remain the same." This advertisement in the October 13th 1956 *Journal* was unduly optimistic as the construction of traffic interchanges at both ends of the bridge continued until November 17th *1957* when service was finally restored.[23]

In 1958 the transit system celebrated its 50th anniversary. The operation covered 57-1/2 miles of trolley overhead using 93 trolley coaches, as well as 106 "gas", diesel and propane motor buses, cruising over 116 miles of routes. Total assets were nearly $4 million with a staff of 456 drivers, inspectors and maintenance men. Transportation was being provided to 34,137,948 passengers over 5,616,641 miles a year on a 10¢ fare. Trolley service was seen by Superintendent MacDonald as being too expensive at $30,000 a wire mile for overhead, for residential areas, but it still held sway in the heavily-travelled core.[24] Even as late as 1961, however, with the increasing use of motor buses, statistics still showed that the trolleys turned in $527,000 revene over expenses. Motor buses ran up a deficit of $785,404 that same year.[25]

With the completion of the new Westwood Garage in 1961, service wire was extended along 118 Avenue west from 101 Street to a loop at the garage at 106 Street. North side trolley bus servicing and storage was then transferred from Cromdale to Westwood.

On January 1st 1962 the Town of Beverly (pop. 6,000) was amalgamated with the City of Edmonton. Any argument against extension of a trolley route into this suburban area no longer held and Beverly residents demanded better transit service.[26] On September 2nd of that year, the south side routes were improved with the splitting of trolley route 1 into two. All south side routes were given letter/number designations. Thus, route 6 became S6 and 1 became S1 to Belgravia and S2 to Parkallen.[27]

---

*Propane had been introduced as an economical fuel several years previously.

Flyer trolley coach No. 224 approaches the 101 Street underpass under the CN Rail tracks a block west of the passenger station. 224 is northbound on route S1.   (Tom Schwarzkopf)

Late in 1962 the city purchased ten used T-44 Brill trolleys from Vancouver at $2,500 each. These twelve- and thirteen-year old vehicles were to be used as spares to replace, in part, the Macks that had been scrapped that year.[28] An Edmonton Journal cartoon showed one of the newly-acquired Vancouver buses pulling up to a stop and discharging a cargo of water and fish from the front doors, presumably left over from its Vancouver days.[29]

At this time the front destination curtains for the Pullmans and T-48 Brills, number 200 through 202 only, were changed for south side service as follows:

105 ST BRIDGE	S1	BELGRAVIA 118 AVE
105 ST BRIDGE	S2	PARKALLEN 118 AVE
LOW LEVEL	S6	UNIV HOSP DOWNTOWN

The left destination was in black, the centre number in yellow and the right destination in red.[30]

Since Can Car (CCF) had stopped producing trolleys nearly five years previously, the supply of electric vehicles had become scarce. Several cities had abandoned them due to electricity costs being higher than diesel fuel. However, with its city-owned power utility, Edmonton had been sheltered from this effect. In March 1963, it was recommended that the Highlands (2) line be extended east in Beverly from 61 Street and 112 Avenue to 50 Street and 118 Avenue.[31] On June 30th, this was put into effect extending the route east on 112 Avenue to 53 Street, then north to 118 Avenue, east to 50 Street, south on 112 Avenue and return.[32]

In 1964 the trolley system grew and shrank. In May, Council approved a budget that included $80,000 for a trolley extension to the Town of Jasper Place (pop. 35,000) which was to be amalgamated into the City on August 17th.[33] This was followed by a retrenchment. Power demands exceeded the supply and due to the high peak-hour ridership on the S6, this route was slated for dieselization. There was also the prospect of considerable roadway changes in that area and more overhead moves would be expensive. This route had the oldest buses on it, the Pullmans, and the wire over the old Low Level Bridge was worn out. Nonetheless, this stretch of wire had to be replaced to keep the system going for the balance of 1964 while two or three of the seven coaches were replaced by the experimental motor buses then under test. The remaining Pullman trolleys were scheduled for removal in mid-1965. However, Superintendent MacDonald was optimistic that the motors from the scrapped trolleys could be used in other bus bodies such as the Japanese Nissan/Fugi/MAAN and the British-built Daimler designs, then under test.[34]

On August 17th 1964, on schedule, service was started into Jasper Place, now a part of Edmonton. This line, route 7, beginning at 115 Avenue and 82 Street, had looped at the old western City limits between 147 and 148 Streets and Stony Plain Road. It now was extended via Stony Plain Road to 157 Street where a terminal had been constructed. This was called by one source at that time, "the last trolley bus extension in Canada and perhaps in North America."[35]

By the year's end concern was mounting that the agitation in Calgary to scrap electric transit there would have repercussions in Edmonton. Superintendent MacDonald came out strongly, stating that Edmonton had no intention of scrapping its fleet of 100 trolleys. Their advantages, including their non-polluting capability, made them a viable transportation form. Peak electricity costs that were troubling Calgary were no problem in Edmonton.[36]

On Saturday, August 28th 1965 the last trolleys were removed from the S6 Low Level Bridge route and Edmonton's first trolley bus line fell victim to the relentless onslaught of the diesel bus.[37] Despite MacDonald's statement, some called this line termination the start of a phasing-out of the trolley bus network. Trolleys were the most efficient bus that the transit system had, but the lack of a bus builder and the disadvantage of being tied to a relatively fixed route were cited as reasons for their gradual disappearance.

Though the Pullmans were the oldest trolleys in the fleet, their passing from the scene was a disappointment to many operators. They were extremely comfortable buses, with excellent heating and a wide driver's compartment that could comfortably fit the most portly operator. Beneath the operator's window was a wide shelf on which one could leave lunches and coffee cups. However this convenience proved a discomfort to operator Dave Fillion one day on the S6 run. The bus had stopped at one end of the Low Level Bridge single span waiting for the light that controlled traffic flow to change. It was a warm summer day and many of the bus windows, including the operator's were open. Dave was eating his lunch when he suddenly noticed that his tomato sandwich was soggy. As he pondered the supposed effect of an over-ripe tomato on untoasted bread, a very irate passenger was coming rapidly up the aisle with a damp shirt front demanding at the top of his lungs "what was the transit company going to do about it?" The explanation suddenly became apparent as Dave noticed in his rear view mirror an open cattle truck passing the end of the bus going the opposite way with one cow's tail lifted. The hapless driver could only think of the standard response for any vehicle encounter, "Did you get the number of that cow, sir?"[38]

By 1966, the fleet was down to 82 buses, ranging in age from 1946 (six buses) to 1954. The Pullmans, Macks and the ACF/Brills, as well as some of the early CCF/Brills, had gone to the scrapyard. The trolley fleet rose to 92 with the purchase of some second-hand units from Regina in March 1966, when that system abandoned its electric buses. The destination blinds for these and some of the ex-Vancouver Brills had added to them:

    S1   105 ST BRIDGE
    S2   105 ST BRIDGE[39]

These buses were repainted in a new colour scheme with a brighter red and white instead of cream for the roof. Most existing units were also repainted in this scheme.

That same month city crews started removing the wires on 100 Street from Jasper to 102 Avenue, down MacDougall Hill over the Low Level Bridge and up Scona Hill to Whyte and west on Whyte to 103 Street. This removed the last reminders of Edmonton's first trolley bus line, 27 years after it had started. Lines were also slated to come down on the University Hospital extension from 109 Street to 114 Street, along 83 Avenue to 112 Street and south to Whyte Avenue.[40]

With the changing of several downtown streets to one way, trolley routes were restructured on July 2nd 1967. Two sections of wire were strung downtown; a single westbound line from 97 Street to 101 Street along 102A Avenue for short turning buses, and a single line west from 101 Street along 103 Avenue to 102 Street, then south on 102 to Jasper. A second section ran along 102 Avenue from 102 Street to 97 Street. The trolley routes were rearranged and renumbered at this time. Routes 2 and 7 were dropped. The new route 3 went from 115 Avenue and 82 Street to Groat Road and 118 Avenue. When going eastbound, it ran south on 101 Street, west on 103 Avenue, south on 102 Street, east on 102 Avenue to 97 Street and north on it. Morning and afternoon extras worked the west end of this line and were numbered route 4 looping east on 102A Avenue, south on 97 Street, west on Jasper Avenue, and north on 101 Street. There were no changes in route 5, but the north terminus of the S1/S2 was moved from the 118 Avenue and 101 Street circle along the former service wire to a loop at 106 Street and 118 Avenue at the south end of WestwoodGarage.[41]

Destination blinds on all T-44 trolley coaches were changed to read:

	Front		*Side*
5	81 St — 118 Ave	5	124 St 112 Ave
5	124 St — 112 Ave	5	81 St 118 Ave
4	Downtown	4	Groat Rd — 118 Ave
4	Groat Rd — 118 Ave		Downtown
3	Groat Rd — 118 Ave	3	82 St 115 Ave
3	82 St — 115 Ave		Groat Rd — 118 Ave
1	Jas Place	1	Highlands
1	Highlands		Jas Place
S1-S2	118 Ave	S2	Parkallen
S2	Parkallen		118 Ave
S1	Belgravia	S1	Belgravia
	107 Ave — 124 St		118 Ave
	Downtown		107 Ave
	Exhibition		124 St
	Garage		Downtown
			Exhibition
			Garage[42]

The future looked bleak but the system held on until the Seventies dawned. Pollution became a popular topic and the environment was being "saved" all over North America. Edmonton, with its fume-free buses, committed itself to prolonging the system. Fifteen trolley buses were purchased from Winnipeg in 1969 to be cannibalized for parts.[43] The system continued to hang on by its teeth.

However, the trolleys' sun was rising in the east. In 1970, the Toronto Transit Commission purchased 151 new bus chassis and bodies to make into new trolleys by installing the indestructible motors from the old Brills. The bus skeletons were to be supplied by Western Flyer Industries in Winnipeg. The Toronto rebuild had been "in the works" with Flyer since 1967 and Edmonton watched the progress of the Toronto experiment anxiously. Maintenance costs on the old trolleys had climbed past that of diesel buses, but "fuel" was still a cent a mile and depreciation costs by now were nil. The costs of wire extensions had risen from $30,000 per mile in the fifties when the last extension had been made, to $60,000. Importation of equipment from Europe was ruled out as too expensive. Toronto was probably the only transit system with extensive-enough shops to undertake the rebuild job itself, since it also maintained Canada's only streetcar fleet in the same facility. Cities other than Toronto would have to order the trolleys factory-built and until there was sufficient volume, the cost of the Flyer trolley coach was deemed uneconomical.[44] The remaining systems were in Vancouver, Toronto and Hamilton with the Calgary network dying a slow death.

In September 1971, MacDonald was appointed City Transportation Director, retaining his position as Superintendent of ETS. He had joined the organization in 1946 and had overseen the gradual replacement of streetcars by trolley buses. He continued the conversion of the trolley coach network after he replaced Thomas Ferrier as ETS Superintendent in 1951.[45] Now he was watching to see if it would experience a rebirth.

The trolleys' supposed salvation arrived in Edmonton in in January 1972. A Toronto Transit Commission/Flyer-built trolley bus (TTC No. 9213) looking much like a GMC diesel in appearance, ran on the 101 Street route on a trial basis. This bus, on a tour of several western Canadian and US cities, was the first built in North America in sixteen years and the first in Canada in eighteen. Toronto was committed to replacing its 153 trolley bus fleet entirely with 152 new Flyers and Edmonton's 92 Brill trolley buses were in no better shape.[46] In 1973 the balance of trolley operations was transferred from Scona to Westwood garage and all but one of the trolley wires through the Scona garage were removed.

By 1973 Toronto had taken delivery of 152 Flyer trolley buses and Hamilton had some also. A factory-built trolley was now an economic reality and Edmonton ordered 37, the start of a planned replacement that would see 75 new trolleys in the next two years.[47] Western Flyer was now known as Flyer Industries and the Manitoba government, through the Manitoba Development Corporation, had taken a controlling interest in it. Several US transit systems were looking seriously at the new trolley and helped boost support for it.[48]

The first shipment of 25 Edmonton buses was due in February 1974 to be followed in June by the remaining twelve.[49] In August Edmonton ordered twenty more coaches worth $1.1 million for delivery in September 1975, and seventeen coaches worth another $1.1 million for September 1976.[50] By December 1974, only one bus (number 213) had been delivered, and the remaining 24 were five months overdue.[51] Technical problems with the controller on bus 213 kept it from being put into service for a time. Flyer was also in the midst of a disastrous strike that was further to delay the balance of the Edmonton order.[52]

In the fall of 1974, ETS purchased some of Calgary's trolleys for parts as they were too rundown to rehabilitate. It also acquired motors, poles, controllers and line hardware from the now-defunct Calgary system.[54]

In May 1975, there were four Flyers in Edmonton and by July the Flyer contingent was up to eight. Delivery problems and many mechanical and electrical problems with the buses prompted ETS to ask for a full financial analysis of maintaining or phasing out the trolley buses. Another factor against the electric buses was increased power costs due to rising natural gas prices. Flyer was having, in addition to labour problems, trouble meeting its delivery dates due to subsuppliers' late deliveries. There were problems with electrical components burning up when the power polarity was changed. Flyer revised its polarity-sensitive components. Other problems surfaced such as the bus heaters drawing so much power that they tripped the power switches in the overhead. The design of the rear spoiler (to hold optional air conditioning) caught the retriever ropes when the poles swung out on a far reach. ETS modified the rear of the buses as each required shopping.

Three more Flyers had arrived but shortly after settlement of the long strike the plant had shut down again for summer vacation. Edmonton was becoming discouraged about the trolley's salvation.

Roller signs on the Flyers as delivered were:

Front (right and left identical)	*Front Centre*	*Side*
blank	numbers 1-10	blank
BEVERLY		GARAGE
EXHIBITION		CHARTER
INGLEWOOD		SPECIAL
JASPER PLACE		RTE. 1 (2-10)
N.A.I.T.		blank
NORTHGATE		
WESTMOUNT		
DOWNTOWN		
GARAGE		
SPECIAL		
CHARTER		
SOUTHGATE		
UNIVERSITY[53]		

On December 8th 1974, an extension from 124 Street west on 114 Avenue through to the new Westmount transit terminal was opened to trolleys.[55] A unique feature of this line was the one block private right-of-way running through the parking lot of the Charles Camsell Hospital. This avoided the buses having to make a jog around the Hospital. No doubt the silent running of the trol-

▫ ▫ ▫ ▫

Photo opposite page:
Brill coach No. 197 turns from 118 Avenue onto 106 Street, after the S1 and S2 routes had been extended to Kingsway Garden Mall. Coach 197 is a T48A Brill. (J.A. Kernahan)

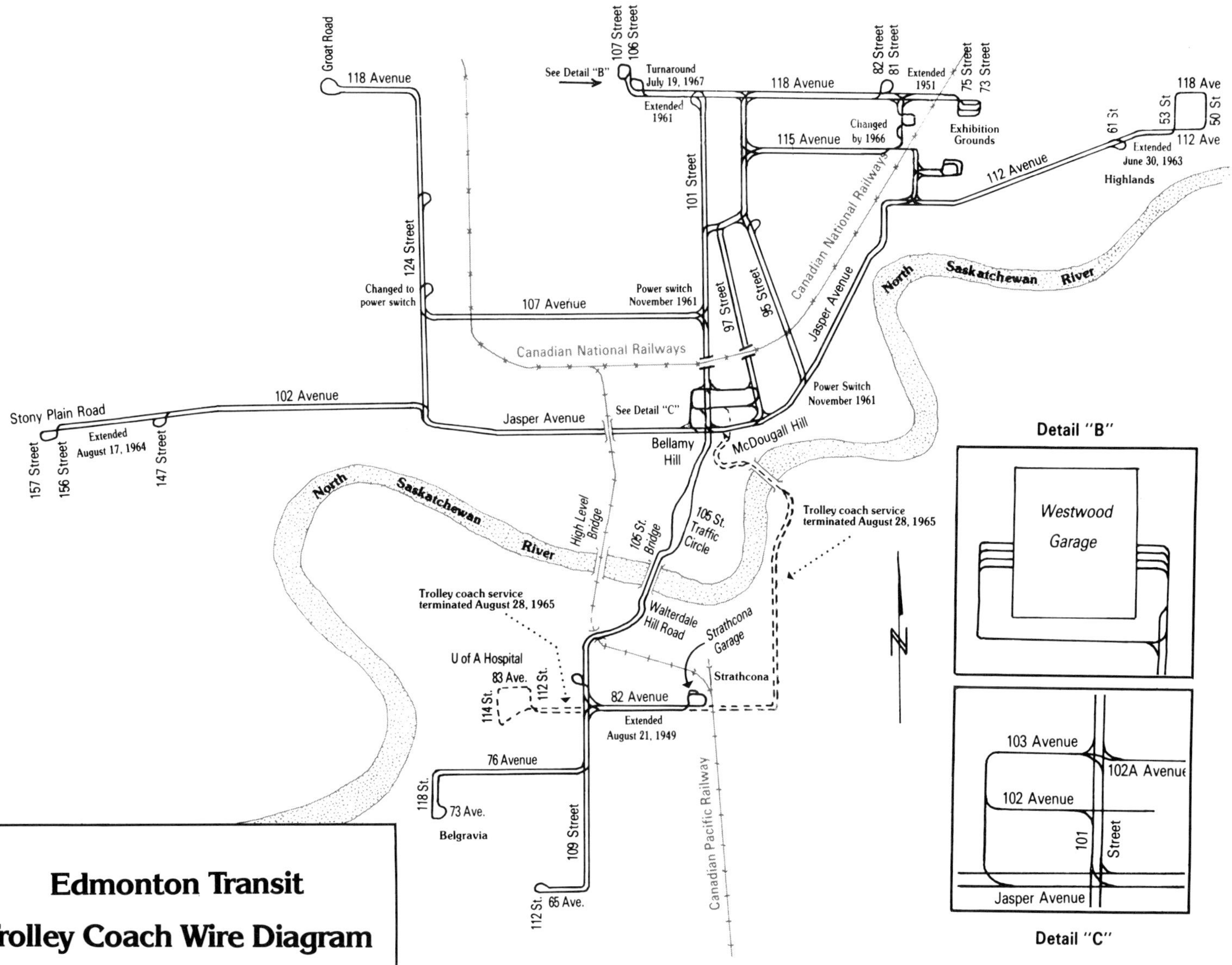

Edmonton Transit Trolley Coach Wire Diagram 1970

Photo above:

The new destination signs were more complete and allowed better signage for the south side routes. No. 222 is southbound on 104 Street south of 97 Avenue. Note the Commonwealth Games logo beside the front door. (Colin K. Hatcher)

Photo above:

On February 19th 1977, a few days after service was extended along Kingsway Avenue, T48A Brill No. 198 heads south near the Royal Alexandra Hospital. Trolley coaches finally provided long-planned (since 1949) service on this thoroughfare. Streetcar rail had been laid in the roadway, but the trackage never saw any service. (Colin K. Hatcher)

Photo below:

Flyer trolley coach No. 248 leaves the north terminus of route 42 (S2) at 106 Street and 118 Avenue near the Northern Alberta Institute of Technology and the Westwood trolley garage. These coaches were still equipped with the early destination signs that were inadequate for the south side routes. Note the female operator. (E.K. Letain)

leys was a plus factor in obtaining permission to run a bus route directly behind a hospital. The line passed through a residential area, and again the trolleys' features helped in winning over the homeowners to having a bus route past their doors. The line looped behind the Westmount Shopping Centre giving passengers immediate access to it. This wire was used by the new route 5 that ran from Westmount Terminal via 114 Avenue to 124 Street, south on it to Jasper Avenue, east on Jasper to 95 Street and north to 118 Avenue and along that to the eastern terminus. At least one truck driver was surprised by this addition when he drove his oversize load through the new overhead as he went down Groat Road, during a Friday rush hour.

In late spring 1975, Jasper Avenue was closed from 102 Street to 100 Street during the construction of the new Light Rail Transit line.[56] At first buses only were allowed. The trolleys ran on temporary overhead suspended from wooden centre street poles. Finally, on June 8th, all traffic was banned and all eastbound trolley routes detoured around the site by going north on 102 Street over a new stretch of wire to 102 Avenue and then to 97 Street. Westbound buses travelled via 97 Street, 102A Avenue and 102 Street. The north/south wire on 101 Street was left intact as it crossed Jasper for the S1/S2 buses.[57] Service was restored on Jasper Avenue in September.

In September 1975, a start was made on extending the 109 Street overhead through to the new Southgate Transit Centre at 111 Street and 54 Avenue. This would allow the new route 9 to be electrified. This route began service with diesels initially on November 9th, 1975, offering fifteen-minute service between Southgate and 118 Avenue and 101 Street. At that same time the north terminus of the S2 route was moved south to 109 Street and 83 Avenue on a half-hour service. The S2 ran only during the peak hours through downtown to the Northern Alberta Institute of Technology. For a time before this, there was a controversy over the routing of route 9 through the residential section of the Southgate area, but eventually the trolleys won and the line was extended south on 109 Street from 65 Avenue to 57 Avenue, west to 111 Street and south to the temporary terminal at 54 Avenue.[58] By the year's end, wire was strung and construction of a new power substation was well underway.[59] On February 1st 1976, the north terminus of route 9 was extended to loop at Westwood garage. At the same time, poles were being erected down 106 Street south past the Northern Alberta Institute of Technology to enter the new Kingsway Garden Mall from 106 Street and loop there. This was the first time that a shopping plaza had allotted space for a transit terminal in the actual mall area for the shoppers' convenience.[60]

By April 1976 feeder cable was strung for the Southgate route 9 extension and the substation completed.[61] In May 1976 regular trolley bus service began on route 9. The NAIT/Kingsway Mall extension was also completed as the north part of the S1.[62] A turning loop was also constructed on 121 Street and 102 Avenue west to 124 Street for the western terminus of an eventual electrified 2 route. Equipment shortages and overhead

Photo below:
On a pleasant day in May, Colin Hatcher photographed Flyer 244 leaving the new Southgate transit centre heading north on Route 9 for NAIT. (Colin K. Hatcher)

Photo above:
Coach 247 in the old colours, but upgraded with the new image decal, pauses in front of the Art Gallery on 102A Street. The Flyer is signed for Groat Road and is making the west run to this terminus. Use of this stretch of wire was limited to the detouring of route during LRT construction.
(Colin K. Hatcher)

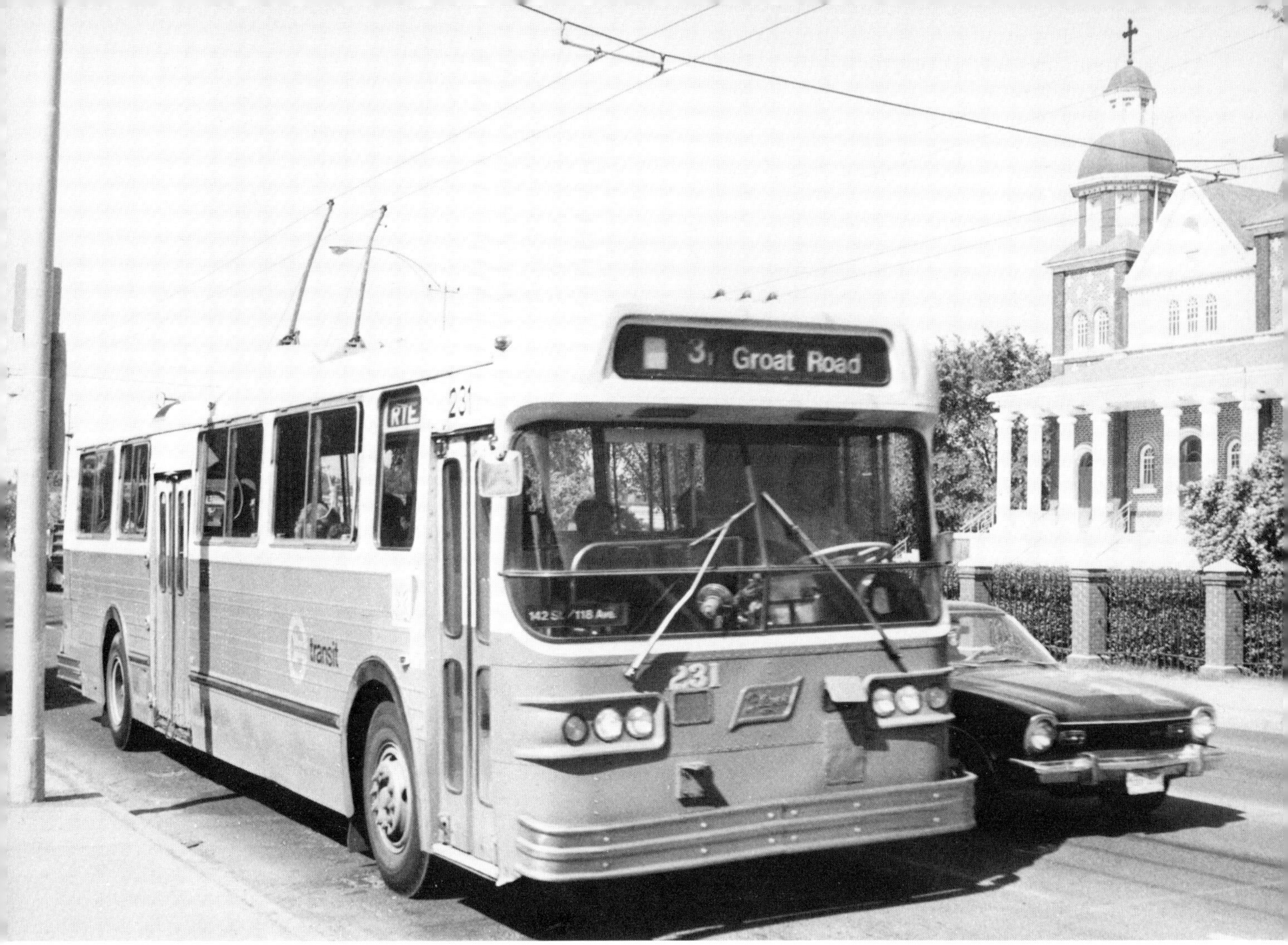
3 Groat Road
RTE
231
transit
142 St./118 Ave.
231

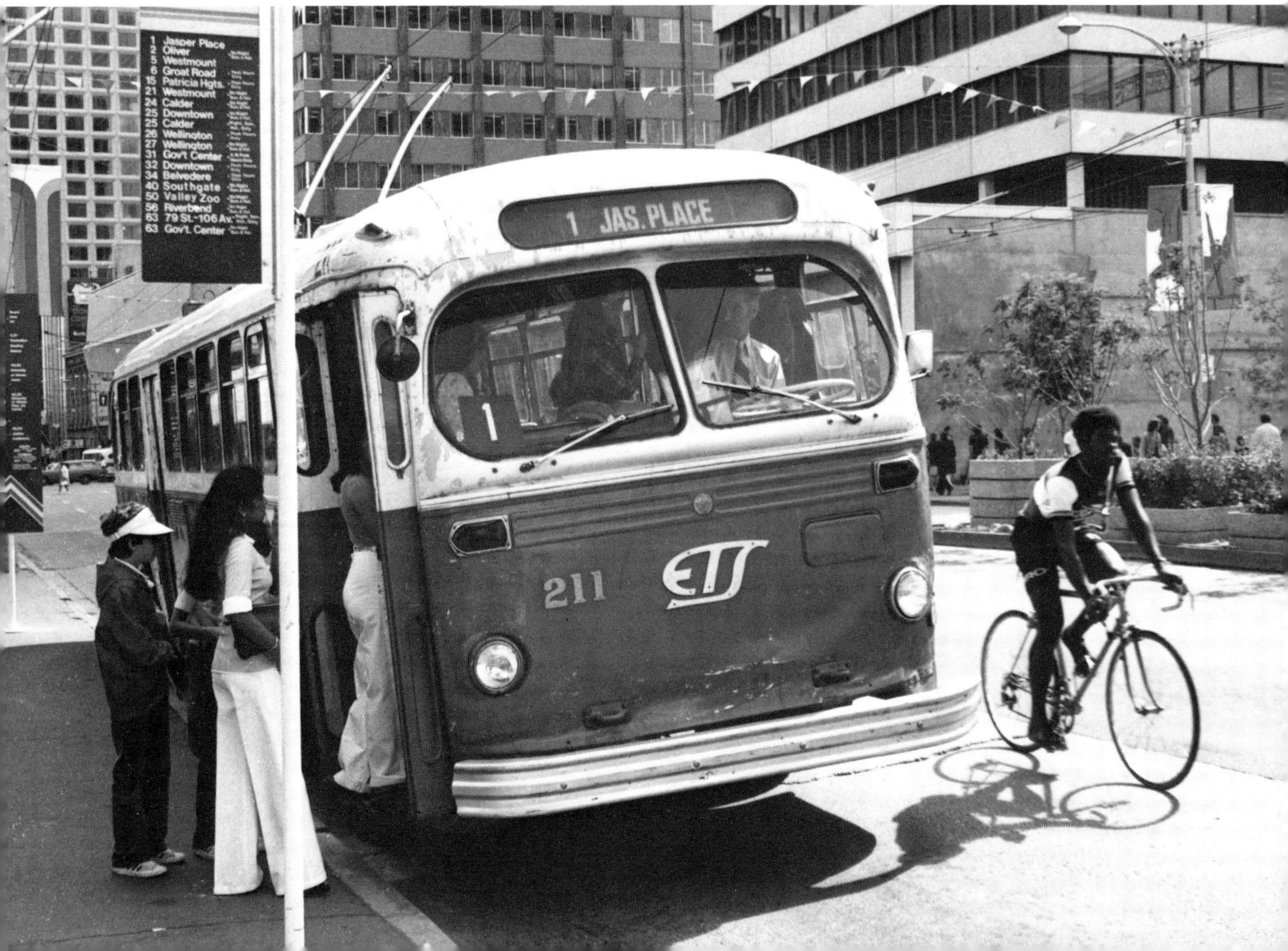
1 Jasper Place
2 Oliver
5 Westmount
6 Groat Road
15 Patricia Hgts.
21 Westmount
24 Calder
25 Downtown
25 Calder
26 Wellington
27 Wellington
31 Gov't Center
32 Downtown
34 Belvedere
40 Southgate
50 Valley Zoo
56 Riverbend
63 79 St.-106 Av.
63 Gov't. Center
1 JAS. PLACE
1
211
ETS

changes has stalled this conversion.[63] On February 1st 1976, route 4 was changed to run to Westmount transit terminal instead of to Groat Road and 118 Avenue. A new route, (6) was introduced to run from Groat Road and 118 Avenue to 81 Street and 118 Avenue along the 5 routing. These two routes, 4 and 6 were peak-hour-only services.[64]

All Flyer buses as received had been painted in the Edmonton Transit System colours of white and red. In 1976 the system dropped the word "System" from its name and adopted an ultra-modern new logo and a blue, white and yellow paint scheme. Since all Flyer trolleys had been fabricated and painted before the change, only those damaged in use were repainted. Bus 232 was the first one dressed up in this new finery.[65]

In September 1976 poles were erected on Kingsway Avenue from 108 Street to 101 Street in anticipation of an extension to the S1 and S2 from the Kingsway Mall to 101 Street.[66]

Another era passed on December 5th 1976, when the old letter/number route designations were replaced with numerals only. The only trolley routes affected were the S1 (41) and S2 (42). In the first part of 1978 all transit buses were equipped with new roller signs to give a consistency to the fleet for the Commonwealth Games. The only exceptions were the Brill trolleys and the GM 5105 diesels. Signs on the Flyers consisted of two numeral rollers at the passenger (left) side and one destination roller as follows:

   blank
   Abbotsfield
   Downtown
   Jasper Place
   Highlands
   Churchill
   Oliver
   Stadium Station
   N.A.I.T.
   Cromdale
   Groat Road
   Northlands
   124 St./108 Ave.
   Downtown
   Westmount
   Coliseum
   81 St./118 Ave.
   N.A.I.T.
   Southgate
   Northgate
   Kingsway Mall
   Belgravia
   Parkallen
   Not in Service
   West Jasper Pl.
   blank

The side signs read as before with the addition of:

   Rte. 18
   Rte. 41
   Rte. 42

These new signs were in upper/lower case lettering as shown and the additional 3 routes on the side sign had this lettering contrasting with the all-upper-case of RTE. 1 through 10. These signs contained some hopeful extensions, ("Northgate", "West Jasper Place") and the names of Light Rail Transit Stations that the line passed by, ("Churchill" and "Stadium"). GARAGE was replaced with N.A.I.T., the closest destination to Westwood Garage.[67]

The extension along Kingsway Avenue came into service on February 13th 1977. It ran from 101 Street to 108 Street where it turned north and joined the loop in the Kingsway Shopping Mall. At this time the north leg of route 42 was reinstated allowing Parkallen residents all day through service to downtown and NAIT. Both the 41 and 42 looped through the Westwood loop, (106A Street and 118 Avenue) and then ran via 106 Street to 112 Avenue through the shopping mall to 108 Street and thence south to Kingsway, 101 Street, Bellamy Hill, 105th Street bridge, Walterdale Hill, 109 Street. At 76 Avenue, route 41 ran west on it to 118 Street and south to 73 Avenue. The 42 continued down 109 Street to 65 Avenue and west on it to 112 Street.[68] On November 22nd 1977, the temporary terminus at the south end of route 9 was moved from 54 Avenue to a permanent transit centre in the Southgate Shopping Mall.

The Kingsway Mall loop was rearranged in April 1978, so that the through wire path was straightened. The loop was broken so that buses could not turn back at the mall and go north unless there was a wire jump. The remainder of the loop was retained in case route 18 should be electrified. Late in 1978, route 1 was rewired to pass by the Stadium LRT station. This involved a jog up 84 Street from Jasper to 111 Avenue, and east on it to join the old wire at 82 Street. The existing outbound wire was retained for short-turning use. In that case, outbound buses would proceed past the new switch at 84 Street along the old wire and turn into the station at 111 Avenue so that all inbound buses were facing the same way. The change in routing, however, only took effect in the summer of 1979.

On November 2nd 1975, members of the Alberta Pioneer Railway Association, a western railway museum group, chartered restored Pullman trolley coach 113, the only surviving one of its kind in Canada, for a "fan trip". Nine years out of service and 31 years from its birth, the old bus ran smoothly over the Sunday-service wires of the system covering most of Edmonton's wire miles. Veteran driver Jack Fleck took the wheel as he had many times when they were in service and local news media chased the trip, recording it for night-

Opposite page, upper:

The trolleys still run in Edmonton. In front of the Ukranian Catholic Cathedral of St. Josaphat, Flyer No. 231 heads south on 97 Street near 108 Avenue on Route 3. The dash sign indicates the extended terminus of the route, 118 Avenue and 142 Street. (Colin K. Hatcher)

Opposite page, lower:

Edmonton Transit CCF/Brill No. 211, somewhat the worse for wear, loads passengers on Jasper Avenue at 102 Street. The date is Friday August 11th 1978, one day before the closing of the Commonwealth games and withdrawal of most of the Brills from service. No. 211 is ex-Vancouver 2009. Note the games location sign in the background. (Colin K. Hatcher)

Photo below:

On a pleasant day in May, Colin Hatcher photographed Flyer 244 leaving the new Southgate transit centre heading north on Route 9 for NAIT. *(Colin K. Hatcher)*

Photo above:

Coach 247 in the old colours, but upgraded with the new image decal, pauses in front of the Art Gallery on 102A Street. The Flyer is signed for Groat Road and is making the west run to this terminus. Use of this stretch of wire was limited to the detouring of route during LRT construction.

(Colin K. Hatcher)

A last fling. "South to the Exhibition" may not ring true, but with a chance to have a stroll after retirement, anything goes. Brill T44 No. 191 in as-delivered configuration leads Pullman No. 113 (116) off the south end of the 105 Street Bridge Sunday September 16th 1979. The occasion is a field trip during the Association of Railway Museums Convention. The operator is Don Clark. (D. Scafe)

time television audiences. One enthusiast travelled from Vancouver for the occasion. The happy photographers had the bus displaying its original S6 route number to the confusion of passengers waiting for a regular bus. Several people with fond memories of the Pullmans commented that they wished that those buses hadn't been retired.[69] Later investigation showed that bus 113 was in fact 116, renumbered when it was added to the ETS historical collection.

Old age took its toll of the Brills, however, and they were slowly pensioned off. Some were stripped for parts to keep healthier sister units going. Many were stored and patched so as to be serviceable for the two weeks of the Commonwealth Games, when all available vehicles would be needed. A small, but vocal public noticed the attrition and kept asking about the state of electric transit in Edmonton. With the advent of the Light Rail Transit System, the logic of maintaining electric surface transit became stronger, but the fleet still dwindled.

What was to become of the oldest continuous running trolley bus network in Canada? The unhappy experiences with the new Flyer trolleys forced the City to commission another evaluation of the advisability of continuing with electric buses. A report by Hu Harries and Associates supported the viability of trolley buses but the question remained, whence will they come? The Brills' day had passed; they lasted longer than most motor buses, but even these venerable war horses would have to be put out to pasture eventually. These questions were put by an Edmonton Journal reporter to E.V. Miller, Edmonton Transit's General Manager, early in 1978. Miller cited the difficulties they had experienced in finding suitable replacements and the fact that the old Brills were falling apart. The possibility of a joint purchase with Vancouver in order to lower the price was being investigated. However, Mr. Miller stated that not only was there money budgeted for new trolleys, but wire improvements were being planned as well. Edmonton Transit, he said, has a firm intention to continue to provide trolley bus service.[70]

Will Edmontonians be able to stand a few years hence on an early frosty winter's morning and hear the stillness broken only by the hiss of carbon shoes on wire and the "clickity-clack" of the poles passing through the switches? Will the only sound as the bus pulls away from the stop be a soft whine from the motor and the thump of the compressor, or will the stillness be broken by the diesel's growl? Certainly the sound will not be that of a Brill, for on November 19th 1978, the last of the breed ran on a special farewell trip in Edmonton. ET bus 202, the last T-48 Brill produced in Canada, was chartered by the Alberta Pioneer Railway Association almost three years to the day after the Pullman trolley bus trip, and sent with much publicity on a grand tour under most of the city overhead. Harry Venecamp negotiated the

bus through numerous pieces of special overhead and posed the bus for the many picture stops. At the conclusion of the trip, bus 202 joined 191, an example of an unaltered T-44 Brill still in the cream roof and red sides paint scheme, and Pullman 113 (116) as part of the Edmonton Transit historical collection. But perhaps the best news was confided to this author by Mr. Miller during the pre-trip press session that at least fifty trolleys would be purchased for delivery over the next two years. These buses would replace the Brills and build the fleet back up to its previous strength. This information was publicly confirmed on the day of the trip and warmly received by the assembled trolley bus supporters.*

Opposite page:

Flyer No. 220 descends Bellamy Hill southbound at the foot of 101 Street in downtown Edmonton. This coach has the most recent paint scheme, roll signs and bobbed tail. Hopefully 220 will be joined soon by the next generation of trolleys from Brown Boveri/GM, maintaining the tradition of the longest continuously-operating trolleybus service in Canada.
(Colin K. Hatcher)

Photo above, left:

Pullman trolley coach 113 (actually 116) on the Westmount private right-of-way, featured in an Alberta Pioneer Railway Association excursion trip November 2nd 1975. (D. Scafe)

Above, right:

The flexibility of the trolley bus was no more evident than during the early LRT construction. It was relatively easy to slide the overhead over on the span wires and continue service. Here Brill 156 passes the Central Station construction westbound on Jasper at 101 Street, June 6th 1975.
(Colin K. Hatcher)

This was a first step in the right direction, but things seemed to move slowly. It wasn't until the summer of 1979 that the next extension took place. In conjunction with reconstruction of Groat Road and 118 Avenue traffic circle, routes 3 and 6 were extended to an off-street loop at 142 Street and 118 Avenue. Work progressed throughout the summer and into the new year. Service started on February 3rd 1980. In addition tenders for one hundred new trolleys were called in the winter of 1979 to commence delivery in 1981. The order was placed with Brown Boveri/GM in August 1980. This order will bring the fleet size up to 137, the largest ever. These positive events coupled with active planning by Edmonton Transit for extensions and electrification of several routes when the new equipment arrives, will put Edmonton once again in the front ranks of Canadian transit systems that rely on the inherent advantages of electricity.

In 1981 and 1982, Edmonton Transit took delivery of 100 new Brown Boveri chopper trolley coaches. See Appendix IV for more details on the new equipment and services.

*As a footnote to Edmonton Transit's historical collection comprising Pullman No. 113, and Brills T44 (Nos. 148 and 191) and T48A (No. 202), the Annual Convention of the Association of Railway Museums was held in Edmonton on September 16th 1979. As one of the convention activities, all three historical trolleys were chartered to take the Association members on a city trolley bus field trip. It is hoped that the transit collection — which includes several motor buses as well — will be used and displayed more often in future.

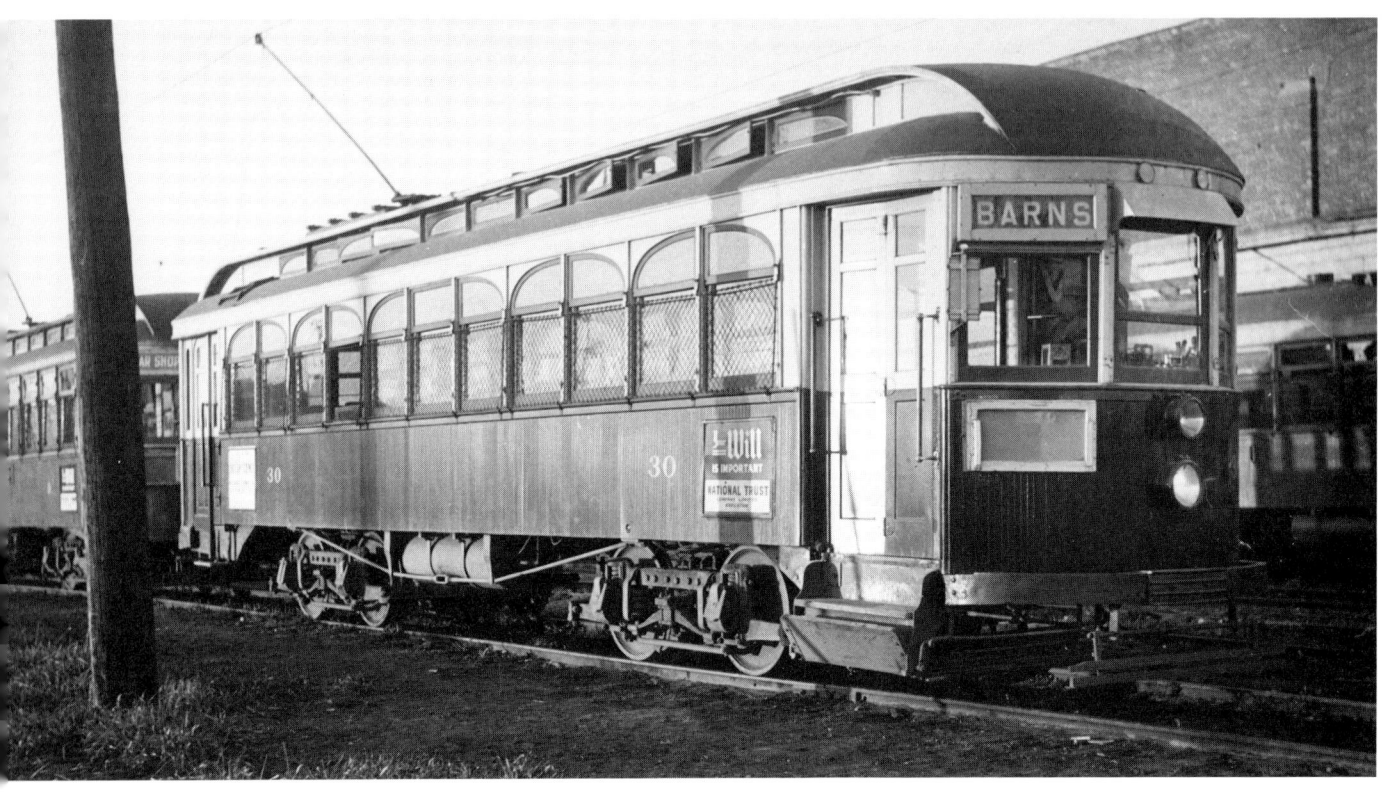

Appendix I
Equipment Roster – Rail

Roster Notes

The roster describes cars as delivered to the railway and, in some instances, as rebuilt for a different type of service. Changes to cars remaining in the same type of service are noted below.

Brakes: All cars were fitted with Ackley Adjustable hand brakes in each vestibule. Preston cars 47 - 81 had Beverly brake wheels installed in the short front vestibule and brake staffs with polished bronze handles for the longer rear vestibule. Type of compressor and motorman's valve for each air-brake-equipped car is noted in the roster. All Westinghouse equipment conformed to schedule S-M-1 except for the 1930 Ottawa-built cars which featured a more sophisticated air brake system co-ordinated with the controller and the centre exit treadle door.

Gear Ratios: On Cars 1 - 31 these are not recorded, but it is thought that this ratio was 69:17.

Car Weights: These figures are based on total weights as noted in the City of Edmonton Street Railway Department Car Weights and Levers chart. It is highly probably, however, that cars in the 47 - 81 series were heavier than this chart indicates. A letter from Preston Car and Coach Company, (dated November 20, 1912 and addressed to W.H. Woodroofe) regarding the shipping weights of these cars, places their weight at 34,000 lbs. each without electrical equipment. Electrical equipment weight tables in the Electric Railway Dictionary 1911, reprinted in 1972 by Newton K. Gregg, Novato, California, USA, establish four motor equipment and controller weight at 12,880 lbs. Total weight of these cars under this formula would have been 46,880 lbs., a weight comparable with similar-sized cars on other street railway systems in Canada.

Dimensions: These have been taken from contract proposals. The dimensions for the 1930 Ottawa-built cars come from the Ottawa Car Catlogue which suggests that this data was based on the cars as completed and ready for service. Heights in all cases are taken from the bottom of the sill to the top of the roof. Widths noted are over sheathing. Library car front platform dimensions are estimated. Observation car dimensions are based on assumption that this car was built on the frame of car 22.

Operation: Double-ended cars had a trolley pole at each end with the exception of car 7 which had one pole mounted on the centre of the car roof, which rotated a full 180 degrees to enable the car to travel in either direction. The cars equipped for double-end operation in the Preston 47 - 81 group were provided with a pole at the rear end only. When the car operated rear end first, the pole was simply turned so that it trailed the direction of travel.

Construction: All cars delivered up to 1914 were sheathed in wood. Cars 32 - 46 had steel-sheathed dashes at each end. The 1930 Ottawa-built cars were completely steel-sheathed. Door sash on all cars was finished in natural cherry wood as was window sash on the wooden cars. The steel cars had brass window sash.

Frame: The wood frame cars all possessed some form of steel reinforcement. This reinforcement consisted of a steel plate extending the full length of the body against each oak side sill. The width and thickness of this plate varied on some groups of cars; hence, some wood-frame cars on the Edmonton Radial Railway did not require truss rods. The first four groups of cars had side sill steel reinforcement 7" wide and 5/8" thick. The fifth, sixth and seventh groups of cars had steel plating 12" X 1/2". The eighth group, St. Louis-built cars 32 - 46, had steel plating 15" X 1/4" with angles 2 1/2" X 2 1/2" X 1/4" supporting the inside and outside bottoms of the sills and the inside tops of the sills.

Opposite page, upper:

In the summer of 1944 Preston-built car 30 is well bathed in the evening sunshine as it stands on the west storage tracks at Cromdale shop. (Bob Walker)

Opposite page, left:

Service car No. 6, stored at Cromdale yard, January 18th 1951. This work unit saw little service during the final days of street railway operations in Edmonton. (A. Clegg)

Steps: Cars in groups 3 and 4 had sliding steps. When the car was operating "A" end first, the steps at the right rear could be drawn out to receive passengers. They were fixed in that position for the duration of the car's trip in that direction. When the direction of the car was reversed so that it operated "B" end first, these steps were slid in under the platform and the steps at the other side and at the other end of the car were drawn out to receive passengers. This was an added safety feature preventing passengers from mounting the step on the wrong side of the car.

Route Markers: Cars 1 - 31 were delivered with no means of route identification. The ERR applied signs to these cars which were generally carried above the centre window at each end of the car. Route markers were standized on all passenger cars in 1912. See notes on individual car groups.

Seats: All cars delivered up to 1914 were equipped with rattan twill-weave seats. The 1930 Ottawa-built cars were fitted with individual leather-cushioned seats. The observation car had wood slat seats. Seating arrangements varied among the groups of cars with most having a combination of longitudinal and transverse seating. Transverse seats in the double-ended cars were reversible so that passengers could sit facing in the direction of travel. Those selected double-end-equipment Preston cars in the 47 - 81 series may have been an exception. It is believed that they all had fixed transverse seats similar to those found in all of the single-end cars on the railway.

Colour Scheme: No official documentation has been found indicating the colour schemes applied to cars 1 - 7 upon delivery. Some sources report a two-tone brown scheme, light above the belt rail and dark below, while others recall a dark green below the belt rail and gold above.

The remaining wooden passenger cars were delivered in Harland's "Coach Painters' Dark Green" on the main body; from the belt rail to the roof, they were finished in Harland's "Birmingham Red". Placement of corporate identification varied on groups of cars. Cars 1 - 7 had the words "EDMONTON RADIAL RAILWAY" spelled out in gold on each side of the body below the windows. Road numbers appeared on each side at each end and on each side of the dash at each end. On Cars 8 - 31, the words "EDMONTON RADIAL RY." appeared in gold letters 6" high with 1" red shading, on either side of the body. The city crest appeared in the centre of each side of the car body flanked by the words "EDMONTON" and "RADIAL". Road numbers of same dimensions appeared on each side of the dash at each end of these cars. Cars 32 - 81 were finished in the same general paint scheme as the previously-described group, except that contracts specified red vestibule pillars. Once again, the city crest appeared in gold on the centre of the car body on each side. On cars 32 - 46 the words "EDMONTON RADIAL RAILWAY" appeared on the letterboard of each side above the windows in gold letters 3 3/4" high. Gold numbers 5" high were placed on each side at each end and on each side of the front and rear dash. Cars 47 - 81 had the same size and colour of letters and numbers found on the previous group of cars; however, only the two words, "EDMONTON RADIAL," appeared on the letterboard on each side. Road numbers were located on the body as in the previous group, but on the car ends road numbers were applied to the bumpers on each side at both ends of the cars. Cars 8 - 81 featured a continuous gold stripe around the bottom of the car 2" above the bottom of the car body. The 1930 Ottawa-built cars were red from the bottom of the sill to the bottom of the belt rail, light cream from the bottom of the belt rail to the lower part of the letterboard, and a red letterboard. No form of railway identification appeared on these cars. Road numbers appeared on both sides of the body at both ends of the body and in the centre of the front and rear dash. The observation car was white with six gold panels on each side each outlined in red. The letters ERR appeared on the front dash. The library car was blue below the belt rail and light cream from the belt rail up. The words "EDMONTON PUBLIC LIBRARY" were displayed on each side of the car where the windows had been blanked out.

Fenders: Cars 1 - 7 were delivered with Providence fenders which were replaced in 1909 with Jenkins fenders. Cars 10, 12, 14 and 16 were delivered with Berg fenders. All other cars subsequently delivered to the ERR with "H.B. Lifeguards". By 1912 all cars were equipped with these lifeguards.

Storm Sash: All cars were delivered with removable storm sash. They were applied to body windows only on wooden cars but on all windows except centre rear vestibule window on the 80 series steel cars.

Rolling Stock: Passenger Cars

Road Number	Builder Date	Roof	Body Windows	Brakes	Trucks	Controller Motors Gear Ratio
1-6	OCC 1908	Monitor Deck	10	Hand	Brill 27-G-1 4'6" wheelbase 34" wheels	K-6 GE-80A (4) 40 hp 69:17
7	OCC 1908	Monitor Deck	8	Hand	Brill 21-E 8'0" wheelbase 34" wheels	K-10 GE-80A (2) 40 hp 69:17
10, 12, 14, 16	Preston 1909	Monitor Bullnose ends	10	Air Westinghouse D-1-EG compressor Valve SX	Bemis 45 4'6" wheelbase 34" wheels	K-6 GE-80A (4) 40 hp 69:17
15, 17, 18-21	OCC 1910	Monitor Bullnose ends	10	Air Westinghouse D-1-EG compressor Valve SX	Brill 27-G-1 4'6" wheelbase 34" wheels	K-6 GE-80A (4) 40 hp 69:17
8, 9, 11, 13, 22, 23	OCC 1911	Monitor Bullnose ends	10	Air Westinghouse D-1-EG compressor Valve SX	Brill 27-G-1 4'6" wheelbase 34" wheels	K-6 Westinghouse 101-B-2 (4) 40 hp 69:17
24-27	OCC 1911	Monitor Bullnose ends	11	Air Westinghouse D-1-EG compressor Valve SX	Brill 27-G-1 4'6" wheelbase 34" wheels	K-6 Westinghouse 101-B-2 (4) 40 hp 69:17
28-31	Preston 1911	Monitor Bullnose ends	11	Air Westinghouse D-1-EG compressor Valve SX	Brill 27-G-1 4'6" wheelbase 34" wheels	K-6 Westinghouse 101-B-2 (4) 40 hp 69:17
32-46	St.L 1912	Arch	11	Air Westinghouse D-1-EG compressor Valve SX	St. Louis 47-B 4'6" wheelbase 34" wheels	K-6 GE-80A (4) 40 hp 69:17
47-74	Preston 1913	Arch	12	Air Allis-Chalmers AA-7 compressor Valve Type C Cars 47-49 Westinghouse D-1-EG compressor Valve SX Cars 50-81	Standard 0-50 4'6" wheelbase 34" wheels	S-4 (Allis-Chalmers) Allis-Chalmers 301 (47-49) 60:17 K-6 GE-80A (50-59) 60:17 K-28-B Westinghouse 101-B-2 (60-81) 60:17
75-81	Preston 1914					
80-81 (2nd) 82-84	OCM 1930	Arch	8	Air Westinghouse Safety Control DH-25 compressor M-28-F valve	Canadian Car & Foundry 5'4" wheelbase 26" wheels	K-35-HH CGE 247J (4) 40 hp 15:58
Observation Car	ERR 1920	Arch	—	Air	Brill 27-G-1 4'6" wheelbase 34" wheels	unknown
Library Car (former number 14)	Preston 1909 Refurbished ERR 1941	Monitor Bullnose ends	4	Air	Brill 27-G-1 4'6" wheelbase 34" wheels	unknown

Rolling Stock: Passenger Cars

Weight (lbs)	Dimensions				Operation	Frame	Step	Seats	Route Markers
	Total Car Length Over Bumpers	Width Height	Platform Length Excluding Bumpers Front	Rear					
38 500	38'6 1/2"	8'6" 9'3"	4'8"	4'8"	Double end	Wood steel reinforced	Fixed single tread	40	
23 000	31'10"	8'6" 9'3"	5'0"	5'0"	Double end	Wood steel reinforced	Fixed single tread	32	
40 500	42'0"	8'6"	6'0"	6'0"	Double end	Wood steel reinforced	sliding	44	
40 000	41'2 1/2"	8'6" 9'4"	6'0"	6'0"	Double end	Wood steel reinforced	sliding	32	
41 000	41'2 1/2"	8'6" 9'4"	5'0"	7'0"	Single end	Wood steel reinforced	Fixed	37	
41 000	43'6"	8'6" 9'4"	5'0"	7'0"	Single end	Wood steel reinforced	Fixed	41	
41 000	43'10 1/2"	8'6" 9'4"	5'0"	7'0"	Single end	Wood steel reinforced	Fixed	41	
42 000	45'0"	8'6" 8'2"	7'3"	7'3"	Double end	Wood steel reinforced	Motorman's fixed, Passengers' folding	36	4 Peter Gray & Son roof mounted illuminated markers. Hunter roll signs roof mounted each end, each side.
42 000	46'3 3/4"	8'11 1/2"	5'0"	7'0"	Double end, one trolley 13 cars. Single end, 22 cars.	Steel	Fixed	44	4 Peter Gray & Son roof mounted illuminated markers. Hunter roll signs upper window sash mounted, window 6 each side and upper right at each end.
40 950	45'11 7/8"	8'3" 8'3 1/4"	7'11 15/16"		Single end, One man, Pay-As-You-Enter.	Steel	Folding	51	Roll signs — Keystone illuminated front centre, Hunter non-illuminated right side. Colour rolls front and rear.
—	41'2 1/2"		5'0"	7'0"	Single end, two man, Pay-As-You-Enter.	Wood Steel reinforced	Fixed	44	
—	40'	8'6"	5'0"	6'0"	Single end	Wood Steel reinforced	Folding	—	Sign "LIBRARY" permanently placed in upper sash of right front dash.

Key to Builders

DuWag	Waggonfabrik Uerdingen AG Werk	Dusseldorf, West Germany
ERR	Edmonton Radial Railway	Edmonton, Alberta
OCC	Ottawa Car Co. Ltd.	Ottawa, Ontario
OCM	Ottawa Car Mfg. Co. Ltd.	Ottawa, Ontario
Preston	Preston Car & Coach Co.	Preston, Ontario
St.L	St. Louis Car Co.	St. Louis, Missouri, USA

Revisions to Cars

Cars 1 - 6
Final installation of trucks, braking and electrical equipment was completed at Edmonton. Jenkins fenders were installed in 1909. Air brakes were installed on these cars between 1910 and 1912. Cast steel wheels replaced iron spoked wheels in 1910. All were converted circa 1912 to pay-as-you-enter cars. Cars 4, 5 and 6 converted to single-end cars in 1912 as noted on 1913 valuation sheet. All were laid out for one-man operation by 1918. Cars 1 and 3 remained in service as double-end cars until the early 1930s, at which time they too were converted to single-end cars. At various times these two cars were equipped with Bemis 45 trucks while they were double-ended cars. Car No. 2 is thought to have been removed from passenger service c1920 and rebuilt to sweeper No. 2. At some time, the rear platforms on cars 1 and 3 to 6 were lengthened 1'4" so that overall length become 39'10½". It is highly probable that this rebuilding occurred as each car was prepared for single-end operation. Cars 3, 4, 5 and 6 retired 1947. Their bodies were stripped and sold. Car 1 remained in service until September 1st 1951 and was held for restoration. The car was stored outside at Cromdale and suffered the effects of weather and vandalism, until it was restored in the 1960s and 1970s, eventually operating again during Edmonton's 75th anniversary celebrations in October 1979, as described in the text. On April 28, 1981, the car was transferred to the Edmonton Radial Railway Society collection at Fort Edmonton Park.

Car 7
Final installation of trucks, braking and electrical equipment was completed at Edmonton. This was the only single-truck passenger car on the ERR roster. Retired from passenger service c1913 to become a line car. Except for the construction of a tower frame over one platform, this car was not rebuilt. About 1937, the body and vestibules were removed and the truck used to build a rail grinding car. It remained on the property in that form until the close of street car service in September 1951.

Cars 10, 12, 14, 16
Final installation of trucks, braking and electrical equipment was completed at Edmonton. Car 12 was refitted c1916 with Brill 27-G-1 trucks and single-end operation. Bemis trucks were refitted again by 1929 and this car converted back to double-end operation again. The Brill trucks were reapplied in the mid-1930s. It was retired in 1947, stripped and sold. Car 14 was rebuilt with short front vestibule for single end operation prior to 1917 and refitted with Brill 27-G-1 trucks. Retired from regular passenger service in 1938 and rebuilt for service as the Library Car in 1941. It was still equipped with Brill 27-G-1 trucks while in service as a Library Car. Retired 1949, stripped at 118 Ave. and 124 St. and sold. Car 16 rebuilt around 1917 with narrow letterboard over front and rear vestibules giving it an appearance similar to the Ottawa Car Co. built cars. At that time it was converted to single end operation and was the first car fully laid out for one-man operation. Apparently it had double entrance/exit front doors. These were replaced with the standard Edmonton-type single front door. Mounted on Brill 27-G-1 trucks, car 16 was retired in 1938. In 1943, it was shopped again and emerged with its original Preston-style wide letterboard over the vestibules, as a single-ended car. Retired permanently from service in 1948, stripped and sold. Car 10 retired from passenger car service about 1938, and scrapped at Cromdale circa 1944. It had been fitted with Brill 27-G-1 trucks in the late 'teens or early 1920s.

Cars 15, 17 - 21
Final installation of trucks, braking and electrical equipment completed at Edmonton. Car 15 rebuilt in 1917 as a single-end one-man car. It had no doors on the blind side and was thought to have had double entrance-exit front doors. These were replaced with the standard Edmonton single entrance/exit front door. Rebuilt without truss rods at unknown time, possibly in 1917. Seating capacity increased to about 40. This car was retired from service in the autumn of 1950. Car 17 was rebuilt at unknown time without truss rods. Retired September 1949, stripped at 118 Avenue and 124 Street and sold. Car 18 retired 1948, stripped at Cromdale and sold. Car 19 rebuilt at unknown time without truss rods. It was retired about 1948 at Cromdale. Car 20 retired about 1948 at Cromdale. Car 21 in accident on October 22nd 1919 at 102 Avenue bridge near 130 Street and scrapped.

Cars 8, 9, 11, 13, 22 and 23
Delivered to the ERR completed and ready to enter service. Cars 8, 9, 11, 13 were rebuilt without truss rods some time during the 1920s. Seating capacity increased to about 43 after conversion to one-man operation in 1917-18. Car 22 burned to the frame while in service on 109 Street on June 13th 1917. Frame possibly used to build the observation car in 1920. Car 23 severely damaged at the Grand Trunk Pacific crossing on 118 Avenue when struck by train switching cars on September 12th 1913. Thought to have been scrapped at that time but a newspaper account reports that same car overturned on the curve onto 100 Street after skidding down 97 Avenue hill on January 16th 1916. Probably car 23 was rebuilt after its 1913 accident and re-entered service; it is unlikely, however, that it was repaired after its reported 1916 accident. Cars 8, 9, 11 and 13 retired from service circa 1948, stripped at Cromdale and sold. The body of car 13 was moved from a farm near Sherwood Park, Alberta to the Alberta Pioneer Railway Museum in 1973. On August 8, 1981 the car body was transferred to the Edmonton Radial Railway Society collection at Fort Edmonton Park.

Cars 24 - 31
Delivered to the ERR completed and ready to enter service. Cars 24 and 27 were rebuilt without truss rods. These cars had squared windows while cars 28 - 31 had semi-elliptical windows on the body. Car 28 destroyed by fire at Cromdale yard March 19th 1943. Rebuilt with arch roof and squared body windows at Cromdale in 1946. Equipped with wood slat seats from the observation car. All cars in this series retired from service c1948. They were stripped at Cromdale and sold. Car 29's body was at Cromdale until 1959. The body of car 31 was moved from Thorhild, Alberta in early December 1980 to Fort Edmonton Park where it is being restored by the Edmonton Radial Railway Society.

Cars 32 - 46
Final installation of trucks, braking and electrical equipment completed at Edmonton. Window sash on this series could be slid up into ceiling. Most cars in this group were converted to single-end operation in 1930-31, but car 33 only converted late in the 1930s. Seating capacity was increased to approximately 50 at this time. There were eleven transverse seats along the left side, ten such seats along the right side, and seating for about eight passengers in the rear vestibule. On cars 35, 41, 43 and 44. the centre window in the front vestibule was widened and the destination sign placed in the letterboard over the centre of that window. Route indicator lights were moved from the centre of the front vestibule letterboard to a position on either side of the destination sign. Window arrangement on the front vestibule of all other cars in the series remained unchanged but the following cars had centre-mounted destination sign: 32, 33, 34, 39, 45. Car 44 retired at Cromdale and body stripped and sold c1949. Cars 35, 36, 38, 40, 41 and 45 were isolated on the Calder stub line in August 1948, providing passenger service until August 1949. All of these cars were stripped at 118 Avenue and 124 Street and sold in September 1949. Cars 32, 33, 34, 37, 39, 42, 43, 46 and 47 remained on the property at Cromdale and were retired from service during 1951. Most of them continued in revenue service up to the cessation of streetcar service in September 1951. They later were stripped at Cromdale and sold. The Edmonton Radial Railway Society moved the body of car 42 from Sylvan Lake, Alberta to Fort Edmonton Park on April 11, 1981. The body of car 38 was moved from Bashaw, Alberta by the ERR Society to Fort Edmonton Park on July 22, 1980. Restoration work is underway on both units.

Below:

Diagram of 80-class cars built in 1930 by Ottawa Car Manufacturing Company Limited.

Photo above:

Car No. 35 stands at the tail of the wye on 118 Street at Calder, on July 8th 1949, ready to back out onto 127 Avenue to head west then south toward 118 Avenue and 124 Street. The roof of the Library Car, parked at the end of track on 127 Avenue, can be seen to the left. (Foster M. Palmer)

Dimensions

Length over Bumpers	45' 11⅞"
Truck centres	21' 2"
Wheel base	5' 4"
Width of seat	34"
Rail to Step	12¾"
Step to Platform	13¼"
Seating Capacity	51
Width of Aisle	24¾"
Diameter of Wheels	26"

Weights and Equipment

Car body	18,400 lbs.
Motors and Equipment	10,350 lbs.
Trucks	12,200 lbs.
TOTAL	40,950 lbs.
Motors and type	Four, C.G.E.-247J
H.P. per motor	40
Gear Ratio	15-58
Control	K-35
Air Brakes	WEST. Safety Control

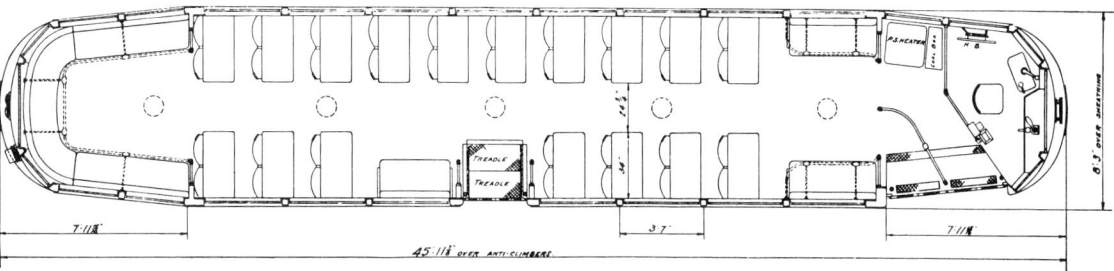

51 Passenger, Double Truck, Single End, Pay Enter, Center Exit, Safety Car, EDMONTON RADIAL RAILWAY

Cars 47 - 81

Delivered to the ERR completed and ready to enter service. Cars in this series were classified by the Edmonton Radial Railway in their 1913 valuation sheets and the Edmonton Street Railway Department in their Car Weights and Levers chart as single-end cars. Allis Chalmers and Canadian General Electric proposals for electrical equipment specified double-end equipment; i.e., two controllers, two trolley bases and poles and two main switches and circuit breakers. As far as can be determined, the cars for which this equipment was intended never operated with two trolley poles while in service in Edmonton. The proposals and contracts for the Westinghouse equipment for these cars could not be located. There is evidence that at least some of these cars were equipped with two sets of controllers. Car 79 is reported to have had a controller on the rear platform until c1939. Reference to K-28-B controllers on the Westinghouse-equipped cars in this series is made in official correspondence. Cars 80 and 81 were sold as operating units in July 1917 to the Oshawa Railway where they retained these numbers, becoming Niagara, St. Catharines and Toronto Railway 327 and 328 in 1943. Cars 50 and 58 were sold to the Toronto and York Radial Railway in the summer of 1918, where they assumed numbers 211 and 213.

Several of the cars in this series were apparently furnished with helical gears in 1926-29. Car 74 was fitted with a treadle-activated rear exit door in 1927 but this feature was later removed. Cars 49, 52, 55, 60, 67, 70 and 77 had rebuilt rear vestibule doorway to accommodate treadle-operated exit but this, apparently, was never installed. In order to facilitate one-man operation the front vestibule was enlarged by moving the front bulkhead about 18" back into the body of the car. This accounts for the two half windows on the left side of the cars in this series. Seating capacity was increased to accommodate approximately 48 passengers in nine transverse seats along the right side of the car, eleven transverse seats along the left side and a circular bench within the rear vestibule. Car 56 was fitted with a K-35 controller in November 1929. Other alterations to the front vestibules of some cars in the series after 1930 included the widening of the centre front window and the positioning of the roller destination sign over the centre front window. Cars 48, 57, 59, 65, 66, 71, 72 and 79 featured the wide motorman's window and the centre destination sign while cars 47, 52, 55, 57, 59, 63, 70, 73, 74 and 78 retained the standard window arrangement on the front vestibule, fitted with the centre destination sign. Car 68 retired about 1947, stripped at Cromdale and sold. Car 61 retired about 1950, stripped and retained off its trucks as a storage shed at Cromdale yard. It was still on the property in 1959. The remainder of the cars in the series were retired during 1951 with most in revenue service at the close of streetcar service. All apparently stripped at Cromdale and sold. The body of car 73 was transferred from Pickardville, Alberta to Fort Edmonton Park on November 14, 1981 where it is being restored by the Edmonton Radial Railway Society.

Photo above:

Motor flat car 4 stands on the extension of the north ladder track along 117 Avenue at Cromdale shop. In addition to carrying street railway supplies, this car switched box cars from the steam railways to points on the street railway system in the early years. This photo was taken in 1941. The car remained on the property until the close of streetcar service in 1951.
(Bob Walker)

Opposite page, upper:

In August 1950, sweeper 1 awaits its last winter of operation, its rattan brooms apparently worn from the previous season's work. *(Doug Parker)*

Opposite page, lower:

The body of ERR observation car mounted on blocks at the east side of Cromdale Shop in 1945. It has been removed from its storage shed on the southeast side of the shop building as preparations get under way for the new trolley coach maintenance garage to be erected on that site. *(Bob Walker)*

Cars 80 - 84

Delivered to the ERR completed and ready to enter service. Cars 80 and 81 were the second streetcars to carry these numbers on the ERR. All cars in this series were in service until the close of streetcar service in September 1951. All 80-series cars remained intact at Cromdale yard (though vandalized) at least until November 1953. Car 80 known to have gone to Dawson Creek for use as a lunch counter. While in service these cars featured full safety equipment. Front entrance-exit doors and the centre treadle exit door were all pneumatically powered and integrated with the braking and control system. The air brake could not be released nor power applied to the motors while any of the doors were open. Closing of all the doors permitted the operator to release the air brakes and apply power to the motors. The motorman had to keep the controller handle down while the car was moving. Failure to do so would cause an emergency brake application, cut power to the motors, sand the rails and open the doors. The body of streetcar 80 was located in Fort St. John, B.C. and delivered to Fort Edmonton Park on August 1, 1981 where it is being restored by the Edmonton Radial Railway Society.

Observation Car

Thought to have been constructed on the frame of car 22. The car went into permanent storage after the close of the 1925 season. It was stored in a shed on the west side of Cromdale shops where it remained until 1945 when the body was moved outdoors to the east yard where it was mounted on piled-up ties for a short time before being scrapped.

Library Car
Passenger car 14 was rebuilt at Cromdale in 1941 for service as a library car. It was used in that service until abandonment of the Calder line in August 1949, at which time it was retired, stripped at 118 Avenue and 124 Street, and sold.

Cars 1001 - 1014
These cars are designated by the builders as Light Rail Vehicle Type RTE 1 of the City of Edmonton. Car bodies are painted in white with blue striping and logo, bright yellow fluorescent band around the bottom of the body, and black letters and numerals. Trucks and roof are in medium grey. Sealed beam headlights are mounted on either side at each end of the cars. Two red lights, mounted beside each headlight, go into service to protect the rear of the train when the direction of travel is reversed. The operator sits in an enclosed compartment at a control panel specially designed for these cars. There are no provisions for fare collection on the cars. Each car has four double-width doors, on each side, for passenger entry and exit. Axle arrangement B'2'B indicates that two axles are powered, the middle two axles are idlers and the trailing axles are powered. Height listed is from top of rail to top of roof.

Cars 1015 - 1017
Body shells arrived in Edmonton in August 1979. Electrical equipment and trucks were shipped with the body shells. Complete wiring and assembly of electrical equipment was completed at Cromdale, as well as all interior finishing and installation of seats. These cars were ordered to accommodate additional traffic expected from the Clareview extension.

Combination Sweeper — Baggage 1
Upon delivery this car carried no road number. It was a standard McGuire-Cummings unit. From 1909 to 1913 it carried a locomotive bell and headlights, all roof-mounted. In summer the sweeper brooms were removed. It later years, a broom was mounted at one end only although the car continued to operate as a double-ended unit. Sweeper — baggage car 1 remained serviceable until the close of streetcar service in Edmonton on September 1st 1951. The car was stripped at Cromdale and sold.

Sprinkler
The sprinkler delivered in 1909 reportedly carried no road number. It apparently remained in service until about 1920 at which time the city's fleet of rubber-tired sprinklers made the street railway units obsolete. Final disposition of this car is unknown but it is thought to have been dismantled at Cromdale in the 1920s. The tank was disposed of but the frame of the car and trucks and equipment may have been used in the construction of plough-spreader 5.

Horse-Drawn Tower Wagon
This wagon was drawn by two horses and used in servicing the overhead line. It was a four-wheel non-rail unit. It is not known when this wagon was retired from service.

Sweeper 3
This single truck sweeper remained serviceable until the close of the Calder stub line in September 1949. It was retired from service at that time having been stripped at 118 Avenue and 124 Street, and sold.

Line Car 7
This was passenger car 7 converted to line car service c1913. Apparently it remained on the property until 1937 when its frame, truck and electrical equipment was used for the construction of a rail grinding car.

Motor Flat Car 4
This car delivered to the ERR in 1912 probably came from a US builder. Since it was ordered about the same time as the St. Louis-built passenger cars, it may have come from that builder; however, it is more probable that it came from the McGuire-Cummings company. Cab rebuilt during service on the Edmonton property. The unit is believed to have been fitted with MCB coupler. It remained on the property until the close of streetcar service in September 1951 and was disposed of at Cromdale.

Rolling Stock: LRT Cars

Road Number	Builder Date	Roof	Body Windows	Brakes	Trucks	Controller Motors Gear Ratio
1001 1014	DuWag 1977	Arch	8 large 1 small at each end of body. 2 piece full-width windshield at each end.	Rheostatic. Mechanical spring brake by Raco. Electro-magnetic track brake by Hanning & Kahl.	DuWag 1,800 mm w.b. 720 mm wheels. Axle arrangement B'2'B Two DuWag/ Rheinstahl gear boxes per powered truck.	Siemens Canada Ltd. & Siemens AG Germany motor driven controller series/parallel starting of traction motors in 20 steps including two field weakening steps and self excited rheostatic braking in 17 steps. SIMATIC running/braking regulator. 2 Siemens AG double shaft motors type 1KB2021-5MB02 218 hp 5.625:1.
1015- 1017	DuWag 1979					

Rolling Stock: Service Cars

Type of Service	Original Known Road No.	Final Road Number	Builder Date	Roof	Brakes	Trucks	Controller Motors Gear Ratio
Sweeper, Freight Hauler, Locomotive.	—	1	McG-C 1909	Arch	Air	McGuire-Cummings Light M.C.B. 10A	K-6 GE-80A (4) 40 hp
Sprinkler	—	—	Preston 1909	—	Hand	Bemis 45 4'6" wheelbase	GE-80A (2) 40 hp
Horse drawn tower wagon, (non-rail)	1	1	OCC 1910	—	—	—	—
Sweeper	—	3	OCC 1910	Arch	Hand	Pedestal 7'0" wheelbase 33" wheels	K-10 Westinghouse 101-B-2 (2) 40 hp
Line Car	7	7	OCC 1908	Monitor Deck	Hand	Brill 21-E 8'0" wheelbase 34" wheels	K-10 GE-80A (2) 40 hp
Motor flat car	—	4	McG 1912		Air	McGuire-Cummings Light M.C.B. 10A	Westinghouse 101-B-2 (4) 40 hp
Centre cab line car	L1	S5	ERR 1912	Arch	Air Westinghouse D-1-EG compressor Valve SX	Bemis 45 4'6" wheelbase	K-6 GE-80 (2) 40 hp
Differential dump car	S5	—	CCF 1913	—	Air	Modified Arch Bar 6'6" wheelbase	GE-80A (4) 40 hp
Sprinkler	S2		McG-C 1913	—	Air	McGuire-Cummings Standard SE 60 4'6" wheelbase 34" wheels	Westinghouse 101-B-2 (4) 40 hp
Plough-Spreader	—	5	ERR 1921	Arch	Air	Bemis 45 4'6" wheelbase	unknown
Wrecker-tool car	—	6	ERR 1925	Arch	Air	McGuire-Cummings Standard SE 60 4'6" wheelbase 34" wheels	unknown
Track Grinder	—	—	ERR 1937	—	Hand	Brill 21-E 8'0" wheelbase 34" wheels	K-10 GE-80A (2) 40 hp
Sweeper	—	2	ERR c1921	Arch	Air	Brill 27-G-1 4'6" wheelbase 34" wheels	K-6

Key to Builders

CCF	Canadian Car & Foundry Co. Ltd.	Montreal, Quebec
ERR	Edmonton Radial Railway	Edmonton, Alberta
McG-C	McGuire-Cummings Mfg. Co.	Chicago, Illinois, USA
OCC	Ottawa Car Co. Ltd.	Ottawa, Ontario
Preston	Preston Car & Coach Co.	Preston, Ontario

Rolling Stock: LRT Cars

Weight (kg)	Dimensions		Operation	Frame	Step	Seats	Route Markers
	Total Car Length Over Couplers	Width Height					
30 600 kg	24 284 mm	2 650 mm 3 320 mm	Double end. Multiple unit.	Welded steel. Articulation by DuWag	No step high level platform loading.	64 plus 97 standing.	Roller sign centered over windshield at each end.

Rolling Stock: Service Cars

Weight (lbs)	Dimensions			Operation	Construction	Special Features
	Total Car Length Body Length	Width Height	Bolster Centres			
—	50' 39'	—	—	Double end	Steel frame Wood body	Sweeper brooms at both ends. Two additional (one at each end) to GE-80A 40 hp motors to drive the brooms.
—	30'0"	—	—	Double end	Wood frame Steel reinforced frame.	3 000 Imperial gallon steel water tank.
—	—	—	—	—	Wood	—
23 600	28'2"	7'0"	—	Single end	Wood body Steel frame.	Sweeper broom at one end. R-28 rheostatic controller to operate the single Westinghouse 101-B-2 broom motor.
23 000	31'10" 21'10"	8'6"		Double end	Wood body Steel reinforced frame.	Wooden frame built on one end of the car to accomodate crews working on overhead lines. Passenger car 7 converted to line car service c1913.
—					Wood deck wood cab steel frame	Used for hauling standard railway boxcars. Equipped with removeable standard M.C.B. couplers.
—	38'0"	8'3"	27'0"	Double end	Wood deck wood frame wood cab	Equipped with Ackley hand brakes. Platform mounted on roof of cab and extends from 14'5 1/2" above top of rail to 20'2 1/2" when raised to limit of extension. Reel stand mounted on one deck, tool box on deck at opposite end.
—					Wood cab steel frame	Equipped with standard railway M.C.B. couplers and train air brakes.
—	28'9"	7'6" 10'11"		Double end	Steel frame steel tank	5 000 gallon steel single compartment water tank. 265 gallon high duty centrifugal pump, 900 rpm delivering water to heads at 35 lbs psi.
—				Single end	Wood frame steel reinforced. Wood deck. Wood cab.	Wing plough mounted on the right side.
—	28'9"	7'6"		Double end	Steel frame. Wood body.	Carried re-railing equipment and towing equipment. Constructed from Sprinkler S-2.
—	21'10"	8'6"		Double end	Wood frame steel reinforced.	Open car with ballast tank on the deck and grinding stones between the wheels on each side.
—	28'2 1/2"	8'6"		Single end	Wood frame steel reinforced. Wood deck. Wood cab.	Broom at one end only.

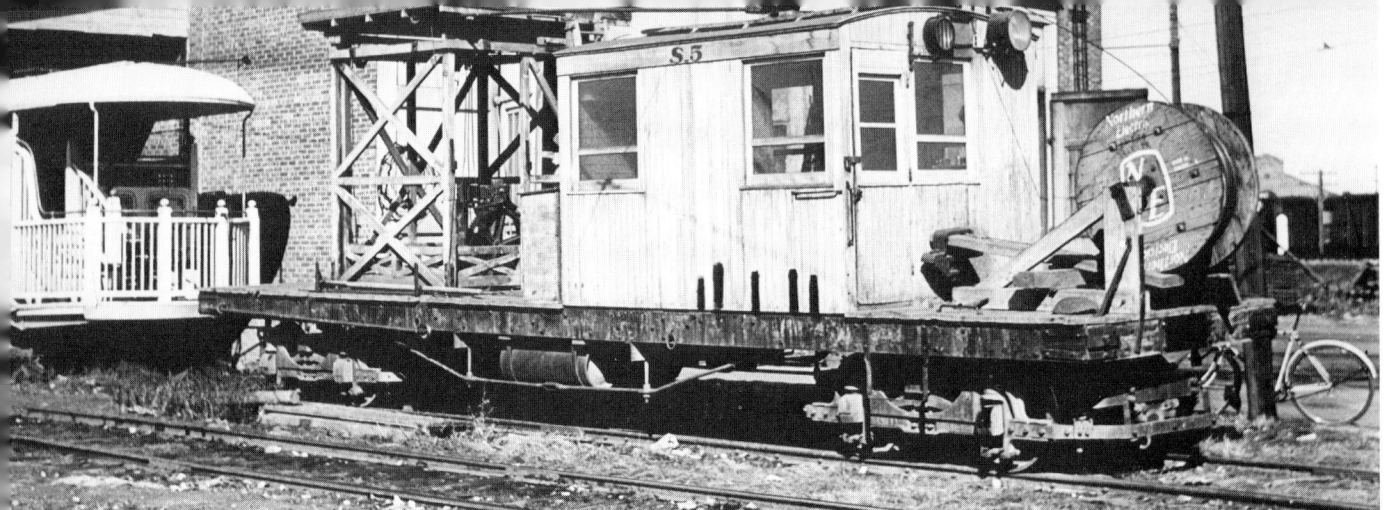

Photo above:

Line car S-5 (formerly L-1) is prepared to move out on a moment's notice to repair overhead line. It is stored at the southwest corner of Cromdale shop. The observation car protrudes from its shelter on the track immediately behind the line car. The line car's cab has been moved off centre and the tower removed from the top of the cab to the rear deck.

(Bob Walker)

Photo left:

Edmonton's home-built sweeper 2 is stored on the east track at Cromdale shop during the summer of 1944. (Bob Walker)

Photo below:

The rail grinder, built on the frame and truck of single truck car No. 7, rests at the end of the Cromdale storage track. This car was still on the property at the close of streetcar service in September 1951. (Eric M. Smith)

Revisions to Cars

Centre Cab Line Car L1
This unit was renumbered c1920 to S5. A rebuilding about the same time involved moving the cab off centre toward the "front" end. The tower was taken from the cab roof and placed on the flat deck at the "rear" of the car. The tower was then equipped with a mechanical lift mechanism. The car became single ended at this time. It was retired at Cromdale in September 1951.

Differential Dump Car S5
While this car is prominent in an early photograph, little is known of its career on the ERR. It is possible that it was sold as an operating unit to another property early in the 1920s. The Edmonton Radial Railway 1913 valuation sheet shows this car as having been constructed by the railway at Cromdale. The Canadian Railway and Marine World reports that the unit was ordered from CCF and in a later issue confirms delivery of the unit from CCF.

Sprinkler S2
Like the earlier sprinkler, this unit seems to have been retired about 1920. Its tank was removed and the frame and trucks used in the construction of wrecker-tool car 6.

Plough-Spreader 5
Possibly constructed about 1921 using the frame, trucks and electrical equipment from the 1909 sprinker. It was on the property at Cromdale at the close of streetcar service in September 1951.

Wrecker Tool Car 6
Built on frame and trucks from sprinkler S2 in 1925. This car serviced disabled streetcars on the road, providing rerailing services, on-the-spot repairs or towing to the barns. It remained in service until the close of streetcar service in September, 1951. Its body and frame remained at Cromdale for some years as an oil storage shed.

Track Grinder
This unit remained intact on the property until the close of street car service. It was built in 1938 from the frame and truck of single-truck passenger car 7 which had also been used as a line car.

Sweeper 2
Possibly built on the frame and trucks of passenger car 2 c1921. It remained at Cromdale until the close of streetcar service in 1951.

KAL-TRAK Switcher 3850
Built in October 1977 by CANRON RAILGROUP of the U.S.A. this unit is powered by a General Motors 453 diesel engine and driven by an Allison 4-wheel drive transmission. It is built on a dump truck type frame, with a gross vehicle weight of 33,500 lbs. The unit can be used either as a road or railway vehicle; four standard truck tires drive the vehicle on either mode. Two flanged wheels are mounted ahead of the front tires and two more behind the rear tires. The flanged wheels can be raised or lowered hydraulically as necessary.

A standard railway coupler can be mounted at the rear to permit box car switching in the yard. In order to switch LRT cars, the railway coupler can be replaced by a Scharfenberg coupler.

A snow blower, sweeper broom or snow plough blade can be mounted at the front of the vehicle. A dump truck box allows it to be used as a ballast spreader as well. The switcher is painted yellow.

Fairmount 6 Cylinder Speeder
This four-wheel single-truck vehicle is used to pull the line equipment.

Overhead Line Equipment
A "scissors" platform is mounted on a four-wheel rigid car frame. The platform is raised and lowered by a hydraulic hoist. The reel car, also mounted on a four-wheel rigid frame, carries one reel for trolley wire and another for messenger wire. The tool box car with tool racks mounted on a four-wheel truck accompanies the train of overhead line equipment. Four hand cars of 5,000 lbs. capacity complete the LRT service car roster. All of the above equipment has insulated wheels. In addition, Edmonton Power has equipped one of its highway tower trucks with a set of railway wheels which can be raised or lowered hydraulically as required for road or railway service.

Standard Revisions to Passenger Rolling Stock

Colour Schemes
The original colour schemes in which passenger cars were delivered has been described. Apparently as cars 1 - 6 were shopped they were painted in the red-and-green colours to match all other cars on the system. In November 1915, four cars introduced a new livery for the streetcars: bright yellow above the window sill and brown from the sill to the bottom of the carbody. The city crest appeared in gold or yellow at the centre of the carbody. Railway identification appeared variously as ERR, EDMONTON RADIAL RAILWAY and EDMONTON RADIAL on the centre of the letterboard on each side. Road numbers were in yellow or gold and were positioned on the carbody sides below the second window from each end. It is not known if road numbers appeared on the dash at either end of the car in this scheme. Roof colour appeared to vary from white to light grey and black. Car 77 introduced the third and final paint scheme, in June 1926: red on the carbody below the window sill and cream from the top of the sill to the roof, with a black beading separating the two contrasting colours. In this livery, cars carried no railway identification. Road numbers, in gold or yellow edged in black, appeared on each side below the second window from each end. Similar numerals, in a contrasting dark colour thought to have been red or black, appeared at each end on the letterboard above the centre vestibule window. Roof colour was usually black. That paint scheme remained until the cessation of streetcar service. However, at some time after the mid 1930s, the practice of placing the road numbers above the centre vestibule windows at each end was discontinued, and these numerals were relocated on the dash below the left front window. On single-end cars the road number appeared below the rear centre vestibule window. Positioning of the road numbers on the steel 80 class cars varied. On some cars, the front numerals appeared below the headlight; on others above the headlight; still another variation was below the left front vestibule window.

One-man Car Operation
Conversion to one-man operation began in 1916 and continued into 1918 by which time each car could be operated by one man. Two steps replaced the single fixed step at the front door on all single-end cars. The lower step folded up when the operator closed the door. This type of step was applied to all of the double-end cars in the late 1920s. Passengers embarked and disembarked through a single entrance-exit door at the front of the car. The first two seats on the right side were removed to permit freer flow of passengers boarding and disembarking. The single entrance-exit door was typical of all ERR cars except the steel "80 cars". The rear platform floor was raised to the same level as the carbody floor. A circular bench was installed around the rear platform which accommodated about eight passengers. The rear entrance-exit vestibule doors were closed off except for a single width emergency exit door. This exit was used in regular service on most cars from 1943 to 1946 when conductorettes were on duty at these doors on cars on heavily-travelled routes. This permitted passengers to board or leave from both ends of the cars, helping to speed up service. These rear platform features were not applied to double-end cars until they were converted to single-end operation cars. In most cases the front bulkhead was left intact or modified slightly, ususally by opening up the right side or centre doorway bulkheads, but the rear bulkhead was removed completely after conversion to one-man operation.

• • • • • • • • • • •

Heating
All cars were equipped with Peter Smith coal-fired forced-air heaters. In addition, electric heaters were installed as standard equipment on cars 1 - 23 and 80 - 84. Such heaters were not specified for any of the other cars but were installed in the rest of the cars by January 1930.

Route Markers

Main Line Route Colours and Destination Curtains

Coloured Panel Coloured Lights	Roller Curtain West and/or Southbound	East and/or Northbound
1926		
Red	WHYTE AVE. VIA LOW LEVEL BRIDGE	111' AV. VIA 95' ST.
Red-and-white	WHYTE AVE. VIA HIGH LEVEL BRIDGE	114TH AV. & 82ND ST.
Red-and-green	CALDER	105TH AV. & 95TH ST.
Green	102 AVE. & 142 ST. (ATHA. AVE.)	102 AVE. & 142 ST. (ATHA. AVE.)
White	BONNIE DOON	HIGHLANDS
Blue	124' ST. & 112' AV.	NORTH EDMONTON
Blue-and-white	124' ST. & 112' AV.	80TH ST. & 118TH AV.
Red-and-blue	76TH AV. & 116TH ST.	MAIN ST. & WHYTE AV.
May 28, 1933		
Red	WHYTE AVE. VIA LOW LEVEL BRIDGE	
Red-and-white	WHYTE AVE. VIA HIGH LEVEL BRIDGE	114TH AV. & 82ND ST.
White	BONNIE DOON	HIGHLANDS
Blue	124' ST. & 112' AV.	NORTH EDMONTON
Blue-and-white	124' ST. & 112' AV.	80TH ST. & 118TH AV.
Red-and-blue	76TH AV. & 116TH ST.	MAIN ST. & WHYTE AV.
June 24, 1933		
Red	111' AV. VIA 95' ST.	111' AV. VIA 95' ST.
Red-and-white	WHYTE AVE. VIA HIGH LEVEL BRIDGE	114TH AV. & 82ND ST.
Red-and-green	WHYTE AVE. VIA LOW LEVEL BRIDGE	CALDER
White	BONNIE DOON	HIGHLANDS
Blue	124' ST. & 112' AV.	NORTH EDMONTON
Blue-and-white	124' ST. & 112' AV.	80TH ST. & 118TH AV.
Red-and-blue	76TH AV. & 116TH ST. WHYTE AV.	MAIN ST. &
July 26, 1939		
Red-and-white	WHYTE AVE. VIA HIGH LEVEL BRIDGE	114TH AV. & 82ND ST.
Red-and-green	WHYTE AVE. VIA HIGH LEVEL BRIDGE	CALDER
White	BONNIE DOON	HIGHLANDS
Blue	124' ST. & 112' AV.	NORTH EDMONTON
Blue-and-white	124' ST. & 112' AV.	80TH ST. & 118TH AV.
Red-and-blue	76TH AV. & 116TH ST.	MAIN ST. & WHYTE AV.
September 1, 1939		
Red-and-white	WHYTE AVE. VIA HIGH LEVEL BRIDGE	114TH AV. & 82ND ST.
Red-and-green	LOW LEVEL BRIDER VIA 97TH AVE.	CALDER
White	BONNIE DOON	HIGHLANDS
Blue	124' ST. & 112' AV.	NORTH EDMONTON
Blue-and-white	124' ST. & 112' AV.	80TH ST. & 118TH AV.
Red-and-blue	76TH AV. & 116TH ST.	MAIN ST. & WHYTE AV.
July 22, 1945		
Red-and-white	WHYTE AVE. VIA HIGH LEVEL BRIDGE	114TH AV. & 82ND ST.
Red-and-green	WHYTE AVE. VIA HIGH LEVEL BRIDGE	CALDER
Blue	124' ST. & 112' AV.	NORTH EDMONTON
Blue-and-white	124' ST. & 112' AV.	80TH ST. & 118TH AV.
Red-and-blue	76TH AV. & 116TH ST.	MAIN ST. & WHYTE AV.
August 28, 1949		
Blue	WHYTE AVE. VIA HIGH LEVEL BRIDGE	NORTH EDMONTON
Blue-and-white	WHYTE AVE. VIA HIGH LEVEL BRIDGE	80TH ST. & 118 AV.

Over the years the means of identifying car destinations to passengers varied. Originally, the ERR made up simple white boards with black lettering which were hung over the centre vestibule window at each end of the car. Sometimes these destination boards were hung on the right front bumper of the car. A typical but incomplete list of destinations on these boards follows: STRATHCONA/EDMONTON/16TH STREET ONLY/SYNDICATE AVE./CITY PARK VIA ALBERTA AVE. Cars 1 - 31 used these boards. In 1911, the ERR began to place Hunter roof-mounted roller signs to the front and rear ends of these cars. In 1912 the railway also began to place four Peter Gray & Son roof-mounted illuminated markers on serviceable passenger cars 1 - 31. These markers carried lenses coloured red, green, blue and white. These installations gave a uniform means for passengers to identify the route of a car from the front or from the rear. Typical but again incomplete destinations on the Hunter roof mounted roller signs on cars 1 - 46 were as follows: ATHABASCA AVE./FIRST ST./STRATHCONA/JASPER AVE. VIA LOW LEVEL BRIDGE/JASPER AVE. VIA HIGH LEVEL BRIDGE/WHYTE AVE. VIA HIGH LEVEL BRIDGE/WHYTE AVE. VIA LOW LEVEL BRIDGE/ALBANY AVE./CAR BARNS/PACKING PLANT/HIGHLANDS/NAMAYO AVE./CITY PARK VIA JASPER E./NELSON AVE./7TH ST. WEST/SYNDICATE AVE. St. Louis-built cars 32-46 carried roof-mounted roller signs on each side and these carried, among many others, the following destinations: JASPER HIGH BR./JASPER LOW BR./WHYTE HIGH BR./WHYTE LOW BR. The "big Prestons", cars 47-81, carried some of the following signs: BARNS/NELSON/PACKING PT./24 ST. VIA SYNDICATE/WHYTE VIA HIGH BR./WHYTE VIA LOW BR./JASPER VIA HIGH BR./JASPER VIA LOW BR./ALBERTA/SIXTEENTH ST. These roller-type route signs became redundant with the advent of numbered streets and avenues which replaced the named thoroughfares in Edmonton in 1914. The coloured markers were still used but the roller signs for the most part fell into disuse. The latter were replaced for a time with large rectangular dash-mounted boards with the destination lettered over the appropriate route colour. Early in the 1920s, cars began to show new roller sign destinations. With the advent of the new paint scheme in 1926 all the roof-mounted destination equipment was removed. Lighted route markers were built into the letterboards above the centre vestibule windows at each end of the cars and the roller signs were all mounted in the upper sash of the right front vestibule window of each car. Side and rear roller signs were removed from all cars. After 1926, in addition to the coloured lights and the destination signs, all wooden cars carried a 26 X 14-inch destination board holder on the right front dash and on single end cars on the right rear dash. This holder housed a complete set of coloured, thin sheet metal panels. A mounting bracket at the front of this box displayed the appropriate route colour panel which indicated the car's route. The five steel cars were the only ones not conforming to this practice. They carried the route colour indicator in a roller sign above the lettered destination roller above the front centre window of the car. A similar colour roller was carried above the rear centre window. Typical regular main line routes are shown in an adjacent table.

The colour destination board was yellow; hence, when no colour panel was mounted on the board, it displayed yellow indicating that the car was a special. This designation was often used to identify service to the exhibition grounds or other major special events. In 1943 when service to the Aircraft Repair Depot opened, cars destined for that facility carried a blue-and-white sign with the words "AIRCRAFT REPAIR" lettered on the colour panel. In 1949, after the opening of the loop at 84 Avenue and 109 Street and the loop at the government centre at 98 Avenue and 109 Street, peak hour blue-and-white sign cars carried panels of the same colours lettered "98 AV. AND 109 ST." or "84 AV. AND 109 ST." With the termination of streetcar service, the use of colours to identify routes ceased.

The roller signs on cars 1001 - 1014 carry the following:

   Charter
   Not in Service
   Training Car
   Belvedere
   Central
   Churchill
   Clareview
   Coliseum
   Stadium

Appendix II
LRT Extensions

Three new LRT cars 1015 to 1017 were placed in service early in 1980. They can be distinguished from the original cars only by their frameless upper sash and different type of end bumpers. Otherwise they are, to the casual observer, identical to the other cars. They, too, were completed at Edmonton Transit's Cromdale shop.

Edmonton's LRT was highlighted by a new passenger service feature on November 19th, 1980, advertised extensively under the title "POP." "POP" means proof of payment, a system of fare payment widely used in Europe. A similar fare collection system was also introduced to the Calgary C-Train when it opened for service in May 1981. The POP system permits passengers to freely move onto the boarding platform and to board any LRT train. There are no fare collection attendants at the stations, nor is there any means of fare collection on the trains. All passengers are expected to have a valid proof of payment receipt which can take one of four forms. Individual fare receipts can be purchased by depositing the correct fare into one of the turnstiles located at the entrance to all LRT stations. The turnstile issues a dated, timed, receipt which the passenger must retain throughout the trip. The passenger can use this receipt as a transfer from the LRT to board any Edmonton Transit bus. Other passengers carrying a valid Edmonton Transit bus transfer, a monthly transit pass, or a senior citizen transit pass, simply walk through the station entrance, onto the boarding platform and onto the train.

In order to ensure that the system is not abused, uniformed personnel carry out spot-checks on trains and platforms, requesting passengers to present evidence of payment. Persons standing on the station platforms may also be requested to present their POP receipt. Failure to produce a valid receipt on demand may result in a stiff financial penalty. The system has the advantage of moving passengers quickly on and off the trains, as well as minimizing the number of personnel and facilities required to check fares.

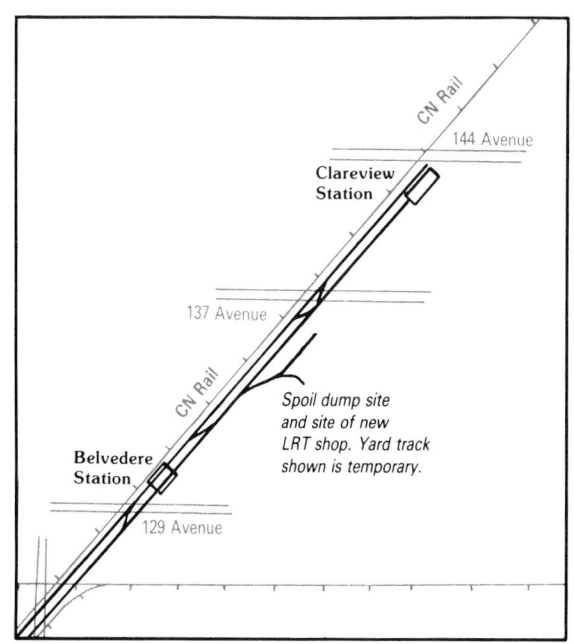

Clareview LRT Extension: 1981

The 2.2 kilometer extension north from Belvedere station to Clareview station opened for regular service on Sunday, April 26th, 1981. The theme of the advertising campaign leading up to the opening was "LRT On Track to Clareview Station." Passengers were encouraged to familiarize themselves with the new extension on Saturday, April 25th, between noon and 6 pm, when all LRT trains operated for the first time beyond Belvedere station to the new Clareview station. All rides on the LRT were free during that period. Travel time between Clareview and Central is fifteen minutes. Several northeast Edmonton bus routes were diverted to serve the new station effective with the opening of the line.

Rolling Stock: LRT Locomotive

Fleet Number	Type	Rebuilt	Built	Builder	Serial No.
2001	Steeple cab electric locomotive	ET 80-09	1912 Weight: 60 tons	ALCO/GE	ALCO 51069 GE 3808 *Previous reporting marks* British Columbia Hydro 961 British Columbia Electric Railway 961 (1946) Oregon Electric 21 (1912)

Rolling Stock: LRT Service Equipment

Fleet No.	Type	Rebuilt	Built	Builder	Previous Reporting Marks
2101	32' Flat	ET 80-03	?	AC&F	NAR 15005, possibly USRA
2102	40' Flat	ET 80-04	17-09	Barney & Smith	NAR 15508 (Boom Car), ACL
2103	40' Flat	ET	1981	Parts by C.W. Carry	Running Gear from NAR 15504 (flat), CN 404958 (Gondola)
2201	Depressed Centre	KML 80-04	?	AC&F	NAR 15009 (Ballast Plow Flat), C&NW
2301[a]	Dump	KML 80-05	?	CC&F	NAR 16024 (tank), CGTX 8505
2302	Dump	KML 80-07	17-08	CC&F	NAR 16022 (tank), CGTX 8824
2303	Dump	KML 80-07	16-04	CC&F	NAR 16023 (tank), CGTX 8652
2304[b]	Dump	KML 80-08	?	?	NAR 15602 (idler), CP 173288 (Fowler Patt. Outs. Fr. Box)
2305	Dump	KML 80-08	?	CC&F	NAR 16020 (tank), BAOX 665
2306	Dump	KML 80-09	?	ATCC	NAR 16018 (tank), GATX
2307	Dump	KML 80-09	?	PSF	NAR 16017 (tank), GATX
2308	Dump	KML 80-09	?	?	NAR 15600 (idler), CP i73589 (Fowler, Patt. O/F. Box)
2309[c]	Dump	KML 80-09	?	CC&F	NAR 16019 (tank), BAOX 206
2310	Dump	KML 80-10	?	?	NAR 20020 (stock)

[a] Upset at spoil tip site 1981-07-13. Body scrapped. Body from 2304 mounted, renumbered 2304.
[b] Frame collapsed 1980-12.
[c] 32' frame, no end platforms.
KML: K.M.L. Custom Fabricators Ltd., Edmonton, Alberta
ET: Edmonton Transit Cromdale Shop, Edmonton, Alberta

Capacities
— Flat Cars 50 tons
— Dump Cars 30 cu. yd.
— Flat Cars 144,000 lbs. gross capacity
— Dump Cars 144,000 lbs. gross capacity
AAR Running Gear

A unique freight service began operating on a completed portion of the Clareview extension about one year before the extension was opened for passenger service. Plans had been drawn up to build two major roadway over-passes across the new extension and to build a large new LRT shop facility about mid-way between Belvedere and the new Clareview station. These projects required considerable landfill. At the same time, a means of disposing of the spoil from the tunneling work on the westbound LRT extension under Jasper Avenue was being considered. A logical means of dealing with the problem was to have a train carry the spoil from the tunnel to the dump site where the landfill was required. Edmonton Transit negotiated with British Columbia Hydro for the acquisition of a retired electric locomotive. The unit arrived in Edmonton on March 15th, 1980 and was immediately sent to Cromdale shop were the unit was restored to serviceable condition. Several steel-underframe tank cars and box cars were purchased from the Northern Alberta Railways. These cars were all stripped to the frame at Cromdale. Eleven of these frames were then transported to KML Custom Fabricators Ltd. in Edmonton where ten steel dump bodies of thirty cubic yard capacity were built and mounted on ten of the frames. From the eleventh frame, KML built a depressed-centre flat car. Three car frames were left behind to be converted to fifty ton capacity flatcars by Edmonton Transit Cromdale shop staff.

Once enough equipment was available and tunnel excavation had begun, locomotive 2001 — brightly decked out in standard LRT passenger car colours — began shuttling between downtown and the dump site. The train made about four trips per day. The locomotive would run down into the tunnel with empty cars, spot them on a loading track, then pick up the loaded cars and haul them out to the dump site. The flatcars carried a variety of construction materials. They often carried pallets designed to carry the lagging and frame members for the tunnel rings. These rings were installed to prevent cave-ins as the round tunnel bore progressed forward. The loaded flatcar was pushed to the end of the track in the tunnel. Here the pallet was lifted off and placed on a low-deck car to complete its journey to the end of the bore where the lagging and frame were installed. Upon completion of the tunnel bore work, the regularly scheduled trips with 2001 and its train ceased, although the equipment is used occasionally for other construction projects.

The LRT extension under Jasper Avenue, west to 107 Street, is expected to open for service in June 1983. Some new cars have already been shipped from DüWag in Dusseldorf, West Germany, for completion. Most of the new Edmonton cars on order will be completed at Calgary Transit's Anderson Road shop. Edmonton Transit ordered sufficient cars to serve a proposed South Edmonton extension. Many of these cars will be surplus for some time, however, as work on the south side extension for which they were intended has been held up pending a final decision on bridging the North Saskatchewan River and the route to be followed upon reaching the south side. In the meantime, Edmontonians will be pleased to see three-car trains on the LRT line. The current two-car trains must sometimes pass by waiting passengers during peak periods, when the trains are over-crowded.

Photo below:

A train of three dump cars has tipped its load of spoil, most of which has already been removed by a loader working at the land-fill site, on April 27, 1982. (Colin K. Hatcher)

Appendix III: Trolley Coach Roster

Fleet Numbers	Manufacturer	Model Number	Serial Number	Quantity Purchased	Year Built	Seats	Notes
101-103	AEC/EEC	663T	087-089	3	1939	38	AEC chasis/English Electric-Preston bodies/EEC 115 HP motors/6 wheels, scrapped 1951
104-106	Leyland		302343-45	3	1939	38	Park Royal bodies/GE (U.K.) 135 HP motors/6 wheels, scrapped 1951
107-109	Leyland		305970-72	3	1942*	39	Same as numbers 104-6
110-112	Mack Truck Co.	CR	1276-78	3	1943*	40	Scrapped 1962. Serial numbers preceded by NOCR1943
113-120	Pullman Standard		5497-5504 (see Note 5)	8	1944	44	Retired 1963-66 and used for parts except No. 116 preserved in operating condition and renumbered 113
121-128	Pullman Standard		5679-86	8	1945	44	Del'd. 1946; ret'd. 1963-66; used for parts
129-130	ACF/Brill	TC44	164-165	2	1945	44	Scrapped 1965
131-152	CCF/Brill	T44	5023-44	22	1947*	44	131-135 serial numbers preceded by 46-, rest by 47-. See Note 6
153-177	CCF/Brill	T44	5176-200	25	1947	44	See Note 4
178-179	CCF/Brill	T44	5503-04	2	1948	44	See Note 4
180-187	CCF/Brill	T44	5242-49	8	1948	44	See Note 4
188-192	CCF/Brill	T44	5675-79	5	1949	44	See Note 4
193-196	CCF/Brill	T48A	8276-79	4	1952	48	Double width front doors. See Note 4
197-202	CCF/Brill	T48A	8340-45	6	1954	42	Double width front doors. See Note 4
203-212	CCF/Brill	T44	5241-50	10	1947	44	Acquired 1962 from Vancouver (Nos. 2001-2010 in order). See Notes 4 and 7
121-130	CCF/Brill	T44	(see Note 1)	10	1949	44	Acquired in 1966 from Regina. See Notes 1 and 4
213	Flyer Industries	E800	E10240395	1	1974	49	40' long/102" wide/rebuilt GE motors
214-237	Flyer Industries	E800	396-419	24	1975*	49	All serial numbers preceded by E10240
238-249	Flyer Industries	E800	420-431	12	1976*	49	All serial numbers as above
100-199[a]	Brown Boveri	GMT6H5307N		100	1982	42	a: Second numbers 101-199

* Indicates the year delivered. Some units may have been partially or completely fabricated the year before.

Data for CCF/Brill and Brown Boveri Trolley Coaches

Bus Type	Wheel Base	Length	Width	Height	H.P.	Circle Radius	Weight — Ratio Front Axle	Weight — Ratio Rear Axle	Weight	Passengers
Canadian Car Brill T-44 121 to 192, 203 to 212	198 1/2"	36'1"	8'6"	10'4 1/2"	140	43'0"	6435	12075	18510	44
Canadian Car Brill T-48A 193 to 202	247"	38'9 1/2"	8'6"	10'6 1/4"	140	39'4"	7300	12220	19170	48 (or 42)
Brown Boveri 100 to 199 (2nd)	7233 mm	12167 mm	2585 mm		360 max. 184 cont.				9700 kg. 21385 lbs	42

Data supplied by Don Mann, Edmonton Transit, from 1972 bus records, and D. Pagett, Supervisor Electrical, Edmonton Transit, from BBC Technical Specifications 1982.

Roster Notes

Note 1:

Ex-Regina units.

Edmonton No.	Regina No.	Serial No.	
125	125	5653	
122	127	5655	
124	128	5656	
123	133	5661	
121	134	5662	
126	135	5663	(serial plate reads CCF-T44-47-5663)
127	136	5664	
129	137	5665	
128	141	5669	
130	146	5674	(TBB)

Note 2:

Ex-Winnipeg 1947 T-44 units bought on November 4, 1969 for parts. Winnipeg numbers/serial numbers:
1610/5075 1614/5077 1616/5078 1618/5079 1624/5082 1628/5084 1632/5086 1634/5087 1640/5090 1642/5091 1650/5505 1652/5506 1654/5507 1656/5508 1658/5509. (TBB)

Note 3:

Ex-Calgary T-44 and T-48 (*) units purchased July 1974 for parts. Calgary number/serial numbers:

401/5139 403/5141 404/5142 405/5143 412/5150 413/5151 415/5153 416/5154 428/5166 429/5167 435/5216 453/5234 454/5235 466/5688 469/5691 477/8168* 479/8163* 480/8164* 481/8320* 482/8321*. (TBB)

Note 4:

All CCF/Brills out of service as of November 17, 1978. The following remained at end of service:

121, 125, 127, 128, 129, 132, 135, 142, 144, 145, 148, 149, 153, 155, 161, 162, 163, 168, 170, 174, 176, 183, 185, 186, 189, 192, 195, 197-201, 203, 204, 208, 211, 212.

T-44 Nos. 148, 191, and T-48A No. 202 preserved. Balance sold to auto wrecker for scrap or storage sheds.

Note 5:

Serial number for No. 116 is 5500 (from serial plate, built June 2, 1944) and the balance of the series is extrapolated from this though not confirmed.

Note 6:

Series probably built in late 1946 and continued into 1947 since serial numbers are in sequence.

Note 7:

Garage records show no builder's plate for No. 209 but sequence is assumed to be continuous.

Information for Table 1 compiled from:
• Trolley Coach News, Trolley Bus Bulletin No. 105, Harry Porter, editor, (TBB).
• Edmonton Transit: Don Mann, Supervisor, Ferrier Division; Jack Fleck, Superintendent, Transit Services; Bob Rynerson, Marketing and Development.

Appendix IV: Trolley Coach Extensions

Extensive changes have taken place in the trolley coach scene in Edmonton during the years between the retirement of the CC&F Brills and the arrival of the Brown Boveri coaches. Some of these changes have been brought about by the planned redirection of roadway traffic, resulting in the need to alter bus routes. Other changes have been necessitated by major construction projects. Finally, some changes have come about due to the extension of the trolley coach network to areas never before served by electric transit vehicles.

In an effort to maximize the use of existing roadways, the City of Edmonton instituted an extensive system of one-way streets approaching the High Level Bridge and Walterdale Bridge over the North Saskatchewan River. This was called Project Uni. The project affected north-south trolley coach routes. The High Level Bridge connecting 109 Street across the river became one way southbound and the Walterdale Bridge (105 Street bridge) became one way northbound. New wire for southbound coaches was strung from the foot of Bellamy Hill at 97 Avenue, west to 109 Street, and then across the traffic deck of the High Level Bridge to connect again with the existing southbound wire on 109 Street at 88 Avenue. Subsequently, southbound trolley coach overhead was removed from Walterdale Hill, Walterdale Bridge, the 105 Street traffic circle and 104 Street to 96 Avenue.

Project Uni went into effect on November 16th, 1980. It was May 4th, 1981, however, before south side bus routes 9, 41 and 42 were electrified again. The stringing of trolley coach overhead across the traffic deck of the High Level Bridge with its low clearances posed some difficulties but these were overcome. The wires are suspended from a corrugated panel fixed to the bridge members and running the full length of the bridge. The panel is slightly wider than the wire track. It serves to prevent the trolley poles from flailing up against the cross members of the bridge should the poles become de-wired. Coincident with this new overhead construction, a short-turn loop at the Renfrew Park Baseball Stadium was built. The former southbound wire from Bellamy Hill across 97 Avenue to 104 Street was left in place as far as 96 Avenue. From this point, the wire was extended one block east on 96 Avenue to connect with the northbound line at Rossdale Road where the Renfrew Stadium is located.

During the summer of 1980, Jasper Avenue was closed from 99 Street to 96 Street to allow construction of the Edmonton Convention Centre. This necessitated the rerouting of all transit services in this area. Since trolley coach overhead was not in place on the detour routes, diesel buses were assigned to routes 1, 5 and 6. Effective with this rerouting, trolley coach operation in Edmonton was restricted for a period of almost one year to occasional assignments on route 3. Trolley coach assignment to this route was possible as, effective December 23rd, 1979, it operated on 102A Avenue between 97 and 101 Streets where overhead was already in place.

Two further closures of sections of Jasper Avenue resulted in additional rerouting of transit services. The first detour took effect on October 26th, 1980, when Jasper Avenue from 106 Street to 109 Street was closed to allow work on the extension of the underground LRT stations to progress. The second stage of the Jasper Avenue LRT construction detour became effective March 1st, 1981 when Jasper Avenue was closed to all transit traffic from 102 Street to 109 Street. Most of these transit services were rerouted to 102 Avenue.

During the period when trolley coach operations were severely restricted, considerable work was undertaken to prepare for the delivery of the 100 new Brown Boveri trolley coaches. Westwood shop was extended and the overhead line in and around the shop was completely rebuilt. Westwood will continue to be the base for trolley coach operations. Edmonton Power crews were also busy installing new overhead wire in the downtown area. The first of these new installations involved an eastbound extension of the overhead on 102 Avenue from 97 Street through to the intersection of 95 Street and Jasper Avenue to connect with northbound wire on 95 Street and eastbound wire on Jasper Avenue. The existing westbound wire on Jasper Avenue was routed into 102A Avenue and extended west along 102A Avenue to connect with existing wire at 97 Street. Wire was also installed on both sides of 102 Avenue from 102 Street to 109 Street and south on 109 Street to Jasper Avenue. Completion of this work enabled Edmonton Transit to assign trolley coaches to the detoured route 6. Westbound buses on this route detoured via 102A Avenue from 95 to 102 Street, south to 102 Avenue, then west into a Contra-Flow bus lane on 102 Avenue (as that avenue is one way eastbound) to 109 Street and south to Jasper Avenue where they continued their westbound trip. The eastbound

Photo above:
Coach 103, one of the 100 new Brown Boveri Canada Edmonton trolley coaches, operates on Route 9 Southgate looping through Southgate terminal on April 13, 1982.

(Colin K. Hatcher)

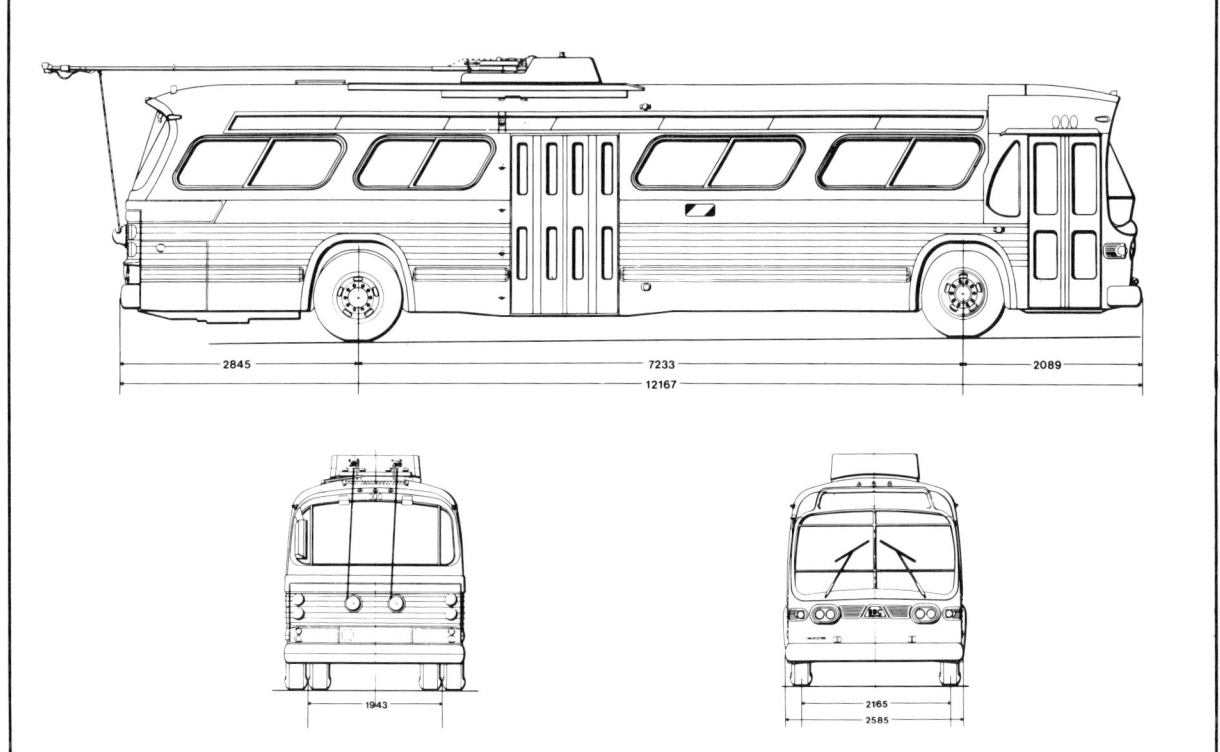

route 6 buses detoured off Jasper Avenue at 109 Street travelling north to 102 Avenue and then running east to 95 Street where they turned north to pick up their regular route again.

Once the LRT construction advanced far enough to allow the re-opening of Jasper Avenue, most transit services returned to that thoroughfare in two stages. During the first phase, while transit traffic was still very light on Jasper Avenue, the overhead line was replaced on both sides of the avenue between 102 Street and 109 Street. New wire was installed north on 99 Street from Jasper Avenue to existing wire on 102 Avenue, affording an eastbound connection onto 102 Avenue. For westbound service, the line was extended north on 99 Street to connect with the 102A Avenue line, enabling westbound trolleys to branch off the 102A Avenue line and run south on 99 Street to Jasper Avenue.

By April 25th, 1982, all of the above installations were completed, and effective with that date, most transit services were restored to Jasper Avenue with the exception of the three-block Convention Centre detour. Since new overhead wire was constructed along the detour route, trolley coaches began to appear again on routes 1 and 5 for the first time in almost two years. With the return of route 6 to Jasper Avenue at that time, the new line on 102 Avenue from 102 Street to 109 Street, and on 109 Street from 102 Avenue to Jasper Avenue, became surplus to any regular service. It remains intact, however, as an alternative route in case of an emergency, offering the flexibility necessary to maintain an efficient service in the downtown area. The delivery of most of the new Brown Boveri trolley coaches combined with the installation of the previously described overhead wire has enabled Edmonton Transit to assign trolley coaches to all of the route formerly served by that mode.

A major extension of overhead line in the west end from the route 3 terminal at 118 Avenue and 142 Street has enabled trolley coaches on that route to extend their trips west on 118 Avenue to 156 Street and south on 156 Street to the Jasper Place terminal at Stony Plain Road. Since route 3 trolley coaches now share this terminal with the route 1 coaches, overhead wiring in the terminal area has been extended and extensively upgraded. It has been designed to accommodate the intended electrification of two additional bus routes now using the terminal. The terminal is therefore now laid out to handle a total of four trolley coach routes. Most of the new overhead in Edmonton is suspended with European K&M fastenings but most of the turnouts, except for a few new electric turnouts throughout the system, are of the Ohio Brass design. The Jasper Place terminal area, however, uses the European suspension and turnouts exclusively. One route 3 bus operates over this new extension every half-hour, while fifteen-minute base and ten-minute peak hour service is maintained on the balance of the route.

Service on the extension commenced on Sunday, September 5th, 1982. Due to Edmonton Transit's practice of serving all routes with diesel buses on Saturdays, Sundays and holidays, the first revenue trolley coach operation was delayed until Tuesday, September 7th, 1982. Route 3 and route 4 service also returned to Jasper Avenue effective September 5th, 1982 after an absence of almost three years. Westbound trips operate via 102A Avenue, west to 99 Street, south to Jasper Avenue, then west to 101 Street where they turn north to continue along their former routes. Also effective September 5th, 1982, westbound route 1 trips travel along Jasper Avenue to 121 Street only. Here they turn north to 102 Avenue then proceed west to the Jasper Place terminal. This change eliminates the left turn at the busy intersection of 124 Street and 102 Avenue. The overhead at 124 Street and 102 Avenue was altered to accommodate the route change.

The Brown Boveri trolley coaches were built by General Motors at Ste. Thérèse, Quebec to T6H 5307N specifications. GM also designed the roof reinforcement to support the trolley pole assembly. The coaches seat 42 passengers. Single cross seats along the left side leave a wide aisle to provide for a free movement of passengers entering or leaving the coach on the heavily-travelled main line routes to which these coaches are assigned. The completed bodies were shipped to Edmonton on railway flatcars during the closing months of 1981 and throughout 1982. Final installation of the Brown Boveri chopper control electrical equipment was carried out by Bennett and Emmott Ltd., in Edmonton. The chopper control reduces maintenance and energy consumption, as well as offering extremely smooth starting and braking. Powerful dynamic brakes reduce the need to use air brakes, resulting in increased brake lining life. A transistorized converter supplies the low voltage system and charges the batteries. It is a self-contained naturally-cooled unit. For ease of access and maintenance the electrical equipment is mounted on a readily-removable cradle in the rear of the bus. The heating system ensures passenger comfort during those occasions when Edmonton temperatures dip as low as minus 40 degrees on either the metric or Fahrenheit scales. Passenger safety is enhanced by the double insulation of all systems connected to the line.

The prototype coach number 100 underwent extensive testing on city streets before being placed in revenue service. On November 10th, 1981, coach 100 was officially accepted by Edmonton Transit. It began revenue service on November 19th, 1981. By mid-January 1982, several of the new coaches were operating in regular service. Soon the Brown Boveri coaches greatly out-numbered the 37 Flyer coaches which had held a three-year monopoly on trolley coach assignments in Edmonton since the November 1978 retirement of the CC&F Brill coaches. Once again the major Edmonton Transit routes are served by quiet, efficient trolley coaches.

Appendix v:
Footnotes

Footnotes for Chapter I

1. Northwest Territories Ordinances, Fourth Session, Second Legislative Assembly, 1893, No. 32. An Ordinance to Empower the Municipality of the Town of Edmonton to Construct and Operate a Tramway. Assented to September 16, 1893, O. 278.
2. Op cit., p. 285.
3. Edmonton Journal, November 2, 1908, p. 3.
4. Loc. cit.
5. Loc. cit.
6. Loc. cit.
7. City of Edmonton, Meeting No. 11, Special Meeting of Council, March 7, 1907.
8. City of Edmonton, Meeting No. 12, City Council Meeting, March 12, 1907.
9. City of Edmonton, Meeting No. 33, City Council Meeting, June 11, 1907.
10. Edmonton Bulletin, September 18, 1907, p. 8.
11. City of Edmonton, Meeting No. 54, City Council Meeting, Committee of the Whole, Sept. 26, 1907.
12. Edmonton Bulletin, September 21, 1907, p. 7.
13. Northwest Territories Ordinances, Third Session, Fifth Legislative Assembly, September, October, 1904, Chapter 34. An Ordinance to incorporate the Strathcona Radial Tramway Company, Limited; Assented to October 8, 1904, p. 255.
14. Edmonton Bulletin, September 18, 1907, p. 2.
15. Edmonton Bulletin, October 4, 1907, p. 2.
16. Op. cit., September 27, 1907, p. 2.
17. City of Edmonton, City Council Meeting No. 56, Minutes, October 8, 1907.
18. Edmonton Journal, October 8, 1907, p. 5.
19. Edmonton Journal, October 23, 1907, p. 7.
20. Edmonton Bulletin, November 1, 1907, p. 2.
21. Op. cit., November 4, 1907, p. 1.
22. Statutes of Alberta, Canada 8 Edward VII, Chapter 33, 1908, An Act respecting the *Edmonton Radial Tramway*.
23. City of Edmonton, City Council Meeting No. 6, January 29, 1908.
24. Op. cit. No. 15, March 10, 1908.
25. Loc. cit.
26. City of Edmonton, Council Meeting No. 19, April 7, 1908.
27. Cross Section and Plan Shewing Street Railway Track Construction, City Engineer's Office, Edmonton, November 1909. APRA Archives at Provincial Archives of Alberta.
28. The Edmonton Bulletin, July 30, 1908.
29. City of Edmonton, Council Meeting No. 42, August 4, 1908.
30. Loc. cit.
31. Edmonton Bulletin, July 30, 1908.
32. Edmonton Evening Journal, August 28, 1908, p. 5.

Footnotes for Chapter II

1. Edmonton Bulletin, August 14, 1908.
2. Edmonton Bulletin, August 7, 1908, p. 8.
3. Edmonton Bulletin, August 13, 1908, p. 1.
4. City of Edmonton, City Council Meeting No. 44, August 18, 1908.
5. City of Edmonton, Contract Agreement, Gorman, Clancey & Grindley, and Ottawa Car Company Ltd. dated August 20, 1908.
6. Edmonton Journal, August 18, 1908, p. 1.
7. Edmonton Bulletin, September 4, 1908.
8. Insurance Plan of Edmonton, June 1913, City of Edmonton, Parks and Recreation, Historical Branch.
9. Edmonton Journal, October 13, 1908, p. 8 and Monday, October 26, 1908, p. 7.
10. Edmonton Journal, October 26, 1908, p. 7.
11. Apmonton Journal, November 2, 1908, p. 3.
12. Edmonton Journal, October 29, 1908, p. 4.
13. Edmonton Journal, October 30, 1908, p. 1.
14. Edmonton Journal, October 31, 1908, p. 3.
15. Loc. cit.
16. Loc. cit.
17. Edmonton Journal, November 2, 1908, p. 3.

Footnotes for Chapter III

1. Edmonton Journal, November 2, 1908, p. 1.
2. Edmonton Daily Bulletin, November 7, 1908, p. 1.
3. Edmonton Journal, November 10, 1908, p. 3.
4. Edmonton Journal, November 11, 1908, p. 1.
5. Edmonton Bulletin, November 11, 1908, p. 8.
6. Edmonton Journal, November 11, 1908, p. 3.
7. Edmonton Journal, November 21, 1908, p. 3.
8. Edmonton Journal, November 23, 1908, p. 1.
9. Edmonton Bulletin, November 30, 1908, p. 1.
10. Edmonton Bulletin, December 8, 1908, p. 1.
11. Edmonton Daily Bulletin, December 4, 1908, p. 1.
12. Edmonton Daily Bulletin, December 23, 1908, p. 2.
13. Edmonton Daily Bulletin, December 4, 1908, p. 1.
14. Edmonton Daily Bulletin, December 4, 1908, p. 1.
15. Edmonton Daily Bulletin, December 8, 1908, p. 6.
16. Edmonton Daily Bulletin, December 10, 1908, p. 2.
17. Loc. cit.
18. Edmonton Journal, December 14, 1908, p. 8.
19. Edmonton Daily Bulletin, December 16, 1908, p. 10.
20. Edmonton Journal, December 26, 1908, p.
21. Edmonton Journal, December 29, 1908, p.
22. Edmonton Daily Bulletin, December 28, 1908.
23. Edmonton Journal, December 28, 1908, p. 6.
24. Edmonton Daily Bulletin, December 4, 1908, p. 1.
25. Edmonton Journal, December 28, 1908, p. 1.
26. Edmonton Daily Bulletin, December 21, 1908, p. 1.
27. Edmonton Evening Journal, December 11, 1908.
28. Edmonton Daily Bulletin, December 21, 1908, p. 1.
29. Edmonton Daily Bulletin, January 3, 1909, p. 2.
30. Edmonton Daily Bulletin, April 19, 1909, p. 2.
31. Edmonton Daily Bulletin, January 3, 1909, p. 2.

Footnotes For Chapter IV

1. Edmonton Daily Bulletin, December 23, 1908, p. 16.
2. Edmonton Daily Bulletin, May 13, 1909, p. 1.
3. Edmonton Daily Bulletin, December 11, 1908, p. 10.
4. Edmonton Daily Bulletin, December 11, 1908, p. 10.
5. Binns, R.M. Montreal's Electric Streetcars, Railfare Enterprises Ltd., Montreal, 1973, p. 44.
6. Edmonton Daily Bulletin, December 11, 1908, p. 10.
7. Edmonton Daily Bulletin, December 30, 1908, p. 8.
8. Edmonton Daily Bulletin, January 7, 1909, p. 1.
9. Edmonton Daily Bulletin, January 11, 1909, p. 1.
10. City of Edmonton, City Council Minutes, Meeting No February 7, 1909.
11. Edmonton Daily Bulletin, February 2, 1909.
12. Edmonton Daily Bulletin, March 25, 1909, p. 8.
13. Loc. cit.
14. Edmonton Daily Bulletin, April 15, 1909, p. 8.
15. Edmonton Evening Journal, September 20, 1909, p. 1.
16. City of Edmonton, City Council Meeting No. 6, January 20, 1909.
17. Edmonton Daily Bulletin, February 2, 1909, p. 1.
18. City of Edmonton, City Council Meeting No. 7, February 2, 1909.
19. City of Edmonton, City Council Meeting No. 10, February 8, 1909.
20. Edmonton Daily Bulletin, April 2, 1909, p. 8.
21. Edmonton Daily Bulletin, March 31, 1909, p. 8.
22. Edmonton Daily Bulletin, March 15, 1909, p. 1.
23. Edmonton Daily Bulletin, May 13, 1909, p. 3.
24. Edmonton Daily Bulletin, May 26, 1909, p. 8.
25. Edmonton Journal, Tuesday, July 20, 1909, p. 8.
26. Edmonton Daily Bulletin, June 1, 1909, p. 8.
27. Edmonton Evening Journal, June 29, 1909, p. 1.
28. Edmonton Evening Journal, Loc. cit.
29. Edmonton Daily Bulletin, June 1, 1909, p. 8.
30. Edmonton Daily Bulletin, November 6, 1908, p. 1.
31. Edmonton Daily Bulletin, June 1, 1909, p. 8.
32. Edmonton Daily Bulletin, June 17, 1909, p. 8.
33. Edmonton Evening Journal, 1909, p. 8.
34. Loc. cit.
35. Edmonton Evening Journal, July 3, 1909.
36. Edmonton Daily Bulletin, July 5, 1909, p. 8.
37. Edmonton Evening Journal, July 27, 1909, p. 3.
38. Edmonton Evening Journal, June 19, 1909, p. 10.
39. Edmonton Evening Journal, July 19, 1909, p. 8.
40. Edmonton Evening Journal, July 12, 1909, p. 8.
41. Edmonton Evening Journal, July 10, 1909, p. 8.
42. Edmonton Evening Journal, July 12, 1909, p. 8.
43. Edmonton Daily Bulletin, July 19, 1909, p. 8.
44. Edmonton Daily Bulletin, September 15, 1909, p. 10.
45. Edmonton Daily Bulletin, September 23, 1909, p. 8.

46. Edmonton Daily Bulletin, September 21, 1909, p. 8.
47. Edmonton Daily Bulletin, September 9, 1909, p. 1.
48. Edmonton Evening Journal, June 21, 1909, p. 1.
49. Edmonton Evening Journal, July 7, 1909, p. 1.
50. Edmonton Daily Bulletin, March 25, 1909, p. 8.
51. Edmonton Daily Bulletin, July 23, 1909, p. 2.
52. Edmonton Daily Bulletin, September 9, 1909, p. 1.
53. Edmonton Daily Bulletin, September 10, 1909, p. 2.
54. Edmonton Daily Bulletin, November 16, 1909, p. 12.
55. Edmonton Daily Bulletin, November 23, 1909, p. 4.
56. Edmonton Daily Bulletin, November 16, 1909, p. 12.
57. Edmonton Daily Bulletin, November 19, 1909, p. 12.
58. Edmonton Daily Bulletin, March 31, 1909, p. 2.
59. Op. cit.
60. Edmonton Daily Bulletin, April 2, 1909, p. 2.
61. Edmonton Daily Bulletin, April 13, 1909, p. 2.
62. Edmonton Daily Bulletin, April 21, 1909, p. 2.
63. Edmonton Evening Journal, August 9, 1909.
64. Edmonton Evening Journal, November 10, 1909, p. 10.
65. Edmonton Daily Bulletin, October 28, 1909, p. 2.
66. Edmonton Daily Bulletin, April 2, 1909, p. 8.
67. Edmonton Evening Journal, August 13, 1909, p. 8.
68. Edmonton Daily Bulletin, September 13, 1909, p. 2.
69. Edmonton Daily Bulletin, October 2, 1909, p. 2.
70. Edmonton Daily Bulletin, October 6, 1909, p. 2.
71. Edmonton Daily Bulletin, June 19, 1909, p. 1.
72. Edmonton Daily Bulletin, September 2, 1909, p. 1.
73. Edmonton Daily Bulletin, September 23, 1909, p. 8.
74. Edmonton Daily Bulletin, September 25, 1909, p. 6.
75. Edmonton Daily Bulletin, December 14, 1909, p. 2.
76. Edmonton Journal, December 13, 1910, p. 1.

Footnotes For Chapter V

1. Edmonton Daily Bulletin, October 12, 1909, p. 8.
2. Edmonton Daily Bulletin, October 13, 1909, p. 2.
3. Edmonton Daily Bulletin, June 28, 1910, p. 8.
4. Edmonton Evening Journal, August 8, 1910, p. 8.
5. Edmonton Journal, November 7, 1910, p. 1.
6. Edmonton Journal, August 5, 1910, p. 1.
7. Edmonton Daily Bulletin, January 4, 1910, p. 8.
8. City of Edmonton, Council Meeting Minutes No. 10, February 28, 1910.
9. Edmonton Daily Bulletin, March 19, 1910, p. 8.
10. City of Edmonton, Council Meeting Minutes No. 10, February 28, 1910.
11. Edmonton Daily Bulletin, March 19, 1910, p. 8.
12. Edmonton Daily Bulletin, January 11, 1910, p. 4.
13. Edmonton Daily Bulletin, March 11, 1910, p. 1.
14. Edmonton Daily Bulletin, March 22, 1910, p. 8.
15. Edmonton Daily Bulletin, March 17, 1910, p. 4.
16. Edmonton Daily Bulletin, March 31, 1910, p. 8.
17. Edmonton Daily Bulletin, June 1, 1910, p. 1.
18. Edmonton Journal, June 21, 1910, p. 1.
19. Edmonton Journal, August 20, 1910, p. 1.
20. Edmonton Journal, August 26, 1910, p. 1.
21. Edmonton Journal, August 27, 1910, p. 1.
22. Edmonton Journal, August 29, 1910, p. 1.
23. Edmonton Journal, November 18, 1910, p. 1.
24. Edmonton Journal, December 2, 1910, p. 1.
25. Edmonton Journal, November 11, 1910, p. 1.
26. Edmonton Daily Bulletin, February 15, 1911, p. 5.
27. Edmonton Daily Bulletin, January 30, 1911, p. 1.
28. Municipality of City of Edmonton, Financial and Departmental layouts for year end October 31, 1909, p. 96
29. Op. cit., October 31, 1910.
30. Edmonton Daily Bulletin, July 6, 1911, p. 2.
31. Municipality of City of Edmonton, Financial and Departmental Reports for year end, October 31, 1910, p. 110.
32. Edmonton Daily Bulletin, January 26, 1911, p. 8.
33. Edmonton Daily Bulletin, January 12, 1911, p. 1.
34. Edmonton Journal, May 2, 1911, p. 12.
35. Strathcona Plaindealer, February 3, 1911, p. 1.
36. Strathcona Plaindealer, April 28, 1911, p. 1.
37. Edmonton Daily Bulletin, April 7, 1911, p. 1.
38. Edmonton Daily Bulletin, April 26, 1911, p. 2.
39. Edmonton Daily Bulletin, April 4, 1911, p. 12.
40. Edmonton Daily Bulletin, May 3, 1911, p. 8.
41. Edmonton Daily Bulletin, May 27, 1911, p. 1.
42. Edmonton Journal, July 28, 1911, p. 9.
43. City of Edmonton, City Clerk's Contract Files, Contract and related correspondence with the Preston Car and Coach Company Limited, December 7, 1910.
44. City of Edmonton, City Clerk's Contract Files, Contract with the Preston Car and Coach Company Limited, February 6, 1911.
45. City of Edmonton, City Clerk's Contract Files, Contract with Ottawa Car Company Limited, December 30, 1910.
46. City of Edmonton, City Clerk's Contract Files, Contract with Ottawa Car Company Limited, February 14, 1911.
47. Edmonton Daily Bulletin, September 14, 1911, p. 3.
48. Edmonton Daily Bulletin, November 23, 1911, p. 8.
49. Strathcona Plaindealer, September 8, 1911, p. 1.
50. Edmonton Daily Bulletin, October 26, 1911, p. 2.
51. Statutes of Alberta, Canada, 2-3 George V 1911-12, Edmonton Strathcona Amalgamation Act, Chapter 66, Section 27.
52. Edmonton Evening Journal, September 28, 1911, p. 1.
53. Edmonton Daily Bulletin, October 26, 1911, p. 2.
54. Edmonton Daily Bulletin, December 27, 1911, p. 10.
55. Edmonton Daily Bulletin, February 10, 1912, p. 12.
56. Edmonton Daily Bulletin, February 29, 1912, p. 10.
57. Edmonton Journal, August 11, 1911, p. 5.
58. Edmonton Journal, September 11, 1911, p. 1. — see also Edmonton Daily Bulletin, October 4, 1911, p. 9.
59. Edmonton Journal, October 3, 1911, p. 1.
60. Edmonton Daily Bulletin, September 29, 1911, p. 8.
61. Edmonton Bulletin, December 19, 1911, p. 12.
62. Edmonton Daily Bulletin, October 26, 1911.
63. Edmonton Daily Bulletin, October 26, 1911, p. 2.
64. Edmonton Daily Bulletin, February 10, 1912, p. 12.
65. Edmonton Daily Bulletin, December 30, 1911, p. 9.
66. Edmonton Daily Bulletin, December 28, 1911, p. 8.
67. Edmonton Daily Bulletin, December 22, 1911, p. 10.

Footnotes For Chapter VI

1. Statutes of Alberta, Canada, 2-3 George V, 1911-12, Edmonton-Strathcona Amalgamation Act, Chapter 66, Section 39.
2. Op. cit., sections 27 and 29.
3. Op. cit., sections 26 and 29.
4. Op. cit., sections 28 and 29.
5. Op. cit., section 30.
6. Op. cit., section 35.
7. Op. cit., section 34.
8. Op. cit., section 33.
9. Op. cit., section 34.
10. Edmonton Daily Bulletin, February 29, 1912, p. 4.
11. Edmonton Daily Bulletin, June 15, 1912, p. 16.
12. Edmonton Daily Bulletin, March 21, 1912, p. 2.
13. Edmonton Daily Bulletin, February 14, 1912, p. 2.
14. Edmonton Daily Bulletin, May 31, 1912, p. 2.
15. Edmonton Journal, September 1, 1911, p. 12.
16. Edmonton Daily Bulletin, September 1, 1911, p. 11.
17. Edmonton Daily Bulletin, June 4, 1912, p. 11.
18. City of Edmonton, City Clerk's Contract Files. Correspondence from St. Louis Car Company to City Commissioners, March 11, 1912.
19. Loc. cit.
20. Edmonton Daily Bulletin, June 8, 1912, p. 16.
21. Loc. cit.
22. Edmonton Daily Bulletin, June 24, 1912, p. 10.
23. Edmonton Daily Bulletin, March 25, 1912, p. 11.
24. Edmonton Daily Bulletin, April 12, 1912, p. 8.
25. Edmonton Daily Bulletin, May 21, 1912, p. 8.
26. Edmonton Daily Bulletin, June 18, 1912, p. 12.
27. Edmonton Daily Bulletin, July 5, 1912, p. 12.
28. Edmonton Daily Bulletin, June 28, 1912, p. 14.
29. City of Edmonton, Annual Report, 1912, Street Railway Department, p. 206.
30. Edmonton Daily Bulletin, July 3, 1912.
31. Edmonton Daily Bulletin, July 6, 1912.
32. Edmonton Daily Bulletin, July 10, 1912, p. 4.
33. Edmonton Daily Bulletin, July 15, 1912, p. 4.
34. Edmonton Daily Bulletin, July 1, 1912, p. 1.
35. Edmonton Daily Bulletin, July 5, 1912, p. 12.
36. Loc. cit.
37. Edmonton Daily Bulletin, July 23, 1912, p. 10.
38. Edmonton, Daily Bulletin, June 6, 1912, p. 12.
39. Edmonton Daily Bulletin, June 8, 1912, p. 12.
40. Edmonton Daily Bulletin, June 15, 1912, p. 16.
41. Edmonton Journal, August 22, 1912.
42. Edmonton Daily Bulletin, September 23, 1912, p. 2.
43. Edmonton Daily Bulletin, July 24, 1912.
44. Edmonton Bulletin, August 13, 1912, p. 5.

45. Edmonton Daily Bulletin, August 20, 1912, p. 5.
46. Edmonton Daily Bulletin, August 2, 1912, p. 2.
47. City of Edmonton, Annual Report, Street Railway Department, January 31, 1913, p. 206.
48. Edmonton Daily Bulletin, October 31, 1912.
49. Edmonton Daily Bulletin, May 28, 1912, p. 6.
50. City of Edmonton, Annual Report, Street Railway Department, December 19, 1912, p. 150.
51. Loc. cit.
52. City of Edmonton, Annual Report, Street Railway Department, December 19, 1912, p. 150.
53. City of Edmonton, Annual Report, Street Railway Department, January 31, 1913, p. 207.
54. Loc. cit.
55. Loc. cit.

Footnotes For Chapter VII

1. Edmonton Daily Bulletin, November 28, 1912.
2. City of Edmonton, Contract with the Preston Car and Coach Co. Limited, Preston, Ontario, November 27, 1912.
3. City of Edmonton, Contract with the Canadian General Electric Limited, Peterborough, Ontario, January 20, 1913.
4. City of Edmonton, Contract with the Preston Car and Coach Co. Limited, Preston, Ontario, November 27, 1912.
5. General Electric Company, Schenectady, N.Y., Railway Department, January 1907, Bulletin No. 4421 A. re G.E. 80 Railway Motor.
6. City of Edmonton, Contract with the Preston Car and Coach Co. Limited, Preston, Ontario, November 27, 1912.
7. Edmonton Daily Bulletin, May 16, 1913, p. 7.
8. Edmonton Daily Bulletin, September 25, 1913, p. 1.
9. Traction Heritage, Vane A. Jones Co., 6710 Hampton Drive E., Indianapolis, Indiana, 46226. Vol. 3, No. 2, March 1970, pp. 21-24. (Reprint from 1914 Electric Railway Journal).
10. Edmonton Daily Bulletin, May 16, 1913, p. 12.
11. Edmonton Daily Bulletin, May 1, 1913, p. 5.
12. Edmonton Daily Bulletin, May 13, 1913, p. 2.
13. Edmonton Daily Bulletin, May 14, 1913, p. 10.
14. Edmonton Daily Bulletin, May 15, 1913, p. 4.
15. Edmonton Daily Bulletin, May 27, 1913, p. 8.
15A. Edmonton Daily Bulletin, October 17, 1913, p. 1.
16. Edmonton Daily Bulletin, October 17, 1913, p. 1.
17. City of Edmonton Street Railway Department, Annual Report, March 17, 1914, p. 286.
18. Edmonton Daily Bulletin, June 3, 1913, p. 8.
19. Loc. cit.
20. Edmonton Daily Bulletin, June 20, 1913, p. 9.
21. Edmonton Daily Bulletin, June 19, 1913, p. 8.
22. Edmonton Daily Bulletin, July 9, 1913, p. 10.
23. Edmonton Daily Bulletin, August 12, 1913, p. 1.
24. Edmonton Journal, August 11, 1913, p. 1.
25. Loc. cit.
26. Edmonton Daily Bulletin, August 30, 1913, p. 14.
27. Edmonton Daily Bulletin, July 26, 1913, p. 16.
28. Edmonton Daily Bulletin, May 29, 1913, p. 5.
29. Edmonton Daily Bulletin, June 4, 1913, p. 10.
30. Edmonton Daily Bulletin, July 21, 1913, p. 1.
31. Edmonton Daily Bulletin, July 31, 1913, p. 2.
32. Loc. cit.
33. Edmonton Daily Bulletin, August 5, 1913, p. 1.
34. Edmonton Daily Bulletin, August 19, 1913, p. 8.
35. Edmonton Daily Bulletin, August 22, 1913, p. 3.
36. Edmonton Daily Bulletin, September 26, 1913, p. 12.
37. Edmonton Daily Bulletin, August 30, 1913, p. 14.
38. Edmonton Daily Bulletin, September 26, 1913, p. 1.
39. Loc. cit.
40. Edmonton Daily Bulletin, September 6, 1913, p. 9.
41. Edmonton Daily Bulletin, October 7, 1913, p. 1.
42. Edmonton Daily Bulletin, October 14, 1913, p. 2.
43. Edmonton Daily Bulletin, November 10, 1913, p. 2.
44. Edmonton Daily Bulletin, November 17, 1913, p. 12.
45. Edmonton Daily Bulletin, December 31, 1913, p. 7.
46. Edmonton Daily Bulletin, October 23, 1913, p. 10.
47. Edmonton Daily Bulletin, November 18, 1913, p. 9.
48. Edmonton Daily Bulletin, October 29, 1913, pps. 1 & 2.
49. Edmonton Daily Bulletin, November 18, 1913, p. 9.
50. Edmonton Daily Bulletin, September 26, 1913, p. 5.
51. Edmonton Daily Bulletin, November 1913, p. 22.

Footnotes For Chapter VIII

1. Statutes of Alberta, 1910, Chapter 49.
2. Op. cit., section 4.
3. Op. cit., section 11.
4. Op. cit., section 4.
5. Statutes of Alberta, 1911-12, chapter 36.
6. Op. cit., section 5.
7. Op. cit., section 4.
8. Edmonton Daily Bulletin, October 18, 1912, p. 11.
9. Loc. cit.
10. Loc. cit.
11. Edmonton Interurban Railway, A Report by M. Polet, September 14, 1917.
12. Edmonton Daily Bulletin, November 2, 1912, p. 12.
13. Edmonton Daily Bulletin, October 18, 1912, p. 11.
14. Edmonton Daily Bulletin, October 18, 1912, p. 11.
15. Edmonton Daily Bulletin, May 30, 1913, p. 4.
16. Edmonton Daily Bulletin, July 12, 1913, p. 20.
17. Edmonton Daily Bulletin, May 30, 1913, p. 4.
18. Corley, R.F., The Edmonton Interurban Railway, A Documented History, June, 1973.
19. Edmonton Daily Bulletin, July 12, 1913, p. 20.
20. Edmonton Daily Bulletin, September 30, 1913, p. 8.
21. Edmonton Daily Bulletin, October 8, 1913, p. 1.
22. Edmonton Daily Bulletin, October 1, 1913, p. 8.
23. Edmonton Daily Bulletin, October 8, 1913, p. 1.
24. Loc. cit.
25. Loc. cit.
26. Edmonton Daily Bulletin, October 15, 1913, p. 9.
27. Agreement between the City of Edmonton and the Edmonton Interurban Railway Company, November 7, 1913 and signed by representatives of both parties.
28. Edmonton Daily Bulletin, December 19, 1913, p. 1.
29. Edmonton Daily Bulletin, December 22, 1913, p. 9.
30. Loc. cit.
31. Edmonton Daily Bulletin, January 3, 1914, p. 18.
32. Edmonton Daily Bulletin, May 18, 1913, p. 1.
33. Edmonton Interurban Railway, A Report by M. Polet, Superintendent of the Company, Edmonton, September 14, 1917.
34. Loc. cit.

Footnotes For Chapter IX

1. Edmonton Bulletin, January 30, 1914, p. 2.
2. Edmonton Bulletin, February 9, 1914, p. 4.
3. Op. cit., p. 5.
4. Edmonton Bulletin, March 6, 1914, p. 14.
5. Edmonton Bulletin, March 9, 1914, p. 12.
6. Edmonton Bulletin, March 18, 1914, p. 6.
7. Edmonton Bulletin, April 1, 1914, p. 10.
8. Edmonton Bulletin, March 11, 1914, p. 9.
9. Edmonton Bulletin, April 24, 1914, p. 10.
10. Edmonton Bulletin, May 13, 1914, p. 1.
11. Edmonton Bulletin, May 18, 1914, p. 1.
12. Edmonton Bulletin, June 9, 1914, p. 2.
13. Edmonton Bulletin, June 20, 1914, p. 1.
14. Edmonton Bulletin, May 22, 1915, p. 2.
15. Edmonton Bulletin, June 9, 1915, p. 4.
16. Edmonton Bulletin, October 6, 1915, p. 1.
17. Edmonton Journal, September 17, 1915, p. 6.
18. Edmonton Journal, September 17, 1915, p. 11.
19. Loc. cit.
20. Loc. cit.
21. Loc. cit.
22. Loc. cit.
23. Loc. cit.
24. Edmonton Journal, November 23, 1915, p. 3.
25. Edmonton Journal, December 1, 1915, p. 12.
26. Edmonton Journal, May 16, 1916, p. 1.
26a Edmonton Journal, May 31, 1916.
27. Edmonton Interurban, A Report by M. Polet, Superintendent of the Company, September 14, 1917.
28. Edmonton Journal, May 19, 1920, p. 8.
29. Edmonton Interurban Railway, A Report by M. Polet, Superintendent of the Company, September 14, 1917.
30. Edmonton Journal, August 29, 1916, p. 8.
31. Edmonton Journal, September 24, 1915, p. 3.
32. Edmonton Journal, November 24, 1915, p. 3.
33. Edmonton Journal, February 2, 1916, p. 1.
34. Edmonton Journal, April 24, 1916, p. 2.
35. Edmonton Journal, May 17, 1916, p. 1.
36. Edmonton Journal, June 26, 1916, p. 1.
37. Edmonton Journal, July 26, 1916, p. 1.
38. Edmonton Journal, July 5, 1916, p. 2.

39. Edmonton Journal, July 7, 1916, p. 6.
40. Edmonton Journal, August 19, 1916, p. 23.
41. Edmonton Journal, September 19, 1916, p. 1.
42. Edmonton Journal, September 22, 1916, p. 3.
43. Edmonton Journal, October 25, 1916, p.
44. Edmonton Journal, August 19, 1916, p. 23.
45. Edmonton Journal, September 16, 1916, p. 8.
46. Edmonton Journal, September 14, 1916, p. 3.
47. Edmonton Journal, October 18, 1916, p. 12.
48. Edmonton Bulletin, August 2, 1917, p. 3.
49. Edmonton Journal, September 1, 1917, p. 1.
50. Loc. cit.
51. Edmonton Journal, September 4, 1917.
52. Edmonton Journal, September 6, 1917.
53. Edmonton Journal, September 7, 1917.
54. Edmonton Journal, September 11, 1917, p. 1.
55. Edmonton Journal, August 26, 1918, p. 8.
56. Edmonton Journal, September 22, 1916, p. 3.
57. Edmonton Journal, February 28, 1917, p. 24.
58. Edmonton Journal, January 9, 1917, p. 2.
59. Edmonton Journal, March 7, 1917, p.
60. Edmonton Journal, July 6, 1916, p. 1.
61. Edmonton Journal, April 6, 1916, p. 1.
62. Edmonton Journal, October 9, 1916, p. 3.
63. Edmonton Bulletin, April 18, 1917, p. 3.
64. Edmonton Journal, April 19, 1917, p. 1.
65. Edmonton Journal, March 23, 1917, p. 2.
66. Edmonton Journal, April 19, 1917, p. 1.
67. Edmonton Journal, June 8, 1917, p. 2.
68. Loc. cit.
69. Edmonton Bulletin, June 9, 1917, p. 3.
70. Loc. cit.
71. Edmonton Journal, June 11, 1917, p. 1.
72. Edmonton Bulletin, June 12, 1917, p. 3.
73. Edmonton Journal, January 2, 1917, p. 2.
74. Edmonton Bulletin, July 6, 1917, p. 3.
75. Edmonton Journal, June 14, 1917, p. 12.
76. Edmonton Bulletin, July 28, 1917, p. 3.
77. Edmonton Journal, October 17, 1917, p. 1.
78. Edmonton Journal, October 13, 1917, p. 3.
79. Loc. cit.
80. Edmonton Journal, October 17, 1917, p. 1.
81. Edmonton Journal, October 13, 1917, p. 3.
82. Edmonton Journal, October 17, 1917, p. 1.
83. Edmonton Journal, October 13, 1917, p. 3.
84. Edmonton Journal, October 17, 1917, p. 1.
85. Edmonton Journal, October 13, 1917, p. 3.
86. Loc. cit.
87. Edmonton Journal, March 9, 1918, p. 1.

Footnotes For Chapter X

1. Edmonton Journal, January 1, 1918.
2. Edmonton Journal, April 29, 1918, p. 4.
3. Loc. cit.
4. Edmonton Journal, July 19, 1918, p. 3.
5. Edmonton Interurban Railway, A Report by M. Polet, Superintendent of the Company, September 14, 1917.
6. The City of Edmonton, City Council Meeting Minutes, March 30, 1918.
7. Loc. cit.
8. Edmonton Journal, March 27, 1918, p. 6.
9. The City of Edmonton, City Council Meeting Minutes, April 18, 1918.
10. Loc. cit.
11. The City of Edmonton, City Council Meeting Minutes, May 28, 1918.
12. Edmonton Journal, April 10, 1919, p. 1.
13. Edmonton Journal, April 15, 1919, p. 2.
14. Edmonton Journal, April 22, 1919, p. 1.
15. Edmonton Journal, July 17, 1919, p. 6.
16. Edmonton Journal, August 22, 1919, p. 1.
17. Edmonton Journal, October 22, 1919, p. 1.
18. Edmonton Bulletin, October 28, 1919.
19. Edmonton Journal, October 22, 1919, p. 1.
20. Edmonton Bulletin, October 23, 1919.
21. Edmonton Journal, October 27, 1919.
22. Edmonton Bulletin, October 25, 1919.
23. Edmonton Journal, September 26, 1919, p. 11.
24. Edmonton Journal, June 30, 1919, p. 6.
25. Loc. cit.
26. Loc. cit.
27. Edmonton Journal, July 2, 1920, p. 8.
28. Edmonton Bulletin, February 16, 1926, p. 10.
29. Edmonton Journal, May 25, 1920, p. 20.
30. Loc. cit.
31. Loc. cit.

Footnotes For Chapter XI

1. Edmonton Journal, April 28, 1921, p. 5.
2. Loc. cit.
3. Loc. cit.
4. Edmonton Journal, April 26, 1921, p. 8.
4a. Edmonton Journal, July 6, 1921, p. 6.
5. Edmonton Journal, July 16, 1921, p. 6.
6. Edmonton Journal, October 5, 1921, p. 6.
7. Edmonton Journal, February 10, 1925, p. 9.
8. Edmonton Journal, March 25, 1925, p. 9.
9. Edmonton Bulletin, June 1, 1926, p. 9.
10. City of Edmonton, Commissioner's Correspondence, Cunningham to Commissioners, February 28, 1926.
11. Canadian Railway and Marine World, January 1929, p. 34.
12. City of Edmonton, Commissioners Correspondence, Wentworth to Robertson, May 6, 1927.
13. City of Edmonton, Commissioners Correspondence, Commissioners to Robertson, May 18, 1927.
14. Edmonton Bulletin, July 4, 1927, p. 11.
15. City of Edmonton, Commissioners Correspondence, Cunningham to Mitchell, September 28, 1927.
16. Diary Extract, November 14, 1929, H. Ward, Electrical Foreman, Edmonton Radial Railway.
17. Edmonton Journal, March 10, 1930, p. 9.
18. Loc. cit.
19. Edmonton Journal, May 5, 1930.
20. Edmonton Journal, May 8, 1930, p. 13.
21. Op. cit., p. 15.
22. City of Edmonton, Commissioners' Correspondence, Cunningham to Commissioners, August 18, 1930 and March 13, 1933.
23. Edmonton Journal, November 5, 1930, p. 20.
24. City of Edmonton, Commissioners' Correspondence File, Commissioners to Cunningham, June 7, 1926.
25. City of Edmonton, Commissioners' Correspondence File, Commissioners to Robertson, June 21, 1926.
26. City of Edmonton, Commissioners' Correspondence File, Commissioners to Alderman A. Farmilo, June 21, 1926.
27. City of Edmonton, Commissioners' Correspondence File, Cunningham to Mayor Douglas, April 24, 1930.
28. Edmonton Journal, April 25, 1931, p. 1.
29. Edmonton Journal, December 15, 1930, p. 18.
30. Edmonton Journal, December 23, 1930, p. 14.
31. Edmonton Journal, April 25, 1931, p. 1.
32. Edmonton Journal, May 21, 1931, p. 15.
33. Edmonton Journal, May 2, 1931, p. 11.
34. Edmonton Journal, January 22, 1932, p. 13.
35. Edmonton Journal, January 29, 1932, p. 16.
36. Loc. cit.
37. Loc. cit.
38. Edmonton Journal, April 26, 1932.
39. Edmonton Journal, January 22, 1932, p. 13, and April 26, 1932, p.
40. Edmonton Journal, May 22, 1933, p. 13.
41. City of Edmonton, Commissioners Report No. 27, June 26, 1933.
    Edmonton Journal, June 22, 1933, p. 13.
42. City of Edmonton, Commissioners File, Street Railway General, Cunningham to Commissioners, November 16, 1933.
43. Loc. cit.
44. Edmonton Journal, December 16, 1933, p. 15.
45. Edmonton Journal, February 26, 1934, p. 13.
46. Edmonton Journal, January 29, 1934, p. 11.
47. Edmonton Journal, February 26, 1934, p. 13.
48. Edmonton Journal, June 25, 1934, p. 13.
49. Edmonton Journal, November 26, 1935, p. 13.
50. Edmonton Journal, December 19, 1935, p. 13.
51. City of Edmonton, Edmonton Transit Report, Mileage and Passenger Statistics 1908-1965.
52. Edmonton Journal, December 4, 1935, p. 9.
53. Edmonton Journal, June 25, 1934, p. 17.
54. Edmonton Journal, June 11, 1938.
55. Edmonton Journal, July 16, 1938.

56. City of Edmonton, City Commissioners Files, City Commissioners from Thomas Ferrier, Superintendent, Street Railway Department, May 16, 1939.
57. City of Edmonton, City Commissioners Files, Commissioners Answers to Inquiries, April 24, 1939.
58. City of Edmonton, Commissioners Files, Street Railway General, March 31, 1939, Chief Constable A.G. Shute to City Commissioners.
59. Edmonton Journal, July 26, 1939, p. 13.
60. Edmonton Journal, August 31, 1939, p. 13.

Footnotes For Chapter XII

1. Edmonton Transit, Mileage and Passenger Statistics Summary, 1908-1965.
2. Edmonton Journal, June 6, 1940, p.
3. Personal conversation with Les Irvin, Supervisor of Schedules, and Alec McSporran, Supervisor of Inspectors, both former motormen with ERR. December 1, 1973.
4. Edmonton Bulletin, February 22, 1943.
5. Edmonton Journal, October 9, 1941, p.
6. Edmonton Journal, October 14, 1941, p. 13.
7. Edmonton Journal, October 18, 1941, p. 14.
8. Edmonton Journal, October 23, 1941, p. 9.
9. Edmonton Bulletin, August 14, 1944, p. 9.
10. Edmonton Journal, August 12, 1944, p. 13.
11. Edmonton Journal, December 1, 1944.
12. Loc. cit.
13. Edmonton Bulletin, October 13, 1943.
14. Edmonton Bulletin, August 18, 1943.
15. Edmonton Bulletin, September 23, 1943.
16. Edmonton Journal, November 15, 1945.
17. Edmonton Bulletin, July 20, 1945. p. 15.
18. Edmonton Bulletin, August 13, 1945, p. 9.
19. Edmonton Bulletin, October 5, 1945, p. 11.
20. Edmonton Bulletin, July 16, 1946, p. 9.
21. Edmonton Bulletin, August 30, 1947, p. 13.
22. Edmonton Journal, August 8, 1947, p. 1.
23. Edmonton Journal, September 24, 1921, p. 6.
24. Personal conversation with Bob Campbell, Retired Motorman from McKernan's Lake line, December 1, 1973.
25. Loc. cit.
26. Edmonton Journal, August 8, 1947, p. 1.
27. Loc. cit.
28. Edmonton Journal, October 4, 1947, p.
29. Edmonton Journal, August 27, 1948, p. 1.
30. Edmonton Bulletin, September 23, 1947.
31. Edmonton Bulletin, May 1, 1948, p. 2.
32. Edmonton Journal, August 7, 1948, p. 8.
33. Loc. cit.
34. Edmonton Journal, August 28, 1948, p.
35. Edmonton Bulletin, February 22, 1949.
36. Edmonton Journal, August 20, 1949, p. 1.
37. Loc. cit.
38. Loc. cit.
39. Edmonton Journal, August 27, 1949, p. 33.
40. Edmonton Journal, September 1, 1951, p. 2.
41. Loc. cit.

Footnotes For Chapter XIV

1. MacGregor, J.G., *Edmonton, A History,* Hurtig Publishers, Edmonton, 1967, p. 327.
2. Loc. cit.
3. *Rapid Transit for the City of Edmonton,* Canadian Bechtel Limited, June 1963, p. 1.
4. Op. cit., p. 2.
5. Loc. cit.
6. *Light Rapid Transit, The Immediate Answer for Edmonton,* Researched and Created by: The University Practicum in Rapid Transit, Fall 1972, Edmonton, Alberta.
7. DuWag Specification Sheet, *Light Rail Vehicle RTE 1,* Edmonton, Canada.
8. Loc. cit.
9. Siemens Specification Sheet, *Light Rail Vehicle RTE 1,* of the City of Edmonton, Ref. E1, E4-477/19.
10. Loc. cit.
11. Loc. cit.

Footnotes For Chapter XV

1. City of Edmonton Archives City Commissioners Files, A73-52 Box 151, Report on Edmonton Street Railway and Recommendations for 1938 Program, December 22, 1937.
2. *Ibid.,* Minutes of Edmonton City Council, February 28, 1938.
3. *Ibid.,* Report of Wilson and Bunnell, April 30, 1938.
4. *Ibid.,* "Report on Street Railway Improvements" by Commissioner R. J. Gibb to City Council, June 20, 1938, pages 3 and 4.
5. *Ibid.,* Copy of call for tenders for 6, 38 to 44 passenger trolley buses for the City of Edmonton, July 21, 1938.
6. *Ibid.,* Recommendation of Commissioners to Council, October 11, 1938.
7. *Ibid.,* Council's decision, October 11, 1938.
8. *Ibid.,* — Supplement to EEC proposal dated September 21, 1938, meeting held October 13, 1938.
   — Supplement to Leyland proposal, October 15, 1938.
   — Letter to Associated Equipment Co. Ltd. Canada, re: exterior paint scheme, lettering, destination signs, etc., December 16, 1938.
   — Letter to Gorman's Ltd. (representing EEC) from Commissioner R.J. Gibb, re: interior paint and upholstry, January 5, 1939.
9. *Ibid.,* Letter to AEC Co., referred to above, December 16 1938.
10. *Ibid.,* Letter from A.W. Haddow, City Engineer, to City Commissioners, November 25, 1938.
11. *Ibid.,* Letter from Commissioner R.J. Gibb to R.D. Parsons, J.G. Brill Co., Chicago, April 19, 1939.
12. Edmonton Journal, May 19, 1939.
13. *Ibid.,* September 4, 1939, and subsequent accounts.
14. Edmonton Bulletin, September 12, 1939, page 1.
15. Edmonton Journal, September 21, 1939.
16. Edmonton Bulletin, September 20, 1939, page 1.
17. Edmonton Journal, September 23, 1939, page 18.
18. South Edmonton Weekly News, September 21, 1939, pages 1 and 2.
19. Edmonton Journal, September 23, 1939, page 15.
20. — *Ibid.,* September 25, 1939.
    — Edmonton Bulletin, September 25, 1939, page 1.
21. Edmonton Journal, October 4, 1939, page 9.
22. *Ibid.,* October 11, 1939, page 10.
23. Edmonton Bulletin, October 24, 1939, pages 1 and 16.
24. Commissioners, *Op. Cit.* Council Minutes, November 27, 1939, Item 10.
25. *Ibid.,* Letter from Commissioner R.J. Gibb to C.R. Garnett, Gorman's Ltd., December 8, 1938.
26. *Ibid.,* — Letter from R.J. Gibb to S.L. Wilson Goode, H.M. Trade Commissioner, Vancouver, October 24, 1940.
    — Reply to above, October 26, 1940.
    — Letter from R.C. Humphry, Leyland, Toronto, to Commissioner R.J. Gibb, October 4, 1940, re: Canton buses.
    — Subsequent correspondence through balance of 1940.

Footnotes For Chapter XVI

1. Canadian Transportation, January 1948, pages 32 to 35.
2. City of Edmonton Archives, City Commissioners Files, Transit Controller G.S. Gray to Commissioner R.J. Gibb, May 21, 1942.
3. *Ibid.,* Letter from T. Ferrier, Superintendent E.R.R., to H.C. Glunz, Assistant General Manager, Mack Trucks Canada, re: paint, destination signs and bus numbers, September 16, 1942.
4. — Edmonton Bulletin, February 10, 1943.
   — *Ibid.,* February 15, 1943.
5. Commissioners, *Op. Cit.* Telegram from Commissioner R.J. Gibb to Controller G.S. Gray, August 3, 1943.
6. Bulletin, *Op. Cit.,* August 16, 1943.
7. *Ibid.,* — September 14, 1943, page 1.
   — October 5, 1943, page 16.
   — October 13, 1943.
8. Commissioners, *Op. Cit.* Letter from Controller G.S. Gray to Commissioner R.J. Gibb, May 29, 1944.
9. *Ibid.,* Decision of Council, June 12, 1944.
10. Edmonton Journal, December 1, 1944.
11. Commissioners, *Op. Cit.,* G.S. Gray to R.J. Gibb, January 9, 1945.

12. *Ibid.,* R.J. Gibb to G.S. Gray, January 17, 1945.
13. *Ibid.,* ACF-Brill Motor Co. Philadelphia, Penn. to R.J. Gibb, March 16, 1945.
14. *Ibid.,* Letter from G.S. Gray to R.J. Gibb, January 22, 1945.
15. *Ibid.,* Letter from ACF-Brill Motor Co., Philadelphia, to R.J. Gibb, March 16, 1945.
16. Bulletin, *Op. Cit.,* March 6, 1945.
17. Commissioners, *Op. Cit.,* Letter from G.S. Gray to R.J. Gibb, April 2, 1945.
18. *Ibid.,* Canadian Car/Brill, Toronto, Ontario to R.J. Gibb, July 24, 1945.
19. *Ibid.,* Report to Transportation Committee (City of Edmonton) by: A.D. Ainley, Mayor; R.J. Gibb, Commissioner and J. Hodgson, Commissioner; February 17, 1945.
20. *Ibid.,* Letter from G.S. Gray to R.J. Gibb, September 24, 1945.
21. *Ibid.,* Minutes of City Council, February 1, 1946 (reaffirming decision of August 13, 1945, pages 230 to 232).
22. *Ibid.,* Letter from Winnifred Audley to Mayor J. Fry, February 23, 1945.
23. *Ibid.,* Reply to Miss Audley from R.J. Gibb, February 27, 1945.
24. "The Trolley Coach", A Symposium held during the 41st Annual Meeting — Canadian Transit Association, June 12, 1946, from a talk by Thomas Ferrier, Superintendent, Edmonton Radial Railway, pages 17 to 24.
25. Commissioners, *Op. Cit.,* Recommendations, R.J. Gibb to Transportation Committee, May 10, 1945.
26. Edmonton Bulletin, July 20, 1945, page 15.
27. Alberta Provincial Archives, Collection 75-11 Box 11, Carbon of Newspaper ad copy.
28. Commissioners, *Op. Cit.,* Copy of requests for bids, August 20, 1945.
29. *Ibid.,* Reply to tentative order for Edmonton, from Canadian Car and Foundry/Brill, Toronto, August 13, 1945.
30. *Ibid.,* Reply to bid from Mack Trucks of Canada, Toronto, August 20, 1945.
31. *Ibid.,* Reply to bid from Twin Coach, Kent, Ohio, August 23, 1945.
32. *Ibid.,* Reply to bid from Pullman-Standard, Chicago, August 28, 1945.
33. *Ibid.,* Reply to bid from MCI (Motor Coach Industries), Winnipeg, August 23, 1945.
34. — *Ibid.,* City Council Minutes, re: Transportation Committee Report No. 6, Section 2 dated September 29, concurred on October 9, 1945.
    — Letter from R.J. Gibb to E.J. Cosford, Sales Manager, Canadian Car and Foundry Ltd., Toronto, Ontario, October 10, 1945.
35. *Ibid.,* Letter from R.J. Gibb to Twin Coach, October 10, 1945.
36. *Ibid.,* Letter from R.J. Gibb to Mack Trucks of Canada, October 10, 1945.
37. *Ibid.,* Letter from W.J. Beatty ACF-Brill, Philadelphia to R.J. Gibb, October 4, 1945.
38. Roll sign in collection of C.K. Hatcher.
39. Commissioners, *Op. Cit.,* City Council Minutes, February 18, 1946.
40. *Ibid.,* Memo from R.J. Gibb to Superintendent T. Ferrier, March 20, 1946.
41. Archives, *Op. Cit.,* Carbon copies of newspaper ad copy used in 1946, 1949, 1950 and 1951.
42. Commissioners, *Op. Cit.,* Memo, D.B. Menzies Commissioner, to Chief Constable R. Jennings, City Police, re: bus route changes, March 27, 1947.
43. Edmonton Transit, Telegrams from CCF/Brill to Superintendent T. Ferrier, re: shipments of units T44-47-5176 through T44-47-5193, September 4 to 17, 1947.
44. *Ibid.,* Telegrams, re: shipments of units T44-47-5023 through T44-47-5044, January 8 to February 6, 1947.
    Ibid., Letter to R.R. Mills, District Manager, Canadian Ohio Brass Co. Ltd., Niagara Falls, Ontario, from Superintendent T. Ferrier, July 31, 1947.
45. Edmonton Journal, October 4, 1947 and Archives carbon of newspaper ad copy.
46. *Ibid.,* page 1.
47. Transit, *Op. Cit.,* Letter from Assistant Superintendent D.L. MacDonald to Associated Equipment Co. of Canada, March 15, 1948.
48. *Ibid.,* Letter to E.J. Cosford, Sales Manager, Canadian Car and Foundry Ltd., Toronto, from Assistant Superintendent D.L. MacDonald, April 21, 1948.
49. Edmonton Bulletin, May 1, 1948, page 2, and Archives carbon of newspaper ad copy.
50. Edmonton Journal, August 28, 1948 and Archives carbon of newspaper ad copy.
51. Commissioners, *Op. Cit.,* Telegram from Mayor H.D. Ainley (Edmonton) to Mayor Garnet Menzies (Regina), January 24, 1949.
52. Transit, *Op. Cit.,* Letter from D.L. MacDonald, Assistant Superintendent ERR, to D.J. Monroe, Superintendent Equipment, Montreal Tramways, January 21, 1949.
53. Commissioners, *Op. Cit.,* Recommendations of Commissioners, re: Report of N.D. Wilson, part B reference pages 22 and 23 of Wilson Report. Recommendation (1).
54. *Loc. Cit.,* Recommendation (2).
55. *Loc. Cit.,* Recommendation (3).
56. *Ibid.,* Report "1951 — Final Conversion from Street Railway to Coach Operation", page 2.
57. Recommendations, *Op. Cit.,* Recommendation (6).
58. Commissioners, *Op. Cit.,* Proposed 1948 Conversion, April 26, 1948, Item 3.
59. *Ibid.,* Council Minutes, July 11, 1949.
60. Transit, *Op. Cit.,* Letter to A.E. Jennings, Assistant Sales Manager, Bus Division Canadian Car, Montreal, from D.L. MacDonald, Assistant Superintendent, May 12, 1949.
61. Edmonton Journal, August 20, 1949, page 1, and Archives carbon of ad copy.
62. *Ibid.,* August 29, 1949.
63. Archives, *Op. Cit.,* carbon of ad copy dated November 12, 1949.
64. Edmonton Journal, January 27, 1950.

Footnotes For Chapter XVII

1. Commissioners, *Op. Cit.,* Report "Edmonton Transit System Streetcar Conversion Program — 1951 — Final Conversion from Street Railway to Coach Operation", March 1951.
2. Alberta Provincial Archives, Collection 75-11 Box 11.
3. Edmonton Journal, March 12, 1951.
4. *Ibid.,* January 18, 1951, page 1.
5. Commissioners Report 1951, *Loc. Cit.*
6. Commissioners, *Op. Cit.,* Council Minutes, C.R. No. 16 Item 8, April 9, 1951.
7. Edmonton Journal, August 29, 1951.
8. Dated photograph, N. Corness collection.
9. Edmonton Transit to R.E. Fielder, G.M. Truck & Coach Div. Pontiac, Mich., from T. Ferrier, June 22, 1951.
10. City Archives, *Op. Cit.,* undated clipping probably Spring 1952. "Study Busline to South Side for Conversion to Trolleys."
11. *Ibid.,* Council Minutes, Item 3 — Answers to Enquiries, February 9, 1953.
12. Trolley Coach News, Trolley Bus Bulletin No. 105 and Edmonton Transit Garage Records.
13. Route Map, Edmonton Transit dated September 1953.
14. Commissioners, *Op. Cit.,* City Council Minutes, Commissioners Report No. 24, Item 10, August 9, 1954. Note of concurrence dated August 9, 1954.
15. Edmonton Journal, March 28, 1966.
16. Edmonton Journal, August 9, 1954.
17. City Archives, Edmonton Journal clipping only dated 1954, "Both Bridges Open But Cars Using One."
18. *Ibid.,* October 18, 1954.
19. Commissioners, *Op. Cit.,* petitions by 512 Parkallen residents in favour of and 45 objecting to trolley poles on 65th Avenue, May 19, 1955.
20. Edmonton Transit, paper "History of Route Extensions and Systems Expansion", no date — c. 1958, page 3.
21. *Loc. Cit.*
22. Edmonton Journal, October 13, 1956.
23. — *Ibid.,* October 13, 1956 (advertisement).
    — Commissioners, Memorandum from D.L. MacDonald to City Commissioners, etc., November 15, 1957.
24. Journal, *Loc. Cit.,* March 4, 1958.
25. *Ibid.,* March 28, 1962.
26. Edmonton Transit, paper "History of Trolley Coach Route Installations, Extensions, Removals", no date — c. 1965, page 2.
27. Edmonton Transit System "New Improved ETS South Side Routes Effective September 2, 1962" (Schedule).

28. Commissioners, *Op. Cit.,* Memo from D.B. Menzies, Commissioner, to D.L. McDonald, Superintendent Transit System, November 7, 1962.
29. Edmonton Journal, Editorial Cartoon, November 1962.
30. Observations and from photo collection C.K. Hatcher.
31. Commissioners, *Op. Cit.,* Letter from W. Robertson, Director Operations, Edmonton Transit to Commissioner D.B. Menzies, March 7, 1963, and Edmonton Journal, November 8, 1962.
32. Transit, History of Trolley Coach, *Loc. Cit.,* page 2.
33. Edmonton Journal, *Op. Cit.,* May 12, 1964.
34. Commissioners, *Op. Cit.* — Memo from D.L. McDonald to C.Z. Managhan, Supervisor Electrical Distribution System and W.D. Kirland, Supervisor Power Plant, Edmonton Power, May 14, 1964.
    — Memo from D.L. McDonald to D.B. Menzies, Commissioner, June 2, 1964.
35. C. R. H. A. "Rattler" (Canadian Railroad Historical Association — Rocky Mountain Branch), September 12, 1964, page 3.
36. Edmonton Journal, December 21, 1964, page 34.
37. *Ibid.,* August 27, 1965, page 22.
38. Personal recollections of D. Fillion as related by his son-in-law, R. Rynerson.
39. Personal observations by C.K. Hatcher.
40. Edmonton Journal, March 28, 1966.
41. *Ibid.,* June 30, 1967, page 23.
42. Alberta Pioneer Railway Association, Edmonton, Edmonton Transit Collection — rollsigns.
43. Trolley Coach News, No. 10, August 1970, page 57.
44. Edmonton Journal, August 14, 1970.
45. Edmonton Transit, List of Superintendents of the E.T.S.
46. Edmonton Journal, January 7, 1972, page 22.
    Loc. Cit., October 18, 1972.
47. *Ibid.,* October 12, 1973.
48. Edmonton Journal, November 3, 1973, page 30.
49. *Ibid.,* August 9, 1974.
50. *Ibid.,* October 25, 1974.
51. *Ibid.,* December 7, 1974, page 8.
52. *Ibid.,* August 1, 1975, page 7.
53. Memo for file, R. W. Rynerson, Edmonton Transit, August 1977 (taken from rollsign on bus 238 built 1976).
54. Edmonton Journal, August 1, 1975, page 7.
55. Personal observations by author (T.S.).
56. Personal observations, both authors.
57. Edmonton Journal, June 5, 1975, page 21.
58. Alberta Pioneer Railway Association (APRA) "Marker", September 1975, page 7.
59. *Ibid.,* October 1975, page 4.
60. *Ibid.,* November-December 1975, page 13.
61. *Ibid.,* April 1976, pages 46 and 47.
62. *Ibid.,* June 1976, page 71.
63. *Ibid.,* September 1976, page 102.
64. Edmonton Journal, January 31, 1976.
65. Personal observations by author (T.S.).
66. Personal observations by author (T.S.).
67. Memo for file, R. W. Rynerson, Edmonton Transit, February 14, 1977 (taken from bus 219).
68. Edmonton Journal, February 8, 1977, page 29.
69. "Marker", *Op. Cit.,* November-December 1975, page 8.
70. Edmonton Journal, February 22, 1978, Section B, first page.

Appendix VI:
Acknowledgements

The compilation of the story of the Edmonton Radial Railway and of the electric vehicles of its current successor, Edmonton Transit, has involved many people. The search for information about Edmonton's streetcars began in earnest in 1973 after considerable encouragement from Don Currie. John Meikle, a local trolley enthusiast who had developed an historical sketch of both the streetcars and trolley coaches of Edmonton, introduced Wilf Robertson. Wilf's father, A. Robertson, had begun work for the Edmonton Radial Railway in 1909 and by the late 1920s, had risen through the ranks to become Traffic Manager. Following in his father's footsteps, Wilf joined the ERR in the 1930s; when he retired in the early 1970s, he was Assistant Superintendent of the ETS. Wilf arranged meetings with Alan Manly and H. Gilbert Sorenson, retired street railway men. The late Mr. Manly provided a rare photograph of Edmonton's observation car while Mr. Sorenson who had been in charge of construction and maintenance of the overhead line system on the ERR, clarified many questions related to the early layout of the street railway system. He recounted many interesting stories about the installation of the overhead line and loaned several photographs depicting early construction on the street railway.

In an effort to compile information about the ERR, J.A. Ross, formerly Operations Director with Edmonton Transit and now General Manager of Saskatoon Transit, had gathered photographs, tickets, transfers and information of historical interest about the streetcars and buses. These he shared to assist in this work. Mr. Ross also made available a newspaper clipping book from the ET office.

L.A. Lawrence, now Director of Operations for ET has taken a great deal of interest in the project. Llew arranged interviews with employees who had operated or worked on the streetcars. Among this group was Les Irvine, now retired but then Supervisor of Schedules; the late Alex McSparron, then Supervisor of Inspectors; the late Ernie Cliff, then Mechanical Supervisor; and Bob Campbell and Bob Lane, both retired motormen and bus operators.

W.L. Mack, Business Agent and Bill MacLean of the Executive of the Amalgamated Transit Union, Local 569, provided an opportunity to reach more retired men at an annual Ladies' Night-Retired Men's Banquet. Previous contacts were renewed and new contacts made. Among the latter was Percy Maines, a retired motorman and former track worker, since deceased.

That evening initiated contacts with Nelson Fisher and Keith Stothert who provided more details about freight and passenger operations on the ERR. Richard T. (Doc) Morrow, a retired streetcar and trolley coach mechanic, offered some interesting insights into the maintenance aspects of keeping the cars ready for service and dealing with emergency repairs on the road.

An interview with Nelson Crampton arranged by John Reid, Cromdale Division (LRT) Supervisor, shed further light on early streetcar operations. Robert Farrants, a former ERR motorman (1911-1917), supplied helpful information and kindly loaned some early streetcar photographs from his album.

Street railways have always attracted a group of enthusiasts and Edmonton was no exception. Photographs were willingly provided by five prominent ERR enthusiasts who had made a hobby of taking an interest in the cars. Les Corness, N.F. Corness, R.J. (Bob) Walker, Eric M. Smith — all native Edmontonians and still residing in the Edmonton area — and George Bergson, now a resident of Richmond, B.C., all shared photographs, information and memorabilia that they had collected as the streetcars were being phased out. As a teenager, Eric Smith was a "scratch builder" of Edmonton streetcar models. The Edmonton cars also attracted the cameras of such noted traction photographers as Foster M. Palmer of Watertown, Mass., and W.C. Whittaker of Mill Valley, California. The

Photo opposite page:

For many years trolley coaches shared centre-of-the-street running space along Jasper Avenue with the streetcars: both utilized the same overhead for their source of power. In 1947, shortly after delivery of the first Brills, the trolley coach overhead was moved from the centre to both sides of the streetcar overhead along Jasper Avenue. This enabled the rail and non-rail electric vehicles to operate independently of one another, and permitted the trolley coaches to pull over to the curb to pick up passengers. Here blue-and-white-sign, Ottawa-built car No. 80 poses for the photographer on May 27th 1947, alongside Brill trolley coach No. 142 at its curbside stop on Jasper Avenue and 97 Street.

(Provincial Archives of Alberta)

Photo above:

Body of Edmonton Street Railway No. 80 in use as a lunch counter at Dawson Creek, B.C. June 1959. *(Omer Lavallée)*

results of their fine work are evident in the book. Historic photographs came from the Glenbow-Alberta Institute in Calgary where Assistant Chief Archivist Georgeen Klassen made available the resources of the McDermid photograph collection and other photographs in the Archives. John Gilpin, Peggy Small, Esther Kreisel, Karl Kaesekamp, Dennis Hyduk, Jean Dryden and Brian Speirs of the Provincial Museum and Archives of Alberta have all at various times assisted in the search for photographs, as well as obtaining the best possible prints from the Ernest Brown Collection and from a variety of other acquisitions as these came to their attention. Mrs. Helen LaRose, Mrs. Honey and other members of the staff at the City of Edmonton Archives often directed the authors to productive sources of information, notably the City Commissioners' Reports. Through the efforts of Ted Tennison — then of Edmonton Transit's Marketing Section and now in the City of Edmonton's Business Development office — and C.J. McGonigle, City Clerk, access to equipment contracts, diagrams, internal correspondence related to various aspects of streetcar operations and City Council minutes was made possible.

The archival material collected by the Alberta Pioneer Railway Association over the years provided information about track layouts, special trackwork and tracklaying methods employed in the early days of development. That collection also yielded considerable route and timing information related to the conversion from streetcars to trolley coaches. Access to the files of D.L. MacDonald, former Superintendent of the ETS, was productive as well. The considerable collection of drawings and correspondence in the possession of the Edmonton Radial Railway Society proved extremely helpful as well. Douglas V. Parker's diary of work progress on the Edmonton Radial Railway Society equipment established arrival dates of streetcar bodies at Fort Edmonton Park.

Microfilm copies of the *Edmonton Bulletin* and the *Edmonton Journal* at the Edmonton Public Library and actual copies of the latter publication in the Provincial Legislature Library also clarified many issues. Files of *Canadian Railway and Marine World,* stored on microfilm at the University of Alberta's Cameron Library, provided helpful information and was a source of many local newspaper leads.

Trolley coach information originated from many of the above noted sources, but further information came through research shared by George Buck, as well as the photographs of Dr. J.A. Kernahan and E.K. Letain. Bob Rynerson of Edmonton Transit's Marketing Section provided overhead line diagram information and anecdotes related to trolley coach operations. McGregor Telephone and Power Construction Co. Ltd. provided photographs which illustrated early trolley coach line layouts. Basic trolley coach roster information came from the North American Trackless Trolley Association's (NATTA) all-time trolley coach roster and updates in its quarterly, *Trolley Coach News.* Most of that material has been substantiated and extended through the cooperation and assistance of Al Romaniuk, Utilities Crews Foreman, Cromdale Garage; Don Mann, Ferrier Division Supervisor and Jack Fleck, Superintendent Transit Services for Edmonton Transit. Many persons already mentioned — particularly John Meikle — have read and corrected various parts of the manuscript and accompanying diagrams. Thanks is acknowledged for the careful scrutiny given the trolley coach portion of the manuscript by Jane Schwarzkopf.

The final chapter on the Light Rail Transit system is based on information provided by Robert R. Clark, originally Supervisor Rail Operations and now Supervisor of Special Services for Edmonton Transit. Encouragement in the final stages of this work has come from E.V. Miller, General Manager, Edmonton Transit.

Several persons previously acknowledged generously assisted with the gathering of information for Appendix II and Appendix IV. Further assistance came from Rondo Wood, Supervisor of Promotion and Advertising, D. Pagett, Technical Supervisor-Electrical and R.J. Charles, Director of Equipment, all of Edmonton Transit. A technical specifications sheet titled *Chopper Trolley Bus City of Edmonton* from BBC Brown Boveri Traction North America was the source of most of the information on the new Brown Boveri trolley coaches.

Special thanks is due to Paul R. McGee for offering his photographic dark room skills and resources. Paul's interest helped to obtain the best possible results from a number of loaned negatives and prints. Considerable help and advice has come from the collections and knowledge of three of Canada's leading railway historians: Anthony Clegg, Ray Corley and Omer Lavallée. Messrs. Clegg and Lavallée edited the manuscript for final publication. The book's layout and artistic design are the work of David Henderson, who coordinated and directed its production.

Research and writing of the electric railway services was carried out by Colin Hatcher. Tom Schwarzkopf researched and wrote the section on trolley coach operations.

Colin K. Hatcher,
Tom Schwarzkopf.

Edmonton, Alberta, December 1982.

Appendix VII:

Bibliography

Binns, Richard M., *Montreal's Electric Streetcars,* Railfare, Montreal, Canada, 1973.

The Bulletin, Edmonton, Alberta, 1907-1948.

Canadian Railway and Marine World, Acton Burrows Ltd., 70 Bond Street, Toronto, Canada, August 1912 - December 1936.

Canadian Transportation, Acton Burrows Ltd., 70 Bond Street, Toronto, Canada, January 1937 - January 1948.

City of Edmonton, Archives, Annual Financial and Department Reports, Street Railway Department.

City of Edmonton, Archives, City Commissioners' Files.

City of Edmonton, Archives, Insurance Plan of Edmonton - Map 1913.

City of Edmonton, City Clerk's Office, City Council Meeting Minutes, 1907-1918.

City of Edmonton, City Clerk's Office, Commissioners' Correspondence, 1926-1942.

City of Edmonton, City Clerk's Office, Contract Agreements and Specifications of Cars and Equipment.

City of Edmonton, Edmonton Transit, Various Route Schedules and Transit Guides, 1976-1979.

City of Edmonton, Edmonton Transit System, New Improved E.T.S. South Side Routes, Effective September 2, 1962.

City of Edmonton, Edmonton Transit System, Route and Transfer Guide, January 1949.

City of Edmonton, Edmonton Transit System, Transit Guide, September 1953.

City of Edmonton, Edmonton Transit System, Various Route Schedules and Transit Guides, 1966-1976.

City of Edmonton, Provincial Archives of Alberta, Alberta Pioneer Railway Association Accession, Engineering Department Track Special Work Diagrams and Track in Pavement Sectional Diagrams.

City of Edmonton, Street Railway Department, Correspondence, Cars and Car Material, January 1, 1923 to December 31, 1951.

City of Edmonton, Street Railway Department, Correspondence, Trolley Coaches, January 1, 1947 to December 31, 1951.

City of Edmonton, Street Railway Department, Street Railway Timetables, January 1937.

Corley, R.F. *The Edmonton Interurban Railway,* A Documented History, 1973.

DüWag Specification Sheet, Light Rail Vehicle RTE 1 of the City of Edmonton, Ref. E1, E4-477/19.

Dorman, Robert, *A Statutory History of Steam and Electric Railways of Canada,* 1836-1936, The Queen's Printer, Ottawa, Canada, 1938.

Ferrier, Thomas, *The Trolley Coach,* a paper presented to a symposium held during the 41st Annual Meeting of the Canadian Transit Association, June 12, 1946.

Forty Years of Public Service, 1911-1951, 40th Anniversary Booklet, Local 569, Amalgamated Association of Street and Electric Railway and Motor Coach Employees of America, Edmonton, Canada.

Photo above:

Car 81 stops for an official photograph in January 1931, shortly after its delivery to the Edmonton Street Railway Department. *(Glenbow Archives)*

Hitt, Rodney, *Electric Railway Dictionary,* McGraw Publishing Company, New York, N.Y., U.S.A., 1911. Republished by Newton K. Gregg, Navato, California, U.S.A., 1972.

The Journal, Edmonton, Alberta, 1907-1979.

Light Rapid Transit, The Immediate Answer for Edmonton, The University of Alberta Practicum in Rapid Transit, Edmonton, Canada, 1972.

MacGregor, J.G., *Edmonton, A History,* Hurtig Publishers, Edmonton, Canada, 1967.

The Marker, Alberta Pioneer Railway Association, Box 6102, Station C, Edmonton, Canada, T5B 4K5, 1975.

Northwest Territories Ordinances, 2nd Legislature, 4th Session, 1893.

Northwest Territories Ordinances, 3rd Session, 5th Legislative Assembly, September - October 1904.

The Ottawa Car Catalogue, Ottawa Car Manufacturing Co. Ltd., Ottawa, Canada. Reprinted by Trains and Trolleys, Montreal, Canada, 1968.

Palmer, Foster M.; Mitchell, Edwin; Holcomb, Bruce; Headlights, Volume 12, Number 1, January 1950, Edmonton, *North America's Northernmost Electric Line,* The Electric Railroaders' Association, Inc., 145 Greenwich Street, New York, N.Y., U.S.A., 10006.

Polet, M., *Edmonton Interurban Railway, A Report,* September 14, 1917.

Railway and Marine World, Acton Burrows Ltd., 70 Bond Street, Toronto, Canada, January 1908 - July 1912.

Rapid Transit for the City of Edmonton, Canadian Bechtel Limited, June 1963.

The Rattler, Canadian Railroad Historical Association, Rocky Mountain Branch, Edmonton, Canada, 1964.

Richey, Albert S., *Electric Railway Handbook,* McGraw-Hill Book Company Inc., New York, N.Y., U.S.A., 1915 and 1924. Reprinted by the Illinois Railway Museum, Union, Illinois, U.S.A., 1978.

Sebree, M.; Ward, P., *The Trolley Coach in North America,* Interurban Special 59, Volume 31, Number 1, Summer 1974, Interurbans, 17309 Alexandra Avenue, Cerritos, California, U.S.A.

Sebree, M.; Ward, P., *The Trolley Coach,* Transit Stepchild, Interurban Special 58, Interurbans, Cerritos, California, U.S.A.

Siemans Specification Sheet, Light Rail Vehicle RTE 1 of the City of Edmonton, E1, E4-477/19.

Statutes of Alberta, Canada, 8 Edw. VII, 1908.

Statutes of Alberta, Canada, 9 Edw. VII, 1909.

Statutes of Alberta, Canada, 2-3 Geo. V, 1911-1912.

Strathcona Plaindealer, Strathcona, Alberta, 1908-1909.

South Edmonton Weekly News, Edmonton, Alberta, 1939.

Trolley Coach News, The City of Edmonton Transit System, Volume 2, Number 4, August 1970, The North American Trackless Trolley Association, 1042 Bardstown Road, Louisville, Kentucky, U.S.A., 40204.

T.T.C. 211 and 213, (formerly Toronto and York Radial Railway 211 and 213, originally Edmonton Radial Railway 50 and 58), Bulletin 51, Upper Canada Railway Society, Toronto, Canada, December 1958.

Woodroofe, W.T., *New Carhouse and Shops at Edmonton,* Electric Railway Journal, 1914. Reprinted by Traction Heritage, Volume 3, Number 2, March 1970, Vane A. Jones Co., 6710 Hampton Drive E., Indianapolis, Indiana, U.S.A., 46226.

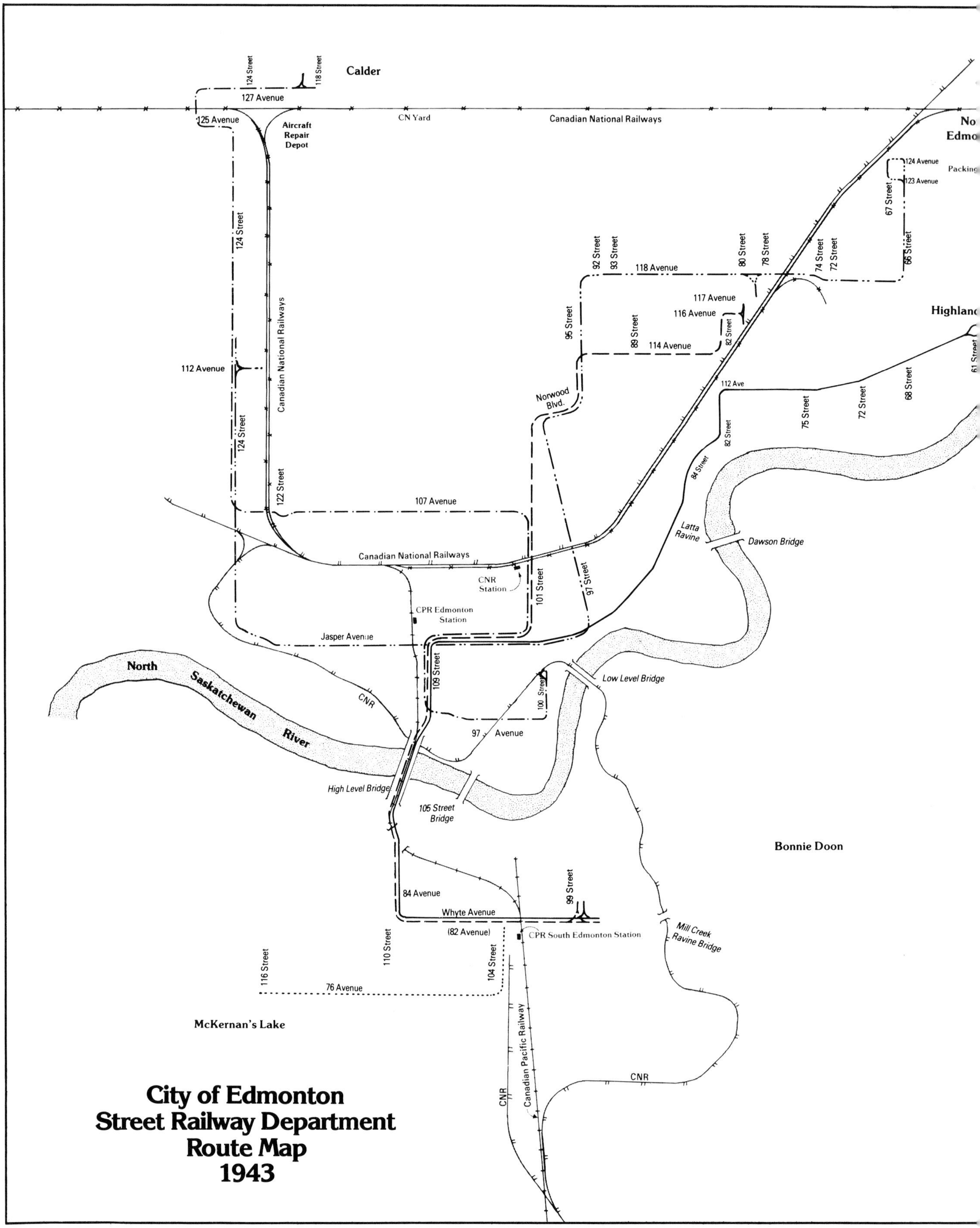

City of Edmonton Street Railway Department Route Map 1943

Key to Streetcar Routes

— White route: from Highlands to South Edmonton
— — — Red and White: from 114 Avenue and 82 Street to South Edmonton
—··— Red and Green: from Calder to Rossdale (near Low Level Bridge)
—·—·— Blue: from 124 Street to North Edmonton
········· Red and Blue: from Whyte Avenue, South Edmonton, to McKernan's Lake
—··—··— Blue and White: from 124 Street and 112 Avenue to 118 Avenue and 82 Street

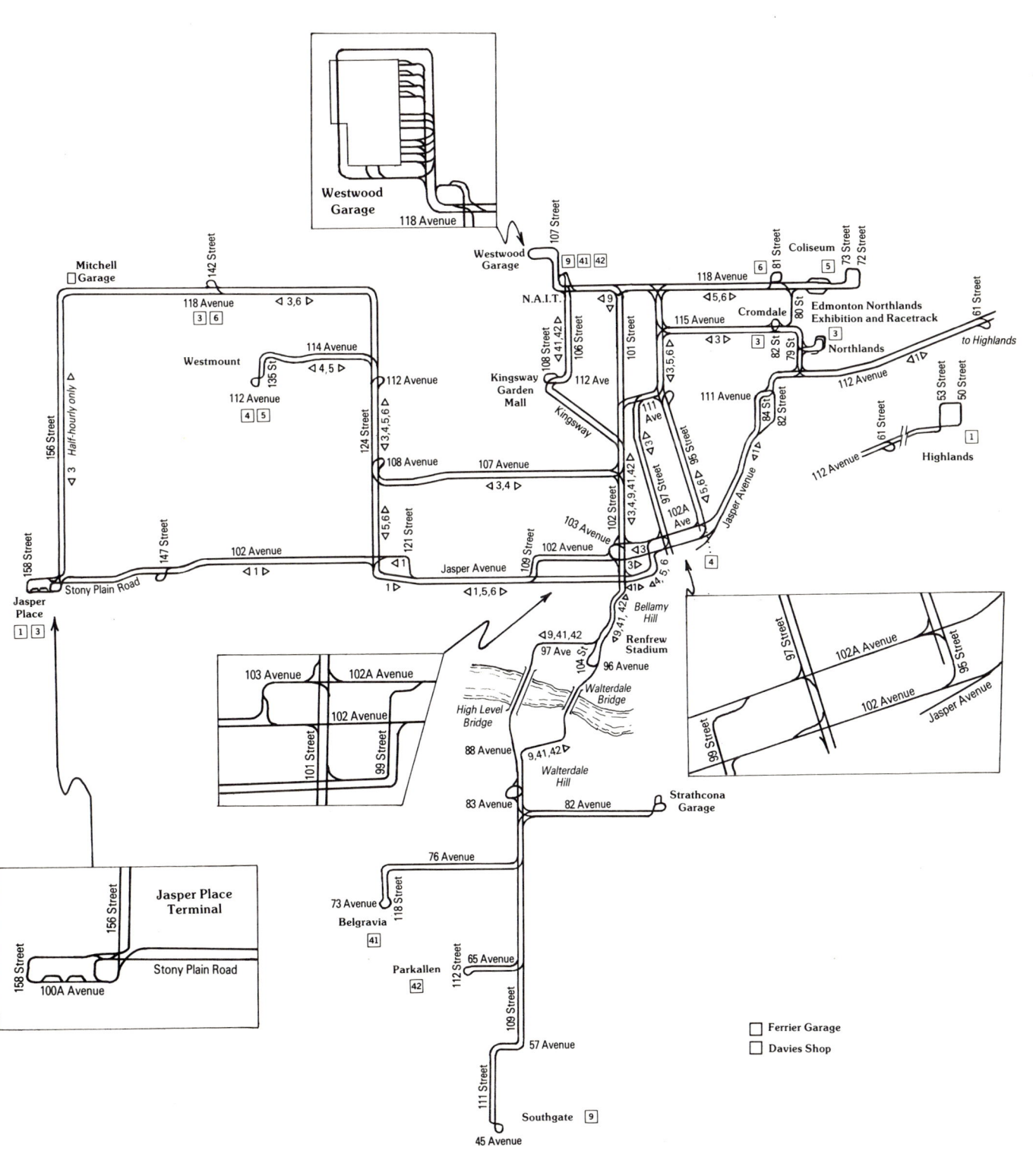

Edmonton Transit Trolley Coach Wire Diagram 1982

Mitchell Garage is expected to be one of the future trolley coach areas. Davies Shop is the main Edmonton Transit shop. Many major repair works are done on the trolley coaches at this location. The vehicles are towed to the facility by Edmonton Transit equipment with special towing hooks. Ferrier Garage is across the street from Davies Shops. It has storage facilities for diesel buses only.

The temperature was hovering around 25° below zero on January 19th 1951, as one of Edmonton's steel, 80-class trams was photographed leaving the south end of the High Level Bridge. (A. Clegg)

Photo below:

Edmonton Transit Brill trolley coach 130 heads north across 105 Street Bridge. (Colin K. Hatcher)